Henry Stedman was born in Chatham, Kent. After studies at Bristol University confirmed that yuppiedom, stripy shirts and braces were not for him he became an impoverished traveller. His wanderlust – which annual family holidays to Bexhill-on-Sea had done nothing to cure – has taken him to numerous far-flung places, and quite a few near-flung ones too. There are leeches in Borneo, Nepal, and Madagascar that have enjoyed hearty meals at his expense, and a thief in the Philippines who's probably still wearing his jeans.

Henry's first trip to the Near East was in 1990 and he has visited the region on three occasions since, the last time for five months during the research for this book. He now lives in London, where he is gradually being introduced back into polite society.

His other publications include contributions to *Trekking in the Annapurna Region*, also from Trailblazer, and Rough Guides' *Indonesia*.

Istanbul to Cairo Overland
First edition 1997

Publisher
Trailblazer Publications
The Old Manse, Tower Rd, Hindhead, Surrey, GU26 6SU, UK
Fax (+44) 01428-607571
E-mail trailblazer@compuserve.com

British Library Cataloguing in Publication Data
A catalogue record for this book is available from the British Library

ISBN 1-873756-11-9

Editor: Patricia Major
Typesetting: Anna Jacomb-Hood
Cartography and index: Jane Thomas

Printed on chlorine-free paper from farmed forests by
Technographic Design & Print Ltd, Colchester, Essex, UK

★ TRAILBLAZER

ISTANBUL
TO
CAIRO
OVERLAND

HENRY STEDMAN

WITH CARTOONS BY ANDREW OWGAN

TRAILBLAZER PUBLICATIONS

For my father

Acknowledgements

As with any guidebook, a whole team is necessary to ensure that it is both accurate and comprehensive. I'm just the one who receives the glory and collects the royalties. To ease my conscience over this injustice, the following is a list of these other hard-working souls.

First, I'd like to express my gratitude to the following whom I met during my time in the region, whose advice was as essential as their company was enjoyable. In no particular order: Ben Lyons (US), Chris Starace (US) – sorry I didn't get back to London in time, Kathryn Doran (Aus), Terry Deane (UK), Kate Mitchiner (UK), Maria de Wit and Martin Schiere (Netherlands) – are we still going to buy a camel?, Mac Duncan (Aus), Andrew Pearl (Aus), Danny Hajjar (Lebanon) – for the football match, Zeina Maasri (Lebanon), Glenn Davy (NZ), Mark Cornwall (UK), Renata Bialkowski (Aus) – hope the cold's better, Tarek Zoobi (Aus), Khaled Hamse (Syria) – for getting my money back, Anne-Marie Culvenor (Aus), Bryan Tierney and Christine Diehl (US), Ted, Aidan and the staff of the *Traveller* (Israel), Paul Kendel (US), Angus Rule (SA), Joel Yakir (Can), Lisa Groarke (US), Tony Neiss (Ger), M Saleh al-Helow (Jordan) for the worry beads, Gorm K Gaare (Nor), Bendik Sorvig (Nor), Inge Sollerud (Nor), Ward Vansteenwegen (Bel), Eugene Dimitriou (Can), Mark Moran (UK) – for letting me win at backgammon, Douglas Baird, Jaq Greening and Brendan McDonnell, Mossad Saad Shaban (Egypt), Alex Morris, Jonas Grenberg and Alex Ball (UK), Robyn (Aus), Ayman Youssef (Egypt), Hanne Finholt (Nor), Basheer Sultan and Abdul-Hamid Mourad (Syria), Craig Speziali (Aus), Andrew Helm (Aus), Linda Corfield (Aus), Warren O'Brien (Aus), Andrea Szabo (Can).

Back in Blighty there have been just as many contributors. Again in no par-ticular order I wish to thank the following for their advice, encouragement, input and insults: Andrew Owgan for the cartoons; Martyn Porter for tiffin, printing and talking rubbish; John Gilbert for checking the contract; Giulia Matozza for the computer; Mum, Dad, Ed and Bungle for proof-reading; Troy and Linda Pearce for the printouts (and the curry); Wendy, Sam and Steve Turner; Alison Bourassa for the research; Philip Riddett for the computer; Abdallah Jarrah and the Lebanese Tourist Office for the translations; also Paul Williams at the Egyptian Cultural Office and Norma Al-Tahan from the Palmyra Kebab Restaurant in Fulham; Lizzie Bradbury for Errol Flynn, help with travel details and the cheese plant.

At Trailblazer, thanks to Jane Thomas for drawing the maps, Patricia Major for editing the text, and Anna Jacomb-Hood for typesetting. And, finally, hearty thanks to Bryn Thomas for giving me the opportunity in the first place.

A request

The author and publisher have tried to ensure that this guide is as accurate and up-to-date as possible. Things change quickly in this part of the world, however: prices rise, hotels come and go, and countries start wars with each other. If you notice any changes or omissions that should be included in the next edition of this book, please write to Henry Stedman at Trailblazer Publications (address on p2). A free copy of the next edi-tion will be sent to persons making a significant contribution.

Front cover: Camels remain the main form of transport in the Wadi Rum (Jordan)

CONTENTS

INTRODUCTION

Every night at 9pm a bus leaves Cairo's Midan Abdel Minnim Riyadh bus station. If the gods of punctures and potholes are on their side the passengers will alight $3^1/_2$ days later in Istanbul. While it's now possible to speed overland on this route, this guide is for travellers who want to spend rather longer in the fascinating region that lies between these two cities; an area comprising the six countries of the Near East.

To travel through the Near East is to follow some of the earliest routes in history. Down the centuries scores of pilgrims, traders, armies and empires have passed through on their way to pray, profit, pillage or plunder, with many stopping to settle in the region permanently. Most left some mark on the landscape, and it is this historical evidence – over 7000 years worth from the prehistoric ruins at Byblos to the 20th century rubble of Beirut – that is the main attraction for modern visitors.

As well as acting as a conduit between three continents, the Near East has also been the source of many new ideas and beliefs that have spread throughout the world. This is the Holy Land, the birthplace of both Judaism and Christianity. It is also where Islam grew and flourished, and the region is full of wonderful buildings dedicated to the glory of Allah. Then there is the pantheon of gods who have long since been consigned to history but whose legacy lives on in temples, such as the Roman ruins at Baalbek, or the pharaonic sites along the Nile, that simply take the breath away.

Religion not your cup of chai? Then how about the natural beauty of the Near East. Both Egypt and Lebanon have a landscape so varied that one can scramble to the top of 2000m-plus mountains in the morning and then plunge into the warm blue waters of the sea that same afternoon. Jordan has the majestic, eerie desolation of Wadi Rum, whilst it also shares with Israel the unique geographical freak that is the Dead Sea. And Turkey has not only a landscape that is as diverse as it is dramatic but can also boast of the prettiest stretch of coastline in the Mediterranean.

Yet, even if the Near East had none of the above, it would still worth visiting to experience a society, culture and way of life that is so alien to anything one encounters in the West. It looks different. The noise generated on the streets, a cacophony of screeching radios, wailing muezzins and vociferous peddlers, sounds different, too. With its combination of dust, diesel and felafel it even smells different. And acquainting oneself with all things alien is, of course, the greatest pleasure of travelling.

The region has suffered more than its fair share of bad press over the years and is often portayed as little more than a dustbowl governed by dictators and populated solely by religious extremists and terrorists. This perception is, of course, inaccurate. Those who visit will be amply rewarded by what they encounter: 70 centuries of visible history, exquisite food, diverse and colourful scenery, warm and friendly locals, and glittering bazaars – all within a journey that can be done in $3^1/_2$ days by bus.

❏ How to use this book

This book makes no claims to being a complete guide to the Near East. If it were it would run to several volumes and there'd be no room left in the rucksack for your pyjamas. Instead, we've distilled the highlights of the region into a single meandering course. We provide the skeleton of a journey but leave it to you to flesh out the details. This skeleton includes all the major sites (and a few of the less well-known ones) but we don't expect you to follow our route religiously. By linking sections together you should be able to fashion your own itinerary.

Abbreviations used are as follows: **sgl/dbl/tpl** – single/double/triple rooms; **comm/att** – common/attached bathrooms; **stu** – students; **U26** – under 26 years of age; **concs** – concessions; **o/w** – one way; **rtn** – return.

PART 1: PLANNING YOUR TRIP

Routes, costs and when to go

WITH A GROUP OR ON YOUR OWN?

Travelling with anyone is a very ticklish business...What is your thrill may be my bore....I cannot imagine what fire and pillage I would commit if anyone were in a position to keep me looking at things longer than I wanted to look. **Cornelia Stratton Parker** *English Summer*

This has to be one of the best regions in the world for travelling independently. It is very safe and, once the language barrier has been overcome, relatively easy to travel through. If you are travelling solo and worried about feeling lonely, don't be: most of this route is a well-trodden path and you'll come across fellow travellers nearly everywhere you go. In less visited countries like Syria and Lebanon the locals are undoubtedly the friendliest, kindest people I have ever encountered.

Consequently, it hardly seems worth the extra expense that comes from taking an organised tour. Nevertheless, there are plenty of agencies willing to take your money and guide you through parts of the region (see p12). There is not, as yet, any company that offers one tour through all six countries.

WHICH WAY?

This is purely a matter of choice. There is no particular advantage with starting in either Istanbul or Cairo. The route in this book begins in Istanbul because this is where most travellers start their journey.

❏ **Advice for women travellers**
Women (particularly blonde women) will find themselves subject to a lot of unwanted attention in the Near East. This should not, however, deter women from travelling alone. Nearly all of this attention is harmless, and a quick *'Imshi!'* ('Go away!' in Arabic) usually does the trick. Some women even prefer to travel through the Near East on their own, and their advice is always the same: provided you do not draw attention to yourself with skimpy clothes or outrageous behaviour you will be treated with respect by everyone, whatever their nationality. If somebody is being a little over-aggressive in his approaches, don't hesitate to humiliate him by shouting. Embarrassment is a most effective weapon in cooling Eastern ardour.

HOW LONG?

Six to eight weeks will enable you to visit most of the main attractions in the Near East, although this won't allow you much time to lie on a beach and work on your tan. Three or four months is probably best if you plan to make a fairly thorough exploration of these six countries.

WHEN TO GO

March and April are my favourite months for travel through this region. The weather is usually fine, the tourist shoals have not yet come ashore and the prices are low. Nevertheless the Near East is one of the few areas in the world where it is both possible and enjoyable to travel at almost any time of the year.

For five of the countries on this route the weather varies little between the seasons. Egypt is hot and dry all year round, and whilst Israel, Jordan, Syria and Lebanon experience cold evenings and heavy downpours in winter this shouldn't prevent you from travelling at this time. The excep-

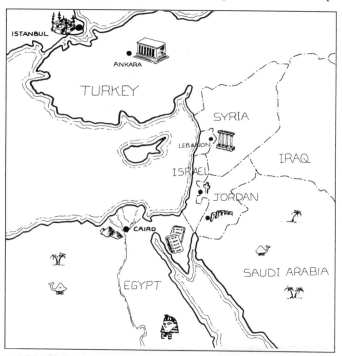

tion is Turkey. Between October and February a few resorts on the Turkish coast close down altogether and the interior is quilted in snow. It is still a pleasant enough experience travelling through Turkey in winter, but you should bring warm clothing and have a very flexible itinerary.

It is also advisable to avoid the Islamic holy month of Ramadan (see p40) if possible. Travelling can be problematic at this time: food, drink and cigarettes are difficult to come by during the day, opening hours are short and erratic and so are tempers. The Islamic calendar is a lunar one, so the dates differ from the Western Gregorian calendar. Dates for 1997-9 are 31 December 1997 to 31 January 1998 and 20 December 1998 to 20 January 1999.

BUDGETING

It is never easy to give an estimate on how much it's all going to cost. Much depends on the season since accommodation prices rise in most places during summer. Your budget also depends on your travelling style: are you going to buy souvenirs, are you willing to use the black market and patronise street stalls etc. In short, travelling through the Near East can cost as little or as much as you want. Arriving at Istanbul with US$1800 in your pocket you could suffer six months of dreadful privations until you reach Cairo, or blow it all on one night at the Istanbul Hilton. Whilst the latter option has much to recommend it, this book is aimed at those who are travelling on a fairly tight budget, although some mid-range and top hotels are included for those who need a break from penny-pinching.

As a very rough approximation, it is possible to scrape by on a minimum of UK£7 or US$10 per day in the low season. If you avoid Israel and Lebanon then it can be even cheaper. In the summer you should allow for a minimum of UK£12 or US$18. Take a lot more than this, however, to cover any unforeseen circumstances.

❏ **Useful Web sites**
Sites which can be helpful for planning a trip include the following:

• Lonely Planet's very comprehensive site (**www.lonelyplanet.com**), where you can leave messages for other travellers on their 'Thorn Tree'. Also check Rough Guides' site – **www.roughguides.com**
• You can reach tourist office sites and other sites which give information for travellers via **www.efn.org/~rick/tour**
• Get up-to-the-minute rates of exchange on **www.xe.net/currency**, for all the countries in this book except Syria.

Via the Web you can also read local newspapers and contact local groups.

❏ GUIDED TOURS

Australia

Adventure World (☎ 9956 7766, fax 9956 7707) 73 Walker Street, North Sydney, NSW 2060.

Gateway Travel (☎ 02-9745-333, fax 9745 3237, e-mail: gatrav@magna.com.au) 48 The Boulevade, Strathfield NSW 2135.

Peregrine Adventures (☎ 03-663 8611, fax 03-663 8618) 258 Lonsdale St, Melbourne Vic 3000 Sales agents for The Imaginative Traveller.

Top Deck Travel Wholesale (☎ 02-299 8844, fax 02-299 8841) 8th floor, 350 Kent St, Sydney NSW 2000.

Canada

Trek Holidays (☎ 403-439 9118, fax 403-5494) 8412-109 Street, Edmonton T6G 1E2 Sales agent for Imaginative Traveller.

Travel Cuts (☎ 416-979 2406, fax 416-979 8167) 187 College St, Toronto Canada M5T 1P7.

UK

Acacia Africa (☎ 0181-960 5747, fax 0181-960 1414) 27d Stable Way, Latimer Rd, London W10 6QX. They concentrate on Africa only and offer a variety of tours from 10-15 days around Egypt.

African Trails (☎ 0181-742 7724, fax 0181-742 8621) 3 Flanders Rd, Chiswick, London W4 1NQ, are now running a six-week tour between Istanbul and Cairo for a very reasonable UK£600 plus kitty. The tour travels via the lakes of Central Anatolia rather than around the coast and excludes Israel and Lebanon; apart from that, their route is similar to the one described in this book.

Contiki (☎ 0181-290 6422) Offers a 16-day tour combining Egypt and Israel.

Encounter Overland (☎ 0171-370 6845, fax 0171-2449737, telex 916654) 267 Old Brompton Road, London SW5 9JA offers a seven-week Cradle of our Civilisation tour from London via Istanbul to Cairo, a journey of some 6000 miles. (They also do a 16-week tour that continues on to Kathmandu). Once again Lebanon and Israel are omitted. They can also offer an Egypt-only tour, and a 10-week Cairo-Kathmandu journey, which travels via Jordan and Syria to Göreme before heading east.

The Imaginative Traveller (☎ 0181-742 8612, fax 0181-742 3045) 14 Barley Mow Passage, Chiswick, London W4 4PH. One of the few companies to offer tours to all six countries on our route but, infuriatingly, not in one package. The nearest they do is an Istanbul-Cairo overland, missing out Israel and Lebanon.

Top Deck (☎ 0171-370 4555, fax 0171-373 6201, telex 8955339), 131-135 Earls Court Road, London SW5 9RH offer a large variety of tours around the south-ernmost three countries of the Near East, including a combination tour of all three.

USA

Himalayan Travel (☎ 203-359 3711, fax 203-359 3669 e-mail worldadv@netaxis.com) 112 Prospect St, 2nd Floor, Stamford CT 06901. Agents for Imaginative Traveller.

African Explorers (☎ 908-870 0223, fax 908-870 0278) 179 Wall St, West Long Branch, NJ 07764.

Getting to the Near East

Most important: do **not** enter the region via Israel. If you do, it will be impossible to hide this fact from Syrian and Lebanese border staff and you'll be prevented from travelling in these countries (see Visas, p15).

FROM THE UK

By air

For up to the-minute prices check the travel pages of the Sunday newspapers or magazines such as *Time Out* and *TNT* since prices vary considerably according to season. Check that the agency you are buying from is bonded by ABTA, otherwise you may not be compensated if it goes bust.

● **To Istanbul** If you're flying to Istanbul, try to buy your ticket back from Cairo before you leave home; tickets in Cairo are expensive. Many airlines – British Airways, KLM, Lufthansa and Air France for example – sell discounted open-jaw tickets (ie London-Istanbul, Cairo-London), although most insist that, to get a discounted fare, you have to be student or Under 26. Sample open-jaw fares are: students/U26: UK£240 low season, UK£350 high (British Airways); others: UK£300 low season, UK£450 high.

● **To Cairo** Flights out of Turkey are very cheap (approximately UK£75 to Heathrow). Consequently, it is usually better to book a one-way fare to Cairo, then buy your return ticket in Istanbul. Some charter companies sell last-minute one-way fares to Sharm al-Sheikh and Luxor that are incredibly cheap (approx UK£100), although usually you can only buy these one week before departure. Sample one-way fares to Cairo on scheduled flights are: students/U26: UK£138 low season, UK£198 high (British Airways); others: UK£180 low, UK£263 high.

Recommended travel agents to try include **STA Travel** (London ☎ 0171-937 9962, Bristol ☎ 0117-929 4399, Manchester ☎ 0161-834 0668, Cambridge ☎ 01223-366966, Oxford ☎ 01865-792800), **Trailfinders** (London ☎ 0171-938 3366, Birmingham ☎ 0121-236 1234, Bristol ☎ 0117-929 9000, Glasgow ☎ 0141-353 2224, Manchester ☎ 0161-839 6969), and **Campus** (London ☎ 0171-730 8111, Manchester ☎ 0161-273 1721, Edinburgh ☎ 0131-668 3303).

By bus

There are no direct buses to Istanbul from England anymore. You can catch a bus to Bucharest (UK£140 o/w) and then a bus or train from there but it's cheaper to fly direct to Istanbul.

By train

Phone ☎ 0171-834 2345 for the latest rail information. There are no direct trains to Istanbul. Instead, one must go via Munich and catch the daily service to Istanbul from there. The train leaves Munich at 13.38, arriving at Istanbul's Sirkeci Station at 08.15. Booking your ticket from the UK costs UK£133, plus UK£16 for a couchette from Budapest to Istanbul.

To get to Munich, travel either by Eurostar via Brussels (UK£77.50 Waterloo to Brussels, UK£103 Brussels to Munich) or by ferry (UK£136 London-Munich). If you're under 26 the Eurostar fare is UK£34.50.

A popular option for under-26 travellers is the Inter-Rail ticket, which allows one month's unlimited travel on Europe's trains. Currently it costs UK£275. There is also an over-26 pass for the same price, although this is not valid in certain countries, for example France and Belgium. Non-Europeans who have lived in Europe for less than six months are not eligible for the Inter-Rail pass. Instead there is the Eurail pass, allowing unlimited travel for 15 days in certain selected countries.

The Orient Express

For those who wish to travel in style the Orient Express is still running, although unfortunately it now terminates in Venice rather than Istanbul. The trip takes two days and one night from London; the cheapest fare is UK£1060. You'll have to make your own way to Istanbul from there.

FROM USA AND CANADA

The Sunday newspapers are a good source of information for cheap flights from North America. If you intend to fly to Cairo, consider the possibility of buying a cheap return to London and a discounted flight from there. From **New York**, a one-way flight to Istanbul/Cairo costs about US$500/600; a low-season open-jaw ticket (New York-Istanbul and Cairo-New York) is about US$110. Flights from **Toronto** cost about 10% more. Travel agents to try include **STA Travel** in the US (branches in most major cities; New York office ☎ 212-627-3111) and **Travel Cuts** (☎ 416-979-2406 Toronto, ☎ 604-681-9136 Vancouver) in Canada.

FROM AUSTRALIA AND NEW ZEALAND

Once again it is usually cheaper to buy a return flight to London and then sort out travel arrangements to the Near East from there.

One-way flights from **Sydney** to Istanbul/Cairo cost approximately A$1000; an open-jaw ticket (Sydney-Istanbul, Cairo-Sydney) is around A$1800. Travel agents to try include: **Trailfinders** (Cairns ☎ 070-41 1199, Brisbane ☎ 07-3229 0887), **STA Travel** (many branches; phone Sydney ☎ 02-212 1255 and Auckland ☎ 09-309 9995 for details of the other offices) and the **Flight Centre** (Brisbane ☎ 07-3229 9211).

Before you leave

VISAS

A list of embassies is given on p312. Ensure that your passport has plenty of pages left for visas. Most consulates insist that you allow a double page for their visa, and that your passport has at least six months left before it expires. Make sure, too, that you do not have any Israeli stamps in your passport or your overland tour will end at the Syrian border.

● **Turkey** Many nationalities do not require a visa and those that do, US and UK citizens among them, have to buy them at the airport/border and pay in their own currency (UK£10 for British citizens, US$20 for Americans). A six-month multiple-entry visa currently costs the same as a regular single-entry visa.

● **Syria** Required by all and obtainable from Syrian consulates only, **not at the border.** This can be the trickiest of all the visas to obtain but provided all your paperwork is in order it should be no problem. The rules are simple. First, you will not be able to buy a visa if there is any evidence that you have been to Israel, **or plan to go there.** If you have an Israeli stamp in your passport, get a new passport. Secondly, some Syrian consulates insist that you can get a visa from them only if you live in that country. Only residents in Jordan can get a Syrian visa from the consulate in Amman, for example. Other Syrian consulates may follow suit so, if you can, get your Syrian visa before you leave home.

To get a Syrian visa en route (currently only available from consulates in Istanbul and Cairo), you need to obtain a letter of recommendation from your own embassy in advance. This usually costs UK£7-9 or US$10-15.

● **Lebanon** The Lebanese visa is required by all, and available only from consulates, **not at the border**. Like Syria, Lebanon refuses entry to anyone who has visited Israel. If you are starting your trip in Istanbul, buy your visa at home if you can since it costs US$40 in Istanbul and currently about half that price in the UK or US. If you start in Cairo, both the Cairene and Amman consulates are fine. There is no Lebanese consulate in Syria. Contrary to popular rumour, it is possible for American citizens to visit Lebanon, although visas should be sorted out before leaving the States.

● **Jordan** Required by all. Although you can buy a visa at the border, it is cheaper to get one at a consulate. If you're beginning your journey in

Istanbul buy your visa there – the consulate in Damascus can be expensive. Coming from the south, the Jordanian consulate in Cairo is OK.

● **Israel** Most nationalities (including Australian, Canadian, British and American passport holders) do not require a visa.

● **Egypt** Visas are required by all. Curiously, it is cheaper to buy one at the airport/border (US$15) rather than at a consulate (US$20). If you do wish to buy beforehand wait until Aqaba - the consulate in Istanbul is way out of town, and in Damascus and Amman there is usually a scrum.

HEALTH PRECAUTIONS AND INOCULATIONS

Make sure that you are inoculated against typhoid, tetanus, polio and hepatitis before you go. The risk of catching any of these is small but it's better to be safe than to suffer. There is a minute risk of malaria in Turkey and Egypt, but the chances are so slim that it is not worth taking anti-malarial prophylactics, which, after all, have their own risks attached to them. Instead take insect repellent.

If you have come from an area affected by yellow fever within the last six months, you'll need a certificate showing proof of inoculation.

INSURANCE

Travel insurance is vital. The risk of being robbed or falling ill here is negligible but Sod's Law dictates that something horrible will befall anyone who isn't insured. Cover falls into two basic categories: health and luggage. If you are not too worried about losing your luggage, you can buy health cover only. Remember to read the fine print in the policy, and check these details:
● How much is deductible if you have to claim?
● Can the insurers compensate you immediately, while you are still in the Near East, or do you have to wait until you get home?
● How long do you have to make a claim, and what evidence do they require (receipts, police reports etc)?
● If you plan to go climbing or diving are these activities covered?

Many insurance companies charge the cheaper European premiums for countries bordering the Mediterranean. If you wish to take out this cheaper cover please note that you may not be covered for Jordan. Beware also of credit card companies that advertise free travel insurance if you book a flight with them. You may find that you are covered only for what you've paid for on the card, ie your flight. Leave a copy of the policy, or at least the policy number, with a friend or relative at home. There are numerous companies; I've always been very happy with the policy offered by **STA Travel** (UK ☎ 0171-937 9971).

What to take

Money

Travellers' cheques are the safest way of carrying money in the region. American Express (AMEX) and Thomas Cook are two of the more recognisable brands. AMEX have at least one office in every country should you run into any difficulty. Leave a copy of the serial numbers at home and keep an up to date record of the ones that you have used.

Many travellers also bring credit cards. Most of the more expensive hotels and bigger souvenir shops accept some form of credit card. The majority of countries on the route now have ATM's (automated teller machines) for credit card advances. Turkey, Israel, Lebanon and Egypt all have them and some should be installed in Jordan soon. You will find your credit card of little use in Syria, however.

It is also important to bring some cash, especially if you wish to change money on the black market. US dollars are by far the most acceptable, followed by German deutchmarks and British pounds. With many insurance policies now providing cover for cash (usually up to the value of about US$250) it is almost as safe as carrying travellers' cheques.

Student/youth cards

Either of these will save you pounds, liras, shekels, dinars etc. The International Student Identity Card (**ISIC Card**) is the most widely-accepted form of student ID. There is a reduction of at least 50% on entrance fees in most countries (except Israel, where the discounts are lower), and it could save you a little on bus tickets and train fares too. The Under 26 Card (also called the **FIYTO Card**) is less useful in five of the countries, but in Turkey it allows you into almost every tourist attraction free of charge!

You can pick up both of these cards at home, or in Istanbul or Cairo at the beginning of your trip (where they are less fussy about proof). If you're travelling without either card wave any form of ID (even a credit card) in front of the guard's face; occasionally it works.

The basic essentials

The old travelling maxim: 'pack the absolute minimum only – then throw half away' applies as much to the Near East as it does to any other part of the world. First, a checklist for toiletries: **toothbrush/paste**, **soap/shampoo**, **deodorant**, **tampons** (sometimes very hard to come by in the Middle East), **pill/condoms**, **toilet roll**, and a **towel**. A small **medical kit** may be useful too, filled with **plasters**, **antiseptic ointment**, **paracetamol**, **sun cream** (which is vital) and an **anti AIDS kit** (syringes and needles). Some people also take along **vitamin tablets**, as the nutritional value of a *shwaarma*-and-*felafel* diet is fairly limited. I have never had any trouble drinking tap water in any of the cities on this route, but if you are travelling to more remote destinations, particularly in Egypt, a bottle of **iodine** or **purification tablets** are essential. Bottled water is available almost everywhere.

What to wear

The *Handbook for travellers in Syria and Palestine* advised 19th century travellers that the adoption of Arab dress by European visitors was 'an effectual way of rendering oneself ridiculous'.Whilst there is certainly no need to don a jalabiyyeh, it is only good manners that you respect the wishes of the locals when choosing your attire. All of these countries have large, conservative Muslim populations. Away from the beach resorts short sleeves and short trousers are often frowned upon, and bare arms and legs are forbidden in all mosques and holy places. Women travellers with bare legs will either offend or excite the locals. Neither reaction is to be recommended so cover them up.

What you bring depends on the season. If you're travelling in winter bring at least one warm **jumper** and a **coat** or **waterproof jacket**. A **woolly hat** and **thick socks** are invaluable items too. In summer a few **T-shirts** and a pair of **lightweight trousers** are all you need. Travelling in this region will almost certainly result in an invitation to somebody's home for a meal; having one set of **tidy clothes** is a good idea. As well as day-to-day **walking shoes/boots**, a pair of **sandals** is recommended.

Other items you may consider taking include: a **torch/flashlight** (very useful), **sunglasses, penknife, books, plastic bags, cards, water bottle, string, chain and padlock, Walkman, earplugs**. A few **passport photographs** for any visas you may need to buy along the way would also be useful, as would an **alarm clock** and a **box of matches**. If you plan to camp out (or sleep rough) then a **sleeping bag** is essential.

Cram the above into a rucksack, preferably one with an internal frame for comfort. A small **daypack** for your camera, water bottle and guidebook is useful. With your moneybelt (**passport, cash, insurance certificate, tickets**, and any **prescriptions** that may be necessary) safely strapped to your person....you're ready to go!

Camera equipment

'There are tourists incapable of looking at a masterpiece for its own sake. They bow into a camera, snap experiences never had, then rush home and develop these celluloid events so as to see where they've been' (Ned Rorem *Music from inside and out*, 1967). Whilst Mr Rorem's opinions undoubtedly contain a kernel of truth most people bring a camera with them. The region's bright sunlight ensures both good lighting conditions (especially at dawn and dusk) and a continual supply of interesting, sun-wrinkled faces. Some of the sights are pretty photogenic too! Although every major brand of slide and print film is stocked in the region you may have to search to find your favourite. You can check the sell-by date but you can't be sure that it has been kept in a cool, dry place out of the sun, so it's wiser to bring as much as you can from home. Try to avoid the X-ray machines at the airports and borders. A polarising filter is useful, as is a camera-cleaning kit; there's a lot of dust and sand out here.

BACKGROUND READING

Instead of taking just one book on your trip, you should seriously consider taking 66 – the 66 books of The Bible. Part historical document, part religious treatise and part swashbuckling adventure story, it's the most relevant literary companion one could take. Most of the less-weighty suggestions below are available in bookstores throughout the region.

Travel narratives
● *The Innocents Abroad*, by Mark Twain, is the most well-known and the best travel narrative covering this area. It is a very personal account of a cruise taken in 1867 with a band of pilgrims to the Holy Land, written with Twain's typically jaundiced, sarcastic pen. It is often very funny. It's now out of print but you may be able to track down a second-hand copy.
●*Arabia through the Looking Glass* (Pan) – Jonathan Raban describes his expedition around the Arab world, including much of the Near East.
● *Holidays in Hell* (Picador) – PJ O'Rourke's irreverent account of his experiences in some of the world's troubled hotspots. As you might expect, Israel and Lebanon feature prominently.
●*A Fez of the Heart* (Picador) – Jeremy Seal describes his experiences in Turkey. Thankfully, the humour rises above the awful pun of the title.
● *Egyptian Journal* (Faber and Faber) William Golding's record of his travels down the Nile, a journey conducted soon after he had won the Nobel Prize for Literature. Some of Golding's more exasperating experiences will strike a chord with anyone who has visited the country.
● *An Antique Land* by Amitav Ghosh (Granta Books). Part-travelogue, part-Egyptian history, wholly enjoyable.
● *Beyond the Pyramids* by Douglas Kennedy (Abacus) A simple traveller's tale, but no less enjoyable for that.
● *The Gates of Damascus* (Lonely Planet) is Lieve Joris's study of the country and her experiences of staying with a Syrian family. It's one of the few travelogues that deals with Syria in detail.
● *Travels in Syria and the Holy Land* by Johann Ludwig Burkhardt is worth tracking down; a facsimile was produced by Darf Publishers of London in 1992. The language may be a little archaic in places but the experiences of this great explorer and adventurer who discovered Petra and Abu Simbel are without equal.

Chronicle Books have published collections of travelling essays on some of the world's great cities; *Cairo* and *Istanbul* among them.

War and politics

● **Lebanon** There are plenty of accounts of the Lebanese civil war written from many different perspectives. Most of the hostages have written of their ordeal; I found Brian Keenan's *An Evil Cradling* (Hutchinson) the most interesting. For an overview, Coughlin's *Hostage – the Complete Story of the Lebanese Captives* (Little Brown) is good, and includes a thorough account of the sinister Irangate affair.

Robert Fisk's *Pity the Nation* (Oxford University Press) and Thomas Friedman's *From Beirut to Jerusalem* (Fontana) are both tremendous. The latter is an account of the plight of the Palestinians, from their eviction in 1948 to their part in the Lebanese war.

● **Israel/Palestine** If it's an analysis of the Palestinian affair you're after you have plenty of choices, although most are polemics rather than straightforward historical accounts. If you read only one book on the subject, it should be *Arab and Jew: Wounded Spirits in a Promised Land* (Bloomsbury) by David K Shipler. Perceptive, accurate and well-balanced, it offers a very precise description of the troubles. For a simplified account, Larry Collins' and Dominic Lapierre's *O Jerusalem* retells the story of the 1948 War of Independence and the birth of Israel.

Israel's most famous author, Amos Oz, has published his thoughts on the troubles in *Israel, Palestine and Peace* (Vintage Press). If you have read this, then tuck into Edward Said's *The Question of Palestine* (Vintage), which details the arguments of the other side. For a better understanding of the plight of the Palestinians, read *Gaza, Legacy of Occupation – a Photographer's Journey*, by Dick Doughty and Mohammed el-Aydi (Kumarian Press), a photo-journal of Doughty's time in a refugee camp. Entertaining and distressing in equal measures.

Biography

TE Lawrence's compelling memoirs of his war-time exploits with the Bedouins in the Arab Revolt, *Seven Pillars of Wisdom* (Cape), is another classic. The elegant prose is difficult to get in to at first; once you do, reading becomes a pleasure. Lord Kinross's *Atatürk, Rebirth of a Nation*, (Phoenix) remains the most authoritative biography of the great man. PJ Newby's *Saladin in his Time* (Faber and Faber) is a good study of the man behind the myth. Read it to see what all the fuss was about.

History

● *Ancient Egypt – a Complete Guide to Exploring the World of the Pharaohs* by Hobson (Thames and Hudson), is one of the best.
● *Byzantine Civilisation* is an enormous two-volume opus by A Vasiliev (University of Wisconsin Press). It's scholarly and highly detailed.

● *Soldiers of Fortune – the story of the Mamlukes*, is an exceptionally well-researched book concerning this oft-ignored empire by JB Glubb (Glubb Pasha), the leader of the Arab Legion protecting Jordan following its independence in 1923. It can be heavy going but it is useful to dip into now and again (for the chronological order of their empire, for example).

● *The Ottomans* by Andrew Wheatcroft (Viking) is not a complete history but is the most readable of all the studies of the Turkish empire.

● *The Bible as History* by W Keller (SPCK) is a classic dealing with the archaeology of much of the area in relation to the Bible.

Fiction

The most famous piece of fiction from Arabia is the *Tales of a Thousand and One Nights*, currently published by Penguin Books (ed. NJ Dawood). These tales were originally told to the Abbassid Caliph Harun al-Rashid. Two of Agatha Christie's greatest novels, *Death on the Nile* and *Murder on the Orient Express*, are set in the Near East.

Amongst fiction by local authors, the best, by quite some distance, are the works of the Egyptian author Naguib Mahfouz, whose Cairene tales earnt him the Nobel Prize for Literature. *Midaq Alley* is probably his best.

Budget guides and phrasebooks

Lonely Planet's *Middle East on a shoestring* is the only other guidebook to include all six countries, and a lot of others too, within its covers. If you prefer a little more detail, they also produce separate guides: *Israel*, *Jordan & Syria*, *Turkey* and *Egypt*. The Harvard-based Let's Go series includes *Israel and Egypt* which also covers Syria and Jordan. They do a *Turkey and Greece* guide, too.

To explore the parts of Turkey not covered in this book, pick up a copy of the *Discovery Guide to Eastern Turkey and the Black Sea* (Diana Darke), published by Haag books; my favourite guidebook on Turkey, however, remains the Rough Guide's *Turkey*. Ms Darke has also written a *Discovery Guide to Jordan* (Immel), which has been recommended.

For Lebanon, Bradt's *Lebanon* is the best budget travel book I have seen on that country. Carlton Press's *Lebanon Guide* is informative, although not really for budget travellers. Ross Burns' *Monuments of Syria – an Historical Guide*, published by IB Tauris is recommended.

There is a wealth of Turkish phrasebooks (Lonely Planet, Rough Guide and Berlitz). Lonely Planet's *Egyptian Arabic phrasebook* is compact and very useful, El-Ghobashy & Wise's *Get by in Arabic* is also fine.

For Arabic, again one has plenty of choices but it's a complex language and no comprehensive Arabic phrasebook/dictionary is compact. Wortabet's *Pocket English-Arabic, Arabic-English Dictionary* (Librairie du Liban) is fairly good, but to use it one really needs to have a working knowledge of Arabic in the first place.

PART 2: THE NEAR EAST

Facts about the region

HISTORICAL BACKGROUND

Prehistory

Man first arrived in this region about 600,000 years ago. By 12,000BC these Stone Age people had learnt basic farming techniques and had begun to settle on the banks of the Nile and on the Mediterranean coast in Palestine and Lebanon. By about 7500BC they had learnt to grow grain, and were using more sophisticated tools than the simple sharpened flints that had been used before.

Semitic migration (3500BC-500BC)

Over the course of 3000 years a number of tribes began to migrate north-wards from the barren wastes of Arabia, or eastwards from turbulent Mesopotamia (the land sandwiched between the Euphrates and the Tigris) to settle in the peaceful, fertile Near East.

The **Phoenicians**, hailing from the Arabian shores of the Red Sea, were one of the first (3500BC) to arrive. Having settled on the Mediterranean coast in Lebanon and Palestine they began to trade with Egypt and its neighbours, and soon built a reputation as skilled seamen and able merchants. Indeed, the Phoenicians called themselves 'Kanaan'ri' – Semitic for merchant, and the Bible frequently refers to the lands of Palestine and Israel as 'Canaanite' land, or simply 'Canaan'.

The Phoenicians were soon followed by the **Aramaeans**, who settled in Syria's Orontes Valley and went on to found Damascus (3000BC); the **Ammonites** (3000BC), of Biblical fame, whose kingdom lay just to the east of the Jordan River; and the **Hebrews**, a tiny Semitic tribe who, under Abraham's guidance, migrated from Sanlurfan in south-east Turkey to Canaan in 1800BC. Finally there were the **Nabataeans** (600BC), whose glorious capital, Petra, is one of the highlights of the region today.

The Egyptian pharaohs (3100-664BC)

Whilst all this was going on in Arabia, to the west in Egypt monumental things were happening. By about 3300BC the small settlements along the Nile had split into two distinct kingdoms – Upper and Lower Egypt – which constantly waged war with each other. This bickering ended in 3100BC when the Upper Egyptian king, Menes, conquered Lower Egypt and united the two lands under his command. His victory paved the way for the prosperous **Old Kingdom era** (Dynasties 3-6, 2686-2181BC). This was the world's first great empire. Many of the Semitic tribes of Syria and Palestine mentioned above fell under Egyptian rule.

The pharaohs were worshipped as gods by their people and this adoration continued even after their death. The pyramids in which they were entombed still stand at Giza and Saqqara, an awe-inspiring spectacle which 4500 years of sand and sightseers have done little to diminish.

The Middle Kingdom (Dynasties 11-17, 2040-1782BC)

A combination of misrule and misfortune ended these golden years. Constructing the pyramids placed a huge financial strain on the economy, and a sequence of droughts and famines eventually took their toll of the country. For the next 400 years the country was more concerned with repelling foreign invaders than expanding its own empire, as foreign aggressors began to appear on the border. Eventually Egypt succumbed to the **Hyskos**, a culturally-backward band of Asiatics who had galloped through to Egypt in their new invention, the horse-drawn chariot.

The New Kingdom (Dynasties 18-20, 1570-1070BC)

By the middle of the second millennium BC the Hyskos had been banished and the country was beginning to enjoy something of a renaissance. A succession of strong and innovative leaders helped to restore it to its former Old Kingdom glory. Thutmose I (1524-1518BC) expanded the empire into Palestine and Lebanon once more; Hatshepsut (1498-1483BC), the widow of his son, Thutmose II, increased the country's wealth by sending trading missions into Africa; and her stepson, Thutmose III (1504-1450BC), pushed the boundaries of the empire even further into Syria up to the Euphrates. Indeed the empire had probably grown too big, and later pharaohs – Sety (I and II), Ramses (I to IX), Tutankhamun and Merneptah – found it difficult to maintain these borders. Nevertheless, the New Kingdom era was the greatest in ancient Egypt. The pharaohs were once more idolised and they used this power to build colossal temples to their gods and, of course, to themselves. Many of these temples have survived to this day; they form the main attraction of Upper Egypt, and in particular Luxor, the site of the New Kingdom capital of Thebes.

❏ **Egyptian kingdoms and dynasties**

Following the work of the third century BC historian Manetho, the three millennia of Pharaonic history are normally divided into 30 dynasties. These 30 dynasties are then parcelled up into five separate periods: the Old, Middle, New, Late and Ptolemaic Kingdoms, each one separated from the next by an intermediate period – the unsettled phases marking the transition between these kingdoms. In order to simplify matters, the above is an extremely brief outline of each era.

The Hittites (1700-1200BC)

The only serious rivals to the Egyptians were the Hittites of Central Anatolia (in Turkey). The Hittites enjoyed a virtual monopoly of the production of iron, which they used to good effect in building an empire covering all of Persia and Syria. Although Hittite settlements have all been destroyed, from the fragments of their temples which sit in the museums of Ankara and Aleppo it appears that they too had a penchant for building on a monumental scale.

As the Egyptian's borders gradually encroached into Syria it was inevitable that the two superpowers would clash, which they did in 1275BC at Kadesh, near Homs in Syria. The result was inconclusive, although the Hittites appeared to have had the upper hand and maintained their influence over Syria after the Egyptians had retreated. You'll find many references to this famous battle, from Istanbul where the peace treaty signed between the two in 1259BC can be seen, to Southern Egypt where Ramses II depicted his brave deeds of derring-do on every public building he commissioned. To seal the peace, Ramses took a Hittite princess as his bride.

The Peoples of the Sea (1200BC)

By the end of the second millennium BC both empires were in trouble: Egypt was beset by the same economic difficulties that had befallen them during the Old Kingdom, whilst Hittite power was being eroded by Greek settlers – the Lycians, Carians, Lydians and others – who arrived on Turkey's southern shore.

Then in 1200BC the whole of the Near East suffered an invasion by the 'Peoples of the Sea'. Although details are hazy, it appears that this group was an amalgamation of Greek tribes from the Aegean Islands who fled following the Trojan War. In Canaan they settled and became known as the Philistines – from which we get the word Palestine. In Anatolia they forced the Hittites to run to the hills for safety, finishing their empire once and for all. And in Egypt they so weakened the Egyptians' defences by their assaults that the Libyans were able to storm through and conquer the land soon after.

The new superpowers (730- 323BC)

For the next 400 years three major empires emerged to fill the vacuum left by the Hittites and Egyptians. The **Assyrians** (722BC) of Mesopotamia were the first, followed in 586BC by Nebuchadnezzar's **Babylonians**. Finally the **Persians** arrived (525-332BC) to annex all Babylon's territories. Indeed they went further, building an empire that stretched from the Hindu Kush in Pakistan to the Volga in Russia. It was the largest empire the world had ever seen but it was soon to be superseded by an even greater one.

Alexander the Great (355-323BC)

In 332BC Alexander of Macedonia (northern Greece) was told by the Delphic Oracle that he was invincible; just three years later, and still a few months shy of his 25th birthday, this son of a prince and pupil of Aristotle had proved the Oracle right. All the lands of the Near East had fallen like dominoes before his charge from Greece to Egypt. Having consulted another oracle at Siwa in Egypt he built a new capital – Alexandria – on Egypt's northern shore before setting off again to conquer Persia and India. By the time of his death in 323BC, his empire covered most of the civilised world from the Libyan frontier to the Punjab in India. It was the greatest military campaign in history.

The Ptolemites and Seleucids (323-31BC)

Following Alexander's death the empire was carved up between his generals. Although they were less competent than he, the so-called Hellenistic era lasted for nearly 300 years in the Near East. It was a prosperous time. The region became a conduit for ideas and merchandise, and market towns such as Aleppo thrived on the passing trade.

Very few Hellenistic buildings have survived. Of those that have, the Ptolemaic temples of Philae and Edfu are the most spectacular. The Ptolemites were followers of Alexander's former general, Ptolemy, who subscribed to the Egyptian religion in such a big way that they built huge temples to the gods, and even used the title of pharaoh for their ruler.

Roman rule (200BC-330AD)

The Romans took the Near East in three stages. Step one had been to take Anatolia, which they had begun to do as early as 200BC. Ephesus, the Roman capital of *Provincia Asia*, on Turkey's Aegean coast, is a fascinating place to visit today. Step two was Pompey's invasion of the Eastern Mediterranean in 63BC; with no united opposition it proved to be a relatively easy task. The final stage was the conquest of Egypt (covered in the Aswan chapter on p272).

The Romans brought stability and a sense of order to the region. Subjugated cities who didn't rebel against Roman rule were rewarded with lower taxes or better rights, and thus most cities were willing to accept them. But despite this, *Provincia Arabia* still proved troublesome. Palestine, in particular, was rebellious. The large Jewish contingent held two successful revolts, throwing off the yoke of Roman rule for a few years each time. And then a radical offshoot of Judaism, Christianity, erupted in the Jewish homeland. The Romans responded with typical ferocity, outlawing the religion and feeding the faithful to the local amphitheatre lions. The Christians, however, continued to be a thorn in the side of the Romans. The empire was slowly beginning to fall apart.

The Byzantine Empire (AD330-1453)

In 324AD the Roman empire split in half. The eastern half moved its capital to Byzantium, a relatively obscure town on the Bosphorus which was renamed Constantinople (now Istanbul) in honour of the first emperor, **Constantine**. The city grew quickly to outstrip the fading Rome in terms of beauty, and the Byzantine Empire he founded soon dwarfed its Roman neighbour.

Constantine was a Christian, converted by his mother, Helena, who had made a ground-breaking pilgrimage to the Holy Land in AD326. Church and state were now bonded together and Constantinople became both the spiritual and administrative centre of the Near East.

For the next two centuries the empire continued to grow. Its greatest emperor was **Justinian** (482-565AD) who, despite being the most zealous of Christians, developed a style of leadership that borrowed heavily from the great pagan emperors of ancient Rome. Under his rule the empire expanded to cover not only all of the Near East but North Africa, Italy and Southern Spain too. Some of Byzantine's greatest treasures – Istanbul's Aya Sofya, for instance – were built on his orders.

After Justinian, however, the empire fared badly. At home the church became embroiled in petty theological disputes, while the state suffocated under mind-boggling bureaucracy. The empire was shrinking; although the Byzantines managed to hold on to Constantinople until the 15th century, their empire in the Middle East folded some 800 years prior to this. A greater power was now emerging, and one that began with an illiterate semi-recluse from a small village in Saudi Arabia.

Islam and the Islamic dynasties (636-1258)

Mohammed's rise to glory is a famous one, recounted on p37. By the time he died in AD632 the Arabian peninsula had fallen to his Muslim followers. The Near East did not have long to wait: Jordan, Syria and Lebanon in AD636, Palestine and Jerusalem in AD638 – all were swept away by the momentum of the Islamic movement.

A succession of Islamic dynasties continued the expansion. The **Ommayad Dynasty** (AD661-750), founded by the Sunni leader Mu'awiya from his base in Damascus, was the first. It was a short but spectacular reign; in 89 years their empire reached Spain in the west, the borders of China in the east, and almost everywhere in between. You'll see plenty of delightful Ommayad buildings on this route through the Near East, including two stunningly beautiful mosques in Jerusalem and Damascus. As public opinion turned against the fat cats in Damascus another Sunni dynasty, the **Abbassids** of Baghdad (750-1258), took control, vowing to return Islam to its original principles.

The Shi'ites had their own dynasty too. The **Fatimids** (AD968-1175) had swept through Egypt from North Africa, re-locating their capital to

Cairo. At its most extensive their empire stretched up to the southern reaches of Syria (including Damascus), and covered most of the Near East. Much of this territory was taken from their Sunni rivals, the Abbassids, rather than the Christian Byzantines.

Seljuks (1071-1243)

The Seljuks helped to maintain the momentum of the Islamic movement which, like most of the great empires before it, was in danger of imploding with internal disputes. This tribe of Central Asian warriors had converted to Islam on their migration towards Europe. By 1071 their insidious empire building had led them to take Central Anatolia from the crumbling Byzantine Empire and snatch Jerusalem from the Fatimids.

The Seljuks were a strange contradiction. Abroad they were known for their barbaric invasions and their intolerance of other religions, (it was they who barred the Christian pilgrims from Jerusalem, an action which led to the First Crusade), yet at home they were one of the most enlightened, progressive societies at that time, and their capital at Konya became a centre for art, poetry and philosophy.

The Christians' revenge – the Crusades (1097-1291)

By 1095 the voracious Seljuks had advanced to within 100 miles of Constantinople. In desperation the beleaguered Byzantine Emperor Alexius called upon his European neighbours, the Holy Roman Empire, for help. They responded with the **First Crusade**, a campaign made by all Christendom to free the Holy Land from the clutches of the Muslims. This turned out to be the most successful of all the Crusades. In 1097 Antioch was captured, and two years later Jerusalem was taken from the Seljuks. By 1124, with the capture of Tyre, all the Levant was in their realm – an area stretching from Edessa (north-east of Antioch) in the north to Aqaba in the south. Despite inferior numbers, the Crusaders were able to keep control over the region by bribing and cajoling the local tribal leaders, establishing a feudal system with themselves at the head.

Subsequent Crusades were less successful, however. A **Second Crusade** was dispatched from Europe in 1148 to strengthen the hold on the Levant, but the Crusaders ran out of food and were defeated almost as soon as they had arrived. A **Third Crusade** under Richard the Lionheart and Philip II of France attempted to regain Jerusalem (which had just been captured by Saladin) but they had to retire defeated three years later. The **Fourth Crusade**, in 1204, proved to be such a fiasco that it was the last. The knights who remained in their huge castles were eventually swept out towards the end of the 13th century by the Mamlukes.

The Mamlukes (1250-1517)

The Mamlukes were fighting slaves from Central Asia, used by Saladin, the legendary leader of the Muslim forces who took Jerusalem from the

Crusaders in 1187. At first the Mamlukes were willing to swear allegiance to their Ayyubid masters and fight on their behalf. (The Ayyubids were the descendants of Saladin who ruled the Near East at the beginning of the thirteenth century – see p292). Soon, however, the tail started wagging the dog. As a procession of weak Ayyubid sultans ascended the throne the Mamlukes began to wield more and more influence in the court until eventually the last Ayyubid leader, Sultan al-Salih Ayyub, died and left his Mamluke widow, Shagarit al-Durr, in charge.

The Mamluke Empire was a truly peculiar one. No matter how high a Mamluke climbed in society, he would still be considered a slave. Even the sultan was still a slave in name. And being slaves they had no hereditary system where titles and fortunes could be passed down from father to son. This led to some bloody battles between potential successors every time a sultan died; the Mamluke era distinguishes itself as one of the most violent the Near East has ever seen.

The most successful Mamluke sultan was **Baybars**, who ruled from 1260-77. Instrumental in sweeping the Crusaders out of the region, he also extended the Mamluke Empire to cover nearly all of the Near East (Turkey excepted) and moved the caliphate from Baghdad to Cairo.

The Mongols (1258-61, 1400-03)

The Mongols were the bane of the Mamluke era, charging down from Central Asia to plunder and rape. You will see no material evidence that they ever passed through this area: destruction, rather than construction, was their forte and they contributed not a jot to the culture and advancement of the region. They were like locusts, swarming onto one town and stripping it bare before moving on to the next.

The Mongols conducted a number of campaigns during the 13th and 14th centuries, including one led by the fearsome **Tamerlane** in 1400-1403. It was typically gory – over 50,000 people were killed at Aleppo alone – and until they were defeated by the Mamlukes in 1260, near Nazareth, they remained the most feared of foreign invaders.

The Ottomans (1453-1917)

The Ottomans were yet another power that swept down from the plains of Central Asia. They were the descendants and relatives of Othman, a 14th-century 'Turkish Saladin' famous for his fighting prowess, virtue and chivalry. Their first capital was at Bursa in Western Anatolia but by the middle of the fifteenth century the last Byzantine stronghold of Constantinople had fallen and the rest of the Near East began to look decidedly vulnerable.

The Mamlukes' bows and arrows proved to be no match for their superior weaponry; in 1516 Syria, Palestine and Jordan all fell. The following year **Sultan Selim the Grim** (1512-20), so called for his record of beheading his ministers at the rate of one per year, had completed the

Near Eastern rout by taking Egypt. Constantinople was now both the religious and administrative centre of the Islamic world, just as it had been for the Christian faith under the Byzantines. But the Ottomans did not stop there. Under Selim's son **Süleyman the Magnificent** (1520-66) the empire reached its apogee: all of Arabia, North Africa, and Europe up to the walls of Vienna became theirs.

To the West the Ottomans remain an enigma. On the one hand they could be outstandingly savage – **Sultan Mehmet II** (the Conqueror) famously ripped open the stomachs of his gardeners to find out who had stolen one of his prize cucumbers, and many a sultan used to stand his subjects on the palace walls to use them for rifle practice – and yet on the other hand they were decadent sybarites who insisted on elaborate and formal ceremony when conducting day to day business, and who spent much of their days dressed in the most luxurious clothes. One day the Sultan could be attacking the walls of Vienna with bloodthirsty vigour, and on the next he could be indulging his passion for horticulture, continuing his quest to cultivate a perfect black tulip.

What is certain is that the fortunes of the Near East, including Anatolia, improved little under their reign. Having conquered, the sultans were content to leave the running of the empire to emirs and pashas; as long as they received all the taxes at the end of the year they saw no point in meddling. As a result, the region began to stagnate.

The Sick Man of Europe

By the end of the seventeenth century the cancer of corruption had taken a hold on the empire. The Janissaries, the sultans' personal soldiers, began to run the empire as they wished. The sultans themselves tended to be weak and ineffectual, their entire childhood having been spent within the cosy confines of the harem to avoid assassination. It left them totally unprepared for the realities of life beyond the palace walls. Early sultans had soubriquets such as Mehmet the Conqueror and Süleyman the Magnificent, later sultans rejoiced under such names as Ibrahim the Debauched (so called for his ability to attend to 24 ladies in one day) or Selim the Sot.

Their refusal to modernise their army – there had been no major changes in Ottoman tactics or weaponry for 200 years – opened the door to the European invaders. From being feared in the West as the Terrible Turk, the empire had disintegrated to become the Sick Man of Europe. The empire survived until WWI, but it was little more than a bloated corpse, propped up by European powers to prevent Russia from controlling the Bosphorus Straits and expanding their territory.

For more than a century the European powers of France, Russia, Germany and Britain gathered on the shores of the Near East, jockeying for the best position, waiting for the Ottoman Empire to finally expire.

The countries of the Near East began to take advantage of the weakening empire too: **Pasha Mohammed Ali** (1805-1839), a soldier of Albanian descent who controlled Egypt for the Ottomans, suddenly turned on his former paymasters and began to conquer the whole of the Near East. He was eventually halted at the gates of Constantinople, not by the Ottomans but by the European powers, who forced him into sharing power with the sultan.

THE NEAR EAST IN THE TWENTIETH CENTURY

World War I (1914-18)

For the Arab world Turkish occupancy had become a boil that needed to be lanced; TE Lawrence and the Arab revolutionaries of WWI were the surgeons who performed the operation. The Arab population, though numerous and brave, had always been too fractious to mount a cohesive revolt before. But during the Great War that situation changed. Guided by the enigmatic Lawrence and the British Army at Suez, and under the loose command of Emir Faisal (son of the Sherif of Mecca), the Bedouin tribes united alongside the Allied effort and together they freed the area from Turkish rule.

The fight for independence in the Near East

● **Turkey – recovery under Atatürk** An attempt by the Allied powers to partition Anatolia, following the Turkish defeat in WWI, led directly to the Turkish War of Independence. The Greek invasion of SE Anatolia in 1918 galvanised the Turks, under the leadership of the charismatic Atatürk ('Father Turk'), into direct action. By 1923 all the Allies had been cleared out of Anatolia, the Greeks had withdrawn and Atatürk, from his base in Ankara, was proclaiming himself the first president of the Independent Republic of Turkey.

To win independence was one thing; to build a united nation from the rubble of the Ottoman Empire was quite another. Following a massive population swap between Greece and Turkey, sweeping reforms were introduced by Atatürk to drag the country into the 20th century. Polygamy and the wearing of the fez (a symbol of subservience under the Ottomans) were both forbidden. The Arabic script was abolished in favour of a modified Roman alphabet, and Islam was no longer the official state religion.

● **Palestine and Syria – The Mandate System** In return for their support against the Turks in WWI, the British and French promised the Arabs their independence. It was, unfortunately, a promise they found difficult to keep. Whilst dangling the carrot of independence in front of the Arabs, secretly Britain and France were agreeing to carve up the Near East for themselves in the 1916 Sykes-Picot Agreement. In what is known as the Mandate system, France gained control of Greater Syria (modern Syria and Lebanon) whilst Britain received the Palestinian Mandate

(Jordan and Palestine). Egypt also remained in Britain's hands, as it had done since the end of the 19th century. It was, of course, a very unpopular arrangement and violent protests followed. In Greater Syria the Arab people installed Faisal, the leader of the Arab revolt in WWI, as their king. It was a move the French refused to recognise, and soon they were bombing Damascus in an effort to suppress Syrian insurgency.

In the same year the Christian Maronites, whom the French saw as their allies, persuaded them to set up a separate state where they could be free from Muslim oppression. This state – Lebanon – not only incorporated the Maronites' homeland in the Lebanese mountains but also the mainly-Muslim coastal towns of Beirut, Tripoli, Sidon and Tyr, included in order to make the state economically viable. The unrest continued in both countries, however. Eventually in the 1940s the French, beleaguered by the war raging in their own country, allowed the two nations to become independent.

Meanwhile, to the south the British were faring little better, although Transjordan – the area to the east of the Jordan River – proved to be the least bothersome of all the Mandate states. In 1920 Britain installed Abdullah, Faisal of Syria's elder brother and the son of the Sharif of Mecca, as the nominal ruler of the land, and in 1947 Jordan finally won full independence. This solved matters to the east of the Jordan River; to the west, however, Palestine was in chaos.

● **Egypt** Egypt's battle for independence was a riotous affair. During the early years of this century the Egyptian people regularly took to the streets in protest at British rule. In an effort to appease them, in 1922 the British appointed a descendant of Mohammed Ali, Fuad, the first King of Egypt. But ultimate power was still held by the British, and as such the unrest continued. Full autonomy arrived only in 1947, after British troops had returned to fight Rommel's tanks at al-Alamein.

Jew versus Arab – the fight for Palestine
● **Jewish immigration** The first rumblings of a revival in Jewish nationalism were heard towards the end of the 19th century. In the World Zionist Conference of 1897 Theodore Herzl, an Austrian journalist, mooted the idea of a Jewish homeland. Their ideal venue was the country that had once been the domain of their most revered king, David. Quite simply, the Jews wanted Palestine. Over the next few decades waves of Jewish exiles arrived on the Palestinian shore, originally pulled not so much by idealistic thoughts of founding a Jewish nation as pushed by the pogroms and persecution of Europe. This continued throughout the British Mandate as anti-Semitism took hold of Central Europe.

The native Arab population felt helpless in the face of this sudden influx and reacted violently. Soon both sides were perpetrating vicious terrorist attacks which increased as the British Mandate drew to a close.

● **The Israeli War of Independence, 1948** In desperation the British turned to the UN. Their solution was to split Palestine into three: the Arabs received the West Bank, Gaza Strip, Jaffa and parts of the Galilee; Jerusalem became an international city; and the Jews, under the banner of Israel, were given the rest of the country.

When Britain finally did leave, in 1948, their departure precipitated a period of open warfare involving not only Jew and Arab but the Palestinians' neighbours too: Jordan, Syria, Lebanon, Egypt and Iraq all piled in, supposedly on the Arab Palestinian's side.

After the dust had settled one year later, the Israelis had taken West Jerusalem, the Jordanians East Jerusalem and the West Bank, and Egypt the Gaza Strip. The Palestinians were now landless, refugees in their own country. What is worse, they had lost the West Bank and Gaza Strip not to their enemies, the Israelis, but their supposed allies Jordan and Egypt! As a result, three quarters of the Palestinian population were forced to re-locate outside their homeland, in Jordan or Lebanon.

● **The Six Day War of 1967** To consolidate their position, the Israelis passed a Law of Return in 1950 which allowed any Jew to settle in Israel. The Jewish population soon outnumbered the native Palestinians by 3:1. In response to this, the Palestinian Liberation Organisation (PLO) was formed in 1964 to further the cause of the Palestinian people.

It was another three years before the Arabs mounted a second concerted effort to win back the land. As in 1948, however, the Six Day War of 1967 proved to be a disaster for the Palestinians and their allies. The Israelis bombed the Egyptian and Syrian airforce whilst they were still on the ground and then went on to capture the Golan Heights from Syria, East Jerusalem and the West Bank from Jordan, and the Gaza Strip and the Sinai from Egypt. Their territory was now four times the size it had been in 1949.

● **The War of Yom Kippur** A third Arab attempt to defeat Israel in 1973 was a little more successful. This time Egypt and Syria mounted a two-pronged assault. Their timing was perfect. October 6th is the Jewish festival of Atonement, Yom Kippur, when most of the regular Israeli soldiers return home or spend the day praying in the synagogues. Although the Israelis eventually retaliated to drive the invaders out, it was the first time they had looked vulnerable and they took heavy casualties.

● **Camp David and the Intifada** As a consequence of the war of Yom Kippur the Israelis were a little more willing to negotiate with the Arabs. In 1979 they got their chance. The Egyptian president, Anwar Sadat, made a surprise visit to the Knesset (Israel's parliament) urging the Israelis to talk peace. The result was the Camp David accords. Israel promised to return the Sinai (which it did in 1982), Egypt promised peace, and the border between the two was opened once more. In Palestine, however, the troubles continued. The PLO responded to a traffic accident in the Gaza Strip, where an Israeli driver appeared to deliberately run down Arab citizens, with the 'intifada', a series of strikes, demonstrations and acts of terrorism against the Jewish nation.

This internal upheaval continued for a number of years; but by now all eyes were on a new conflict brewing just over the border in Lebanon.

The Lebanese Civil War 1975-92

● **Christian versus Muslim** To begin with, the Lebanese Civil War was just that: an internal battle for power between the Maronite Christian and Muslim populations. It had at its roots a census taken way back in 1932 when the country was still under French rule, which found that for every six Christians in Lebanon there were five Muslims. When the French departed in 1943 the Maronite Christians, in the absence of any better suggestions, decided to divide power according to these ratios. Thus for every six Christian MP's in parliament there was to be five Muslims. The Maronites also decreed that the president of Lebanon should be a Christian, whilst the prime minister should be of the Sunni faith and the speaker a Shi'ite.

Unfortunately, in the ensuing years the population ratios changed. Palestinian refugees flooding over the border following Israel's War of independence swelled the Muslim population to such an extent that they soon outnumbered the Christians by 3:1. The Muslims, naturally enough, called for greater political representation in light of this, but their calls were ignored by the Maronites in power.

● **The PLO arrive** In September 1970 King Hussein of Jordan launched an all-out attack on the PLO. Since their inception in 1964 the PLO had used Jordan's capital, Amman, as their headquarters and had launched frequent attacks on Israel from the city. Unfortunately, they had also turned Amman into their own private playground, with law and order deteriorating to such an extent that anarchy now ruled. In response, Jordan's King Hussein (Abdullah's grandson) asked his army to intervene in the month now known as Black September. By July 1971 the PLO had been defeated. In desperation they fled to Lebanon, from where they renewed their attacks on Israel.

This was bad news for the Christian government in Lebanon, for the PLO were natural allies to the Muslims in their battle for a greater share of the power. The besieged government figured that they had but one choice and turned to their militias, private armies such as the Phalangists and the Tigers, to try to break the PLO, King Hussein-style, by force. The Lebanese Muslims sided with the PLO, and in 1975 the fighting between the two sides – the PLO and Lebanese Muslims versus the Maronite government – began in earnest.

One year later, and the war had reached deadlock. The Christians held East Beirut and the Mt Lebanon range, whilst the Palestinians and Lebanese Muslims controlled West and South Beirut. Syria, the first of many foreigners to interfere, held the north of the country.

● **The Israeli invasion** This deadlock held for six years until, on 6th June 1982, the Israelis invaded to try and defeat the PLO. It took them just one week to storm through the south of the country and on 13th June they arrived at the gates of Beirut. There they issued an ultimatum: either the PLO evacuate, or Israel would invade Beirut. To prevent further bloodshed Yasser Arafat, under the supervision of a UN-sponsored MNF (Multi-National Force), led his troops onto a boat bound for Cyprus.

Despite this withdrawal, the Israelis went ahead and invaded the city. Their reason, apparently, was to try to force a peace treaty out of the Lebanese government. Their actions were unforgivable: in one particularly heinous episode they surrounded two refugee camps, Shabra and Chatila, and watched as their Phalangist allies entered and slaughtered over 1000 inhabitants. Many of the refugees inside were Shi'ites, who had fled the PLO-Israeli fighting in Southern Lebanon.

The Israelis' actions had failed to secure a peace treaty, earning instead only worldwide condemnation and the Shi'ites' hatred. Eventually, they agreed to leave Beirut empty-handed but instead of returning home they bunkered down in southern Lebanon. This action provoked even more anger, especially amongst the Shi'ites who considered Southern Lebanon to be their homeland.

● **Chaos** Anarchy now ruled. The simple Muslim versus Christian punch-up had been superseded by more secular squabbles. The Israelis were fighting the Shi'ites in the south; the various militias had turned on each other, settling ancient feuds in their attempt to control the lucrative drug-trafficking industry; and even the US Marines, part of the MNF force that had overseen the PLO evacuation, had been dragged into the war. Over 240 US servicemen were killed when a suicide bomber rammed an explosives-laden truck into a barracks. (President Reagan, mindful of growing unrest at home, withdrew his troops the following year). As an illustration of just how confused the situation had become, the Christian Government started to issue visas to their old PLO enemies to enlist their help in the war against their new enemy, the Shi'ites!

● **Syrian intervention** Finally, in 1987, the Syrians took Beirut and began to restore order. Initially, their proposal for a new constitution, which allowed the Muslims a greater share of power, was rejected by the Lebanese President Michael Aoun. Instead, the president called for a

---

(**Opposite**) The traditional Arabian headscarf provides excellent protection from both desert storms and the over-intrusive camera lens.

'War of Liberation' to rid the country of the Syrian 'oppressors'. One year later Syria took total control, and Aoun was forced to step down.

By 1992 the Syrian and Lebanese army had restored order and had managed to implement the new constitution originally rejected by Aoun. In August of that year free elections were held for the first time in two decades. Shi'ite Hizbollah won the largest number of seats, and billionaire financier Rafik Hariri became the new prime minister. The new president, following the assassination of Rene Moawwad in October, was Elias Hrawi, a Maronite Christian and a good friend of Syria.

The Gulf War, 1991

In December 1990 soldiers from Saddam Hussein's Iraq invaded Kuwait. In response, a UN force was cobbled together to liberate the tiny, oil-rich dictatorship from Hussein's grasp.

The countries of the Near East played an integral part in the success of the UN mission. Syria and Egypt supplied troops and Turkey allowed the UN to use their air bases. Only Jordan supported Iraq, although throughout the conflict King Hussein attempted to play the role of mediator. The Israelis wanted to help with the war effort too, but were prevented from doing so by the UN who feared that any Israeli involvement could fracture the anti-Iraq coalition; after all, no self-respecting Arab would fight on the same side as an Israeli against a fellow Arab.

Aftermath and the future

All were rewarded for their efforts in the Gulf War. Egypt had half of its US$20.2bn debt wiped out, whilst Syria, Israel and Jordan were offered the opportunity of an even greater prize: peace. The conflict had brought the Palestinian problem to the forefront of the UN agenda, and in the following months the Arab and Jew conflict took centre stage. During a conference later that year in Madrid there was a significant improvement in relations between the three nations. Then in 1993, following talks in Oslo, the PLO leader Yasser Arafat and Israel's prime minister Yitzhak Rabin signed a historic agreement in Washington. As a result of this agreement the Gaza Strip and West Bank (excluding existing Jewish settlements) were allowed to govern for themselves for the first time. The Arab state of Palestine had finally been realised. Two years later, in December 1995, the Palestinians were going to the election booths for the first time, overwhelmingly voting Yasser Arafat to be their first president.

In 1996 Rabin and King Hussein also came to an agreement, ending 46 years of hostilities between Israel and Jordan. Israel even went as far as promising their old enemies, Syria, that they would negotiate a deal over the Golan Heights.

(**Opposite**) These Ships of the Desert are on their way to Cairo's massive Imbaba camel market.

And thus by the end of 1994 it looked as if the bloody Near East saga would have a happy ending after all. Unfortunately, as we shall see in the relevant chapters, the actions of one Jewish extremist in 1995 have thrown the whole peace process into jeopardy once more.

THE PEOPLE

Arabs

Most of the native Arab population of the Near East are descendants of those original Semitic immigrants of four thousand years ago, such as the Canaanites or Amorites. Less than 10% of these people still adopt the traditional nomadic lifestyle of the Bedouin – most have now settled permanently to farm the land, or have migrated to work in the cities.

Turks

Originally from Central Asia, where there is a hill called Tuk'ueh from which they derive their name, the Turks migrated south-west to avoid the Mongols about 700 years ago. About 95% of the Turkish population is composed of Turks; most of the rest are either Kurdish or Armenian.

Kurds

With the same religion and features, at first glance the Kurdish people appear remarkably similar to the Turks but they have, in fact, their own distinct culture and language. They occupy an area in Northern Syria, Eastern Turkey, Iran and Iraq, and their push for an independent Kurdistan has seen them come into conflict time and again with the governments of those countries.

Armenians

On the north-eastern border of Turkey is the tiny state of Armenia, a former-Soviet Christian state. The Armenian history is an unhappy one and during WWI they were largely wiped out by the Ottomans on suspicion of being pro-European traitors. Many of those that were not massacred were pushed south to Syria and Lebanon, where they remain today. They are one of the few Christian races in the region.

Hamito Semitics

This group were living on the Nile in pharaonic times. Basically, they are the original Nile settlers. As their name suggests, they probably migrated from the East – Arabia or Mesopotamia – before settling in Egypt.

As well as these peoples one can find a sprinkling of Circassians and Chechens from Central Asia, a smattering of Nubians in Southern Egypt and a light dusting of Russians, Americans, Europeans and Africans who have settled in Israel.

RELIGION

As the centre for the three major monotheistic faiths – Islam, Judaism and Christianity – religion has played an integral part in the history of the Near East and continues to dominate everyday life. It comes as a surprise to many travellers to find out just how closely the three religions are linked, especially as they seem to spend most of their time at each other's throats! But Christianity can be seen as just a radical departure from Judaism, and Islam is little more than an extension of both. All the monotheistic faiths worship the same God. Jesus, Moses, Noah, and Abraham are all Islamic prophets too.

Just as surprising is the fact that many of the beliefs have their roots in the religion of ancient Egypt and other extinct faiths, even though at first sight they appear to have very little in common. See p281 for more information on the ancient Egyptian religion.

The following provides a brief background to the modern faiths.

Judaism

● **Historical background** In 1800BC a group of nomads under Abraham headed west from Ur in Mesopotamia to Canaan. Abraham's grandson, Jacob, had twelve sons, the descendants of whom became the Twelve Tribes of Israel. Drought eventually forced Abraham's Israelites to move on from Canaan to Egypt, but they returned in about 1250BC after years of persecution in Egypt by Pharaohs Sety I (who imprisoned them) and Ramses II.

The journey back to Canaan is the 'Exodus' of Biblical fame, a 40-year tramp through the wilderness in search of the 'Promised Land'. During this time their leader, Moses, received the ten commandments from God and the nation of Israel was born, albeit a few hundred miles to the west of their eventual homeland.

Upon arriving the Israelites set about making Canaan their own. David, the son and heir of the Israelites' first king, Saul, expanded the Jewish domain up to the Euphrates. His son, Solomon, continued the good work. His reign is celebrated as the Golden Age of Judaism, when art, trade and theology reached their apogee. A glorious temple to house the Ark of the Covenant – a chest containing the Ten Commandments given to Moses – was also made at this time, on Mt Moriah in Jerusalem.

Following Solomon's death in 930BC the land was split into two. Ten of the Twelve Tribes broke away to form Israel, a land to the north of Jerusalem. They were eventually obliterated from history by the Assyrians in 722BC. The people were scattered in mass deportations and became known as the Ten Lost Tribes of Israel.

In the south Judah, including Jerusalem, held out until the Babylonians invaded in 586BC. Solomon's Temple was destroyed, and the Judeans were exiled to Babylonia. Only after Cyrus and the Persians had captured Babylonia 48 years later (see p223) were the Judeans allowed to return home.

Under the Romans Palestine was declared a vassal state ruled by Herod – an Edomite whose loyalties lay with Rome. In order to quell any civil unrest Herod curried favour with the Jewish locals by renovating Solomon's Temple. Unfortunately his heirs proved to be less capable at appeasement and after a spate of Jewish revolts the Romans were forced to assume complete control. The Jews rebelled twice during their reign - in AD 66 and again in the Kochba rebellion of AD132 – but each time the revolts were suppressed and the Jews suffered the wrath of Rome. Following the Bar Kochba rebellion Jerusalem was flattened – Herod's temple included – in AD132 and a new Roman city was built.

With no temple and no homeland the Jews recognised that the only bond that they could have was to follow a common law. Thus the Jewish people, wherever they went, followed the same religious doctrine. These Jewish people became known as the Diaspora, or 'the scattered'.

● **The religion** The Jews believe that they are high priests, chosen by God to teach and guide the Gentiles. They believe that God will return to resurrect the faithful on Judgement Day, appearing first at Jerusalem. Their faith is founded on the *Torah*, the first five books of the Old Testament that deal with the creation, the migrations of Abraham and the Exodus of Moses.

Much of the complexity of Judaism arises from the laws that govern it. The *Talmud*, written in the first century AD, is a collection of interpretations of these laws. New laws are still being developed today to cope with the modern age. Some of these rulings are well-known, such as the proscribing of eating pork and non-kosher food for example. When visiting Israel you will find that these laws may impinge on your travelling plans in some way.

Christianity

Christianity grew out of the turmoil into which Judaism had plunged during the Roman occupancy of Palestine. Many of the faithful had become dissatisfied with the way the religion was being run by self-serving leaders creating ever-more ridiculous laws. Essentially, Christianity can be seen as a movement away from the letter of Jewish law and towards its spirit, as exemplified by Christ's Sermon on the Mount, a distillation of all His teachings.

● **Historical background** Historians are now fairly satisfied that there was a man called Jesus, who was born c5BC and lived for about 35 years, mostly in Nazareth. Beyond that, things are a little less certain. According to the Gospels, Jesus was born in Bethlehem to the Virgin Mary but spent much of his infancy in Egypt, where his family had fled to escape the massacre of children by Herod. On his return Jesus was baptised by his cousin, John the Baptist, and settled down in Galilee as a teacher. He became just one of many reactionaries who toured the land at this time. But his outspoken views and crowd-pleasing miracles with the blind and lame set him apart from the others, and soon earned him a large following. Unfortunately, it earned him many enemies too. In AD30 he went to Jerusalem to celebrate the Jewish festival of the Passover. Having criticised the Roman and Jewish governors in many of his sermons, he must have known that his life was in danger. He was eventually arrested in the Garden of Gethsemane, and charged with the capital offence of blasphemy. He was crucified on the Jewish leaders' insistence by the Roman Governor Pontius Pilate.

But of course the story doesn't end there. Three days later he rose from the dead to frighten the life out of his disciples and the rest, as they say, is history.

● **The religion** Unfortunately, the only detailed records of Jesus' life are the Gospels, written by Christians for Christians. They were also written long after Jesus had died; the first is attributed to Mark, AD62.

There is no doubt, however, that the religion held sway in the Near East from the third to the seventh centuries thanks to the Byzantines. During this period the church split down a number of theological lines, which eventually led over the years to the establishment of three major churches: Catholic, Eastern, and Protestant. Most of the Christians in the Near East follow the Eastern Orthodox faith, which can be subdivided into the **Syrian Orthodox** (based in Damascus), the **Maronites** of Lebanon and the Egyptian **Coptic Church**.

Today there are significant pockets of Christianity in Syria, Lebanon, Jordan and Egypt. It comes as a surprise to find the unequal representation between each of the churches in the Holy Land. For instance, the world's largest church, Roman Catholicism, owns very few of Christianity's sacred sites, whereas smaller denominations – the tiny Armenian church, the Greek Orthodox, even the Egyptian and Syrian Copts – are far more visible in Israel. The other major church, the Protestants, barely gets a look in.

More disturbing is how much friction there is between all of them. The squabbling over who owns what in the Holy Land has continued for centuries. By far the biggest chunk is now in the hands of the Greek Orthodox Church, next are the Armenians (over 30% of all holy sites in Israel are Armenian-owned); the Roman Catholics own less than 20%.

Islam

● **Historical background** Mohammed was born in Mecca in AD570. At the age of 40 he began to receive messages from Allah (God) via the angel Gabriel. On these revelations he built a new religion, Islam – 'Submission' to Allah's will.

Having failed to convince the citizens of Mecca, Mohammed and his followers, the Muslims ('surrendered men' as they have surrendered themselves to God), fled to Medina in AD622 to receive a far warmer reception. Whilst there they built a massive following and returned in triumph to conquer Mecca in AD630. Two years later Mohammed died but not before he had communicated all his prophecies and teachings to scribes (he was illiterate) who collated them into a book called the Koran. His forces had conquered all of Arabia with an unstoppable mixture of persuasion and force. Mohammed's successor, Ibn Bakr, continued the Islamic expansion.

Soon after Mohammed's death Islam split into two. Originally the argument was one of succession: the fourth successor to Mohammed was his son-in-law, Ali, who had been implicated in the assassination of the previous caliph, Othman. In revenge Mu'awiya, one of Othman's relatives and the founder of the Ommayads, is said to have had Ali killed; he then established himself as the new Caliph. The followers of Mu'awiya became the **Sunni Muslims**, who maintain that the Caliphate should be an elected position. The followers of the descendants of Ali (the only true descendants of Mohammed) believe that the Caliphate should be hereditary, and they became known as the **Shi'ite Muslims**.

● **The religion** The West's perception of Islam is often a negative one. To many it is a religion followed by extremists, governed by antiquated laws and populated by misogynists who suppress the role of women until they are little more than slaves. If your visit to this region teaches you nothing else, I hope you may at least learn to respect a religion which is not so far removed from Christianity as you may at first have believed.

Although Muslims believe in many of the Jewish and Christian prophets, to them Mohammed is the only prophet to whom God revealed the whole story. From the divine messages he received Mohammed began to establish a religion built on five 'Pillars', the essential tenets on which Muslims should base their lives. The first of these pillars is to profess one's faith in God (Allah) by the phrase 'There is no God but Allah and Mohammed is his prophet'. Five times a day you will hear this phrase intoned by muezzins calling the faithful to prayer from minarets throughout the region.

The act of praying is the second pillar. The faithful can pray anywhere, as long as they pray towards Mecca. (You can buy a prayer mat in Amman with a built-in Mecca compass). The head must be covered, and a set of ritual ablutions should be carried out before praying. A fountain is usually set in the courtyards of the mosques for this purpose. The third pillar is to give a portion of one's income to charity, whilst the fourth is to observe the fasting month of Ramadan (see below). The final tenet is that all Muslims must make a pilgrimage to Mecca at least once in their lives.

● **Islamic sects** Of the two main branches of Islam, **Shi'ite** and **Sunni**, it is the Sunnis who have the largest number of followers. All of these six countries save Lebanon and, of course, Israel have a majority Sunni population. Other Islamic sects you may encounter include the **Alawites**, a Shi'ite sect who worship Ali as a God. They are found nearly exclusively in Syria. President Assad is an Alawite.

A breakaway group from Islam is the **Druze**. Very little is known about this religion, which has as its founder Ismael al-Darazi, a follower of Caliph al-Hakim (see p308). They are tremendously secretive, and only a few elders know the complete litany of Druze beliefs and teachings. The Druze, who are based in the Mountains of Lebanon and Syria, are not permitted to abandon their faith, nor are others allowed to join.

Baha'i
● **Historical background** Sayyid Ali Mohammed was born in Persia in 1820. For most of his adult life he went around declaring that he was the new prophet, the 'Bab' or 'Gateway to the Truth'. Persia at this time did not take too kindly to heretics, and in 1850 he was shot dead; his body was buried in Tehran, and his followers fled the country.

Further exiles and persecutions took place; then in 1863 the stepbrother of Sayyid's successor decided that he too was a Bab and changed his name to **Baha'u'llah** – 'The Splendour of God'. By this time Baha'u'llah and the followers of the faith had landed at Akko (northern Israel), bringing with them the body of Sayyid Ali Mohammed for burial. Baha'u'llah's successor, Abbas Effendi, then transferred the Bab's body to Mt Carmel in Haifa where a beautiful shrine was built. Baha'u'llah himself died in 1892. His shrine in Akko is the Baha'is' holiest.

● **The religion** The Baha'i faith at first appears to be an amalgamation of all the best bits from other religions. Zoroaster, Buddha, Mohammed, Jesus, all are considered prophets to the Baha'is, who believe that religious truth is progressive and develops over time. That is to say, the religious truth of 2000 years ago is not the same religious truth that is relevant today. According to the Baha'is, God revealed to each of these prophets the truth that was relevant to their time, so that they could then guide mankind through that period.

One of the main goals of Bahai'sm is the promotion of peace. It aims to promote understanding between cultures and races, and stresses the need for a single world language in order to achieve this goal. It is still a relatively minor faith, but one that is growing rapidly in every part of the world.

Practical information for the visitor

HOLIDAYS AND FESTIVALS
Islamic holidays
The Islamic calendar dates from the escape from Mecca to Medina by Mohammed, and is known as the Hejira ('flight') calendar. Their holy day is **Friday**; most shops, banks and public institutions close on this day.

● **Ramadan** (Ramazan in Turkey) is the main Islamic festival, although throughout this month of fasting and denial celebrations are a little thin on the ground. During the day Muslims are not allowed to let anything pass their lips, be it food, water or cigarette smoke. Only at dusk, which is traditionally signalled by the firing of a cannon, may they break their fast. This procedure continues for thirty days, and ends with three days of festivities and gorging. In all Islamic countries these three days are national holidays. In 1997 Ramadan will begin on 31Dec, and continue until 31 Jan 1998. In the following Islamic year (1419) it will run from 20 Dec 1998 to 20 Jan 1999.

● **Kurban Bayrami** Celebrating the attempted sacrifice of Isaac by his father Abraham (he was eventually stopped by God), in Turkey this is the biggest holiday of the year. For four days banks and many shops close down, with many locals heading off on holiday.

● **Idul Adha** The time when Muslims should complete the fifth pillar of their faith, the pilgrimage to Mecca. In 1997/98 it will be held in April.

● **Mulid al-Nabi (Mevlid-i Nebi in Turkish)** Mohammed's birthday, which until the end of the millennium will be in July. Mosques are festooned with lights, and special prayers are recited.

Christian holidays
The Julian calendar, used by Christians in the Near East, is up to one month behind the Western (Gregorian) calendar. **Easter** is the most important holiday in the Julian year. **Christmas** is also celebrated throughout the region. Israel is the most popular destination at this time for obvious reasons, but if you fancy a more secular celebration consider heading to Lebanon and join in the fun there.

Jewish holidays
From Friday evening to Saturday evening Israel is on holiday. The Jewish **Shabbat** must be carefully planned for (see p223).

The main annual festivals are **Yom Kippur**, the Day of Atonement, and **Rosh Ha-Shanah**, the 'Head of the year'. Both occur in September-

October time, and Israel comes to a halt on these days. During Yom Kippur observant Jews must abstain from food, smoking, washing and sex in favour of prayer and contemplation. Rosh Ha-Shanah is a two-day festival with more prayer and contemplation involved. Other festivals include **Sukkot and Simhat Torah**, which celebrate the 'wilderness years' of Moses, and **Hanukkah**, which commemorates the first great Jewish rebellion, the Maccabaean Revolt of 167BC against the Greeks.

LOCAL TRANSPORT

Train

Every country except Lebanon offers some sort of rail service. It is possible to travel from Istanbul to Aleppo (part of the classic Orient Express route), and from there on to Aqaba by train. Only in Egypt, however, is it a really useful mode of transport for travellers; for details of the timetable of the Nile trains see the Egyptian chapter.

The historic **Hejaz Railway** used to run from Damascus to Petra and on to the Saudi Arabian province of the Hejaz, for the holy shrines at Medina and Mecca. We give details of the section between Damascus and Amman (see p152). The track was originally laid by the Ottomans but is more famous for its destruction rather than construction. This was the target for Lawrence of Arabia's sabotage attacks during the Arab revolt in WWI. Where once the carriages were full of Haj pilgrims and Ottoman troops waiting to be blown up, today the carriages contain nothing but dust, grime and secret police. Nevertheless, it is a small piece of history, and a must for all railway enthusiasts.

Bus

For most of the journey you will probably have to rely on the buses, which range from the nice (Turkey) to the nauseating (Syria). In Turkey you'll be fed and watered and even entertained with videos. In the Arab world, however, you won't need any televisual entertainment. The Arab flair for interior decoration, which seems to be missing from many of their houses, is unleashed on their beloved vehicles. Prayer beads, photos, slogans, flowers, fake leopard-skin, air fresheners, clocks, more photos, mirrors, compasses, posters, stickers, drawings of Mecca/Swiss chalets/Saddam Hussein/Boney M, tinsels, tassels, bells and whistles – and that's just the dashboard. To accompany this dizzying vision, every chariot-driver will then put on at full blast either the latest in Arabic bubble-gum pop, a medley of traditional Turkish/Bedouin folk tunes, or that old classic, *Verses from the Koran*. It can be quite an experience.

Servis taxi

All countries have a shared taxi arrangement where the cost of the taxi is split between the passengers. In Arabic countries it is called the servis taxi, in Israel it's the sherut and in Turkey the dolmus. Many of these taxis are rusting classics from the fifties: Chevrolets, Rileys, Studebakers – in which it is an honour to feel car-sick. The usefulness of this form of transport varies according to the other options available. They are essential in Lebanon, where the transport infrastructure is still fairly shattered, whereas in Turkey it appears they are gradually being phased out.

POST
Receiving mail
There are two ways of receiving mail abroad in the Near East. Some people use the American Express (Amex) service. For a fee, or free if you have an Amex card, the offices will hold any mail for you. Addresses of all the offices on the route are given in the relevant chapters.

A far more common method, however, is to use poste restante. Simply ask your loved ones to send mail to the major post offices addressed thus:

> Mr Henry <u>STEDMAN</u> (surname underlined)
> c/o POSTE RESTANTE,
> Main GPO,
> Damascus,
> SYRIA

Remember to put a return address on the back. Ask the sender to post the letter two or three weeks before you are due to arrive. When collecting, most GPO's insist on seeing your passport before handing over letters.

MONEY

For rates of exchange and more information about money see the 'Facts about the country' sections at the start of each country chapter.

Bargaining
Whatever your budget, there is one way you can make it cheaper for yourself: Bargain! Westerners always feel awkward, at least initially, about arguing over price but here, without exception, bargaining is the norm. Hotels, souvenirs, bus fares – whatever it is you're after, haggle.

When you do haggle, remember to smile, and keep it friendly – charm is a very potent weapon in these countries. Having agreed on a price you must not go back on your word. And don't regard it as a slight on your ego if you don't get the price you want – lighten up, you're on holiday!

Baksheesh
Another alien concept to most of us is 'baksheesh', the Arabic euphemism for a bribe. In the Near East, baksheesh has been around longer than money and, especially in Egypt, controls nearly every facet of day-to-day life. If applied at the right moment to the right person, it can

work in your favour too. Rules are bent, doors are unlocked, hieroglyphics explained – and all for a few piastres. You'll soon get to know when baksheesh is necessary.

Tipping

Tipping is not common. At the better restaurants and hotels a tip will be expected but taxis and tour guides are not normally tipped. For budget travellers the matter of paying a service charge should not arise too often.

❏ The bargaining process

The procedure for haggling is nearly always the same. First, find something of interest and ask the shopkeeper to name his price. In response, he will point out the exquisite craftsmanship of said item, the painstaking attention to detail and the long hours of labour that have gone into producing such fine quality merchandise. He will tell you everything, in fact, except the price.

When he does finally give a figure, it will be the real price multiplied by a factor greater than two. This figure is based less on how much the item is worth and more on how much he thinks you've got. As is customary, you should offer, at most, half of his original offer. He will laugh in mock disbelief, and then pretend to be insulted. Don't believe any of it.

Foreplay over, this is where the real bargaining begins. Your next step is to ask the shopkeeper to name his best price. He will probably drop his original offer by a third. You should then shake your head and tell him that you're a poor student; in response, he will no doubt tell you that he has a large family. You could try grabbing a couple of small denomination notes from your pocket, explaining that this is all you have left. He will probably tut and throw back his head but it's worth a try.

As a last resort, leave the shop. In all likelihood, he'll call you back. You'll then return, expecting him to quote a lower price, only to hear him quote the same as before. (This part may be played out a number of times).

Eventually, after arguments and much wailing and gnashing of teeth, you'll agree on a price. You'll then head back to the hostel to meet somebody who paid half as much as you did for the same object, while the shopkeeper will probably lock up for the day, and go home to contemplate early retirement.

BODY LANGUAGE

If you've given up on attempting to master the spoken word (see p313), you will be pleased to know that it is a lot easier to be fluent in the body language of the Near East. Knowing certain gestures can make communication easier, and more fun. Here are a few of the essentials:

● **No**: Throw your head back and tut. A raise of the eyebrows is common too. At first it seems terribly ill-mannered, as if the gesticulator is being contemptuously dismissive of the enquiry.

● **I don't understand**: You're asked a question but do not know the Arabic or Turkish for 'No', and so you shake your head instead. Except that in the Near East, a shake of the head means 'I don't understand', and so the question will be asked again, and again, and again....!

● **Wait/Calm down**: Pinch the fingers on one hand together, point them upwards, and hold them out in front of you. For a demonstration, attempt to hurry somebody up. You'll doubtless receive this gesture in reply.

● **What do you want?**: Hold your hand out as if you're about to shake somebody's hand. Now open the fingers, and rapidly rotate the hand so that the palm now points upwards.

● **Come here**: Imagine you've just robbed a fruit machine and the proceeds lie all over a waist-high table. Quickly scrape the coins into a bag by your foot with one arm without bending it at the elbow. You are now making the gesture for 'come here'.

● **Show me your passport/ticket/document**: The official will trace a line across the palm of his hand with the index finger of his other hand.

● **Enough/I am full** (when referring to food): Place your hand on your heart and give a big smile. If it's a drink that is being offered, place your hand over the cup.

It is worth noting too that the Arabs are a demonstrative, tactile people. Do not be surprised, therefore, if somebody takes you by the arm if you have asked them for directions. It is not sexual, just part of the Arab way. The same treatment may be meted out to women; providing it's the hand he is leading you by, there is no need to feel too alarmed.

Etiquette – the art of not causing offence

Even more important than learning which gesture means what is learning which gestures shouldn't be used at all. Pointing at someone is derogatory. Point with your fingers and you're asking for trouble; point with your foot, and you'll probably get it. If you do wish to indicate someone, nod your head in their direction. Don't use your left hand when you're eating either, particularly if you are eating from a communal bowl. The Arabs come up with all sorts of stories about how this tradition came about – there is a devil on your left shoulder, Mohammed ate with his right hand etc – but the main reason is that the left hand is the toilet paper substitute.

Most of the other 'forbiddens' are just simple courtesies common to most of the world: avoid canoodling with your partner(s) in public; don't blow your nose in public or make a great display of picking your teeth in a restaurant (cover your mouth with your other hand); dress conservatively in towns and cities and avoid conspicuous smoking and eating during Ramadan.

When in Turkey, do not insult Atatürk. It causes great offence to Turks to have their hero slandered and there is actually a law against it. There is also a law against insulting Syria's President Assad, so be careful whom you talk to and what you talk about.

Mosque etiquette

Some of the oldest and holiest mosques in the Islamic world are in this region. The etiquette for visiting them is always the same. First, don't visit during prayer times (signalled by the call to prayer five times a day) and avoid Fridays. Second, don't wear revealing clothes. Robes are often provided but it is as well to come prepared. Third, before entering, remove your shoes. Be quiet when inside; there are often people praying, so don't distract them with flash photography or loud conversation.

FOOD

If you have the money, your tour through the region could turn into a gourmet extravaganza. Unfortunately for budget travellers, it is the same few cheap, staple meals that can be relied on, and only in Turkey is it possible to enjoy really varied and exquisite fare at reasonable prices (as long as you're not vegetarian).

Religious standards are as important as hygienic ones in the kitchens of the Near East. For Muslims, all meat must be *halal*, that is to say that it must be drained of blood, should come from animals that have been slaughtered according to certain rules and should not be the flesh of a carnivorous animal or a pig.

According to Jewish law, meals must be prepared according to the tradition of kosher food. This is a very complex set of rules and standards. The following are just a few of the more common. Piggies are once again proscribed: order a BLT sandwich, and you'll get just the L and the T. Indeed animals must chew the cud and have cloven hooves to be acceptable as food according to Jewish law. It must also be completely drained of blood and inspected for the defects – scars, damaged tissue, injuries – that would make it non-kosher.

Local specialities

If you get the chance, don't refuse an invitation to the traditional Bedouin meal, **mansaf**; (women, unfortunately, are rarely invited). This meal of rice, pine nuts and lamb's head is eaten in the traditional way by sitting on the floor round the dishes of food. The eyeballs are usually presented to honoured guests – which usually means you. This is in part tradition, and in part to see if you'll be able to keep them down.

Other dishes to try include the Egyptian's delicacy, **pigeon** (delicious but I hate food that glares back at me – I wish they'd remove the eyes), and **sheep's testicles**: succulent, if a little too salty.

The budget traveller's diet

The following is a list of the top 11 meals that make up 90% of the traveller's diet. This isn't because they're especially delicious, but because they're cheap.

● **Bread** Whatever you eat in the Near East, you'll be eating it with bread. Bread is the cutlery, crockery and napkin on a Near Eastern table (in fact I've even seen somebody use it as a hankie too!). It is usually unleavened, (except in Turkey), round, and the size of a dinner plate.

● **Felafel** The number one Arab staple is felafel, a deep-fried golf ball of mashed chickpeas. These are placed in a pitta bread full of salad and vegetables, hoummus (see below), and all kinds of sauces. Although every country has them, they all vary slightly. In Syria they're a little soggy and the pitta is larger, and wrapped around the filling. In Egypt they're cheap but bland, while in Israel they're more expensive but refillable. In Lebanon, however, the art of felafel-making has been raised to a new and higher plain, and they are frequently delicious.

● **Shwaarma/kebab** A felafel for carnivores. Everywhere you go you will see large skewers of unidentifiable meat (it's probably best not to ask what it is, although it will usually be lamb or chicken). Ask for a shwaarma, and the chef will carve thin strips off this skewer and place them inside the pitta. The shwaarma is the meat; once in the pitta, the dish is called a 'sandweech'. They are often lovely, if a little greasy.

In Turkey, where they are called kebaps, they are truly heavenly. The bread is usually half of a leaven loaf hollowed out to receive the filling. The meat is served in numerous different ways: chunks (shish), slices (doner) or even as meatballs. It may also be spiced.

● **Hoummus** An alternative use for all those chickpeas. This is chickpea paste, usually served swimming in olive oil. Hoummus is yummy for breakfast or as a starter before something more substantial in the evening. It is usually served with bread, or on a felafel/shwaarma.

● **Tahini** Sesame seed paste in olive oil. Delicious, especially when flavoured with garlic, onions or lemon.

● **Baba ghanoush** Take one eggplant, mash it up and add tahini. Voila! baba ghanoush.

● **Goshari** An Egyptian speciality, this is a noodle dish with tomato sauce, chilli, lentils and onions. When you come across discarded paper buckets littering the streets, it usually means a goshari stall is nearby.

● **Baklava** Probably the single biggest cause of tooth decay in the Arab world, baklava is the Western name for all the many different types of honey-drenched pastry/pistachio combinations that one can buy throughout Arabia. Delicious in small quantities, it can be very tempting to purchase enormous bags from the brightly-lit stores. Like so many travellers you'll probably buy more than you can eat and at some time on your trip suddenly come upon a forgotten half-eaten bag of baklava squashed at the bottom of your rucksack.

● **Fuul** Another Egyptian dish, these are simply fava beans, although they are often flavoured with all manner of ingredients; onions and lemon are two of the more popular. Once again served in pitta bread.

● **Roast chicken** You'll find racks of chickens roasting on spits outside many restaurants. Order a half, and you can expect at least some lemon, onions and bread to accompany your meal. Cheap and tasty.

● **Pizza** Every country has a go at making pizza, with varying degrees of success. Syria's and Turkey's efforts are boat-shaped and simple, filled with cheese, lamb and whatever else they can find. They are very inexpensive and can be very good.

And then there is Lebanese pizza. This is a thinner, floppier version of the Italian original. Tomatoes, herbs, onions and cheese are all sprinkled on to a flat piece of bread, which is then rolled up like a shwaarma. The first bite will send your pulse racing and each bite that follows will tap out a tantalising tango on your tastebuds. Worth the price of a Lebanese visa, and yet only 1500LE (about £0.60/US$1).

DRINK

Non alcoholic
Chai is, without a doubt, the number one drink in the Near East. It's simply tea with no milk, lots of sugar, and is served in a small glass. Sometimes it's also flavoured with fruit, such as apple or peach.

The best place to drink chai is in a dim, smoky café, accompanied by a game of backgammon and a puff of *nargileh* (the hubbly-bubbly water pipe used to smoke tobacco; like the chai, the tobacco comes in many different flavours). These cafés are essential parts of Near Eastern society, as much an institution as the Western bar or pub.

The other favourite drink served in cafés is Turkish or Arabic **coffee**, incredibly strong and laced with cardamom. The dregs are so thick that they could cause respiratory problems if swallowed.

Other drinks include **Sahlep** (sweet milk flavoured with powdered orchid tuber) and the Israeli version of **cappuchino**, which is made with whipped cream. The Egyptians have their own speciality, **fruit cocktail**, which is a kind of strawberry and fruit mush, thrown into a pint glass with what seems like a kilo of sugar, and drunk through a straw. It's delicious. Most other countries have their own versions.

Alcohol
Every country has its own beer. Although Syria's **al-Shark** is vile, and Egypt's **Stella** tastes so chemically derived that it's said that two Australians have died from imbibing it, beer in the other countries is reasonable. Turkey and Lebanon both import a lot of well-known beers or even manufacture the stuff themselves under licence. Turkey has **Tuborg** and **Efes Pilsen**, both fine brands, while Lebanon and Jordan have **Amstel**. Israel has its own brands, **Goldstar** and **Maccabee**.

The local spirit is **arak**, a generic term which covers a multitude of alcoholic sins. Usually aniseed-based, arak is the illegitimate offspring of a liquorice allsort and the devil himself. It tastes like the Greek firewater, ouzo, and runs down your throat like volcanic lava. Lebanon makes the best, and the safest.

WORKING IN THE REGION

The number one place to work in the Near East is undoubtedly Israel, but if you do plan to work there see Syria and Lebanon first, otherwise it will be very difficult to see them at all.

Finding a job in Israel is fairly straightforward, and 99% of travellers do not even bother securing a work permit. There is job information everywhere, and sometimes one merely has to wait on a designated street early in the morning to find work.

The Kibbutz and Moshav projects are very popular. Age limits are usually between 18 and 32. The work is usually fairly menial and agricultural-based, and often entails working long hours six days a week. They're OK providing you don't mind working hard for very little money (the Moshav, a privately-run Kibbutz, usually pays more) and can live in the insular camp atmosphere. Jobs can be arranged before you arrive in the Middle East, or when you reach Israel (see pp248/226 for addresses of agencies in Tel Aviv and Jerusalem). If you do sort work out before you leave home, don't carry the documents with you – Syrian officials may find them at the border and refuse you entry.

Travellers who do not end up working in one of these camps often find work on construction sites or in restaurants. A number of caveats need to be heeded for both of these. Firstly, you are doing work that the Israelis do not want to do. The jobs are often dangerous, tedious, tiring and poorly paid. What is more, as you will probably have no work permit, you have no recourse to the law should you become involved in an accident or have some other complaint to make against your boss. Tales of travellers who have done work without ever being paid are legion. If you can, find out from other travellers which employers are reputable before you begin.

Away from Israel, the main profession for travellers in the region is teaching English. These days it is usually necessary to arrange a job before arriving. If you have not pre-arranged anything then the universities are the best places to enquire about the possibilities of work. Cairo is the most popular venue for finding a job, although one should not discount any of the other major cities. (Beirut, in particular, with its large number of English-speakers, would be a good choice).

More and more travellers are finding work with the carpet sellers in Turkey or the restaurants at Dahab. The pay is usually poor, but it can be an interesting way to spend a few months.

PART 3: TURKEY

Facts about the country

These days Turkey is trying to market itself as a package tourist destination in the style of southern Spain or Greece. Most of the holiday adverts you see feature bronzed families lounging lazily round the hotel pool or on spotless sandy beaches under the roasting Turkish sun. Whilst there are some luxurious hotels in this country and some of the beaches are indeed gorgeous, the reality is that the Turkish Tourist Board is selling the country short: there's a lot more to Turkey than sun-drenched coastline and soulless family resorts.

❏ **Country ratings – Turkey**

● **Highlights** Apart from Istanbul, the Cappadocian region must garner more praise from travellers than any other part of Turkey. It is, quite simply, stunning. The tourist resorts down on the west and south coasts are also quite beautiful at times, and a lot less spoilt than the resorts of their neighbour and rival, Greece.

● **Expense $$$ ($$$$** in summer along the coast)

● **Value for money** ✔✔✔✔ Food, transport and accommodation are all very reasonably priced, and if you have a youth card then entrance to most of the major tourist attractions is free.

● **English spoken** ✔✔ Away from the tourist-oriented west coast you may have trouble making yourself understood. A knowledge of German could well prove valuable.

● **Getting around** ✔✔✔✔✔ Buses are by far the most convenient mode of transport.

● **Travellers' scene** ✔✔✔✔ Vibrant, especially in Göreme, a real traveller's hangout, and Istanbul, the beginning of so many Europe-Asia and Europe-Africa overland journeys.

● **Visible history** ✔✔✔✔ Apart from the obvious attraction of Istanbul, historians will also find plenty of interest in the Roman and Greek ruins along the west coast and the capital of the Seljuks at Konya.

● **Woman alone** ✔✔✔ To many Turkish males, a Western women is the ultimate accessory. But their attention, whilst occasionally a little too aggressive, is rarely as persistent or wearying as elsewhere in the Near East.

● **Good food** ✔✔✔✔✔ An excellent choice of food. Once you have wearied of kebabs, try their pizzas at a *pideci* (pizza house), with cheese (*peynirli*) or lamb mince (*kiymali*).

● **Vegetarian friendly** ✔✔ Avoiding meat in Turkey can be a little tricky. Even many salad dishes have meat as a flavouring, but do try *coban salatasi* (a tasty salad made with hot peppers) and *patlican salatasi* (made with eggplant).

The country has over 4000 years of visible history including more ancient Greek ruins than Greece, as well as acres of unspoilt landscape, magnificent mountain ranges, delicious food and a superior transport network. There's also the Turkish coffee, carpets, slippers and delight available in the many labyrinthine bazaars, and, of course, the highlight of any trip to Turkey: Istanbul – the seat of two empires, and the most romantic city in the whole of the Near East.

Modern Turkey

Turkey today is still under the spell of Atatürk, the founder of the republic and its greatest leader. His name is revered throughout the land, his statue stands in the centre of every major city, and every town and village has at least one Atatürk Caddesi or Bulvari. Since his death in 1938, the road has been a rocky one for the Turkish Republic. Mismanagement of the economy and a rise in terrorist activity – whether it be Muslim fanatics, Armenian terrorists or pro-Soviet troublemakers – have twice led to military coups (1960 and 1980), both of which have been fairly brutal.

Despite this, Turkey now appears to be one of the more stable countries in the region. The economy seems healthy: Turkey is a net exporter of food and also boasts a sound manufacturing base and a booming tourist industry. Its progress into the European Union, however, is still blocked by two major obstacles: the country's rampant inflation, and the rise in power of Muslim fundamentalists who today form a coalition government under Necmettin Erbakan. Tansu Çiller, the former prime minister and the country's first female leader, is now the deputy prime minister.

Turkey's relations with its neighbours are also less than cordial. Syria and Turkey fell out initially over the Hatay, a Syrian province ceded to the Turks in 1939 by the French in return for a guarantee of peace. Neither side has done much to repair the damage since. Syria argues that Turkey's plan to dam the Euphrates will have serious effects on their water supply, whilst Turkey accuses Syria of harbouring PKK (Kurdistan Workers' Party) terrorists, whose fight to secure a Kurdish homeland in Eastern Turkey continues to this day.

Turkey's relationship with Greece continues to be difficult, too. In 1974 Turkey invaded and occupied Northern Cyprus in response to a Greek-engineered coup on the island, later declaring the land to be the 'Turkish Republic of Cyprus'. Both sides still hold skirmishes at the UN-controlled border, where as recently as August 1996 one anti-Turkish demonstrator was killed.

GEOGRAPHICAL BACKGROUND

Turkey is a vast and diverse land spanning two continents, several seismic zones, a couple of mountain ranges, a few deserts and lots of vast, fertile plains. Only three per cent of Turkey lies in Europe, an area called

Thrace in the north-west, separated from the rest of the country by the Sea of Marmara and the Bosphorus Straits. Asian Turkey is actually surrounded by four different seas: the Sea of Marmara and the Aegean to the west, the Med to the south and the Black Sea to the north.

In the centre of Turkey is the Anatolian Plain, separated on all sides from the coastal strips by mountain ranges. Turkey's highest mountain at 5122m is Mt Ararat (where Noah's ark landed) in the east of the country. The mountain forms part of the Eastern Highlands, the source of both the Tigris and the Euphrates which flow south into Iraq and Syria respectively.

❑ Practical information – Turkey

● **Visas** Required by UK and US citizens. Available only at the airport or border. UK citizens must pay in sterling (UK£10), and Americans in dollars (US$20).

● **Currency** Turkish Lira (TL). Fully convertible, but rampant inflation ensures that it's difficult to convert Turkish currency outside Turkey. Within the country, it is no problem changing your lira back into another currency at the end of your trip. As in July 1997: UK£1=264,000TL, US$1= 157,000TL. **Prices in this guide are given in US$.**

● **Banks** Because of Turkey's rampant inflation it is wise to change only small amounts at a time rather than one huge amount at the beginning which will subsequently decrease in value. Changing money is a relatively painless affair although the process often involves a lot of paper shuffling. Post Offices (PTT's) in many places have a small exchange counter, but they usually only accept cash in dollars and deutchmarks. Many banks, such as Vakifbank and Akbank, do not charge commission on travellers' cheques. Most banks will allow you to draw out money on your credit card too, although there is a fee for this service.

● **Time** GMT + 2 (+3 from last Sunday in March to last Saturday in September)

● **Electricity** 220 volts AC, 50Hz.

● **Post and telecommunications** PTT (posta, telefon, telegraf) offices are scattered throughout the towns and villages of Turkey; look out for the yellow and black signs. The service is fairly efficient and cheap – US$0.20 for a postcard.

Turkey has now introduced a phonecard system, a far more convenient and cheaper way to phone abroad than using the PTT operator service. Currently a 100 luk (unit) card costs US$3, which will enable you to connect with Europe for two minutes, or the USA, Canada and Australia for one minute.

Local calls can be made from the yellow booths. These take tokens which one can buy from the post office or from vendors on the street. One token will suffice for local calls; put the token in first, then dial. Phonecard booths are gradually being introduced too.

● **Warnings** i) East Turkey is the homeland of the Kurdish people, whose separatist campaign has previously involved the kidnapping of travellers. So far, every tourist has been released unharmed. Our route does not enter any danger areas but those wishing to head further east should check with their consulate for the latest information.

ii) Do not insult Atatürk. See the warning on p44.

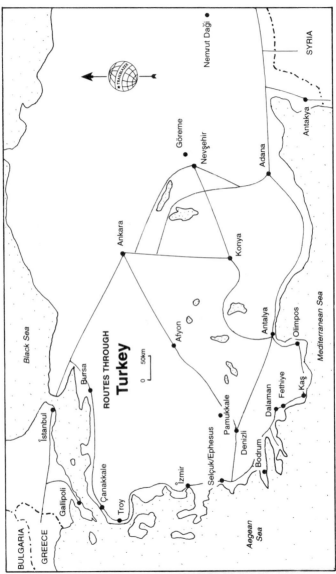

RELIGION

Although Islam ceased to be the official state religion in 1928, 99% of the population are Muslim, mainly Sunni but with a smattering of Shi'ite in the south-east of the country. Of the remaining one per cent a tenth are Christian and about 20,000 are Jewish. Both of these groups are centred in Istanbul.

LOCAL TRANSPORT

Bus

The intercity bus service in Turkey is phenomenal. There are hundreds of bus companies, and the competition is cut-throat. The customer benefits from this warfare in the form of cheap ticket prices and an excellent service aboard some state-of-the-art buses. It is not unusual, particularly on longer journeys, to be served chocolates and drinks throughout the trip, and even on the shorter journeys one is always offered a refreshing splash of cologne. My only gripe is that the bus companies assume everyone in Turkey is a smoker – as I have already pointed out, this isn't far from the truth – and hence the journey can sometimes become a choking, nicotine-filled nightmare. Some companies have started to lay on no-smoking services in response, but even more companies will tell you that the bus is no-smoking when you buy the ticket, only for you to find out otherwise when you climb aboard.

Of the bus companies, Kamil Koç and Pamukkale are two of the more reputable, whilst Kent are one of the smallest and cheapest. Although the ticket offices collude to set a standard price, it is still possible to haggle for a cheaper deal. Avoid the touts who beckon you into the office, otherwise their wages will be incorporated into your ticket price.

Train

There are some top-notch trains operating in Turkey and some real rickety affairs too. Prices vary accordingly. The trains are of little use if you wish to travel along the coast, but if you wish to travel via Central Anatolia and Ankara you have plenty of options. Remember to take your ISIC/U26 card to take advantage of discounts which are sometimes as large as 30%. Book two days ahead during holidays.

❑ **Routes through Turkey**

This guide follows two routes through Turkey. Both begin in Istanbul, head down to Gallipoli and Ephesus, before diverging at Pamukkale. The first route goes east to Ankara, then on to Cappadocia. The second route is more circuitous and follows the coast around to Olimpos, after which it heads inland for a spin with the Whirling Dervishes of Konya before joining the first route at Cappadocia. Both routes then continue to Syria via Antakya.

Istanbul

Istanbul is a thoroughly modern city that cannot forget its past. Wherever you stand there are reminders of the glory-days when the city, first as Byzantium and then as Constantinople, was the centre of two huge empires. It's festooned with dramatic, powerful imperial architecture.

This beauty was bought at a terrible cost to the Near East. Both the Ottomans and, to a certain extent, the Byzantines, drained their Arabian territories with extortionate taxes in order to embellish their capital. Today, with no Middle Eastern taxes to rely on, the city has turned to trade to maintain its sheen. In Istanbul, anywhere that crowds gather, traders gather too. This is what makes a stroll around the streets of Istanbul so fascinating. On Galata Bridge, housewives haggle with fishermen over the day's catch. In Sultanahmet, the bread sellers and shoeshine boys circle around the tram station, ready to pounce on the next unsuspecting, arrival. And almost everywhere you go peddlers pester passers-by, selling everything from clockwork drumming monkeys to pictures of Atatürk, industrial power-tools to flame-proof nighties.

And so the city thrives once more. In the cracks between the old imperial buildings modern Istanbul has germinated and flourished into a vibrant metropolis of over 6.5 million people. It may have succumbed to the new imperial powers – MTV, Sony and McDonald's – but it has lost none of its exotic appeal. This is where Asia meets Europe, the souk culture of the Orient meets the chic boutiques and shopping malls of the West – and it's fascinating.

HISTORY

Lygos and Byzas

Istanbul has enjoyed many incarnations during its 3000-year history. By the time the Megarian colonist Byzas (Megaria was a Greek state) arrived in 650BC, a number of small fishing villages had already sprouted along the shore. Byzas was not slow in recognising the natural advantages of the peninsula, and he established a colony on the site of one of these villages, Lygos, where Topkapi Palace stands today. With due modesty, he named his new city Byzantium.

Constantinople

Byzas was not the last person to be enchanted by the peninsula. As the Roman Empire split in two the Christian Emperor, Constantine, pursued his rival eastwards. One of the cities they passed through was Byzantium;

Constantine was so rapt by what he saw there that he vowed to return to make it the capital of his new empire. In 324AD he did just that and, taking Byzas' lead, renamed the city after himself.

Constantine went to great lengths to convince people that his Constantinople was the new Rome – he even designed the city so that it was built on seven hills – and went to even greater lengths to beautify it. His successors followed suit, and the city became a glorious jumble of Byzantine palaces, colonnaded streets, mosaic ceremonial walkways and, of course, magnificent churches. Such extravagance was only fitting; the city was, after all, not only the capital of a vast Byzantine Empire but also the administrative centre (if not its spiritual home) of the most fashionable religion at the time, Christianity.

The Crusaders

In the early days of the thirteenth century Emperor Isaac had been overthrown in a coup inside the city. His son, Alexius, asked for a Crusade to return his father to the throne. The Crusaders kept their part of the bargain – in 1203 Isaac was restored as emperor – but Alexius did not have the money to reward them. In response the knights went on a rampage throughout the city, raping and pillaging for all they were worth. It was the worst damage ever done to the city, committed by knights who professed to being on the Byzantine's side!

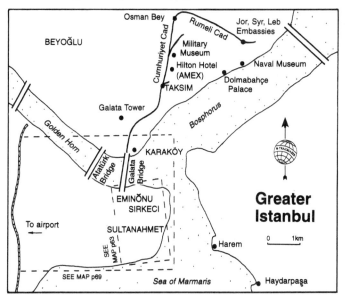

The arrival of the Turks

The story of Christian Constantinople's demise is well known. Although the Byzantine Empire had been shrinking for centuries, it still clung on to Constantinople. Only an outstanding army under brilliant leadership could take the capital. The Ottomans, under the direction of Mehmet Fatih, (Mehmet the Conqueror), were just such an army.

Mehmet was a young man who needed a good victory to confirm his authority. Succeed, and he would be fêted for ever. Fail, and the court strangler was waiting with open hands. Considerable obstacles lay in Mehmet's way, however: the Golden Horn was blocked by an iron chain stretching from one bank to the other, which prevented any boats from passing up the straits and bombarding the city; and if one attempted to attack the city by land, strong, well-fortified walls defended by 10,000 battle-hardened mercenaries, protected the city.

The chain was the first problem. Using guile rather than force, Mehmet avoided it altogether. In May 1453, under cover of darkness his men dismantled their ships, placed the parts onto rollers and dragged them overland around the chains. The operation was a success and the Ottoman cannons began to pepper the Byzantine defences from their re-assembled vessels in the straits.

After failing to breach the walls despite months of bombardment using the biggest cannons the world had ever seen, the city fell after a careless Byzantine citizen left a gate in the city wall open, allowing the infidels to pour in. The Byzantine empire had finally expired.

Ottoman rule to the present day

Mehmet was astute enough to forbid the destruction of any Byzantine buildings by his troops, and he began an architectural trend himself by commissioning Istanbul's first imperial mosque, the Fatih Camii, in 1463.

Subsequent sultans added their own buildings, the most prolific being Süleyman the Magnificent who was fortunate enough to have the Ottoman's most talented builder, Sinan, in his court. Sinan built over 300 of the most beautiful buildings in Istanbul, many of which have survived to this day. Even when the Ottoman Empire began to decline during the 19th and 20th centuries, the capital was still adorned by new palaces. In fact, such was the decadence of later sultans that they would often spend more of the annual budget on their palaces than on the whole of the rest of their empire put together!

After the fall of the Ottoman Empire Atatürk shifted the capital to Ankara, which was not only safe from sea invasions but was also, in his eyes, a more Turkish city. Despite this loss of status, Istanbul today has lost none of its vivacity and continues as the commercial, historical, and cultural centre of the country.

ARRIVAL AND DEPARTURE

The airport

Visas (required by British and American citizens; see p51) must be obtained from a small desk by passport control before joining the lengthy queues at passport control. Within the main foyer of the airport are two 24-hour banks (the rates are better in town, but not significantly so) and a 24-hour Tourist Information Office.

Airport transport A **taxi** to Sultanahmet will set you back about US$4 (US$7 at night), provided you insist that they switch on the meter. A cheaper alternative is the **Havas Bus** (US1.75) which travels between the airport and Taksim Square in Beyoğlu. During winter the Havas Bus runs every hour from 0550 to 2250. In summer they run more frequently and also operate throughout the night, although you pay double for the night service. If you arrive during the day ask to be dropped off at Aksaray, from where you can catch the tram to Sultanahmet.

For the truly budget traveller, the cheapest way to get into town involves a 30-minute walk from the airport to Yesilyurt train station, where you can catch a **local train** to Cankurtaran (daytime only) or Sirkeçi. It costs only US$0.25 on the train, which runs every twenty minutes, although the walk between the airport and Yesilyurt is a bit strenuous with a full pack. A taxi between the two will cost US$1.

If you are travelling from Sultanahmet/Cankurtaran to the airport, the hostels advertise a five-times-a-day **shuttle-bus** service for US$2.50.

LOCAL TRANSPORT

● **Tram** Anyone staying in Sultanahmet should master the tram system, which runs from the train station at Sirkeçi all the way to Zeytinburnu in the west. It's not that difficult. Tickets (US$0.30 per journey regardless of distance) can be brought from the green booths near the platforms. This ticket is then placed in the slot at the platform's entrance. Sometimes you may be fortunate to find a ticket seller who will sell you half-price student tickets on production of an ISIC card (these tickets should really be for Turkish students only). If you do find one, buy a few tickets from him to save money on subsequent journeys.

● **Ferry** The main ferry terminal in Istanbul is at Eminönü, where each of the numbered piers serves a different destination. Tickets for the ferries, which usually run every 20 minutes, cost US$0.30. The most useful ferry for tourists sails between Karaköy (in Galata) and the Asian train station at Haydarpaşa. Most ferries stop running at 6pm.

● **Bus** Istanbul's bus network is vast. Unfortunately, timetables and bus numbers are prone to change, so it is always a good idea to check with the tourist information office for the latest details. Tickets are bought from a booth or stall near the bus stop. On entering the bus, place these into a little box near the driver. Some buses do not accept these tickets, and you must pay for your journey on board the bus. Unfortunately, there is no way of distinguishing between those buses that will accept your ticket and those that will not. Fares are a standard US$0.30 however far you travel. See relevant sections for bus numbers.

● **Taxis** Istanbul's taxis are metered but this does not prevent many drivers from preying on unsuspecting tourists by taking longer routes to reach their destination. Some drivers even refuse to use their meters; if they do, ignore them and wait for another taxi.

● **Dolmus** Many of these shared taxis are classic pre-1970 Chevrolets or Chryslers. They are a tiny bit more expensive than buses. Fares are collected during the drive – just pay the same as your fellow passengers (usually US$0.33). The most useful service runs between Taksim Square in Beyoğlu and Sirkeçi.

● **Metro** The underground system stretches westwards from Aksaray to the Otogar and beyond. As with the tram, tickets cost US$0.30 and are valid for one journey, whatever the distance. To get to Aksaray Station take the tram to Yusufpaşa. The station is just to the north.

ORIENTATION

Istanbul is the only city in the world that spans two continents. A very common mistake, however, is the belief that the Golden Horn is the dividing line between them, whereas, in fact, the Bosphorus is the Asian border. Indeed most visitors do not cross into Asia until they leave Istanbul, since the Asian side is largely residential with few attractions.

The Golden Horn splits European Istanbul into two. To the south is Stamboul, ancient Constantinople. At the tip of Stamboul is Sultanahmet. Most of the major sights, budget hotels and cheap restaurants are to be found here. To the north-west of Sultanahmet lies the district of Çemberlitaş, with the Grand Bazaar and the university. West from here is the district of Fatih, the ancient Byzantine city walls – still largely intact – the new bus terminus and airport. To the north of Sultanahmet the roads slope down to the Golden Horn and the districts of Eminönü and Sirkeçi.

To the north of the Golden Horn is Beyoğlu, consisting of Galata on the shore, and up the hill, Taksim. This is the main business district where most of the embassies and luxury hotels are located.

SERVICES   (Istanbul ☎ **area code** 0212)

● **Bookshops** The supply of English language books is pretty meagre. There's a rather dreadful bookstall-cum-carpet shop just off Divan Yolu, and one stall that deals in very old, overpriced tomes in the small book bazaar of Sahaflar Çarşisi to the west of the Grand Bazaar.

● **Changing money** There are lots of exchange booths amongst the souvenir shops and travel agents on Divan Yolu, although banks usually offer a better rate. There is also a small exchange kiosk in the grounds of Topkapi Palace which does not charge commission on travellers' cheques. A tiny black market for US dollars cash is beginning to emerge in the Grand Bazaar, which may boom if the lira continues to devalue fast. The Istanbul branch of AMEX is inside the Hilton Hotel on Cumhuriyet Caddesi (PO Box Harbiye).

● **Laundry** The Star Laundry, opposite the Orient, is currently the best place to purge your clothes of ingrained travelling grime. They charge a mere US$1 per kilo of washing.

● **Photography** There are some specialist photography stores on Yeni Postane Cad. If you're having photos developed check the print size beforehand or you may find yourself with a fistful of miniature photos.

● **Post** The main GPO is housed in a grand building on Yeni Postane Cad, and stays open from 0830-2000 every day. The Poste Restante Counter shuts from 1230-1330, and closes by 1730. Bring your passport.

● **Telephone** The phone office next door to the GPO sells phonecards, which is the cheapest way of phoning abroad. The office is open 24 hours.

● **Tourist office** There is a smallish tourist kiosk near the toilets in Sultanahmet but it's not staffed with the most helpful bunch of people. A far superior office is situated in Sirkeçi Station; it's open from 0900-1700 every day except Sunday. There's a 24-hour office at the airport.

● **Travel agencies** On Divan Yolu there are a number of travel agencies, all of whom offer a similar service. Nevertheless, shop around: the fares

---

❏ **Embassies and consulates**

The Syrian, Jordanian and Lebanese Embassies are all within 30 seconds' walk of each other. To get here take buses 54 or 69 from Eminönü to Osman Bey. From there, walk up the hill until you see a sign on your right advertising the 'English Centre'; head down this road for about ten minutes to the roundabout. The embassies lie nearby.

• **Australia** (☎ 2577050) Tepeçik Yolu 58, Etiler (Bus 43 from Eminönü, then taxi)

• **Canada** (☎ 2725174) Büyükdere Cad, Begun Han 107/3, Gayrettepe

• **Egypt** (☎ 2636038) Cevdet Paşa 173, Bebek (bus 22, 25 from Eminönü)

• **Jordan** (☎ 2301221) Kalipçi Sok 119, Teşvikiye; **visa**: 0930-1200; 1 photo, collect 1400 same day; costs: Aus free, Can US$45, UK US$15, US US$40.

• **Lebanon** (☎ 2361365) Saray Apt 134/1, Teşvikiye; look for the Lebanese flag by the roundabout; **visa**: 0930-1100, 1 photo, 1 letter of recommendation, collect same day; cost: US$40

• **Syria** (☎ 2326721) Macka Caddesi 59, Teşvikiye (next to the Istankasi Complex); **visa**: 0930-1100 ; 1 photo, 1 letter of recommendation, collect 1400-1430 next day; costs: Aus/Can free, UK US$25, US US$40

• **UK** (☎ 2937540) Meşrutiyet Cad 34, Tepebaşi

• **US** (☎ 2513602) Meşrutiyet Cad 104-108, Tepebaşi

vary even if the products do not. **Pasifik Travel** has been recommended by a few. There is also one agency that sells ISIC cards without bothering to see any proof! Unfortunately, I am not allowed to tell you their name, but ask around. Just down from the Backpacker's Café is **Backpacker's Travel** who stock the U26 cards.

Many of these agencies also deal in Turkish bus tickets; buying tickets from travel agencies is a good idea, for they cost no more than if you buy them at the station and agencies often offer free lifts to the terminus.
● **Visa extensions** If you have any trouble with your Turkish visa, the first place to head is the Tourist Police, opposite the entrance to the Yerebatan Saray.

WHERE TO STAY   [Accommodation keyed to map on p63]

Cankurtaran, the area bounded by Sultanahmet Square to the north and the suburban railway line to the south-east, is chock-a-block with accommodation possibilities to suit every budget and prejudice.

Real cheapskates should go to the *Ilknur Pansiyon* [1] (☎ 5176833), where for US$1.50 you get the chance to sleep on one of twelve lumpy mattresses in this end-of-terrace's attic (US$3 per person on the bunks in the private room). The pension is run by Istanbul's most endearing couple, the elderly and eccentric Zeki and his equally batty wife, Zahide. The dormitory used to have MTV until the telly broke, and a tank full of fish too...until they were over-fed. Indeed, on my last visit even the lock on the toilet door had gone! Still, they have just installed a hot shower system and the view over the Bosphorus is good. Rumours of Zeki chasing non-payers down the street with an hatchet are unsubstantiated, but it is wise to settle your account promptly, just in case.

Those with standards should head one block further north to the ever popular *Orient Youth Hostel* [2] (☎ 5179493). This establishment certainly appears to have everything: clean rooms with central heating, showers with hot water, no night-time curfew and a travel agency in reception. They even hold belly-dancing displays in their rooftop café every week. The boisterous atmosphere that prevails isn't to everyone's taste, but nevertheless they still keep packing them in at US$3.75/5pp dorm/dbl. Just round the corner from the Orient is a new competitor, the *Sultan Tourist Hostel* [3] (☎ 5169260). This hostel can match the Orient for facilities and surpass it in terms of the quality of its rooms. It's begin-

---

❏ **Prices**

Turkey has been suffering from uncontrollable inflation over the last couple of years. Consequently prices are changing every other month in order to keep apace. Although the Turkish lira is still welcome everywhere, **all the prices in this section are quoted in US dollars**.

ning to raise its prices now, however, (US$4/9/13 for dorm/sgl/dbl).

Other cheap hostels in Cankurtaran include the *Hanedan* [2] (☎ 5164869), which survives on the overflow from the Orient next door, the *Bahaus* [4] (☎ 5176697; US$7/15 sgl/dbl), which has been recommended by many, and the tiny, cosy *Troy B&B* [5] (☎ 5177339; US$7.50pp with breakfast), just down the steps from the Ilknur.

The main rival to the Orient Hostel is the large *Yücelt Interyouth Hostel* [6] (☎ 5136150), standing in the shadows of the Aya Sofya. Many find the stringent rules at this hostel rather wearying after a while – on occasions it feels less like a hostel than a boarding-school – and the grumpy staff can be equally vexing. There are compensations, however, in the form of a café, laundry-service, garden and luggage storage facilities. Prices are US$4.50/7/15 for dorm/sgl/dbl.

Outside Sultanahmet and hidden away amongst the shoe shops in Aksaray, the *Piyerloti Family Pension* (☎ 5178070, Piyerloti Cad, Kadirga Hamam Sokak 4) deserves a mention. 'Family Pension' is an apt title, for you are made to feel like one of their own whilst you stay. Come here to get away from it all; prices start at US$10 for a double room.

Medium and top-range hotels

The newly-built *Aladdin's Guest House* [7] (☎ 5162330), fifty metres away from the Backpacker's Café on Akbiyik Cad, is a real gem. All the rooms in this pine-clad hotel are en suite and come complete with a direct-dial phone, while the breakfast terrace is a most pleasant venue for eating one's cornflakes. Prices start at US$20 for a single, US$30 double.

The *Otels Sumengen* [8] (☎ 5176869), *Avicenna* (☎ 5170550) and *Obelisk* (☎ 5177173) stand next to each other on the quiet back-street of Admiral Tafdil Sok. They have a lot in common besides location. All three occupy tastefully-restored 19th century Ottoman houses, all charge roughly the same prices for some very fancy rooms (US$45/55/65/85 sgl/dbl/tpl/suite) and all offer wonderful vistas over the Bosphorus. The Sumengen is my favourite (it even has its own marble bath) but you will not come away disappointed from any of this triumvirate.

The *Istanbul Hilton* (☎ 2314650) is an extraordinarily ugly building on Cumhuriyet Cad, just to the north of Taksim Square. It offers all that you'd expect from a Hilton, however, and the view from the rooms looking out over the Bosphorus is incomparable. Prices start at US$210/240 sgl/dbl, rising to US$1800 for the presidential suite.

WHERE TO EAT

The man who runs the fez stall outside the Aya Sofya claims that you are never more than ten metres from a kebab in Istanbul; a bit of an exaggeration maybe but it's certainly true that it is difficult to get away from kebab-culture in Istanbul. For a little variation on the theme, head down to Eminönü where, next to the ferry termini, a number of absurdly-garbed fish-kebab sellers [a] stand in their traditional fish-kebab-selling boats plying customers with a mixture of bread, fish and bones for US$1.

When dining out, many travellers head to the row of restaurants along Divan Yolu. One wonders why. Some of the smaller places, such as the *Halkin Koftecizi* [b], are not bad, but the majority are more adept at squeezing every last lira out of their customers than they are at cooking food. Amongst them is the *Pudding Shop* [c], once a mandatory stop on the Hippie Trail but now mandatory only if you wish to pay extortionate prices for substandard fare.

Those with more sense than money should head for the string of eateries behind the Blue Mosque. *Gantiep Kebap Salonu* [d] has a wonderful compilation of kebabs, all served with bread and salad, for US$1-2. Next door, the pizzas at *Doy Doy's* [e] truly flatter the palate. Their sheep's cheese pizza is to die for – almost. Next to them is the *Pizza Sun Restaurant* [f], offering a range of traditional Turkish pizzas, and on the corner is the *Café Yildiz* [g], a great place to people-watch.

In Cankurtaran, the *Backpacker's Café* [h] has come up with a winning combination to attract the budget traveller: food, beer and MTV. The sandwiches are enormous half-loaf affairs crammed with meat and salad; the breakfasts are even better. The Orient's *Rooftop Café* has struck on a similar recipe for success, although they haven't got MTV and customers have to make do with watching the boats on the Bosphorus instead. Nearby, the food at the *Green Hotel* [i] has been praised by many, although it's a lot more expensive.

If you're taking the tram up to Çemberlitaş, the *Çennet* is an extremely popular choice. It is one of these 'authentic' Turkish gozleme places, where everybody sits on the floor, the waiters wear fezzes and women cook the gozlemes (light, flaky pancakes) in the centre of the floor. Overpriced, over the top ....and good fun.

If you prefer to cook for yourself, there is the Wednesday fruit and veg market in Cankurtaran, and the Migros chain of superstores has a number of branches throughout the city, including one in Aksaray.

NIGHTLIFE

High on the checklist of things to do for travellers in Istanbul – below visiting the Topkapi Palace but above Dolmabahçe – is a trip to the casino. They offer free food and cigarettes; all you have to do is turn up looking fairly smart, change up some money (which you can change back at the end of the evening) and then stuff yourself with canapés, no gambling required. Some casinos are now wise to this scam and have imposed restrictions, such as a minimum amount of cash that has to be gambled, to prevent freeloaders like us.

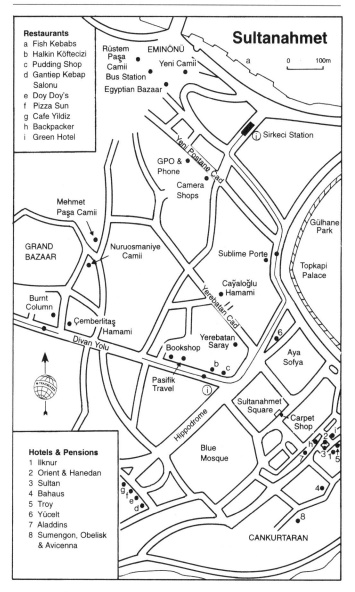

Sultanahmet

Restaurants
a Fish Kebabs
b Halkin Köftecizi
c Pudding Shop
d Gantiep Kebap
   Salonu
e Doy Doy's
f Pizza Sun
g Cafe Yildiz
h Backpacker
i Green Hotel

0   100m

Hotels & Pensions
1 Ilknur
2 Orient & Hanedan
3 Sultan
4 Bahaus
5 Troy
6 Yücelt
7 Aladdins
8 Sumengon, Obelisk
   & Avicenna

Rüstem Paşa Camii
EMINÖNÜ
Yeni Camii
Bus Station
Egyptian Bazaar
Sirkeci Station
GPO & Phone
Yeni Postane Cad
Camera Shops
Mehmet Paşa Camii
GRAND BAZAAR
Nuruosmaniye Camii
Sublime Porte
Gülhane Park
Topkapi Palace
Cağaloğlu Hamami
Yerebatan Cad
Burnt Column
Çemberlitaş Hamami
Divan Yolu
Bookshop
Yerebatan Saray
Aya Sofya
Pasifik Travel
Sultanahmet Square
Carpet Shop
Blue Mosque
Hippodrome
CANKURTARAN

The best place to drink beer is the *Backpacker's Underground Café*, which has a happy hour early in the evening. If it's Wednesday move on afterwards to the *Orient Hostel*, to witness their weekly ritual-humiliation-disguised-as-cultural-exhibition, the **belly-dancing** display. After ten minutes of astounding abdominal acrobatics by a teasingly-tasselled tummy-twitcher the evening takes on a less pleasing aspect, as members of the audience are dragged onto the floor to launch their paunch at the cowering crowd. It's all rather unpleasant.

If beer and bellies aren't your cup of chai, there are plenty of clubs around Taksim Square and near the Bogaziçi Bridge. Ask at the Underground Café or the tourist office for details.

WHAT TO SEE

Sultanahmet Square
The pretty, dog-infested garden with the fountain in the centre is Sultanahmet Square, the centre of Istanbul's tourist heartland. This used to be the Byzantine parade ground and, along with the adjacent Hippodrome, formed the epicentre of the Byzantine Empire. To the south today are the Aya Sofya Baths, now a carpet shop, whilst to the north is the main east-west thoroughfare, Divan Yolu. The star attractions, however, are the two giant, minareted buildings to the east and west: Sultan Ahmet's Blue Mosque, and the legendary Aya Sofya.

Aya Sofya
(Open 0930-1630, closed Mon; US$4.50, US$2.25 students, free for U26)   This is the Byzantine Empire's greatest building, a colossal wonder that is as much a symbol of Istanbul as the Eiffel Tower is of Paris. Today the Aya Sofya (meaning Grand Wisdom) looks a mite tatty, especially when compared to Sultan Ahmet's dazzling Blue Mosque which vies for attention across the square. Its exterior is cloaked in scaffold, the one brown minaret looks out of place amongst three white ones and the whole building could do with a good lick of paint. But to be fair, the Aya Sofya predates the mosque by over a thousand years during which time it has had to endure earthquakes, destructive iconoclasts, voracious crusaders and even a change of religion!

The building's curriculum vitae is a relatively simple one: church for nearly 1000 years, mosque for almost 500, museum for over 50. The Emperor Constantine was the first to build a church on this spot in AD325, not long after his arrival in Byzantium. That church was destroyed by fire in AD404. A second one, built soon after the fire, suf-

---

(Opposite) Top: Istanbul's Aya Sofya has witnessed two empires and undergone a conversion from church to mosque during its colourful lifetime. **Bottom:** Catching the afternoon sun in Antakya (see p111).

fered a similar fate during the Nike Revolt of AD532. And so it was a case of third time lucky. The Emperor Justinian set about restoring a church to the site and in typical Justinian style used the best materials his empire could offer. Some of the pillars are from the Temple of Jupiter at Baalbek in the Lebanon (see p178), the pink granite comes from Aswan, the small columns are from Ephesus and the marble is mainly from Libya and the Peloponnese. After just five years and under the supervision of two mathematicians – Anthemius and Miletus, who designed the building – the work was complete. On Boxing Day AD537, Justinian knelt in awe outside the entrance, proclaimed to the heavens, 'O Solomon I have outdone thee', then entered to consecrate the church.

Although it was the Christians who conceived the building, it is the Muslims we have to thank for its preservation. Mehmet the Conqueror forbade his victorious troops to destroy any Byzantine buildings, including the Aya Sofya. (The women seeking refuge in the church at the time were not so lucky, however, and were raped on the altar.) The church became a mosque, and remained one for 500 years until Atatürk, in 1935, decided that the building should be a museum. It was a sensible step, for both Christians and Muslims would love to claim it as their own.

The building There are two things about the Aya Sofya that captivate. One is the Byzantine mosaics, dating mainly from the tenth century and after (the iconoclasts destroyed those that were here before). The other is the huge central dome which soars 55.6m above the stone floor in the centre of the church. The first dome built by Justinian's mathematicians was even larger; indeed, it was so huge that it appeared to defy the very laws of physics. Unfortunately, it could only defy them for twenty years before it collapsed. The dome we see today was built by Anthemius' nephew. It is narrower, higher and less spectacular – but more permanent.

The mosaics The first great mosaic sits above the Byzantine public entrance. This is at the southern end of the narthex (covered porch) facing Sultanahmet Square. It depicts Mary cradling the infant Christ, whilst on either side the genuflecting emperors, Justinian and Constantine, offer the Aya Sofya and Constantinople respectively.

Most of the other mosaics can be found in the women's gallery upstairs, reached via a ramp which rises from the opposite end of the narthex to the Byzantine entrance. The best mosaic here is the badly battered **Deesis**, depicting Jesus, John the Baptist and Mary. It is on your right, half way along the southern gallery.

(Opposite) **Top:** Dead but not forgotten, Atatürk's memory lives on in street names and statues throughout Turkey, and in his imposing mausoleum in Ankara (see p105). **Bottom:** A souvenir seller, perfectly positioned halfway up the hill between Ankara's two main tourist attractions, the archaeological museum and the Hisar (see p104).

❏ TURKISH BATHS (HAMAMIS)

Baths – the history

It was the ancient Greeks who first realised just how much fun one could have with a bar of soap and a couple of friends. In the early days the Greeks had to rely on natural hot-water springs for their foam-filled frolics; the Romans, however, were able to apply the latest engineering technology to create purpose-built bath houses complete with extensive underground heating systems.

Down the years, the bathing tradition continued. The Byzantines loved to lather, the Mamlukes and Ottomans were keen scrubbers and the tradition has survived to this day. The nearest thing that the West has to the communal bathing concept that I can think of is the pub, a venue for socialising, smoking, drinking and relaxing. The Turkish bath is much the same – although of course, being an Islamic country, the drinks are non-alcoholic.

What to do when you're in one

There is no mixed-sex bathing; women either have their own section, or the bath will set aside women-only times.

On arriving, you'll be shown into a private cubicle for changing. The attendant will furnish you with a cloth to wrap around you and a locker to store your valuables. Proceed from here into the hot room, a mini-sauna for sitting and sweating. You should still be wearing the cloth. Having basted in your own juices for a few minutes you are ready for the essential third stage: the cleaning process. You can either do this yourself or, if you're feeling flush, have somebody do it for you. The amount of dead skin and dirt a professional will scrape off you with his abrasive cloth is often horrendous; it must be the quickest way to lose weight. The experience usually stops just short of being agonising...but not by much. During the whole time the cloths stay on, protecting your modesty. At the end of it all you may feel a little woozy. Whilst you're regaining consciousness, the staff will be wrapping you in a number of towels and leading you by the hand to the cold-room. Here you can sit, drink tea, and relax after your ordeal. If you ordered a massage, this can happen at almost any stage of the bathing process.

Turkey and Syria have the best baths; further south the quality deteriorates, until by the time one reaches Egypt they have become, almost without exception, seedy, salubrious, health-threatening parlours of immorality. Avoid.

Istanbul baths

There are two types of baths. The first is the no-nonsense, get-clean-and-get-out variety, frequented almost solely by locals. These are cheap and offer a more authentic taste of the real Turkish bath, however unpleasant that may be. The second sort of hamamis are lavish temples of hygiene where tourists and locals alike come to immerse themselves in history, wallow in the Ottoman surroundings, enjoying the knowledge that they are bathing where once sultans were soaped.

The 16th-century **Çemberlitaş Hamami**, next to the Çemberlitaş tram stop, is the most famous. The bath is designed with separate sections for men and women. A bath costs US$4 including soap, a towel, a locker and shampoo. For an extra US$6 you can have a massage. You can even get a shave or haircut. Near the Yerebatan Saray the **Cağaloğlu Hamami** boasts of an impressive roll-call of previous clients (Florence Nightingale, Kaiser Wilhelm II, Franz Liszt, Edward VIII), and the 17th-century interior is stunning. It also houses a small café and bar. It is open for women between 0800-2000, and for men from 0700-2200. Prices are similar to those at the Çemberlitaş.

At the end of this gallery there's a mosaic of Jesus, Constantine IX and the 11th-century empress Zoe, who changed husbands frequently and had to alter the mosaic accordingly. The amendments she made are obvious even today. A 12th century mosaic of Empress Eirene, her son Alexius and John II Commenus sits nearby.

Also in the gallery, near the Deesis, is the tomb of the Fourth Crusade's leader, the Venetian Henricus Dandalo. It's somewhat ironic that the man responsible for stripping the Byzantine capital of much of its wealth and beauty should end up buried in its greatest building.

Ottoman Aya Sofya The main body of the church is bare and cold; Mehmet's troops stripped it of its assets, and the furniture that does remain is all Ottoman. This includes the sultan's loge (a section of the mosque separated off for the sultan's personal use), mihrab (the elaborately-decorated niche in the wall which points towards Mecca), minbar (the wooden 'stairway', surmounted by a pulpit, that is used in Friday prayers), and the choir's platform. There are also four giant discs suspended from the walls; on them are written the names of Allah, Mohammed, Ali, and Abu Bakr.

And that's the Aya Sofya. But just before you leave, find the **Weeping Column** which stands in the north-west corner of the church. About four foot up it is a hole; stick your finger inside, and if it comes out damp your wishes will come true... so they say.

Sultan Ahmet Camii – The Blue Mosque

(Open daily, closed at prayer times; free, but donation expected.) Whether or not this mosque was built to rival the Aya Sofya, or merely to complement it, there is no doubt that it provides just as big an impact when viewed from the gardens of Sultanahmet Square. Built in 1619 by Mehmet Ağa, one of Sinan's students, it borrows ideas from both the Aya Sofya and many of the other imperial mosques too.

The entrance to the mosque today is through a side-door, rather than the main gate which faces the Hippodrome. As with all mosques, shoes must be removed. Robes should also be worn if you are exposing too much flesh or if you are too scruffy.

To the left of the entrance a ramp emerges from the mosque wall. It was used by the imperial chariot as it carried the sultan up to the imperial loge. This loge, on the left as you walk inside the mosque, is raised above the floor and surrounded by fine marble latticework to prevent the common people catching a glimpse of their ruler.

The reason why Ahmet's Camii is also called the Blue Mosque becomes apparent as soon as you enter: 21,000 blue Iznik tiles cover the walls and pillars, and blue is the dominating hue of many of the stained glass windows and a number of the prayer carpets. The central dome rises

41m, supported by semi-domes and huge, tiled pillars. Most of the mosque is roped off for worshippers, preventing sightseers from fully appreciating the original 17th century mihrab and minbar.

Outside, the mosque has six minarets. Legend has it that Sultan Ahmet, before leaving on his pilgrimage to Mecca, instructed the architects to build golden ('altin') minarets. The architects, certain that the colossal amount of gold required would bankrupt the project, decided that the sultan must have meant six ('alti') minarets instead. Whatever the reason for their construction, the Shrine of the Kaba'a at Mecca also had six, and this lead to uproar amongst the faithful. To appease everyone, Ahmet sent Mehmet Ağa to Mecca to construct a seventh minaret for the Kaba'a Shrine. Hence today the blue mosque is the only six-minaret mosque in the world, and the Kaba'a Shrine is the only one with seven.

Surrounding buildings

By the Blue Mosque's entrance stands the **Mausoleum of Ahmet I** (open 0930-1630, closed Mon and Tues; US$1, US$0.20 students/U26). Poor Ahmet died, aged twenty-seven, just seven years after his mosque was built. The mausoleum was built at the behest of his son Osman II. Ahmet, his wife and family, including Osman II, are all interred here.

To the south of the Blue Mosque are two small museums. The entrance to the uninteresting **Carpet and Textile Museum** (0900-1200, 1300-1600, closed Sun and Mon; US$1, US$0.50 students/U26) is via the imperial ramp. The **Mosaic Museum** (0930-1630, closed Thurs; US$1, US$0.50 students/U26) has mosaics discovered in the immediate vicinity of the Blue Mosque which used to adorn the floors of the Byzantine palace that once stood here. Unfortunately it is labelled in Turkish and German only. The entrance is through the small tourist arcade.

❑ **Turkish carpets**

If you want to buy a carpet in Turkey you will have plenty of opportunities; if you don't want to, you'll be sick to death of the touts who try to persuade you that you do. My advice to potential buyers is as follows. Firstly, visit one of the free 'classes' that the Yücelt Hostel runs on carpet-making. This gives you an idea of what to look for. Secondly, call in at the government-run, fixed-price Haseki Hurem Hamami, the Aya Sofya's baths-turned-carpet shop, on the southern side of Sultanahmet Square. It's a little expensive but gives you a rough idea of prices and designs. Finally, head to the shops and haggle like crazy. If you are coming back to Istanbul, wait until your return visit before purchasing; every town has a thriving carpet industry, and it is usually cheaper to buy a carpet outside Istanbul. This tactic also gives you more time to hone your bargaining skills to perfection.

After purchasing, you still have to get it home. If the carpet shop is going to send it for you, take a photo of your purchase and make sure you get a receipt. This could save a lot of hassle and help with any claims against the shop later on.

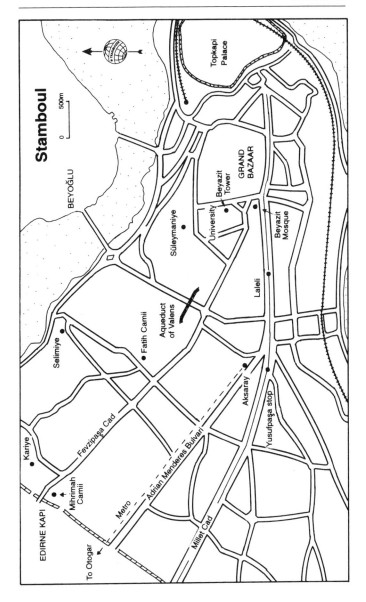

Stamboul

The Hippodrome

Built in AD203 by Septimus Severus and expanded by Constantine in the 4th century, the Hippodrome was the city's main venue for celebrations, protests and rebellions during both the Byzantine and Ottoman eras.

Even the chariot racing for which the Hippodrome was originally intended grew into a form of political expression. Each political party entered a team in the races, and to ally oneself to a certain team was to show support for a political party. One particularly boisterous post-match riot culminated in the Nike Revolt (AD532), a row over the high taxes imposed on the empire, which almost cost Justinian his throne. In response, Justinian put 40,000 rioters to the sword in the Hippodrome. Thirteen hundred years later Sultan Mahmut II topped even that, executing 50,000 Janissaries in the Hippodrome to curtail their influence over the empire. More recently the Hippodrome became a semi-permanent camp established by overlanding hippies, conveniently located within sight of their beloved Pudding Shop. They have since been moved on.

The monuments of the Hippodrome These forlorn-looking monuments are just a few of the many that used to adorn the 400m-long central dividing wall of the Hippodrome, around which the athletes and chariots would run. Unfortunately, the good ol' boys of the Fourth Crusade who looted the city in 1204 took many of the Hippodrome's decorations, including, famously, the bronze Horses of Lyssipus that now adorn St Mark's in Venice. Only the heavier, less-transportable items have survived.

Probably the heaviest of all is the **Limestone Column** at the western end of the Hippodrome. We know very little about this singularly unimpressive monument other than it was built in AD940, and the Crusaders relieved it of the gold plates which once covered its entire surface.

The next monument is the **Obelisk**, built for the New Kingdom Pharaoh Thutmose III and transported from Heliopolis (near Cairo) in AD390 by the Byzantine emperor Theodosius. It was already 1800 years old even then. Amongst the carvings on the obelisk's plinth is Theodosius seated in the royal box in the Hippodrome, which used to connect to the outer court of his palace (where the Blue Mosque now stands).

The beheaded **Serpent's Column** was brought from Delphi by Constantine. Originally made in 479BC by the Greeks to celebrate a victory over the Persians, it's the oldest Greek monument in Turkey.

The last of this string of monuments is a nineteenth-century gazebo, the **Fountain of Kaiser Wilhelm II**, a gift from Germany to the sultan. Before you leave, however, continue straight ahead from the Hippodrome and you come to the tiny **Firuz Ağa Camii**, built in 1491 and one of the oldest mosques in Istanbul.

Topkapi Palace   [Items below keyed to map on p72]

(Open 0930-1700, closed Tues; US$4.50, US$2.25 students, free for U26). Topkapi Palace is an Aladdin's cave of imperial treasures. It is also the oldest and most important of all the sultans' palaces in Istanbul. From within the confines of these walls a whole empire was governed: this was where the sultan and his family lived, his crack troops were stationed and the Ottoman ministers met to discuss affairs of state.

Constantinople's first sultan, Mehmet the Conqueror, built the palace soon after his victory in 1453; Süleyman the Magnificent was the first to move in permanently, and every sultan until 1839 enjoyed the sumptuous comforts of this luxurious residence. It remains the largest of all Ottoman palaces. Nine thousand people lived within the walls including 5000 troops, 1000 gardeners, 800 cooks and 600 craftsmen. Yet it is not the scale or beauty of the palace but the inordinate treasures contained within that people come to see today.

The **entrance** is round the back of the Aya Sofya on the southern side, behind the rococo **Fountain of Ahmed III** (1728). An inscription above the gate states that the defensive walls were built in 1478 by Mehmet the Conqueror. On the left as you walk through the gate is an ancient Byzantine church, **Aya Iran**, consecrated on the same day as neighbouring Aya Sofya. Today it serves as an exhibition hall.

Courtyard of Regiments

You are now in the Courtyard of the Regiments, so-called because the sultan's personal guards, the Janissaries, used to congregate here. They were hired slaves, hand-picked for their fighting abilities. Like the Mamlukes of Egypt, these guards often wielded more power than their sultan paymasters. For 350 years they influenced almost every decision in the court and it was a foolish sultan who dared to incur their displeasure. They were eventually wiped out by the reforming Sultan Mahmut II in 1826 (see the Hippodrome, opposite), who replaced them with a new, European-style army.

In Ottoman times the Janissary Courtyard was as far as the public could venture inside the palace grounds; buy a ticket from the booth on the right of the path and you can go much further. At the end of the path lies the **Gate of Salutations (a)**. In times gone by this gate was often surmounted by the head of some poor unfortunate who had displeased the sultan. The fountain, where the executioner would remove all those troublesome bloodstains from his sword, is near the gate.

Court of the Divans

Traditionally, only the sultan could pass through the gate on horseback; everybody else had to dismount in deference. However you choose to travel through, on the other side is the second of Topkapi's four courts, the Court of the Divans.

To the right are the huge **Kitchens (b)**, housing the biggest collection of Chinese porcelain in the world, 15,000 pieces altogether. The green

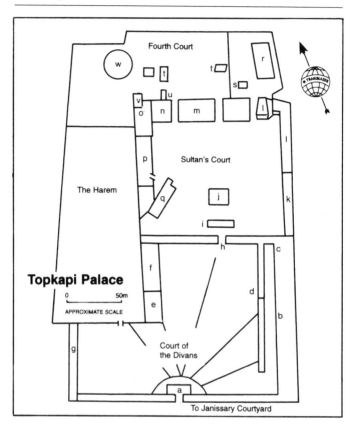

Topkapi Palace

0   50m

APPROXIMATE SCALE

To Janissary Courtyard

KEY

a Gate of Salutations
b Kitchens
c Porcelain Room
d Silver Room
e Imperial Council Chamber
f Collection of Arms
g Stables (Royal Carriages)
h Gate of Felicity
i Audience Chamber
j Library of Ahmed III
k Süleyman Baths
l Treasury

m Portraits
n Clock Collection
o Holy Relics
p Calligraphy Display
q New Library
r Restaurant/café
s Mosque
t Terrace Pavilion
u Revan Pavilion
v Circumcision Room
w Baghdad Pavilion

crockery is made from celadon, a special form of porcelain that would discolour whenever poison was served upon it. This was introduced following the agonising death of Mehmet the Conqueror, who suffered two weeks of unbearable convulsions before he died. All the water jugs are fitted with locks for the same security reasons. Other pieces include the precious yellow-ware collection, which could be used only by royalty.

Opposite the kitchens stands the **Silverware Room (d)**. Two huge silver vases, set with diamonds, dominate the display. One is topped by a red flag – the flag of the state – whilst the other flies a green flag, the flag of Islam, the state's religion. The sultan, as emperor and caliph, was the head of both. Also included in the exhibition is a silver tea set, a gift from the last Tzar of Russia, Nicholas II.

On the western side of the courtyard is the entrance to the **Harem** (see below) and the nearby **Imperial Council Chamber (e)**, where the grand vizier (prime minister) met with cabinet ministers to discuss affairs of state. The sultan could listen in on the conversation from behind a screen. Before leaving the second court, check the notice-board by the chamber to find out the times of the tour round the Harem.

Sultan's Court Passing through the **Gate of Felicity (h)** you enter the innermost sanctuary of the sultan's world and the epicentre of the empire. Very few people were allowed in here. The courtyard was staffed by white eunuchs, the sultan's most trusted slaves. Foreign ambassadors and the grand vizier were received in the **Audience Chamber (i)**, immediately in front of the Gate of Felicity. The sultan would sit on sumptuous pearl-encrusted cushions, shielded from view behind latticework, whilst the visitor knelt deferentially outside, held down by two large eunuchs.

Touring the court in an anti-clockwise direction, the first room, **Süleyman's Baths (k)**, is filled with a display of the sultan's costumes. Next door are the four rooms which, along with the belly-dancer at the Orient, are probably Istanbul's biggest crowd-pleasers. They used to be the living quarters of Mehmet the Conqueror, but after the Harem's construction they became the **Treasury (l)**. Today they house a blinding collection of jewels and precious knickknacks. Everything in here glitters and dazzles: the fabulous gold-tipped arrows, the huge solid-gold candlesticks smothered with over 6000 diamonds, the 200kg of golden throne decorated with emeralds, the world's largest uncut emerald (3.26kg) and, most famous of all, the emerald and diamond-handled Topkapi dagger. This dagger was originally meant to be a gift to the Shah of Persia from Mahmut I (1730-54), but Mahmut decided to keep it for himself (sensible fellow) following a revolt in Persia that saw the Shah toppled. If all this doesn't impress you, check out the Spoonmaker's Diamond in the third room of the treasury; at 86 karats it's the biggest cut diamond in the world. Vulgar or not, this collection's ability to astound is beyond question. Before leaving, don't miss the first of many religious relics on this route through the Near East – **the arm of John the Baptist**. This was brought back from Jerusalem by Constantine's mother Helena during her historical pilgrimage of AD326. You can visit his head in Damascus.

John's arm is not the only relic in Topkapi. Housed in a room in the north-west corner is a display of **Islamic Relics (o)**. There is plenty of Mohammed memorabilia here, including such curiosities as two of his swords, a toenail, a hair from his beard and a footprint. Most of these relics were handed over to Sultan Selim I by the caliph, when he invaded Egypt in 1517. To the sultans these relics were more useful than anything in the treasury: they proved to the Muslim tribes that the Ottoman Empire was now the centre of Islam, thus ensuring their obedience and support.

The Fourth Court To the right of a room housing **Portraits of the Sultans (m)** is a gate to the fourth court, the gardens of the palace. A number of kiosks sprout up from the lawns. Out of sight, the sultan used to inspect the parades that marched past the palace. The view from these kiosks over the Bosphorus is superb.

The Harem (Open 0945-1545, tours every half-hour; US$2, no concessions). The Harem can be visited only with a guide, and a timetable of the tours is printed by the entrance. The name 'Harem' comes from the Turkish 'Haram', meaning forbidden. It was built on the orders of Süleyman the Magnificent after his wife, Roxelana, persuaded him to build living quarters for her within the confines of the palace. Previously, the ladies of the court had been housed in a separate palace where Istanbul University now stands. The Harem was staffed by black eunuchs, and inhabited by the sultan, the *valide sultan* (the sultan's mother), his wives and his children.

Outside the Harem the sultan ruled, but inside he was often subservient to the valide sultan. It was she who chose which four women would be his wives, and ruled over the day-to-day administration of the palace. She also had over 40 rooms within the Harem all to herself.

With such prestige and power at stake, the wives would go to great lengths to become the next valide sultan. The Harem was a hotbed of conspiracy, with each of the wives plotting against the others. If one did give birth to an heir, the others would often plot to have that child killed; more than one infant was boiled to death in the Harem (boiling being a favourite method of disposal). As you walk around the Harem, with its web of secret passages and hidden corridors, you can well imagine the intrigues that went on between the wives and eunuchs who lived here.

Museum complex
(0930-1700, closed Mon; US$2, US$1 students, free for U26). Down the cobbled street behind the Aya Sofya is Istanbul's main museum complex.

Turkey's museums are usually well presented and the three here are no exception. Amongst the exhibits in the **Archaeological Museum** is the Sarcophagus of Alexander the Great (not actually his, but one of his generals) from the Royal Necropolis of Sidon in the Lebanon. Opposite stands the **Museum of the Ancient Orient**. The exceptional item here is the Treaty of Kadesh, an agreement signed between the warring Egyptian and Hittite Empires (see p22). In the centre of the complex stands the **Tiled Pavilion**, built on the orders of Mehmet the Conqueror as a pleasure palace. The pavilion's blue, faience-tiled exterior is most impressive. Inside is a museum dedicated to tiles.

Before returning to Sultanahmet Square walk down to the bottom of the hill. On the right is **Gulhane Park**. Continue down the road and opposite the next bend is the **Sublime Porte**, the gate which lent its name to the Ottoman government. City council offices now stand behind it.

❏ Intrigue in the Harem

The battle to be Süleyman's successor was a typical example of the conspiracies and plots that went on in Ottoman Istanbul. In the early days of the Ottoman Empire there was no fixed law of succession following the death of a sultan. It was customary, therefore, for the sultan to have his brothers and their male children murdered so that his heir would have no rivals to the throne.

Unfortunately for Süleyman the Magnificent the situation was complicated by his devotion to Roxelana, his favourite wife who had two sons – Beyazit and Selim – to rival Süleyman's eldest son Mustafa. It was more than parental love that drove her to promote her sons' claims to the throne. If they were successful, Roxelana would ascend to the position of valide sultan, the most powerful woman in the kingdom. First, she managed to persuade Süleyman to move the Harem inside Topkapi, a canny ploy to put herself in the nerve centre of the empire. Next, she formed an alliance with the grand vizier (prime minister) Rüstem Paşa, a relationship that was cemented when he married her daughter Mihrimah. Together Roxelana and Rüstem managed to turn Süleyman against his son to such an extent that the latter formed a party with rebellious Janissaries and landowners against his father. Süleyman had no choice but to have him killed; in 1553, Mustafa was visited by the court strangler.

Süleyman recognised that Rüstem had a hand in the affair and had the grand vizier dismissed. But two years later he was back, after Roxelana urged Süleyman to have Rüstem's successor, Ibrahim, murdered. Süleyman, still totally besotted with his wife, watched from behind a curtain as Ibrahim was murdered by mutes at the Mihrimah Mosque.

Of Roxelana's two sons it was Selim who emerged victorious in the ensuing power struggle. Beyazit and his family were subsequently murdered. Unfortunately for Roxelana, she never got to be valide sultan. She died eight years before her husband and never saw Selim II become sultan. Her actions had only succeeded in accelerating the decline of the Ottoman Empire. Selim proved to be the first in a long line of cretinous sultans who eventually brought down the empire. He developed a severe drinking habit, became known as Selim the Sot, and eventually died of cirrhosis of the liver.

Divan Yolu

The main east-west thoroughfare bisecting the southern peninsula changes its name frequently along its length but in Sultanahmet it is called Divan Yolu. The road stretches from Sultanahmet to the city walls. Between Sultanahmet and the Metro station at Aksaray it is flanked by many buildings of interest, beginning with Yerebatan Saray, and including the Grand Bazaar and the esteemed Istanbul University.

Yerebatan Saray

(Open 0900-1730; US$1.50, US$0.75 students/U26). A visit to Constantinople's ancient waterworks may not seem the most exciting of prospects but, in fact, this cistern rates as many people's favourite attraction in Istanbul. Built during the reign of Justinian, the ceiling is supported by large pillars topped by fine Byzantine capitals. To dispel the dank, melancholic aura of this subterranean hall the authorities have also introduced schools of fish into the water, and music and coloured lights have been added to heighten the atmosphere.

This cistern is just one of a number discovered in the city but this is the largest and the best of the two that are open to the public. The entrance is by the green to the west of the Aya Sofya, on Yerebatan Cad.

Scorched Column

Continue up Divan Yolu for approximately ten minutes, past the Mausoleum of Mahmut II, the sultan responsible for ending the Janissary guard. Just before the Grand Bazaar is a column which looks to have been scorched by fire. The pillar, Çemberlitaş ('bound column') used to be surmounted by a statue of Constantine, who erected it in 329AD. It was the first Byzantine monument in Constantinople. Next to it is the small **Mosque of Atik Ali Paşa**, a vizier of Sultan Beyazit II (1481-1512).

Kapali Çarşi – The Grand Bazaar

(0830-1800, closed Sun). This is the largest and prettiest of all the bazaars on this route through the Near East, containing over 4000 shops and occupying 200,000 square metres of land. The covered building was built during the reign of Mehmet the Conqueror, although it is almost certain that a Byzantine market existed here before; the plaza on the south-eastern corner of the bazaar by the Çemberlitaş tram stop used to be a Byzantine forum.

To many the bazaar is just too touristy but the fringes, where the rent is lower, have some of the more traditional stalls and are more evocative of Ottoman times. Whatever your thoughts about it, it is an exceptional traveller who comes away from here without buying something.

Incidentally, the gardens you walk through to reach the bazaar are the grounds of the 18th century **Nuruosmaniye Camii**. Very near is the **Mehmet Paşa Camii** (1463), the oldest mosque in Istanbul.

Süleymaniye

It is hardly surprising that a mosque built in honour of the Ottoman Empire's greatest sultan, and which was designed by the Ottoman's greatest architect, is today considered the finest example of Ottoman architecture in Istanbul. Although Sinan later declared the Selimiye to be the best of his buildings, he lived and is buried near this, his most famous work.

The Süleymaniye was completed in 1557. The interior is extremely simple and spacious, the most striking feature being the stained glass windows, the work of one Ibrahim the Drunkard. It is surrounded by arcades, which used to house the city's public buildings such as schools, clinics and libraries.

The **Mausoleum of Süleyman**, which also houses the tombs of his infamous wife Roxelana and his children, lies in the mosque's grounds to the south-west. Ten metres away is Sinan's tomb.

To reach the mosque, walk down Çadircilar Cad and turn left behind the university.

Beyazit Camii and the University

The pigeon-covered mosque of Beyazit II separates Divan Yolu from the University. The university was founded in the 19th century but looks a lot older than that; the date on the gate reads 1453 but this just commemorates the day Constantinople fell to the Muslims.

In the corner of the university campus is the **Beyazit Tower**. Originally it was made of wood and was used as a lookout for town fires; not surprisingly, it burnt down. The present tower was built in 1823; at over 60m it is the tallest structure in Stamboul.

Continuing on Divan Yolu you pass the **Laleli** ('Tulip') **Mosque** (1760), which gives its name to the district, and reach Aksaray, where Stamboul's metro line begins.

Fatih and Outer Istanbul

This area, which stretches north-west of Laleli to the Theodosian city walls, seldom draws the casual sightseer. This is not for the lack of attractions – some of the finest Ottoman and Byzantine buildings are here – but because it can be a pain to reach, bus No 86 from Eminönü to Edirne Kapi (Gate of Hadrian) is the easiest way.

Next to Edirne Kapi are a number of points of interest. The single-minareted **Mihrimah Camii** (1562) is the most obvious. It was built by Sinan for Mihrimah, the daughter of Roxelana and the wife of the grand vizier, Rüstem Paşa. Not too far away is the small **Postern Gate**, which the Byzantines left open, allowing the Ottoman soldiers to flood inside.

Kariye – the Chora Church (Closed Tues)

To the south east of Edirne Kapi stands this pretty red-brick church, the secret treasure of the Byzantines. It was built during the reign of Justinian and originally stood outside the city limits – 'Chora' means countryside. It contains some of the best mosaics outside of a museum. (This is not strictly true, for now the church *is* a museum).

Selimiye According to the architectural genius himself, this is Sinan's masterpiece. It was completed on the orders of his patron, Süleyman the Magnificent, in 1522 and is dedicated to the memory of Süleyman's father Selim I ('The Grim'). Selim's tomb lies in the grounds, as does the tomb of the nineteenth-century sultan, Abdulmecit.

Fatih Mosque If one includes all the attendant buildings, this is the largest mosque complex in Istanbul. It is not, however, the original built for Mehmet Fatih (Mehmet the Conqueror). This fell down in an earthquake; the one you see today dates from the 18th century.

Aqueduct of Valens Stretching across Atatürk Bulvari is this oft-photographed aqueduct, part of a network which used to transport water into the city. Valens was a fourth-century Byzantine emperor, although it is not known whether the aqueduct was constructed during his reign or not. What is known is that it was restored by, yes, you've guessed it, Sinan.

Eminönü

Before the northern banks of the Golden Horn flourished earlier this century, Eminönü was the commercial centre of the city. Today it has five sites of interest to the tourist: the Yeni and Rüstem Paşa Camiis, the Egyptian Bazaar, the local bus station and the ferry terminals.

The **Yeni Camii**, also known as the Pigeon Mosque (it's not difficult to see why), was begun in 1597 by the then valide sultan, but was not completed until 1667 by the mother of Mehmet IV. Nearby is the **Rüstem Paşa Camii** (1561), named after the same Rüstem who helped Selim the Sot ascend the throne.

Follow the path between the Yeni Camii and the bus station to reach the **Egyptian Bazaar** (closed Sun). This is the place to come if you're hankering after those oriental spices you've heard so much about, or just want some respite from the carpet sellers at the Grand Bazaar. It was built in the 17th century with taxes collected from Egypt.

Beyoğlu (Northern Istanbul)

The Genoese first settled in Beyoğlu in the ninth century. As their Byzantine neighbours to the south fell to the Ottoman hordes, the Genoese survived by remaining neutral. During the 1800s, as the Ottoman Empire slowly disintegrated, Beyoğlu became popular with foreign ambassadors who chose to settle in relative safety inside vast, purpose-built foreign compounds in this area. They brought with them money and European style, and soon all the beautiful people of Istanbul were migrating northwards over the Golden Horn. The sultans, recognising that Beyoğlu was a more fashionable address with better amenities, were soon following suit and relocating to the northern shore, where they built a number of palaces. Today the district remains the most populated, modern and vibrant part of town.

Pera, the main business district, lies to the north of Karaköy (Galata). At the heart is Taksim Square, surrounded by all the major hotels. Although there is less of interest on Beyoğlu and Pera than Sultanahmet, there are nevertheless a few sights worth visiting.

Galata Tower (0900-0100; US$1.25, no concessions). In the heart of Istanbul's tiny Jewish Quarter stands this Genoese lookout tower, the most obvious landmark in Galata. It was built in 1348 as part of the Genoese fortifications of their territory, and extended to its present 61m height in 1446. A restaurant/nightclub has been built into one of the nine storeys, so it is now possible, if you have the cash, to dine in style whilst enjoying the views of the Bosphorus some 140m below.

Bus No 74 will drop you near the tower, although it is only a 20-minute walk from Galata Bridge.

Dolmabahçe Palace (0900-1730, closed Mon and Thu; US$2.50, no concessions). You would think, looking at its impressive facade, that this palace was built at the height of the Ottoman's glory but you would be wrong. The palace is a symptom of the empire's disarray in the 1800s, rather than a reflection of its success. By the time the palace was completed Ottoman Turkey had become 'the Sick Man of Europe'. Bankrupt, disorganised, threatened by revolt, the empire was in terminal decline. And as the empire fell apart, the sultan hid inside these luxurious palaces, shutting the awful reality out behind high stone walls.

Dolmabahçe Palace was built at the behest of Sultan Abdulmecit who recognised that Topkapi was beginning to show its age. Draughty, dark, and damp, it was clearly time for a change. The site of his new palace used to be a filled-in harbour (dolmabahçe means 'filled garden') on which stood a pleasure palace belonging to Ahmet I. Abdulmecit's palace took 13 years to complete (1843-56) and incorporated four tonnes of gold and 40 tonnes of silver in the decorations. Small wonder that the total cost was five million gold coins, equivalent today to US$500 million!

Just twenty years after its construction it became the venue for the first Turkish parliament and was later used as the Istanbul residence of Atatürk. Indeed, on 10th November 1938 at 9:05am he died here. All the clocks in Dolmabahçe have been stopped at that time in tribute.

To view the screamingly ostentatious Dolmabahçe, catch buses Nos 22E, 22C, 22, 24, 25E or 30D from Eminönü, all of which will drop you by the entrance. The palace can be viewed only on a guided tour which, provided the guide is fairly knowledgeable, is worthwhile.

Military and Naval Museums (0930-1700, closed Tues; US$1.50 in each museum). The highlight of the Military Museum, which lies to the north of the Hilton Hotel on Cumhuriyet Cad, occurs at 3pm every afternoon when the Janissary band, fitted out in appropriate uniforms, performs a number of period tunes in the gardens. In the museum is the chain which the Byzantines used to close off the Golden Horn, and any number of guns, weapons and uniforms from the Ottoman era.

The Naval Museum, even further up the Bosphorus than Dolmabahçe, is really only for those with an obsessive interest in the subject.

Bosphorus ferry cruise

Every day two boats depart from Pier 3 at Eminönü (at 1035 and 1335) to bounce along both sides of the Bosphorus all the way to the shores of the Black Sea. Here one is allowed to alight and spend a couple of hours, which is enough time to take in the scenery and the fresh sea air. The boats return to Istanbul at 1630 and 1810 respectively. During winter the first boat only is running but in summer they lay on extra trips. Tickets cost US$3 (US$1.50 on Saturdays, Sundays and holidays).

MOVING ON

Bus Heed the advice given under the Travel Agents section on p59 before buying a ticket. The new Istanbul bus terminal, a concrete jungle of ramps, kebab stands and ticket offices, rises out of the wasteland west of the city, with only a nearby prison for company. To get here, take the metro to Otogar ('bus station'). A bus to the next destination, **Çanakkale**, costs US$8. This includes the ferry price across the straits. Buses run approximately every hour, with the 340km journey taking six hours.

Train For those who'd like to go straight to **Ankara**, it's best to take the train. There are eight per day, varying in price from US$3.30 to US$10 (less 30% for students). You can buy tickets from Sirkeçi station (window 9/10). To get to Haydarpaşa station, catch a ferry from Karaköy, or from Eminönü (pier 2) to Kadiköy, which is five minutes south of the station.

West Turkey

ÇANAKKALE, GELIBOLU (GALLIPOLI) AND TRUVA (TROY)

Traveller, halt! The soil you tread once witnessed the end of an era. Listen! In this quiet mound there once beat the heart of a nation. **From a poem by NH Onan, written on the side of a Gelibolu hill facing Çanakkale**

Muslims have Mecca, the Jews have Jerusalem, but for Aussies and Kiwis it seems to be the deserted, pine-clad hills of Gelibolu that represent their spiritual home. Thousands of Antipodeans make the pilgrimage each year to these windswept shores. It was on these blood-soaked battlefields during WWI that the two nations sacrificed thousands of lives for a cause they cared little about and in a war fought thousands of miles from their homeland. It was also here that the two forged their own national identity, and began to drift away from the imperial rulers in Britain. Wherever you're from, however, a tour round these battlefields can be a moving and educational experience.

Orientation and services   (Çanakkale ☎ **area code** 0286)
Çanakkale is just a US$0.60-boat ride away from the Gelibolu port of Kilitbahir. Buses to Çanakkale terminate at the harbour. All the hotels, restaurants and amenities are huddled nearby. By far the easiest way to visit the battlefields and cemeteries of Gallipoli is on a **tour**. Almost every hotel organises one, or at least knows somebody who does, and the quality varies only slightly. The price is usually about US$10 for a one-day tour, which lasts about four hours. Contact **Down Under** on ☎ 814 24 31 or call in at **Troy Anzac Travel** near Çanakkale's clock tower.

Where to stay
Anzac House [1] (☎ 2170156; US$5/9 sgl/dbl) is aiming at the huge Antipodean market: vegemite sandwiches and TNT magazines abound. Although the manager is justly proud of the recent refurbishment – the rooms are immaculate – I have, unfortunately, heard some uncomplimentary reports about the treatment of certain backpackers here. Consider heading to the *Yellow Rose* [2] (☎ 2173343) instead. Though a little overpriced (US$4.50/7.50 sgl/dbl) the rooms are pleasant and the lounge has satellite TV. Another option is the spotless – and, at US$2pp, cheap – *Kervansaray* [3] (☎ 2178192), run by the beanie-wearing, white-bearded brother of the owner of the Yellow Rose. The building is over 200 years old, and used to be the residence of a Turkish paşa. The *Efes* [4] nearby is run by their sister; it is a little dearer.

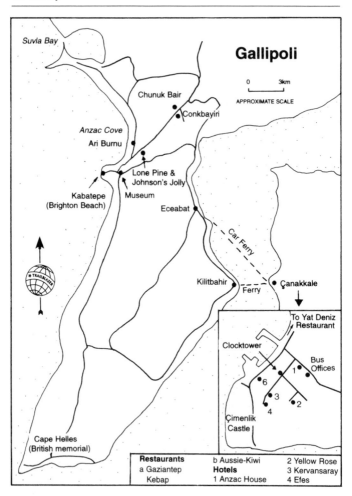

Where to eat

Gelibolu offers the usual Turkish fare. For something other than a kebab, head to the *Gazientep Kebap* by the clock tower and try a lahmacun or four (a small mincemeat and onion pizza, US$0.35). Nearby, the *Aussie & Kiwi Restaurant* is the place to go if you're homesick for vegemite and apple crumble. Moored in the harbour to the north of the town is the recently-opened *Yat Deniz*, basically a bar on a boat that serves a little food too. Their mussels (US$1.50) are particularly fine. They have plans to organise cruises in summer.

Gelibolu

The best place to begin a tour of Gelibolu is the **museum** (0800-1200, 1300-1700; US$0.75, free for U26) perched on top of the hill above **Brighton Beach** (Kabatepe). The first room is dedicated to the late forest manager who died in a fire that raged through the peninsula two years ago. The rest of the museum is concerned with the war. Amongst the displays of shrapnel, uniforms and other paraphernalia there are two rather

---

❏ The Allied Gallipoli campaign

Although the Allied Gallipoli campaign ended up as a bloodbath, the strategic thinking behind the offensive was, initially at least, sound. Not only would a successful negotiation of the Dardanelles leave the Ottoman capital of Constantinople at the mercy of the Allied naval artillery, but it would also open up a vital supply route through to the beleaguered Russians. The Turks recognised the strategic importance of the Dardanelles too. On the 18th March 1915, 18 Allied warships sailed up the straits. They were soon subject to a fierce bombardment from Turkish guns based on the Gelibolu peninsula. By the end of the battle, three boats had been sunk, with another three disabled beyond repair.

The lesson this gave to Churchill, then the first Lord of the Admiralty, was clear: if one was to conquer the straits, one would have to silence the guns of Gelibolu first. With this in mind, on 25th April 1915 a combined force of Australian-New Zealand troops (ANZACs) landed on Gelibolu's western shore, whilst to the south a body of French and British men landed at Cape Helles.

Both landings were a disaster. The British and French were welcomed ashore by a huge body of Ottoman troops and suffered heavy casualties as they struggled to gain a toehold on the peninsula. The ANZACs, meanwhile, had landed three km north of their ideal landing spot at Brighton Beach and were faced by the virtually-insurmountable cliffs at ANZAC Cove. They suffered casualties running into the thousands before a beachhead was established.

As with the western front at Flanders, the battle for Gallipoli soon settled into the miserable stalemate of trench warfare. On the 19th of May the Turks launched an offensive to break this deadlock. It was so gory that four days later a temporary truce was called to enable the troops to clear the bodies from the battleground. The Allies counter-attacked in August and took Conkbayiri (Chunuk Bair), a strategically-important hill affording views over both coasts. They held it for just three days before the Turks under Atatürk (then just plain old Mustafa Kemal) retaliated and won back the land.

Eventually the Allies, depleted by disease and unprepared for the harsh winter, began to evacuate. On the 19-20 December, 83,000 were evacuated from Sulva and Anzac Cove. The following January the last 35,000 were withdrawn from Cape Helles. Amazingly, after eight months of vicious fighting that had seen the Allies lose 43,000 of their 489,000 troops (205,000 casualties), and the Turks lose nearly 100,000 men with 300,000 casualties, the evacuation was accomplished without a single fatality.

poignant letters sent back by the soldiers to their families.

North of Brighton Beach is **Anzac Cove**. Nobody knows for sure why the ANZAC forces landed here. Maybe the current was too strong and forced them to land sooner than they had wished, or maybe in the dark of night they just mistook this tiny cove for the expanse of beach at Kabatepe. Whatever the reason, it was an error that was to cost the lives of thousands of ANZACs in the first days of the fighting.

Nearby are a number of cemeteries: **Beach Cemetery** is an ANZAC burial ground, which includes the grave of John Simpson – the 'Donkey Man' – so-called after he rescued Allied soldiers from the front by carrying them on his donkey to the hospital boats. He survived for just 25 days of the war. Just to the north lies the Turkish cemetery at **Ari Burnu**.

Up in the hills are more cemeteries. At **Lone Pine** one can find the grave of the youngest soldier to die, fourteen-year old James Martin. The pine tree that stands in the middle is a seedling from the original Lone Pine, the last tree left standing after the others had been chopped up for firewood during the harsh winter. On both sides of the road near here are some of the original trenches. In some cases, such as at **Johnston's Jolly** and **Quinn's Post**, the distance separating the Allied and Turkish trenches is just seven metres.

At the top of this hill is **Conkbayiri**, the first goal of the Allied forces. This was where the British/French and Anzac forces were supposed to meet up. There is a monument to the New Zealand troops who captured the hill for three days in August. They were eventually driven off by the Turks under the guidance of a young general called Mustafa Kemal; he was later to become the father of the republic, Atatürk. He was saved at Gallipoli by his pocket watch, which deflected a piece of shrapnel heading for his heart. Another monument on Conkbayiri stands on the spot where Atatürk ordered his men 'not just to attack, but to die'. Twenty-eight thousand men, from both sides, did just that in those three calamitous days.

Çanakkale
There is a small, oft-ignored **Military Museum** housed in the Ottoman Çimenlik Fortress, with a few exhibits that complement the tours of Gelibolu, (0900-1200, 1330-1700; US$0.40, US$0.20stu, free for U26). The park that surrounds it stays open until 6pm.

Truva (Troy)
Before its discovery by the amateur archaeologist Heinrich Schliemann in 1871, it had always been assumed that the Troy of *Iliad* fame was a mythical city, the legends surrounding it mere products of Homer's fertile imagination. The story was, after all, written in c750BC, some 500 years after the battles between Paris, Achilles, Ulysses et al were supposed to have taken place.

Schliemann uncovered not only ruins from Homer's Troy but eight other cities on the same site, built one on top of the other like layers on a cake. These cities date from 3600BC (Troy I) to 550AD (Troy IX); Homer's city is believed to be Troy VII (c1250BC).

There is little to see here today. A ghastly wooden horse has been erected by the side of road so visitors have something to photograph. The ruins of Troys I to IX are contained in an area of 100 square metres, partially enclosed within the walls of Troy VI. It is possible to hire a guide who will explain the relevance of each pile of stones, or you can arrange a tour from Çanakkale.

Dolmuses leave from the centre of Çanakkale (US$0.60) throughout the day, taking approximately 50 minutes to reach Troy.

Moving on
A bus to Izmir, Turkey's third largest city (population 1,757,414), takes approximately five hours and costs US$7.50. From Izmir one can catch a bus to the next destination on this route, Selçuk (US$1.50).

SELÇUK AND EPHESUS

The classical Roman town of Ephesus is the biggest draw on Turkey's Aegean coast. Most of the hotels and tourist facilities are located in nearby Selçuk, a former farming community which is now riding on the crest of the tourist boom.

Orientation and services   (Selçuk ☎ area code 0232)
Atatürk Cad runs from Izmir to Aydin, bisecting Selçuk. The bus station is by the road on the eastern side; to the north of the bus station is the main shopping area. Most of the sights, hotels and souvenir shops lie opposite the bus station to the west of Atatürk Cad. Ephesus is 2km to the west of Selçuk.

The **tourist office** opposite the bus station is packed full of pamphlets with pretty pictures. The hostels, however, usually have much better information. There are plenty of **banks** in the shopping district; the **PTT** (0900-1200, 1300-1630) can be found here too.

Where to stay
There is fierce competition amongst the hotels in Selçuk, which can only be good news for visitors. The only disadvantage is that every hostel doubles as a carpet shop, or is at least affiliated to one. Bear in mind that the wealthier you look, the harder the sell – try to look scruffy!

Most cheap hostels are confined to a small hill to the south of St John's Basilica, behind the Ephesus Museum; ignore the touts at the bus station and head this way. Note that the room rates below are for the low season. The most popular place is the *AUS-NZ Pension* (☎ 8926050) for US$3/3.75/4 dorm/sgl/dbl. Unlike some other hotel owners, the Toparlak family spent twelve years Down Under and their Australian accents are genuine. Their hotel is most comfortable: hot water, spotless rooms, toilet paper (!) and free lifts to Ephesus for the lazy. Their rooftop Diamond Inn pulls in the crowds too.

Nearby is the *Barim Hostel* (☎ 8926923), a restored, 18th-century Ottoman house (US$4.50 pp). The wrought-iron exterior is undoubtedly impressive; the twelve rooms on the inside, however, provide few thrills. But at least one resident appears happy: a stork has taken to nesting on the chimney. Up the hill is the *Homeros Pension* (☎ 8923995), a quieter alternative to the two above (probably because they don't employ touts). Dervis Köse is your helpful host, and his hotel is clean and well maintained (US$4.50/7pp dorm/dbl).

On the other side of Atatürk Cad and to the south of the bus station there's the *NZ Pension* (☎ 8914892), another excellent place (US$3/4.50 sgl/dbl). Kitted out in pine and undergoing refurbishment when I last visited, it can boast a kitchen, pool table, information board, and even a mini-gym in the basement!

The *Hotel Bella* (☎ 8923944) overlooks St John's Basilica. Every room (US$7.50/15 sgl/dbl) is smart, clean and with bathrooms en suite, but the hotel as a whole appears a little shabby.

Where to eat
In Selçuk's market are a number of snack-peddlers who can conjure up a stomach-filling sandwich for about US$0.80. The local delicacy is Turkish pizza, and almost all restaurants specialise in these. The locals' favourite is the *Nur Restaurant*, where an egg and tomato pizza will set you back about US$1.20. The *Pamukkale Pide Lahmacun Salonu* in the centre of town is another good place. Round off your meal with a cake, or similar saccharine-filled treat, from the *Sevni Patisserie*.

Sights in Selçuk
The Artemision (0800-1730, free). The single, giant pillar rising up from the fields on the way to Ephesus was originally one of 129 that surrounded the Temple of Artemis, the first of three of the Seven Wonders you can visit on this route through the Near East. It was built in the sixth century BC, over 400 years before the Romans arrived, and originally covered an area larger than a soccer pitch. The temple was burnt down on the night of Alexander the Great's birth. It was rebuilt by the Ephesians, but Emperor Justinian pillaged much of the temple's marble for St John's Basilica and the rest of the building gradually subsided into the mud. The re-erected pillar today functions both as a local landmark, and as an ideal roost for storks.

Archaeology Museum (Open 0830-1200, 1300-1700; US$2, US$1 students, free for U26). Amongst the exhibits in this interesting little museum are some statues of the multi-breasted Artemis, an ivory frieze of soldiers and their horses from the second century and a room containing reconstructions of typical Roman dwellings from Ephesus.

St John's Basilica (0900-1700; US$1.20, US$0.60 students, free for U26). St John was one of the first apostles to arrive in Ephesus. He is believed to have spent his last few years here, preaching to the Artemis-worshipping population and writing his gospel.

The cruciform basilica, built on the orders of Justinian and his wife Theodora, is constructed around his tomb (marked by a marble slab in the centre) on top of the old Citadel Hill. Currently there are plans to restore it to its sixth-century glory.

Meryemana – House of the Virgin Mary

(0900-1700; US$1). About five km from Ephesus, this is another Christian monument with a curious tale behind it. Catherine Emmerich, an 18th-century German, had visions of this house even though she had never visited the region before, and was able to describe in exact detail the appearance and location of the building. Popes Paul VI and John Paul II have both made pilgrimages to the site, which before Catherine's revelations had been just another hillside shack. Mary's tomb, according to Ms Emmerich, lies nearby but has yet to be discovered. It is possible to walk to the house from the back gate at Ephesus, although it's a stiff climb and only for the very fit. Just follow the signs to Meryemana.

Ephesus

(Open 0800-1700; US$4, US$2 students, free for U26). The Roman town of Ephesus is a pleasant, two-km walk from Selçuk along the tree-lined Dr Sabri Yayla Bulvari. This ruined city was once the capital of Roman Asia and boasted a population approaching 500,000. Thanks to the quality of its restoration, Ephesus today provides us with the best example of a Roman provincial city on our route.

Although most of the buildings in Ephesus are Roman, just before the entrance, however, one finds a Byzantine monument. The tale behind the **Grotto of the Seven Sleepers** is an interesting one (more interesting than the grotto itself). This dormant septet was a band of Christians who escaped persecution in the town by hiding in this hillside grotto. Whilst sleeping the seven were discovered by their tormentors, who sealed the cave with them still inside. The entrance was later unblocked by an earthquake and the seven awoke to return to the town. It was then that they realised that they had, in fact, slept for 200 years. When they eventually died they were buried in the cave and a small Byzantine chapel was built inside. The grotto is a little distance from the path to Ephesus. Signposts point the way.

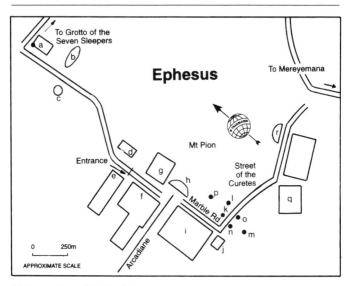

Ephesus

(a) Gymnasium of Vedius From the second century. Both the gymnasium and the next-door **(b) Stadium** are up a hill and invisible from the entrance path.

(c) The Acropolis

(d) Byzantine baths

(e) Church of the Virgin Mary Lying behind the souvenir stalls on the right is this church. The name is important, for churches were named after saints only if that saint happened to live in the area and legend has it that Mary was brought here towards the end of her life (see Meryemana, p87).

(f) Sports Arena There is very little to see in this overgrown wasteland, or in **(g) The Theatre Gymnasium** .

(h) Theatre Cut into the side of Mt Pion at the end of the pine-fringed avenue, this was where St Paul's followers were lynched by an angry mob of silver makers after Paul had condemned the local religion, the worship of Diana (Act 19:23-41). The silver makers manufactured the Diana idols that were used in the religion.

The street that runs straight ahead from the theatre is the **Arcadiane** which used to lead to the harbour. The fact that the sea is now some four km away explains why Ephesus died: the harbour silted up, and the sea trade moved elsewhere.

Perpendicular to this is the **Marble Road**, Ephesus' main street that runs along-side the **(i) Agora** (a Roman arena used for public meetings) and leads to the town's best-restored building, the **(j) Library of Celsus**, built in AD110. Picture-boards inside explain how the restoration was carried out.

Heading away from the library up the hill is the **Street of the Curetes**, which is jam-packed with buildings.

(k) Brothel The first ruins on the left are often referred to as the brothel, although there is little evidence to suggest they were anything more than public baths.

(l) Temple of Hadrian This stands next to the brothel; the reliefs are not original (the real ones are in the Archaeological Museum in Selçuk). Also in the museum is a reconstruction of the **(m) Private Residences**, on the hill opposite the baths.

(n) Fountain

(o) Octagon

(p) Latrines An ancient Roman ruin – so don't use them.

Continuing up the hill, on the right-hand side is the dilapidated **(q) Temple of Diocletian**, the largest of the four temples dedicated to the emperors, which now houses the **Museum of Inscriptions**. At the top of the hill is the **(r) Odeon**, a smaller version of the theatre which was used as a venue for public meetings.

Moving on

Getting a correct fare in Selçuk is nigh on impossible. Like flies around a discarded kebab, bus touts swarm around foreigners at the merest sniff of a well-endowed moneybelt. Even if you manage to avoid them by waiting by the side of the road for a bus you still have to contend with the staff on board. A few buses go all the way to Pamukkale (US$4.50, every hour, 2hr 30min), but most stop at Denizli, 20km before Pamukkale, and charge the same price.

PAMUKKALE

The thermal springs at Pamukkale (Turkish for 'Cotton Castle') are a wonderful natural phenomenon that have, unfortunately, been spoiled somewhat by the excessive development of the town. The water emanating from the springs has been reduced to a trickle and the gleaming white limestone pools have been dulled by soil brought up on the boot-soles of careless tourists. Strangely enough, I've also heard of more backpackers being robbed here than anywhere else in the Near East. Today the chalky-white cliffs and surrounding Roman ruins retain some of their splendour but, one wonders, for how much longer?

The ruined town that lies on the plateau above the springs is Hierapolis. Founded by Eumenes II (c190BC), a king of Pergamum, it was later bequeathed to the Romans in his will before they had a chance to come and steal it. (Pergamum was just one of the Greek kingdoms that flourished in Anatolia following the demise of the Hittites. We shall be encountering towns of the Lycians, Phrygians and Carians later on).

At least three Roman emperors came here to benefit from the soothing, healing waters of the spring. Although later destroyed by earthquakes, the city flourished once more under the Byzantines who built a church in honour of the Apostle Philip, who lived, preached and was martyred here in AD80.

Orientation and services (Pamukkale ☎ area code 0258)

The thermal pools are situated at the top of a cliff to the east of the town, where they form a spectacular white scar on the cliff-face. Above the pools are the **PTT**, a **tourist office** and a few exchange counters. The hotels and restaurants are down in the town; the further down the hill, the cheaper the hotels tend to be.

Where to stay

Many hotels in Pamukkale have their own pool filled with the beneficial water from the hot springs. Unfortunately, the last time I visited *Daisy's* (☎ 2722343) their swimming pool was the colour and consistency of mucus, but they say it will be cleaned for the summer. The rooms, all en suite, cost US$7.50 in summer and less than US$2 in winter. It is one of the cheapest in town, and provided you can put up with the manager's marauding children, it's a good choice.

The *Allgau* (☎ 2722250) is a very popular place, although maybe this is because their network of touts stretches all the way back to Denizli. Again the hotel has a pool, and the prices are similar to Daisy's.

The eponymous owner of *Mustafa's* (☎ 2722240) is a cheerful guy boasting a heavy Birmingham accent. His wife does all the cooking; judging from the size of Mustafa, she's very good at it. Prices start at US$4.50pp with an extra charge for heating. There's also a pool.

The *Kervansaray* (☎ 2722209, US$6pp) is excellent value; all rooms have a balcony, and the terrace restaurant is very pleasant too. The *Weisseberg* (☎ 2722064, US$3.50pp), a cosy, family-run place, and the upmarket *Meltem* (☎ 2722413, US$7.50) have both been recommended.

Where to eat

Most of the restaurants in Pamukkale are overpriced. Amongst the better ones are *Mustafa's*, which does some great kebab meals, and the nearby *Pizzeria*. Seek out this place – with its bright lights, multi-coloured flags and pumping stereo it's hard to miss – for while it's not the cheapest in town (average US$3 for a pizza) their food is some of the best.

Thermal baths

(US$2.50, US$1.50 students, free for U26). These prices assume that you are going to bother paying for the baths. It is a fact of life, however, that most travellers climb up the ridge on the other side of the springs from the entrance where there is no ticket booth. Whatever way you go, be sure to remove footwear and stub out cigarettes before you reach the snowy-white travertines. This limestone is slippery so watch your step.

The water in the pools is supposedly therapeutic, especially if you suffer from kidney and bladder ailments. (Some of the water in the bottom pools appears to have been used by people with *very* severe bladder ailments).

Behind the pools is the **museum**, housed in the excellently-preserved Roman baths (US$0.80; closed Mon). Even further up the hill is the **Pamukkale Motel**, which is built around the gorgeous **Sacred Baths**.

Unfortunately, there is a US$6 charge to use these baths, which have fluted columns and pillars scattered on the bottom. Tickets are available from the exchange counter at the motel entrance.

Hierapolis
Around the Pamukkale Motel are the remains of Roman Hierapolis. The 48-tier **theatre**, to the right of the road as you walk up the hill, is the undoubted highlight, but many of the tombs that lie scattered hereabouts also merit further inspection. Many visitors prefer these ruins to Ephesus; while not as spectacular, there is more to discover, fewer crowds and no entrance fee. There are certainly worse ways to spend an afternoon than to rest on an old tomb in the meadows with a picnic at your side.

Moving on
Most buses terminate at Denizli, some 20km from Pamukkale. A local bus or dolmus from here costs US$0.40. In Pamukkale there are a number of small ticket agencies. For those who have decided to cut through Central Anatolia, the fare to Ankara is US$9 (6hr journey, five buses per day). For those who are going around the coast, buses to Bodrum leave at 1100 and 1500; it's US$4.75 for the 3hr 30min trip.

BODRUM

On Turkey's south-western shore, where the azure waters of the Aegean and Mediterranean merge, stands Bodrum, the most picturesque of all of Turkey's seaside resorts. Not even the proliferation of tacky clubs, English Pubs and package holidaymakers can detract from Bodrum's beauty. This is ancient Halicarnassus, capital of the Greek kingdom of Caria. One of their kings was the egocentric Mausolus (376-353BC), whose tomb was so magnificent that it warranted inclusion in Pliny's list of the Seven Ancient Wonders. Mausolus lent his name to every monumental tomb ('Mausoleum') built thereafter. Although his famous sepulchre has long since been destroyed, Bodrum still has plenty – Crusader castles, sandy beaches, good food, temperate climate – to keep the traveller occupied.

Orientation and services   (Bodrum ☎ area code 0252)
The bus station is about 500m uphill from the harbour along Çevat Şakir. About halfway along road is the junction with Atatürk Cad, the main tourist street in Bodrum which runs alongside Kumbahce Bay. The **GPO** and **banks** are on Çevat Şakir. The **tourist office** nestles underneath the walls of St Peter's Castle.

Where to stay and eat
Bodrum is not cheap. The least expensive accommodation I could find was *Titiz* (☎ 3160701), which in winter cost US$4 for a single (US$6 dbl)

but even here the summer prices are frightful (US$13/20 sgl/dbl). The rooms are shabby although they do all come with a sink and toilet.

The *Gözde* (☎ 3165377) is a personal favourite. Though double the price of the Titiz in winter and US$16pp in summer, it's staffed by people who will bend over backwards to make your stay as enjoyable as possible. The rooms are very pleasant; try to get a south-facing room.

Also recommended is the *Elvan* (☎ 3162490), which offers boat trips out to the nearby islands. The rooms (US$7.50 winter, US$15 in summer) are adequate only, but the food they serve here is very good. It's at 20 Atatürk Cad, about thirty metres east of the mosque. Also on Atatürk Cad, behind the Captain Bodrum Restaurant, is *Emiko* (☎ 3165560), a pleasant, clean, Japanese-run hotel (US$7.50/15 winter/summer).

Surprisingly, perhaps, the *café* inside the entrance to the Castle of St Peter is one of the cheaper places to eat in town. It is always packed, particularly with local schoolchildren at lunch-times, but is none the worse for that. For vegetarians, the *Bugday* in town has a large menu and appetising food.

What to see
The Mausoleum of Halicarnassus (0800-1200, 1300-1700, closed Mon; US$1, US$0.50 students). For fifteen hundred years Mausolus' tomb stood as one of the Seven Wonders of the World. Although Mausolus had talked about building a monumental tomb for years, the project was eventually undertaken by his wife upon his death. Today the remnants of the Mausoleum lie scattered in museums throughout the world (in particular the British Museum in London), but the original site is still open to the public. Picture boards displayed in a nearby shelter suggest how the mausoleum may have looked. Its estimated size was 32m by 38m, with a height of about 55m when surmounted by the original statue of a four-horse chariot, a feature described by Pliny the Elder.

St Peter's Castle (0800-1200, 1300-1700, closed Mon; US$2, US$1 students, free for U26). Much of the stone from the mausoleum was used to construct this Crusader fortress. The Crusading Knights of St John arrived from Rhodes in the wake of Tamerlane's Mongol invasion of 1402, when the Ottoman Empire had been rocked back onto its heels by a series of heavy defeats. Construction began in 1406 on the site of an old Byzantine castle, and was subsequently used by the Ottoman Empire after the Crusaders had been chased from the Turkish mainland by Süleyman the Magnificent in the 1500's. Towards the end of the last century it was converted to a prison.

Today it houses the not-to-be-missed **Museum of Underwater Archaeology**, winner of the 1995 European Museum of the Year Award. The museum traces the history of sea trade since 4000BC, when the Greeks first began to deal with the Egyptians. Included in a separate display is the **Glass Wreck** (1000-1100, 1400-1600, Tues-Fri only; US$1, free for U26), one of the oldest shipwrecks ever raised. It sank in 1025 during the Fatimid/Byzantine era, and was only discovered 948 years later, in 1973, by sponge-diver Mehmet Askin. The boat's cargo consisted of a lot of smashed glass, plenty of which has been recovered.

At the entrance to the museum are two monuments celebrating two famous former residents of Bodrum. One is the twentieth-century author Çevat Şakir Kabauğacli, and the other is Herodotus, the 'Father of History', so-called because he was one of the first historians to record events without recourse to gods or mythical beasts.

Moving on
There are three buses daily to Fethiye, at 0730, 0915 and 1830. The fare is US$8; the trip takes 4-5hrs (275km).

FETHIYE AND OLÜDENIZ

One of the larger resorts on the southern coast, Fethiye stands on the site of ancient Tessos, once a major Lycian town (c400BC). The Lycians were one of the many Greek tribes who invaded Anatolia's west coast following the demise of the Hittites.

Everywhere you go in Fethiye you will find evidence that the Lycians once lived – or at least died – here, for there are numerous sarcophagi scattered throughout the town: by the post office, in back gardens and cut into the cliff face that overlooks the town.

Fethiye's downtown area is quaint, despite the presence of a large number of souvenir and carpet shops. There is also a small **museum**, a good place to while away the hours. Despite these attractions, most travellers prefer to stop just one night at the most at Fethiye before catching the dolmus to Olüdeniz.

Built round a clear-blue lagoon that is invisible from the sea, Olüdeniz is the archetypal Turkish resort: a perfect two-km swathe of golden sand backed by steep, pine-draped mountains. Senseless development has taken a toehold but has not yet spoiled the place. If you think Olüdeniz is one step away from paradise, take that step by joining one of the tours to the verdant Butterfly Valley (approx US$4).

Enjoy Olüdeniz while you can. The developers are slowly taking over more and more land, and plans are afoot to charge beach-users a fee, probably about US$2 per day.

Orientation and services   (Fethiye/Olüdeniz ☎ **area code** 0252)
Fethiye's bus station is some four km east of the centre of town and the harbour area; a dolmus between the two costs US$0.20. About half way between the two is the Olüdeniz dolmus station (US$0.75). Both the **GPO** and the **tourist office** also lie on this main road.

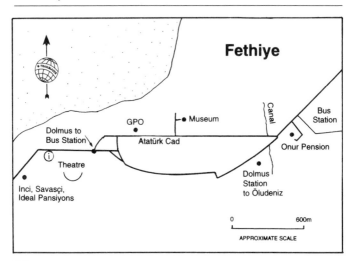

Where to stay

Fethiye Just west of the town centre is the main hotel area. The **İnçi** (☎ 3325144) and *Savaşçi Pension* are both to be recommended. Both charge about US$15 in summer but are closed in winter. Alternatively, haul your-self uphill to the *Ideal Pansiyon*, (☎ 6141981, US$15 dbl with breakfast). There's a great view over the water, and all the rooms are spotless and spacious.

If you arrive late at night or wish to stay near the bus station, call the *Onur Pension* (☎ 6122841). The owner will pick you up in his car and take you to his comfortable pension (US$3pp low season), which has hot showers and clean rooms. You can also use the kitchen here.

Olüdeniz is a summer resort only; in winter it closes down completely. The small *Susie's Place* is one of the more charming places to stay. The sparsely-furnished wooden huts cost about US$15 in summer. It is in the centre of the tourist village, 100m from the beach opposite a small shop.

Moving on

A bus from Fethiye to Kaş costs US$2.50, and takes approximately two to three hours. There are eight buses per day.

KAŞ

The southern coast of Turkey is studded with picturesque harbours and small fishing villages, and gilded with pine-clad hills and deserted, sandy beaches. There are some perfect get-away-from-it-all resorts here. Kaş, although more popular than most, is just such a place. There is very little to do in Kaş except browse amongst the jewellery and carpet shops, visit the small Roman amphitheatre, climb to the nearby Lycian tombs, or sit in one of the restaurant terraces and watch the world and his donkey go by. There are, however, a couple of excursions you may consider taking: a boat trip to the even more picturesque fishing village of Kekova; or a trip to Ptarra, the home of Father Christmas.

The bus station is at the top of the hill to the north of the town. At the bottom of the hill is the harbour. Walk to the harbour and turn left to reach the **tourist office**.

Where to stay   (Kaş ☎ area code 0242)
One block behind the tourist office is *Smiley's Restaurant* (☎ 8362812). The manager, Smiley, has an unusual ploy for pulling in customers: eat here, and you can sleep upstairs for free. The dorms are nothing special, sometimes just a mattress on the floor. Other places to try include the *Meltem Pension*, on the small estate below the bus station, and the *Koyum* (☎ 8361373), up the hill from Smiley's. A double in the latter costs US$17 including breakfast, which is actually a good deal as the rooms come complete with a mini-kitchen and a coffee machine.

Ptarra
Saint Nicholas (aka Father Christmas) was a fourth-century Byzantine bishop who spent most of his time further up the coast at Demre. His church still stands there, and is very popular with sightseers. In Ptarra itself, don't expect to find elves and red-nosed reindeer; there is little to see except some overgrown Roman ruins. The beach, however, is vast (18-km long!) and deserted. From Kaş, take a dolmus from the station (US$1.50) for the one-hour trip to Ptarra.

Moving on
A bus to the turn-off for Olimpos is a three-hour journey along the coastal road. Buses run throughout the day and cost US$3.

There are, unfortunately, no buses that travel down to either Olimpos or Cheurali from the main road. You can hitch, although you may have to wait a long time for a car to pass, or phone up the tree-house (see below) of your choice before you arrive and arrange for them to meet you at the top. Ensure that a lift *back* to the highway is included in the price of your room too, or you'll end up paying another US$12-15 for a taxi.

OLIMPOS AND CHEURALI

Eleven km down from the coastal road lie Cheurali and Olimpos. The attractions here are some overgrown Roman ruins, the Chimaera (eternal flame) of Mt Olimpos, a wide sandy beach and the unique treehouse accommodation for which Olimpos is famous.

Orientation and services   (Olimpos ☎ **area code** 0242)
There is no post office, tourist office or bank in either village. Stock up
on cash before you arrive.

Olimpos is little more than a collection of shacks and tree-houses hugging a meandering stream as it winds its way down from the hill. The
Roman ruins are just before the stream empties into the sea. One km
along the beach to the east is Cheurali, a larger village with a couple of
shops. Six km further on up the hill behind Cheurali is the Chimaera.

Where to stay
In Olimpos make a beeline for *Yoruk Camping II* (☎ 8921250), not
because of the accommodation (although the open tree-houses by the
stream, where one can fall asleep to the sound of croaking bullfrogs and
chirruping crickets, are wonderful), but because of the phenomenal quality and quantity of the food: massive amounts of cordon-bleu cuisine
heaped on to the plate at every meal-time. The price is US$16 per person
including breakfast and dinner.

A little nearer the beach is *Yoruk Camping I* and *III*, for those who
prefer bungalows to tree-houses. About 500m before the ruins is *Gypsy's*
(☎ 8921223), another bungalow option which is currently undergoing
renovation. When it's complete they plan to charge about US$20pp.

More orthodox bricks-and-mortar accommodation is available in
Cheurali. The *Yildiz* (☎ 8257160), *Nadir* (☎ 8257180) and *Deniz* (☎
3157030) have all been recommended. Prices are negotiable, but are
about US$15pp per night.

The Chimaera
If you happen to be an Ancient Greek, you probably believe that under
the summit of Mt Olimpos lies Chimaera, a fire-breathing lion-cum-goat-
cum-serpent creature, who was killed by Bellerophon and his winged
horse Pegasus. And as scientists have yet to agree on which combination
of gases causes these inextinguishable flames to rise from the cracks of
Mt Olimpos, your explanation is as good as any other. What we do know
is that the mountain once burnt much more fiercely, sending flames six
feet high into the air, but today the summit looks to be concealing little
more than a small collection of Bunsen burners underneath the rocks. To
witness this eternal phenomena, follow the signs from Cheurali.

Olimpos
Olimpos is an ancient Lycian city, whose inhabitants, perhaps unsurpris-
ingly given that the mountain nearby was forever ablaze, worshipped fire.
The largely unimpressive ruins of this city lie scattered all around the

(Opposite) The restored Agora and Library at Ephesus (see p87).

stream and up the hillside. They are so overgrown they remind one of the abandoned Inca monuments in the jungles of South America. They mainly date back to the Romans who arrived here in the first century AD. As with the Chimaera, there is no entrance fee.

Moving on

The next major town to the east is Antalya, a major package-tourist spot. Pass through quickly in order to get to the more delightful destinations of Konya and, best of all, Cappadocia. A bus from the Olimpos turn-off to Antalya costs US$0.80, and takes just forty-five minutes. From Antalya, a bus leaves regularly to Konya (5hrs 30mins, US$6).

KONYA

Konya is one of Turkey's more conservative and friendly cities. Situated at the heart of the Central Anatolian Plain – a vast fertile steppe often referred to as Turkey's breadbasket – the city today survives on agriculture and light industry, supplemented by a small but burgeoning tourist industry.

Tourists come to Konya to see the former capital of the Seljuk Sultanate of Rum, the last vestige of a Seljuk Empire which once spanned Iran, Iraq and stretched down through the Near East far enough to knock on – and then knock down – the gates of Jerusalem.

The Seljuks were an ambitious bunch who fancied themselves as the rightful successors to the Roman Empire (which is where the 'Rum' of their sultanate comes from). In the 1100s their capital at Konya became a refuge for thousands of people from the Middle East and Central Asia who had fled from the twin threats of the Mongols and the Crusaders. Indeed Godfrey de Bouillon and his knights of the First Crusade occupied the city for a time, but for once showed restraint and did not injure either the buildings or the people.

One such refugee was Celaleddin Rumi (the Mevlâna), who arrived from Afghanistan with his parents in 1221. After studying in Aleppo and Damascus he returned to Konya where he fell under the influence of Mehmet Şemseddin Tebrizi, a Sufi (mystic follower of Islam). Combining the teachings of Tebrizi with his own orthodox theological background, Rumi began to write, setting down in poetry his beliefs about God, the universe and mankind. He is best known in the West for his epic poems, longer than anything in English literature, and the Whirling Dervish order he founded, where the faithful spin themselves into a giddy, ecstatic trance representing man's union with God. (Displays

(**Opposite**) Two different approaches to the problem of living on a hillside. **Top:** The troglodyte dwellings of Göreme (see p108). **Bottom:** The stacked houses of Maalula in Syria (see p151).

of the Mevlâni worship ceremony can be seen during the December Festival, as well as in Cairo (see p300).

The Mevlâni order continued to flourish long after the Seljuk Sultanate had been crushed by the Mongols. Many of the Ottoman sultans became members of the order. But by the twentieth century the Mevlâni sheikhs had grown lazy, undisciplined and self-serving. Atatürk outlawed the order for that reason in 1925. Nevertheless they still exist today, supposedly as a purely cultural, rather than religious, tradition.

Many of the mosques and religious buildings built during the Seljuk era still form the major landmarks of the town; they may lack the imperial lustre of ancient Constantinople's camiis, but then they do predate them by at least three hundred years.

Orientation and services

(Konya ☎ **area code** 0332)

The hill, Alaettin Tepesi, that rises like a pimple on the flat face of Konya, marks the centre of town. It's made from the collected detritus built up during Konya's 4000-year existence (Bronze Age man settled here long before the Turks arrived). To the north is the bus station; catch a tram to the centre for US$0.25 (half-price for students), or a dolmus for the same price. To the east of Alaettin Tepesi, along Alaettin Cad, is the main area of interest to tourists. The major sights, hotels, **PTT** and **tourist office** are all around here. To get from here to the bus station, catch a dolmus (US$0.30) from behind Serafeddin Camii on Alaettin Cad.

Where to stay

Nearly all hotels in Konya have the government-fixed price-list displayed in reception, and nearly all ignore it too. The best-value hotel in Konya is the *Olgün Palas Oteli* [1] (☎ 3512587). Ali Alici runs the show here, and his immaculate rooms are excellent value at US$3/6 sgl/dbl – the cheapest in town. For once, however, the cheapest is not the most popular with backpackers; that award goes to the *Ulusan* [2] (☎ 3515009) and with some justification. The staff are amicable, the rooms (US$6/8 sgl/dbl) newly-decorated and sunny, and there is a large communal TV lounge in the centre.

The *Çesme* [3] (☎ 3512426) is pleasant too. Although the first prices they ask for are high (US$9/11.50 sgl/dbl, plus US$1.50 for en suite), if they're not full they seem more willing than most to lower them.

In contrast, the *Otel Yasin* [4] (☎ 3511624) at 25 Yusufaga Sok off Istanbul Cad, is overpriced (US$7.50/12 sgl/dbl) and they're less receptive to bargaining. Their rooms do come complete with TV, however, so you can watch all your favourite black-and-white Turkish films at night.

Moving up a notch, the *Otel Huma* [5] (☎ 506618), to the north of Alaettin Tepesi on Ankara Cad, is a smart little establishment. Prices here are US$40/60 sgl/dbl; add US$4 for breakfast.

Where to eat
The first place to look for food is along Cikrikcilar Cad, where there are a few cheap lokantasis and pide salonus. The favourite along here is the **Lokanta Bahceli Bokazici** [a], run by two Kurdish brothers who used to work in Germany. The kebabs they make are cheap and delicious.

Mevlâna Museum
(0900-1730, 1000-1730 on Mon; US$1.50, US$0.75 students, free for U26). The green-domed mausoleum of the Mevlâna was the first religious building to be converted into a museum by Atatürk's reforms of 1925 (the Aya Sofya is another example). You will find that this conversion has not altered the Turk's perception of the sanctity of this building one iota. Very few come to view the museum's treasures housed inside, but plenty still come to pray at Rumi's sarcophagus. Dress modestly and respect the wishes of the faithful who flock here.

Formerly the complex was a monastery for the Dervish order; you can still see their cells surrounding the main building today. The fountain on the right is Mevlâna's wedding fountain, so called as the Mevlâna always referred to his death as a wedding, uniting him with God. Every December the Dervishes whirl around this fountain to celebrate the anniversary of Mevlâna's 'wedding'. Inside the mausoleum the wooden

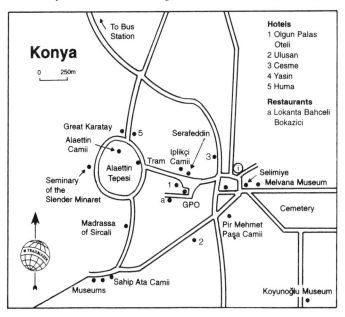

Konya

0   250m

To Bus Station

Hotels
1 Olgun Palas Oteli
2 Ulusan
3 Cesme
4 Yasin
5 Huma

Restaurants
a Lokanta Bahceli Bokazici

Great Karatay
Alaettin Camii
Alaettin Tepesi
Seminary of the Slender Minaret
Madrassa of Sircali
Sahip Ata Camii
Museums

Serafeddin
Iplikçi Camii
Tram

GPO

Pir Mehmet Paşa Camii

Selimiye
Melvana Museum

Cemetery

Koyunoğlu Museum

Sarcophagus of Rumi is beautifully engraved with verses from his poetry. The tombs of his son, Sultan Veled, and his father lie nearby. His father was in fact the first to be buried here, when the plot of land was just a garden. The buildings were added only after the death of Rumi's son.

The vaulted hall next door is still used for the devotional dances of the Sufi. Amongst the display of musical instruments and sacred robes held within are a couple of real treasures: the huge gold, silver and bronze **April Cup** from Baghdad, used to collect rainwater during that month; and possibly **the world's finest carpet**, 500 years old and said to contain 144 knots per square centimetre.

Opposite the entrance to the museum is the **Selimiye**, which, unlike the exquisite version in Istanbul, was made for Süleyman the Magnificent's stepson, Selim II (1566-74) rather than Süleyman's 'grim' father, Selim I. While still just the governor of Konya, Selim II presented it as a gift to his father.

Other mosques around the Mevlâna Museum

Konya's oldest and plainest mosque is the **Iplikçi Camii**, built in 1202. Despite the bungled restorations, the mosque remains one of the most revered in Konya since the Mevlâna regularly preached here. In contrast, the **Serafeddin Camii** is one of Konya's newest, an Ottoman building (1636) constructed over the ashes of a Seljuk original. It faces northwards with its back towards Alaettin Cad.

Koyunoğlu Museum

(0900-1700; US$0.75, no concessions). This museum is housed in one of the ugliest buildings in Turkey. Inside, the exhibits (all donated by one collector of very eclectic taste) range from a display on calligraphy to one on art, a mineral section and a small compilation of prehistoric bones. If the man at the ticket-office mutters something unintelligible to you he is probably saying: 'Don't miss the quaint Konyali House next door. It gives a good idea of how my ancestors lived in Konya in the 19th century. Oh, and by the way, I've got the key, so come and find me when you're ready'. Or words to that effect.

To get here, cross the road to the south of the Mevlâna Museum, walk alongside the graveyard (keeping it to your left), then turn right down Koyunoğlu Sok. The museum is at the end, opposite a green mosque.

Other sights

Most of Konya's other sights surround Alaettin Tepesi like satellites.

● **Great Karatay Museum** lies to the north of the Tepesi. It used to be a seminary or madrassa (an Islamic theological school), but nowadays it houses the tile museum (Karaköy Cinesler Muzesi), containing a rich collection of blue faience tiles (0930-1230, 1330-1700; US$0.80). The seminary was built in 1251 but abandoned in the nineteenth century.

● **Seminary of the Slender Minaret** (Inceminare Medresesi) stands to the west of Alaettin Tepesi, and is now the home of Konya's woodcarving museum. Built in 1264 by Vizier Sahip Ata Fahrettin, as with so many Seljuk buildings the glorious entrance is a lot more impressive than the building inside. The slender minaret, from which the mosque takes its name, stands outside. The seminary is 600 years old, but was partially destroyed in 1901 by lightning. Both this and the Karatay above have the same opening hours (0900-1230, 1330-1730, closed Mon; US$0.60, US$0.30 students, free for U26).

● **Madrassa of Sircali** This madrassa lies in the jumble of streets to the south of the Tepesi. The highlight is undoubtedly the distinctive Seljuk doorway. Inside is a small collection of Seljuk/Ottoman gravestones in the madrassa's courtyard. Prices and opening hours are as above.

● **Sahip Ata Camii** Head due south along the road from the Sircali madrassa, past a number of vividly-painted Ottoman terraced houses, and eventually one comes to this Camii. Next door are the **Archaeological** and **Ethnographic Museums**.

● **Alaettin Mosque** is actually on the Alaettin Tepesi, amongst the parasols of the outdoor cafés. It's a truly bizarre structure where little thought appears to have been given to harmony or style. It was built for Alaettin Keykubat I, the greatest Seljuk Sultan of Rum (1219-1231). It has recently been reopened, though the extensive restoration work is still very much in progress. To the north are a few remains of the sultan's palace.

Moving on

As with most cities in Turkey, it is possible to catch a bus to almost anywhere from Konya. The bus to Göreme/Nevşehir (see p105) costs US$5 and leaves frequently, taking four hours.

Ankara and Central Turkey

ANKARA

The Republic of Turkey's capital city is like one huge metropolitan shrine to its founder, Atatürk. Apart from the obligatory statues of the great man and the usual Atatürk Caddesis and Atatürk Bulvaris, one can also spend time wandering around the Museum of Liberation or Museum of the Republic to admire his work, visit his mansion to the south of the city, and his mausoleum on the western outskirts.

Before Atatürk there was Angora (where the goats come from), founded by the Hittites and owned successively by the Phrygians, Romans, Byzantines, Seljuks, Mamlukes and Ottomans. Ankara enjoyed fleeting moments of fame and influence during these occupations, thanks mainly to its position on a major caravan trail, but by the time Atatürk had moved in Ankara had dwindled to little more than a downtrodden Ottoman village. Today it is a vibrant town of some three million.

Orientation and services (Ankara ☎ area code 0312)

If you arrive in Ankara by bus, your ticket should also enable you to catch a local bus into town, which is about 9km away. The train station is far more convenient. As you walk out of the station the road straight ahead, Cumhuriyet Bulvari, leads up to the equestrian statue of Atatürk in the centre of town, Ulus Meydani, 1.5 km away. The road that runs perpendicular (north-south) to Cumhuriyet Bulvari is Atatürk Cad. The **post office** is on this road, just two minutes south of the statue, and there are many **banks** nearby. The embassy enclave, Gaziomanpaşa, lies five km to the south of the centre, east of Atatürk Cad. Unfortunately, the **tourist office** is very inconveniently located between Atatürk's mausoleum and Atatürk Bulvari on Gazi Mustafa Kemal.

❑ **Embassies and consulates**
- **Australia** (☎ 4461180-87) Nenehatun Cad no83, Gaziomanpaşa; a letter of recommendation, costing US$15, takes a couple of hours
- **Canada** (☎ 4361275-79) Nenehatun Cad no75, Gaziomanpaşa
- **Israel** (☎ 4263904) Mahatma Gandhi Cad no85, Gaziomanpaşa
- **New Zealand** (☎ 4679054) Level 4, Kav Aklidence; a letter of recommendation costs US$15 and can be collected the same afternoon
- **Syria** (☎ 4409650) Abdullah Cevdet Sokak 7, Çankaya
- **UK** (☎ 4686230) Şehit Ersan Cad no46A, Çankaya
- **USA** (☎ 4686110-28) Atatürk Bulv no110, Kavaklidere

Local transport

There are three colours of buses in Ankara. With both the green and red buses, tickets must be bought before boarding (US$0.25, US$0.15 students). For the blue buses, however, tickets are available on board and cost approximately the same.

To get to the Otogar, look for the acronym ASTI on the front of the bus (bus Nos 623 from Kizilay and 198 from Ulus both pass through the centre of town). Bus Nos 112, 114 and 603 travel along Atatürk Cad between the embassy section and Ulus Meydani. Buses to the capital's attractions are mentioned in the relevant sections below.

Where to stay

Most of Ankara's budget hotels are grim, dank and – with so few travellers bothering to make it here – lonely too. The *Nursaray Otel* [1] on Kevğirli Sokak ranks as the best, if only because the staff are a little less brusque with foreigners than most of the others. It can be a little noisy here, but it's well located and the rooms are comfortable, if not exactly

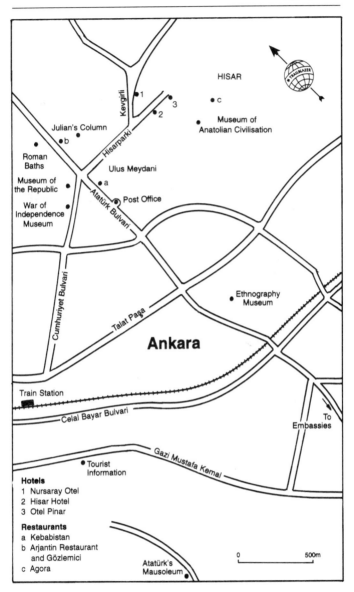

HISAR

Julian's Column

Roman
Baths

Museum of
the Republic

War of
Independence
Museum

Kevgirli

Hisarparki

Ulus Meydani

Atatürk Bulvari

Post Office

Museum of
Anatolian Civilisation

Cumhuriyet Bulvari

Talat Paşa

Ankara

Ethnography
Museum

Train Station

Celal Bayar Bulvari

To
Embassies

Gazi Mustafa Kemal

Tourist
Information

Atatürk's
Mausoleum

Hotels
1 Nursaray Otel
2 Hisar Hotel
3 Otel Pinar

Restaurants
a Kebabistan
b Arjantin Restaurant
   and Gözlemici
c Agora

0   500m

exceptional (US$3.75/8.30 sgl/dbl comm, US$6.75/12.50 att).

If you wish to take a small step down in price, then be prepared to take a giant leap down in quality. The ***Hisar Hotel*** [2] (US$3/7.50 sgl/dbl) is nearby, just off Kevğirli on Hisarparki Cad. It stands next door to a Turkish bath, which is just as well for the price of the cheaper rooms does not include washing facilities.

A better bet is the ***Otel Pinar*** [3] (☎ 311 8961) just 20m away (US$3.20/5.50 sgl/dbl). It's not much of an improvement – some of the rooms are draughty and the water is often cold – but at least you're made to feel more of a guest and less of an inmate during your stay.

Where to eat

Of all the themed restaurants in the world, there can't be that many that are dedicated to the noble sport of weightlifting. ***Kebabistan*** [a], however, is. The kebabs here (US$1-2) are very good though some are extremely spicy. The restaurant is tucked away in a shopping arcade off Atatürk Bulvari. As you walk down from Ulus Meydani, look into the shopping courtyards on your left; it's about the third one down.

Another essential kebab house is the ***Arjantin Restaurant and Gözlemici*** [b]. Popular with locals (ie very smoky), this establishment overflows with customers and atmosphere. Their servings are equally generous (US$2 for a huge kebab, gozleme US$0.40, a beer only US$0.50); this is undoubtedly one of the best cheap restaurants in Turkey.

Amongst the terraced houses on the Hisar are some seriously beautiful restaurants. Expect to pay about US$10-12 for an evening – a lot of money, perhaps, but if you're only going to eat out once in Turkey then it should be here. The ***Agora*** [c] is recommended; try their swordfish kebab for US$7.50 or their chicken agora for US$3.10.

Museum of Anatolian Civilization

(0830-1700, closed Mon in winter; US$1.50, US$0.90 concessions). For those with only a day to kill in Ankara, a walk up to the Hisar on the hilltop, calling in at this museum on the way, is as good a way as any of killing it. This museum gives what is probably the best overview of the ancient history of Ankara (up to about the sixth century BC). All the exhibits have English explanations, and the museum is well organised and undaunting.

Hisar

Looking very out of place in a modern city like Ankara – indeed, it looks very out of place in the 20th century – the Hisar is the capital's charming old quarter. The Byzantines built many of the fortifications, although the fortress that stands on the pinnacle is Seljuk, and the terraced houses that surround it are mainly Ottoman and date from the last century. It's very picturesque, and offers a good vantage point over the city.

Atatürk's Mausoleum (Anitkabir)

The imposing mausoleum bears down on the city from its hilltop location, a reminder of the influence Atatürk still has over the country some 60 years after his demise. It's a very impressive monument, containing a huge enclosed courtyard with his sarcophagus (all 40 tonnes of it) at one end. The rooms surrounding the courtyard detail his life and work.

The mausoleum lies to the west of the city. To get here, catch a bus to Bachilievler or Emek from the centre of town. Jump off at Tandoğam Square, then walk up the hill for five minutes. Bring your passport with you, for the guards will probably wish to see it.

Other Atatürk buildings

Near Atatürk's statue in Ulus is the **Museum of the Republic** (0830-1200, 1330-1700, US$0.50) the second parliament building of the republic. Unfortunately, the labels are all in Turkish, but they do hand out a free leaflet which details the history of the building and the republic. (The present parliament is just off Atatürk Bulvari, to the north of the embassy enclave).

Just up the hill is the **War of Independence Museum** (same times, prices), which describes the heroic efforts of the Turks in their struggle to regain their country from the victorious WWI allies. Once again the labels are in Turkish only.

For those who aren't completely 'Atatürked out', the **Ethnography Museum** above the Atatürk Bulvari with Talat Paşa junction contains a room used an office by Mustafa Kemal, and at the far end of Atatürk Bulvari is his former mansion.

Roman baths

(0830-1200, 1300-1700; US$0.40, no concessions). This field to the north of Ulus Square contains the foundation of Ankara's early Roman baths. It is a good example of its kind, but is really only of interest to scholars and those with a passion for Roman personal hygiene. Nearby are a couple more Latin relics including **Julian's column**, erected following a visit by the Byzantine emperor Julian in the fourth century.

Moving on

Nevtur run nine buses per day to the next destination, Göreme (US$5.80), beginning at 0730, with the last leaving at 0100. You will probably have to change in Nevşehir, so keep your ticket; they may well check it again.

GÖREME AND CAPPADOCIA

The former Central Anatolian kingdom of Cappadocia is a fantastical land of underground cities and fairy chimneys, populated by troglodytes and enclosed within a surreal, windswept, semi-arid moonscape. It is a unique attraction, and a real geological oddity. Today, especially in summer, this Tolkeinian world is overrun by armies of tourists enjoying the roasting sun and unique attractions. But in winter it can be bitterly cold and desolate. At this time, however, especially on a crisp, sunny day after a heavy flurry of snow, this geological freak of nature can appear at its most enchanting.

Whatever time of year you come here, give yourself at least three days in Cappadocia. It will take two days to explore the official sights, especially as public transport is minimal and hitching or hiking is often the only option. A third day is necessary to recuperate and write postcards. Many travellers end up spending longer than this, and it is not surprising: the area is perfect for exploring, and many of the valleys conceal beautifully decorated churches that escape the attentions of the less thorough sightseer.

History
Around thirty million years ago three active volcanoes, which today form the tallest peaks in the region, spewed lava and ash over a vast area of Central Anatolia. When compressed this ash became tufa, a soft, erodable and easily-worked rock which forms the strange moon-like landscape of the region.

Man discovered just how easy it was to carve into this rock as early as 4000BC and began to excavate cave dwellings from the stone. The arrival of Christianity in the region in the second century elevated the design of these caves to a new artistic level. Elaborately-decorated churches were scooped into the rock, cunningly concealed from the gaze of their Roman persecutors by hidden entrances and tunnels. As Christianity became the accepted religion there was no longer any need to hide these churches, and their frescoes became even more elaborate.

Later still, as the Arabs arrived and converted the region to Islam, the locals relocated underground to vast, impenetrable subterranean cities. It was an effective form of defence: only when the Ottoman Empire disintegrated, and the lands of Turkey and Greece were split along ethno-religious lines, did Christianity finally lose its tenure in Cappadocia.

Orientation and services   (Göreme ☏ area code 0384)
To most travellers Cappadocia is Göreme, a small laid-back village where many of the pensions have rooms hewn out of the soft, sandy rock. It is an excellent base from which to explore the region. Not only is it set amongst some of the prettiest scenery, where the sandy hills are divided by verdant, fertile valleys, but it is also near the main transport hub at Nevşehir, the underground city of Derinkuyu and the open-air museum at Zelve.

In the village itself is a small bus station, dozens of hotels and a number of restaurants. The **post office** is down the hill to the north of the town, opposite the turn-off to the Open-air Museum. To **change money** head to the Rose Pension, where the last time I visited they were offering the best rate with no commission charges. Try to change enough before you arrive, however, for occasionally the Rose runs out of money.

Local transport

Many tour agencies have now opened in Göreme, all offering a similar tour around the sights of Cappadocia. These are excellent if you have a limited amount of time in the region.

When deciding which tour to take, there are several factors worth considering. Does the price include entrance fees? (If you have an U26 card all the sights are free anyway). Is lunch included? Does the tour include a guide, or is it transport only? Most tours cost US$10-20, depending on the specifications. I recommend Mustafa at **Yama Tours**, whose knowledge of the area is second to none. **Turtle Tours** has been praised by many too.

For those who prefer to travel on their own there are plenty of options. Bikes can be hired for US$6 per day, motorbikes for US$16 (not including petrol). Some agencies even offer horses for hire (US$15 for two hours) and donkeys (US$5).

Public transport is minimal. There is a half-hourly bus from Göreme to Nevşehir (US$0.25), and buses on the hour to Avanos (last one 5pm).

Where to stay

As Göreme village is so compact it is possible to hop from one pension to another until you find one that suits. There is a small accommodation office by the bus station that will help you if you get stuck. Although winter is the low season for tourists the heating costs are higher, so prices do not vary between seasons.

Most of the hostels in Göreme are of a very similar standard, and charge similar rates – usually US$3.50-4pp in a dorm, US$5pp upwards in a double. Consequently, it is difficult to go wrong here. If I had to select five places above all the others, my top five would be as follows.

The *Köse Pension* (☎ 2712294) is the first on my list for a number of reasons: the excellent food conjured up by Mehmet, the knowledge and enthusiasm of the area displayed by Mehmet's Scottish wife Dawn, the large comfortable rooms and the best-informed traveller's book on our trip. Sadly the hotel does not have any cave-rooms, but instead is built on wasteland near the post office. If it is caves you're after then head to the *Kelebeck* (☎ 2712531) which, owing to its hillside location, can also boast a wonderful panoramic view over the village. It is a very popular choice, but the manager can be a little unwelcoming sometimes.

The *Phoenix* has stunning rooms. It is the kind of place where the toilet roll – which has been folded into a triangle at the end for that extra special touch – matches the bedspread.

At the other end of town on the way to the open air museum stands the quaintly-named *Ufuk Pension* (☎ 2712157 – 'Horizon' in Turkish), which is currently undergoing renovation. It feels more like a home than a hotel and most of the rooms are doubles with showers. Last on the list is the *Peace Pension* (☎ 2712487), a small place near the bus station. Whilst the rooms are only adequate, Mustafa the manager is a fun-loving chap who often organises barbecue trips into the valleys in summer.

Where to eat

The *Köse Pension* does some terrific food; if you are not staying there, call in during the day to tell them you're coming for dinner.

Of the restaurants, the *Sedef* near the main road is by far the best. Their pizzas (US$2) are a delight. Their neighbours, however, are not so competent. The *Tardelli*, which claims to specialise in authentic Italian dishes, is particularly dreadful.

The *Göreme Café* is across the road. Don't be put off by the emaciated condition of the chef, for the menu is large and the food is very good.

There are a number of bars and clubs opening in Göreme, of which the *Flintstones* and the *Duck Bar* are currently the most popular.

Göreme Open-air Museum

(0830-1630 winter, -1800 in summer; US$2.50, US$1.30 students, free for U26). Although one can find frescoes of a similar quality in the Rose Valley (where there is no entrance fee) and even in the museum's bus park, the Open-air Museum houses a remarkably high concentration of churches, monasteries and other caves which offer the best introduction to the peculiar architecture of Cappadocia. The frescoes in the museum range from the sophisticated – look for those of Christ's birth and Crucifixion on the roof of the **Dark Church** (Karanlik Kilise), and the figures on the supporting pillars of the **Apple Church** (Elmali Kilise) – to the simple: around the back of the Apple Church is the small eighth-century **Church of St Barbara**, where the naive geometric patterns are clearly the work of artists restricted by the severe impositions of iconoclasm (see p25).

In most instances the frescoes still appear fairly vivid, as the sunlight that manages to penetrate these caves is minimal. The shallow hollows dug in the floor of many of the churches are graves.

The museum is 1.5km from Göreme village, a pretty walk flanked by a number of enticing multi-storey caves which are well worth exploring.

Zelve

(0800-1700; US$1.50, US$0.75 students, free for U26). Whereas Göreme's open-air museum was a purely ecclesiastical settlement, Zelve used to be a village of peasants who farmed the land. Christian and Moslem lived here in harmony right up until 1923, when the Christians left following the creation of the Turkish Republic. The Muslim villagers remained until they were forced to evacuate in the 1950s by the authorities, concerned about the fragile nature of some of the eroded caves.

The only free-standing structure in Zelve is the pointed roof of a mosque. The caves that flank it, however, are complex labyrinths which are great fun to negotiate. Opposite the mosque is a semi-spherical hollow pockmarked by small windows. It is possible, via a series of navigable tunnels, to look through every one of these windows; just watch out for the resident bat population.

If you're walking from Göreme to Zelve along the main Göreme-Avanos road you'll pass through the village of **Çavuşin**. A little further on and on the right hand side is the turn-off for Zelve. The fairy-chimney landscape of **Paşabag**, a monk's village, lies beside this turn off. These phallic elevations were formed when basalt rocks settled on top of the soft tufa; as the weather gradually eroded the ground around the rock, the tufa underneath remained untouched, forming these weird, elongated toadstools.

Rose Valley

One of the more established hikes in Cappadocia is the Rose Valley walk, which begins at Çavuşin then heads south-east up the valley to a panoramic viewpoint. It's not very strenuous and offers the perfect stroll for the novice hiker.

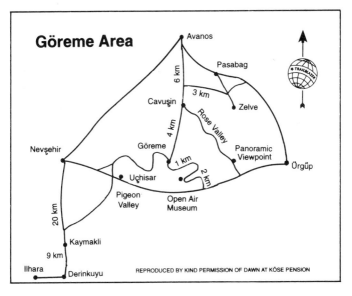

Pigeon Valley

So-called because of the thousands of pigeon shelters hewn out of the rocks by the villagers which fleck the cliff-face on both sides of the valley. Pigeons still use these shelters today.

Ilhara Valley

This is one of the most stunning and least explored gorges in Cappadocia. It is also one where I'd recommend you take a tour, for many of the frescoed churches are very difficult to spot without a guide. Mehmet and Dawn at the Köse run two-day camping trips up the valley. For those equipped to tackle the valley by themselves, there are two buses from Aksaray to Ilhara.

Avanos

About ten km north of Göreme is the pottery town of Avanos. It's not that attractive, but if you have signed up for a tour it is very likely that your guide will lead you to one of the pottery manufacturers, since they get commission on every piece you buy.

Derinkuyu Underground City

(0800-1700, -1800 in summer; US$1.50, US$0.75 students, free for U26). Most of our knowledge of Cappadocia's subterranean cities comes from a French Jesuit priest who arrived here at the turn of the century. He counted over 30 such underground dwellings on his visit. Unfortunately he never wrote down where they were; only eight have been found so far, including one found by a farmer out ploughing his fields last year.

Derinkuyu is the biggest of the eight, and the best of the three which are open to the public. All the cities were built from the sixth to the tenth centuries to protect the Christian villagers from the Arab invaders. It was possible to remain in these cities for up to six months and in some of the larger dwellings, such as Derinkuyu, up to 5000 people could be housed within.

These cities were totally self-contained communities: schools, hospitals, cemeteries, prisons, police stations, churches – everything necessary to maintain an orderly society was included in their design. It was not until the twelfth century and the arrival of the Seljuks – who allowed the Christians to continue practising their faith as long as they paid higher taxes – that the fashion for underground living faded.

The city The city covers some four square km, and descends 70 metres below the surface. Originally only the first three floors were dug, but as the population grew further floors were added. The first floor was used as a toilet and animal storage section and, bizarrely enough, a school too. On the final floor is a cruciform (cross-shaped) church and an adjacent confessional box. In the church, look for two holes in the wall, from where they hung offenders as punishment. A narrow corridor on the left leads to the cemetery, where the dead were kept until it was safe to resurface.

Moving on

In order to get to Antakya, the final stop on this route through Turkey, one must travel via noisy, dusty Adana, a large town with little of interest to the sightseer. Two buses depart every day from Göreme to Adana (calling at Nevşehir) for US$4.80. The departure times are 0800 and 1200, and the journey takes five hours. From Adana, buses leave every 30 minutes to Antakya. The three hour trip costs US$2.80.

ANTAKYA (HATAY)

Some towns are fated to play an important role in history; Antakya, formerly Antioch, is one of them. The capital of the Seleucid Empire, a vital Roman trading town, the first organised centre of Christianity and the capital of the Crusader's Principality of Antioch – it's been all of these at some point or another.

The town was founded in 300BC by Seleucus Nicator, who named it after his father. Like their rivals the Ptolemites, the Seleucids were a Greek empire founded by one of Alexander's generals, Seleucus, following Alexander's death. During Roman times the town flourished, like so many on our route, as an important caravan stop feeding off the trade that passed through the region. By the third century it boasted a population of half a million and was the third most important city, after Rome and Alexandria, in the whole of the Roman Empire. The Byzantines who followed made it a bishopric and the capital of their Middle Eastern holdings. The gorgeous mosaics which are housed in the archaeological museum date from this time.

Today the city has a large Arab-speaking population. This is not surprising when one considers that the town is so close to the border and was, until 1939, part of Syria. In that year the French, who ruled over Antakya as part of their Syrian Mandate, handed the town over to Atatürk in return for his promise of peace.

Orientation and services

(Antakya ☎ area code 0891)

The city is split down the middle by the Asi River, a continuation of the Orontes in Syria. To the east lies the old Ottoman quarter and on the west bank stands the thriving modern city. The **post office** and **museum** huddle around the roundabout on the western banks of the Asi. The **tourist office** (0800-1200, 1330-1730, closed Sun) is 10 minutes north of the roundabout along Atatürk Cad, which runs parallel to the river on the western side. To change money, go to one of the **banks** along Istiklal Cad. For Syrian pounds, ask your hotel manager if he has any contacts, or ask (discreetly) in the old quarter's small souk.

Local transport

A dolmus between the centre of town and the bus station is US$0.30

Where to stay

The *Seker Palas Oteli* [1] (☎ 2151603) sits opposite the bus station on Istiklal Cad. Whilst the resemblance to a 'palas' is minimal – the rooms (US$3.25pp) consist of one grimy sink, one rusty iron bed, two rock-hard pillows and a cold, tiled floor – the hirsute manager is friendly and helpful and it's probably the best of the hotels around the bus station. For a tad more comfort the *Jasmin Hotel* [2] (☎ 2143530), also on Istiklal Cad but nearer the main roundabout, is a lot more pleasant (US$5pp). Come here in winter as there's central heating.

Also on the eastern side of the river, on Hurriyet Cad is the *Atahan Hotel* [3] (☎ 2142040). With the exception of the luxury Buyuk Antakya Hotel this has the smartest rooms (US$23/31 sgl/dbl), and ranks as the best-value hotel in town.

Where to eat

The Atahan Hotel is conveniently situated next to some very good restaurants. The *Nuri Restaurant* [a], *Altin Köse Kebap* and *Caglayan Restaurant* are all very reasonable.

Of all the restaurants and cafés near the station, the *Dort Ortak Lokantasi* [b] opposite the Seker Palas is probably the best.

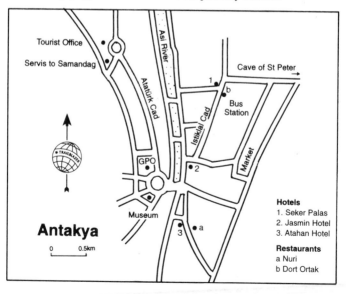

Archaeological Museum

(0830-1200,1330-1700, closed Mon; US$1.50, US$0.75 students, free for U26). With its wonderful collection of Byzantine mosaics, this museum by the main roundabout is Antakya's most-visited attraction.

After a small display of weapons and a collection of bath shoes (the lofty footwear designed to prevent bathers from slipping on the wet floors of the public baths), there's a number of rooms dedicated to the splendid mosaics. Note the fine details in some of the works, in particular the folds in the dresses in 'Ipheginia in Aulis', and the expression on the face of Soteria, who confronts you as you enter the first salon. A coin collection and a room devoted to the Hittites complete the exhibits.

Cave of St Peter

Dug into the hill on the edge of town, this is believed to be the cave where St Peter lived and preached. Antakya has had a considerable Christian population since the very early days of Christianity, and according to Acts 11:26 it was at Antioch that the disciples were first called 'Christians'. The cave was converted into a church during the Byzantine era, although the arches and mosaics we see today are the work of the Crusaders and the altar is a 20th-century addition. The Capuchin monks still worship at the cave. Following the path away from the church and the town one finds the **Lion's Gate**, affording beautiful views of the valley.

On the coast

Although they are not really worth the effort unless you have time to kill, there are a number of excursions from Antakya. Just 29km away is **Samandağ**, the gateway for Antakya's seaside resorts; a dolmus from the roundabout near the tourist office costs US$0.30. Seven km north of Samandağ is **Çevlik**, Antioch's ancient port, **Seleucia ad Peria**. Check out the series of large halls, the **Tunnel of Vespasian**, cut into the rocks.

Moving on

For buses to the Syrian border and Aleppo, see p114. Heading in the other direction, buses leave regularly to Adana (US$12.50), where you can continue to Nevşehir (for Cappadocia) or Antalya.

❏ **Other attractions in Turkey**

Eastern Turkey is an area of stunning mountain scenery, rich in history and culture. Although in winter it is all but cut off by heavy snows, in summer this area is delightful. Lake Van, Mt Ararat (where Noah's ark grounded), and the mountain-top statues at Nemrut Daği are just a few of the delights on offer, but heed the warning on p51 before setting off.

The Black Sea Coast is probably the least explored region of Turkey. Although there are few major sights, the pretty coastal scenery is dotted with small fishing villages. In western Turkey Bursa, the Ottoman's capital before they conquered Constantinople, is still an important attraction.

THE BORDER – TURKEY AND SYRIA

Turkey to Syria
Don't arrive at the Syrian border without a visa; it's a long way back to
Istanbul or Ankara. Make sure you spend your last Turkish lira too, for
they're virtually worthless abroad.

The cheapest way to cross is to catch a dolmus from Antakya to
Reyhanli (US$0.60). Ask to be dropped off at the junction (next to the
petrol station) before Reyhanli, from where you can hitch to the border
(Cilvegozu). Hitching is usually very easy.

On leaving Turkey fill out a departure card, then hitch to the Syrian
border at Bab al-Hawa. Remember: you have **not** been to Israel, and you
have no intention of going there. The Syrians post their most miserable
personnel at this border who like to show you who's boss by making you
wait and sweat. Just grit your teeth and smile. You'll be given a yellow
immigration card. Fill it out, have it stamped, and keep it safe. There is
an exchange counter, but it accepts US dollars cash only.

Hitching from the Bab al-Hawa to Aleppo is straightforward, and
often one of the customs' inspectors will stop a passing coach for you.

Syria to Turkey
There is no dolmus to the border, despite what they tell you in Aleppo.
Instead, catch one to the village of Bab al-Hawa باب الهوى (S£15, 1hr) and
hitch the five km from there. Leaving Syria is no problem, and there
should be no troubles at the Turkish border either. There is an official
kiosk for you to change money – useful if you need to buy a Turkish visa.

Hitching from the Turkish border can be difficult; the Turkish taxi-
drivers wait at the arrival gate to persuade passing vehicles not to pick
you up. If you can, sort out a lift before you leave border control.

PART 4: SYRIA

Facts about the country

Farewell, O Syria, and what an excellent country this is for the enemy! – Attributed to the Byzantine **Emperor Heraclius**, following the Battle of Yarmouk in AD636 which ended Byzantine rule in Syria.

Syria is the Near East's best kept secret, a tantalising trove of ancient treasures untainted by tourists and left to the intrepid to enjoy at their leisure. It is a fascinating land which has suffered more than most from the swords of marauding invaders, nearly all of whom have left some mark on the barren landscape.

Despite this continual abuse the people of Syria still haven't learnt the basic lesson: never trust the foreigner. They are, quite simply, some of the

---

❏ **Country ratings – Syria**

● **Highlights** If you don't like history you may think Syria has little to offer but you'd be wrong. Both the Crac and Palmyra are more than just historical attractions; they are unique sights that really take the breath away. Syria's towns too, especially Damascus and Aleppo, are exciting and have their own supercharged atmosphere. And overlaying all of this is the hospitality of the locals, which makes the hefty visa fee (for UK citizens at least) somewhat more palatable.

● **Expense $$**

● **Value for money** ✔✔✔✔ Accommodation, whilst rarely expensive, is artificially high, thanks to various laws and taxes imposed by the government.

● **English communication** ✔✔ Try speaking French if attempts to communicate in English get you nowhere.

● **Getting around** ✔✔✔✔ Buses are by far the most convenient form of transport on this route through Syria.

● **Travellers' scene** ✔✔ The 'scene', such as it is, is mainly in Palmyra or at the al-Haramain/al-Rabie hotels in Damascus.

● **Visible history** ✔✔✔✔✔ Palmyra (the Bride of the Desert), and the Crac are just two of Syria's many historical treasures.

● **Woman alone** ✔✔✔✔ Although Western women are still objects of curiosity here, you are far more likely to be asked to share a meal or a cup of tea than you are to be propositioned.

● **Good food** ✔✔ Not Syria's strong suit. A cross between over-greasy Turkish cuisine (with added dust) and stale Lebanese food, without the invention or artistry of either. For some reason Hama is the exception, and their desserts, especially sweet cheese pudding, are definitely worth trying.

● **Vegetarian friendly** ✔✔✔ Felafel, felafel, felafel, hoummus, felafel.

warmest and most hospitable folk you will ever encounter. Sometimes it is difficult to walk more than a few yards down a street without being offered a cup of tea, and it is a rare traveller indeed who is not invited to at least one meal with a Syrian family.

So don't be put off by the profusion of portraits of President Hafez Assad (he's the one with the comb-over) and his late son (the smouldering one in the shades), which grin at you from every building and vehicle in the country. It *is* a police state with an antiquated transport system and bureaucracy to boggle the mind but you will probably leave Syria with nothing but good memories of wonderful days, terrific sights and warm, exuberant people (and a bladder full of tea). Emperor Heraclius may have been a lousy general but he sure knew a good country when he saw one.

Modern Syria

President Assad is just the latest in a long line of dictators who have risen to power in the 52 years since the country won its independence. Many of these regimes have been memorable only for their incompetence and ruthlessness. Whilst Assad has undoubtedly maintained the tradition of the latter – as we shall see in the Hama chapter, Assad does not suffer opponents gladly – his 27 years in charge is the longest of any president and proves that he is at least a little more competent than the others.

Since Assad and his Baath Party took over following a coup in 1970 (Syria rarely bothers with elections), they have had to negotiate plenty of crises both at home and overseas. When you have Lebanon exploding on your front doorstep, the Gulf War raging over the garden fence and your neighbours are either tampering with your water supply (Turkey) or stealing your land (Israel), you know your hands are going to be full during your term in office. Throughout all these troubles their Soviet-style government has not changed. Posters everywhere remind you that Big Brother is watching you; the only difference being that this brother is small, balding and has an oversized moustache.

By the mid-1990s things were looking rosy for Syria. The government, whilst brutal and inhumane, has at least brought a modicum of stability. New oil finds have helped to bolster the largely-agricultural economy, a vital discovery following the demise of Syria's former sugar-daddy, Russia, in 1991. It also looked as if the various factions in Lebanon had at last found some sort of *modus vivendi*, and peace began to return to the troubled land.

Unfortunately, things have soured since then. The election in Israel of the hard-line president Binyamin Netinyahu could stall the peace process and end Syrian hopes that the Golan Heights will be returned. Relations between Turkey and Syria are still not cordial following the building of a Turkish dam on the Euphrates. And the West appears to have turned against Syria once more, accusing Syria of sheltering, and even funding, international terrorism – a claim it has consistently denied.

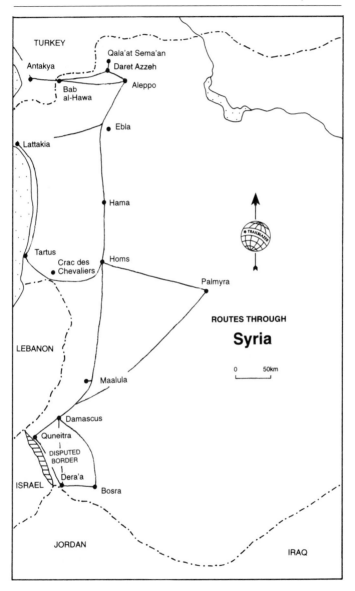

TURKEY

Qala'at Sema'an

Antakya

Daret Azzeh

Bab
al-Hawa

Aleppo

Ebla

Lattakia

Hama

Tartus

Crac des
Chevaliers

Homs

Palmyra

ROUTES THROUGH

Syria

0   50km

LEBANON

Maalula

Damascus

Quneitra

DISPUTED
BORDER

Dera'a

ISRAEL

Bosra

JORDAN

IRAQ

GEOGRAPHICAL BACKGROUND

Syria's total land area is 185,050 square km. To the west lies the Anti-Lebanon mountain range including Mt Hermon, Syria's highest peak at 2814m. To the north of this is some 180km of coastline. To the south the range tapers off into the disputed Golan Heights on the Israeli border.

There are two major rivers in Syria. The north-east of the country is bisected by the Euphrates, which flows from Turkey via Syria to Iraq. Syria's second river, the Orontes ('Rebel', as it flows in the opposite direction) begins in Lebanon and ends in Turkey. Most of the bigger cities lie along the Orontes Valley.

❑ **Practical information – Syria**

● **Visas** Single-entry 15-day visas can be bought en route from embassies in Istanbul or Cairo. A letter of recommendation from your own embassy is always required. Multiple entry is twice the price but valid for six months. Once in Syria, it is easy to extend your visa in Damascus or at any major city.

● **Currency** Syrian pounds (S£), divided into 100 piastres (virtually obsolete). Fixed exchange rate, and a flourishing black market. Officially US$1=S£42, UK£1=S£64.3. Unofficially, US$1=S£50, UK£1=S£75.

● **Banks** Only the Central Bank of Syria is authorised to change money, and it can take ages. You may find plenty of their branches in town but often only one of these will be able to change foreign currency. Always ask for small denomination notes, as larger notes can be difficult to break up. The **black market** for foreign currency flourishes in Syria. There is usually no need to look for the exponents: they will come to you. US dollars are the most readily accepted currency, although you should be able to find someone willing to change other currencies in the big towns. Be very careful: rip-offs do happen, and the police are not very forgiving if they catch you dabbling in illegal exchanges. **Credit cards** are not widely accepted except in a few of the top hotels and in the tourist souks.

● **Time** GMT + 2 (+ 3 from April to September)

● **Electricity** 220 volts AC, 50 Hz.

● **Post** The postal service and telephone networks are both pretty dire. Letters sent from Syria take ages to reach their destination (two weeks to Europe); parcels take even longer. If someone sends you a letter addressed to Poste Restante, you have only a 50-50 chance of receiving it; if it's a parcel, forget it.

● **Telephone** The easiest way to make international phone calls is to buy a phonecard; a 1000-unit card costs S£900. Currently the rates per minute are: Europe S£110 (S£60 between 0100-0600); Australia S£125 (S£75 from 1400-1900); USA and Canada S£135. For local calls use the battered orange phone boxes. These phones take lots of S£1 coins; there is usually somebody standing nearby selling rolls of them.

● **Warning** Syria is a Soviet-style police-state. As such the secret police force (Mukhabarat) – or rather, the eight secret police forces – are big employers. So be careful whom you talk to and, more importantly, what you say to them. If somebody asks your opinion on President Assad just smile, look ignorant, and talk about the weather.

RELIGION

Syria's population is approximately 70% Sunni Muslim. There are small pockets of other Islamic sects too, including Shi'ites, Ismailis and Alawites. Nearly all the rest are Christians, primarily Greek and Armenian Orthodox, or Druze. There are also a few thousand Jews, most of whom are desperate to leave the country.

LOCAL TRANSPORT

Karnak is the national bus company, and they offer a cheap and reliable service around the country. Of a similar standard are the privately-owned **Pullman buses**, costing a little less. (They usually have 'Pullman', or 'Poulman', written on the side to aid identification.) Cheaper still are the **local buses**, which are approximately half the price of the Karnak buses. Comfort is minimal in these machines but they are frequent and reliable.

The yellow, rusting **servis taxis** operate all over Syria. As usual, they leave when full. The small white **microbuses** operate in the same way. They tend to run to small destinations not served by the big buses.

Syria also has a fairly extensive **train** network. The main problem is that, almost without exception, the train station is a long way out of town. Prices are fairly cheap.

> ❏ **Route through Syria**
> The route through Syria begins at Aleppo, and heads due south along the Orontes to Homs, where you briefly stray from this southerly course to visit the oasis town of Palmyra. Continue back to Damascus and down to Bosra.

North Syria

ALEPPO (HALEB) حلب

Aleppo is, first and foremost, a market city. The hotel lobbies of Haleb (the local name for Aleppo) are regularly converted into a temporary trade fair by travelling salesmen from every part of Russia and Central Asia; outside these hotels shifty-looking smugglers from Armenia sell contraband to lucky Aleppians; and in the centre of town stands the city's biggest tourist attraction, a huge bazaar that rivals – in terms of grandeur and atmosphere – any other you'll see on this tour.

The Greeks were the first to fully realise Aleppo's potential as a market town. Before they came in 331BC it was the capital of the scavenging Amorite kingdom, which survived on the bounty captured from nearby cities. But once the Hittites arrived to trample all over the city in 1650BC, the beleaguered Aleppians recognised that their future lay not in stealing fortunes but in earning them.

Natural forces and envious neighbours have all conspired to thwart Aleppo's prosperity at various times down the years: the Persians decimated and devastated it in AD614, the Mongols arrived in 1260 to emulate the Persians and enjoyed it so much that they returned for a repeat performance under Tamerlane in 1400; and a huge earthquake in 1822 reduced much of the city to rubble. All these destructive forces, however, devastating as they may have been at the time, have proved to be only temporary setbacks to the commercial success of the city.

There is a lot more to Aleppo besides markets. Four hundred and seventy mosques, thirty-nine churches, sixty-eight caravanserais and fifty-eight public baths to be precise, many of which have been built according to the exquisitely simple geometric rules of Mamluke architecture. Swarming amongst these buildings is a noisy population of 1.5 million, amongst the most charming people you could hope to meet anywhere. Their colourful, cosmopolitan city is one of which they are justly proud.

Orientation and services   (Aleppo ☎ area code 021)

Buses from the Turkish border terminate opposite the tourist office in the centre of the city. Buses from the south arrive at the main bus station, about 500m to the south of the tourist office on Baron St شارع بارون .

The **tourist office** is open from 0800-1530, closed Fridays. The **GPO** and **telephone office** are on al-Jala'a St by the large roundabout west of the park. The GPO stays open from 0800-2000 (the telephone office is open one hour later) but both are closed on Friday. You can also phone from the **DHL** office downtown, where you don't have to wait so long.

The branch of the **Bank of Syria** which changes money is up a flight of stairs on Baron St. Although it advertises opening hours in the evening, it is usually open in the morning only.

Where to stay

You won't have to walk too far to find a hotel in Aleppo but finding one that is not also a brothel or a flea-pit is more difficult. Unfortunately, as most of the other hotels are filled with traders from the CIS, the poor backpacker must often rely on these hovels and whorehouses for a bed. The **Yarmouk** فندق اليرموك [1] (☎ 217510) on al-Maari St شارع المعري is neither of the above. It is also warm and friendly and at S£200/375 sgl/dbl great value too. Unfortunately, it is usually full up with Armenians.

Just up the road, the **Hotel Syrria** فندق سورية [2] (☎ 219760) also plays host to our former Soviet chums – even the telly in reception shows programmes beamed from Moscow – but at least they will usually find you a room (S£200/375 sgl/dbl), albeit one that is cramped and smothered with nasty flock wallpaper.

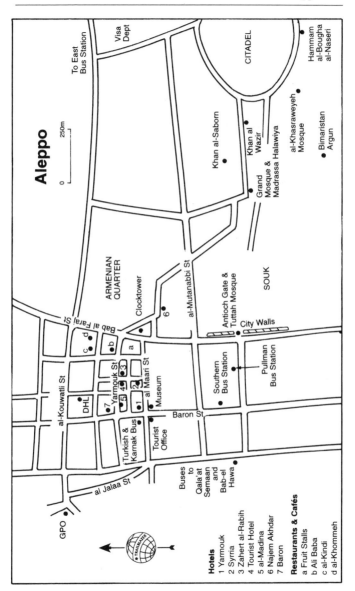

The **Zahert al-Rabih** فندق زهرة الربيع [3] (☎ 212790) is currently Aleppo's cheapie, at about S£125 per person, but here you get what you pay for: a light-free, air-free room. Opposite this near-death experience is the **Tourist Hotel** فندق السواح [4] (☎ 216583) which advertises itself as a backpackers' hostel. Run by the house-proud Madame Olga and decorated with her collection of Constable prints, it is without doubt one of the better places in Aleppo. The price, however, (S£300pp) reflects this.

The **al-Madina** المدينة [5] (☎ 210990) is an agreeable option too; you probably won't be raving about it on your postcards home but the staff are amiable, the rooms are comfortable and the price is fair (S£200/350 sgl/dbl). Another good place is the **Najem Akhdar** فندق النجم الاخضر [6] (☎ 239157) in the heart of the Armenian ghetto behind the clock tower. Popular with the Japanese, it's well-maintained – a moustachioed chap comes round with his feather duster every morning – and remains one of the better hotels in a fairly ordinary bunch (S£250pp).

With such a mediocre selection of budget hotels you may wish to splash out and stay at Aleppo's finest, the octogenarian **Baron Hotel** [7] فندق بارون (☎ 210880). Down the years a number of dignitaries (Atatürk, Teddy Roosevelt, the odd potentate or two) have rested their eminent heads on the plump pillows of the hotel's sumptuous bedrooms. On display in the lounge are a few reminders of these halcyon days, including Lawrence of Arabia's bill and a letter he sent to England 'from this beautiful hotel'. Nowadays the Baron could do with a lick of paint, and it's spookily quiet. But this place is swathed in history, and for US$29/39 sgl/dbl, including breakfast, you could be too. It's worth having a look around, even if you cannot afford to stay.

Where to eat
For cheap eats head for the junction of Bab al-Faraj St and Yarmouk St, where there are a number of juice and felafel stands [a]. You can concoct your own cocktail of juices for upwards of S£20, or settle for felafel for S£10.

If you hanker after hoummus, squeeze your way past the Armenian crowds and nab a table at the **Ali Baba** [b] restaurant, opposite. They do many salad and hoummus dishes, each costing about S£10-15.

One block north of here are a number of fairly good restaurants in very noisy competition with each other. The **al-Kindi** [c] is probably the best, although the **al-Khommeh** [d] is very good value too; the decor is over-the-top in both but the price of the food is not.

The Old City
The walls of the Old City were built by the Romans and Byzantines, though the west, south-west and south-east walls that remain today date from Mamluke times. Within the Old City are the citadel and the souk, as well as a whole host of mosques, madrassas, and maristans (hospitals).

The Souk (Closed Fridays). Whilst a shade smaller than Istanbul's Grand Bazaar, Aleppo's souk feels a whole lot more authentic, probably because it is not as crammed full of mass-produced tourist trinkets. Historians suggest that the market may have begun in the 15th century as just a few nondescript covered shops but today it is a vast, gay (in both senses of the word in some parts) souk that has grown to house approximately 13km of covered streets. These streets are organised into different sections named after the products sold there. Amongst them are some beautiful caravanserais: the 17th-century **Khan al-Wazir** خان الوزير – situated between the citadel and the Grand Mosque – and the nearby **Khan al-Saboun** خان الصابون are two of the more elaborate.

Despite these landmarks, it is almost inevitable that you will get lost in the souk. But who cares? Just throw yourself headfirst into the chaotic amalgamation of narrow twisting lanes and dimly-lit alleys, breathe in the pungent aroma of herbs, spices, cardamom, diesel and donkeys, avoid the cyclists, scooterists, barrow-boys, mini-vans and strident, burqa-clad Aleppian housewives, drink any chai, coffee or sahlep that is proffered – and enjoy this overwhelming assault on your senses.

The Citadel (0900-1600, closed Tues; S£200, S£25 students). The Citadel is an awesome example of Medieval architecture that completely dominates Aleppo's skyline. Construction on the tell (hill) was begun by Nehruddin, Saladin's predecessor, in the 12th century, on the site of an earlier Arab citadel that had tumbled down during a massive earthquake. The work was continued under the Ayyubid king al-Zaher Ghazi, and was finally re-fortified and completed by the Mamlukes 200 years later. It still wasn't impregnable and the Mongols proved as much in 1400, when Tamerlane conquered the city and allowed his troops to run amok for three grisly days. During Ottoman times a village of 3000 people was established inside the walls, until, as at the Crac des Chevaliers, they were booted out by the French.

The ruins today are part-Mamluke fortress, part-Ayyubid palace and part-Ottoman village, representing each of the important phases of the citadel's history. To enter, it is first necessary to penetrate the defences of the Mamluke fortress. A drawbridge used to stand between the first two gates of the main entrance; buy a ticket here if you wish to proceed.

A huge **moat**, 20m deep and approximately 40m wide, now stands between you and the citadel. Even if you manage to cross this (via the stone ramp is the easiest way), you still have to negotiate a twisting corridor – its ceiling punctured by burning-oil holes, its course blocked by yet another steel-enforced gate – that runs between the **Snake Gate** and the fifth and final barrier, the **Lion Gate**.

Survive all this, and you will find yourself at one end of the village street. On the right is a stairway leading down to the **cisterns**, whilst on the left are some **baths**. Next to the baths stands a small **mosque** from the early Ayyubid era (1175-1250), and at the end of the street lies another, this time dating from the 13th-century and the Mamlukes.

From here, turn right and cut across the middle of the citadel, across an incongruous 15-year old **Roman-style theatre**, to reach the final section, the 13th-century Ayyubid **royal palace** which lies near the main entrance. This was the home of King al-Zaher Ghazi; the restored **throne room**, with its elaborate Damascene ceiling, looks out of place amongst the bare rocks of the rest of the citadel.

To leave the citadel, take the stairs that lead down to a **control room**. This was the defensive nerve-centre of the castle, from where the generals could see all five gates. A secret passage from the **armoury** next door leads back to the Snake Gate.

Hammam al-Bougha al-Naseri حمام البوغا الناصري (0900-2200) On your left as you walk down the citadel ramp is a large, yellow-domed building. Inside are Aleppo's showpiece **public baths**, built in the 14th century and restored in 1985 by the Ministry of Tourism.

A full scrub-down and massage costs approximately S£300. The baths are open to women only during the day on Saturday, Monday and Wednesday.

Ommayad (Grand) Mosque المسجد الأموي Although the Grand Mosque was originally an Ommayad Mosque dating from AD715, and the one free-standing minaret dates from 1090, the building we see today is actually attributed to the Mamlukes. It's a beautiful mosque with a large open courtyard, which comes as something of a relief after the cramped confines of the souk which borders it. In Arabic the mosque is called Jami'a Zakariyyeh, as the head of John the Baptist's father, Zacharias, is reputedly buried here.

Other sight in the Old City

● **Madrassa Halawiya,** next to the Grand Mosque, still contains parts of a sixth-century Byzantine cathedral.

● **Tuttah Mosque** مسجد التوته Aleppo's oldest mosque (dating from the twelfth-century) stands by the Antioch Gate باب انتاكية .

● **Bimaristan Argun** بيمارستان أرغون Difficult to find, this Mamluke lunatic asylum and hospital was built in 1354. The open courtyard is very pleasant, with the central fountain still in working order. The dark and dingy cells that surround it are quite eerie.

Archaeological Museum

(0900-1600, closed Tues; S£200, S£25 students). Just over the road from the tourist office and guarded by a pair of ninth century-BC black basalt lions is Aleppo's renowned Archaeological Museum. There are rooms devoted to the nearby excavations of Ugarit, Mari and Ebla. Upstairs is a quite dreadful contemporary art gallery, often kept under lock and key because of the blatant images of nudity contained within.

All the artefacts are labelled in English, although explanations are minimal; the guide book on sale for S£200 gives more details.

Christian quarter حي النصارى

The large Christian quarter, founded by the Armenian refugees who fled here to escape Russian and Turkish persecution in their homeland, lies to the north-east of the clock tower. It is an area full of stately homes – some of which, for a little baksheesh, you may be able to visit – as well as a few Armenian churches and cathedrals. Look out too for **Orient House**; this is a bazaar of the bizarre, a fascinating junk shop full of kitsch collectibles and curiosities.

Qala'at Sema'an قلعة سمعان

(0830-1700; S£200, S£25 students). The remains of the Basilica of St Simeon, 25km outside Aleppo, are one of the 'must-sees' in Syria. St Simeon was an ascetic whose pursuit of enlightenment through self-inflicted pain reached excruciating proportions.

Born in 392AD, he was flung out of his first monastery at thirteen for embarking on a fasting regime which made even the senior monks wince. This did not curtail his masochistic tendencies, however. Summers would find him buried up to his chin in sand, for the rest of the year he sported a girdle of spikes which made him to bleed every time he moved. During Lent he would add to his discomfort by walling himself up in a cell.

But whilst he could endure copious amounts of physical pain, he could not bear the simple company of people. After failing to escape their attentions by living as a hermit, in 423AD Simeon struck upon the idea of residing atop a pillar to avoid them. It was only a partial success, and a vicious circle was formed: as crowds flocked to see this weird guy stuck on top of a pole, Simeon extended the pillar to distance himself from them; as the pillar grew, even more came to see. Eventually his column stood at 64ft, and there St Simeon (or Simeon the Stylite as he is better-known) stayed for over 30 years, surviving on food brought up to him once a week by monks. Pilgrims, sightseers and freak-show fanatics from as far away as England were all drawn to the spectacle and soon Simeon, a true pillar of the community, was conducting two masses per week for the pilgrims.

Living the high life eventually weakened Simeon's health and in AD459 he passed away. His pillar has survived, although now it is just an ungainly boulder, much reduced in size by memento-seekers and looking out of place amongst such carefully-wrought stonework.

This masonry is the ruin of a Byzantine basilica completed in AD490 and built to house the pilgrims who continued to flock here after Simeon's death. In its day it was the largest in the world. It was designed in a cruciform style, although this shape is somewhat obscured by the remains of a monastery adjoining the east wing of the church.

Reaching Qala'at Sema'an can be a time-consuming affair depending on your hitch-hiking capabilities. A minibus from Aleppo to Daret Azzah (دار العزة) costs S£10. The basilica is 5km from here; try to hitch at least one way as the walk can be very tiring in the sun.

Moving on
● **Bus** The Karnak bus station is opposite the tourist office on al-Maari St. The fare to Hama is S£55 (six buses per day). The station for local and Pullman buses heading south is on Baron St. A pullman to Hama is S£35, or it's S£25 by local bus (90 minutes).
● **Train** The station is to the north of the town. There are two trains heading south each day, both at inconvenient times: 0039 and 0213. For Hama (just over two hours) the fare is S£34/23/18 for first/second/student.

HAMA حماة

Hama is situated right on the Orontes River and, unlike some other towns in Syria, it seems very proud of that fact. The river runs through the very centre; the citadel, Old Quarter, museums, hotels and restaurants all huddle along its banks. Indeed Hama's most famous monuments are the river's ancient wooden waterwheels, the norias, that groan through their labours each day.

The quaint, laid-back serenity of Hama masks a bloody past. As early as the ninth century BC the Aramaeans, who were enjoying a certain amount of prosperity through their trade with the Israelites, came to blows with Assyrians who had arrived to appropriate their spoils. In 722BC, after decades of failure, the Assyrians finally broke through and devastated Hama, sending the hapless Aramaeans into exile. This story has been repeated in Hama countless times down the centuries; only the names of the assailants and victims have changed. The most recent was in 1982, following an attempt on President Assad's life in June 1980 by the Muslim Brotherhood. The assassination failed; Assad himself deftly kicked one of the grenades thrown at him out of the way.

The president bided his time, waiting for the appropriate moment to exact his revenge. In February 1982, after a coalition of revolutionaries,

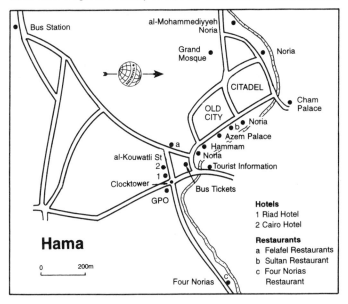

al-Mohammediyyeh Noria

Bus Station

Grand Mosque

Noria

CITADEL

OLD CITY

Cham Palace

Noria

b

Azem Palace

a

Hammam

al-Kouwatli St

Noria

2

1

Tourist Information

Clocktower

GPO

Bus Tickets

Hotels
1 Riad Hotel
2 Cairo Hotel

Restaurants
a Felafel Restaurants
b Sultan Restaurant
c Four Norias Restaurant

Hama

0   200m

Four Norias

including the Brotherhood, published an anti-government manifesto, that moment was at hand. The government closed off the city, ordering first an aerial bombardment and then a land invasion by the army. Because of a news blackout details are still hazy but it is believed that between 15,000-25,000 civilians died in the massacre. Many more were subsequently killed in Syria's prisons.

Today, although the government continues to keep a very close eye on the town, there appears to be peace. The town thrives once more as the centre of the steel and iron industry, and yet it does not resemble a major industrial centre. Indeed it is almost idyllic, and the combination of pretty parks, good food, pleasant accommodation and an easygoing atmosphere entices many a traveller to stay longer than originally planned.

Orientation and services   (Hama ☎ area code 033)
Almost everything of interest in Hama lies to the south of the river. The ghastly electronic clock tower is the focus of Hama: the **GPO**, **bank**, and the Riad and Cairo hotels are all within earshot of the chimes. A bridge to the north of the clock tower leads over the river to the **tourist office**. Nearly all the major attractions, save for the Four Norias, line the river to the west of this bridge.

Where to stay
Look no further than the ***Riad Hotel*** فندق الرياض [1] (☎ 239512) for a place to rest those travel weary bones. For S£125 you get to sleep in an immaculate dorm with fans, central heating and balcony (S£600 dbl with TV, fridge and mini-bar, S£800 in high season). Breakfast is S£75. As a bonus, some of the most knowledgeable guys in Syria hang around reception fielding questions on every aspect of their country. The hotel is near the electronic clock tower (which is the only disadvantage, as the tinny chimes can be heard from some of the rooms). Next door is the ***Cairo*** [2] (فندق القاهرة ☎ 222280), not a bad alternative, although at S£150/225/350 dorm/sgl/dbl it cannot really compete with its neighbour. Round the corner from these are one or two scruffier alternatives.

Where to eat
Hama's food is the nation's best. Opposite the western end of al-Kouwatli St are a number of stalls [a] offering the usual Syrian snacks, but with a difference: they are either half the price of anywhere else in Syria, or double the quality. For more upmarket nosh, the ***Sultan*** [b] in the Old City has a fixed-price menu but does not serve alcohol; try their barboush, an eggplant and garlic combination (S£55). At the other end of town the

---

(**Opposite**) **Top:** The best views of the Crac des Chevaliers (see p132) are from the hill south of the castle. **Bottom:** The Citadel, Aleppo (see p123).

Four Norias Restaurant النواعير الاربعة [c] does serve alcohol but sometimes the staff have problems adding up your bill. Check everything carefully.

All over town you will also see the local delicacy, halawit al-jubit (sweet cheese pudding) dangling from the cafés' chairs in preparation for that evening's consumption. The dish is a mixture of water, millet and sugar, and is often served with ice cream (S£25 per roll). It's delicious.

The Norias
The best way to become acquainted with Hama is to walk along the river-bank. The wooden water wheels that line the banks of the Orontes have come to symbolise Hama. They were used to supply water from the river, which was then conveyed by a system of aqueducts throughout the town. Nobody is exactly sure when these norias first appeared, but a second-century mosaic depicting an early version of them has been unearthed nearby. The design of the present ones dates back to the 13th-century Mamlukes. Near the Grand Mosque, you can see the remains of one aqueduct adjoining the main **al-Mohammediyyeh Noria**. At over 20 metres in diameter, it is the largest in Hama.

The Grand Mosque
Unfortunately, this is a lot less grand than it used to be. Its history is similar to that of the Grand Mosque in Damascus: Byzantine church built on site of pagan temple, then converted into a mosque by the Ommayads during the seventh century. Hama's version, however, which had retained many of the old Byzantine features, was smashed in 1982 and is still being rebuilt.

The Old City
The remains of the Old City lie on the southern bank of the river. It is really little more than one street, and even this did not fully escape Assad's bombardment. However, there is still a fair bit to see. The **Azem Palace** (قصر عازم S£200, S£25stu) is an older, smaller version of its namesake in Damascus. Both were built as pasha's residences by the same man, Assad Pasha al-Azem, who ruled Hama from 1700-42. (Ironically, this pasha is an ancestor of President Assad, who almost destroyed the building 240 years later).

Also in the palace is a small **museum**. Pride of place here goes to a second-century mosaic of six women playing musical instruments which, in terms of detail and subject matter, is quite unlike any other mosaic you'll see on this route through the Near East.

To the south of the palace is a medieval **hammam**, still in use (S£100). Women can use the bath from 1200-1800 every day.

(Opposite) The fierce Syrian sun manages to penetrate even the narrowest and gloomiest of alleyways in Damascus' Old City (see p146).

The Citadel

Many of the artefacts in the museum were found buried on this artificial mound that rises from Hama like a miniature volcano. The summit is now landscaped and furnished with picnic tables; views over the city are good.

Moving on

● **Bus** The Karnak buses leave from outside the ticket offices by the river. There are four Karnak buses per day to Homs, which is just half an hour away (S£25). By local bus the fare is S£11.

● **Train** There are two early morning trains to Homs, at 0230 and 0400. The fares are S£15/10/9 for first class/second class/student.

Central Syria

HOMS حمص

There is nothing of great interest in Homs but the city is such an important transport hub that most travellers find themselves staying here for at least one night. There are good connections not only along the Orontes Valley but also westwards to the Crac des Chevaliers and Lebanon and east to Palmyra.

Homs is steeped in history, and it's disappointing that so little evidence of it remains today. It began as an Aramaean village c1100BC, which grew to be an important religious centre for the cult of Baal, the Sun God. At one time Emesa (as Homs was then called) even had a fabulous Baal Temple to rival Baalbek's in importance. Towards the end of the Roman Empire one of the temple priests even became emperor, and the cult of Baal became the official religion of the empire.

But you will see nothing vaguely Roman, Graeco-Roman or Aramaean in Homs today. On Hama St is the **Khalid ibn al-Walid Mosque** مسجد خالد ابن الوليد , nothing special but a little less of an eyesore than the rest of the town. Built at the beginning of the century, it houses the tomb of the eponymous Muslim commander who was instrumental in the introduction of Islam to Syria in 636AD.

Orientation and services   (Homs ☎ area code 031)

It is easiest to imagine Homs as a triangle. At the northern apex of this triangle is the bus station. The two main roads that run south-west and south-east from here – al-Korniche St شارع الكورنيش and Hama St شارع حماة respectively – form two sides of the triangle. The third side is Shukri al-Kuwatli St شارع القوتلي . The best hotel, **tourist office** (0830 -1400, 1600-2030, closed Friday) and **GPO** (0800-1700, closed Friday) are all near here. For foreign exchange, there's a small branch of the **Bank of Syria** in one of the little side streets near the al-Nasser al-Jadid Hotel.

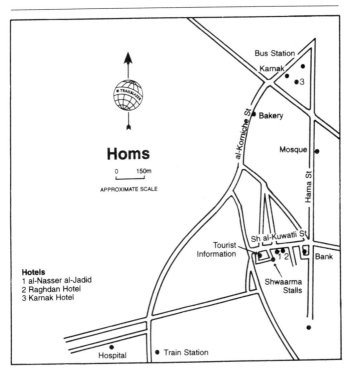

Hotels
1 al-Nasser al-Jadid
2 Raghdan Hotel
3 Karnak Hotel

Where to stay

Most travellers head for the *al-Nasser al-Jadid Hotel* فندق النصر الجديد (☎ 227423) on Sh al-Kuwatli. Having checked out the alternatives, I definitely advocate following the herd. The rooms, all with sink, are spacious and cleaned daily. The Nasser's lugubrious owner will show you around the hotel, pointing out facilities such as a Western-style toilet for 'the rich people'. He will also state that: 'The cost is S£175 single, S£300 double. If you do not like this there are other places in town'; so I guess bargaining is out of the question.

Most of these 'other places' are definitely substandard, but all have the temerity to charge as much as the al-Jadid: the *al-Khayam* (tel 223959) next door (no sgls, S£300 dbls) and the *Hotel Ebn al-Walid* (☎ 223953) off Hama St (S£175/275 sgl/dbl) are two.

The vast *Raghdan* (☎ 225211), just up from al-Nasser on Kouwatli St, is a little better than these in terms of quality but is hugely overpriced at US$17sgl, US$23dbl, US$28 tpl.

Finally, there is the **Karnak Hotel** (☎ 233099) above the Karnak ticket office next to the bus station. It's a very ugly concrete cylinder with bags of cement littering the hallway, but the rooms are OK, if a little characterless (US$24/31sgl/dbl, +5% tax).

The Crac des Chevaliers كراك دي شائليه

Known in Arabic as Qala'at Hoseyn, this is the Crusaders' greatest legacy and probably the finest example of military architecture in the Near East. It is massive. During its heyday it held 4000 soldiers and 400 knights. Today it still dominates the scenery for miles around.

The 'Castle of the Knights' served two purposes. The first was strategic: it overlooks a large gap in the Lebanese mountains which was once the major thoroughfare between the Orontes and the coast. But it was also designed, like the posters of President Assad today, to intimidate.

The Crusaders started to build their castle in 1142, and remained within for 129 years. During their tenancy they resisted 12 assaults, including attacks by Nehruddin in 1164, and Saladin in 1188. They were eventually starved out following a 45-day siege by the Mamluke Sultan Baybars in 1271. Once the Mamlukes had left the castle was rarely used in any military capacity, and during Ottoman times a village of 10,000 people grew within its walls. When the French expelled them in 1936, they built a new village below the Crac with materials stolen from the castle.

Visiting the Crac (Open 0900-1700; S£200, S£25 students. Bring a torch). The Crac is 40km from Homs. A bus from Homs station costs S£20-25. The last bus back to Homs leaves at 1530, so try to reach the Crac as soon after 9am as possible to enjoy a full day here. The castle is split into two sections. At the centre of the castle are the living quarters, and surrounding them is the defensive outer section.

This outer section used to contain a moat which surrounded the living quarters. Today only stagnant vestiges remain. By the entrance ramp on the left is a secret subterranean passage which led out of the castle, a typical Crusader feature. The towers which stand on the south side of the castle both date from the Mamluke era.

After a complete circuit of the defences, go through the gate that leads into the second section, the living quarters. Everything that the knights needed to be completely self-sufficient is here. There's a canteen, a meeting hall, a church, a large storage section and plenty of smaller rooms. The huge hole at the back of the large meeting-hall was once a bread oven. Try not to fall in here, nor, for that matter, into the latrines that lie to the north. Beyond the latrines a small entrance leads into a chapel, converted to a mosque by the Mamlukes. A staircase nearby leads up to the top of the castle, overshadowed by three towers that were once the office, salon and bedroom of the Crac's chief knight. As you can imagine, the view of the surrounding area is breathtaking from here.

Moving on

Bus All the buses leave from the same vermin-infested bus station to the north of the town, although the Karnak terminus is separated off and has its own entrance. Be warned: you are more likely to be ripped off here than anywhere else in Syria.

● **To Lebanon** Karnak runs three buses daily (0230, 0300, 1200) to Beirut for S£150 (4 hours), and five to Tripoli (same times as Beirut plus 0900 and 0930) for S£100. Microbuses also run to Tripoli (S£200, 3 hours) and Beirut (S£300), throughout the day; they take less time at the border.

● **To Palmyra** (not Sunday, Tuesday or Friday). There is one Karnak bus at 0915 for S£50 (2hrs), and seven local buses (S£45). Minibuses charge S£60. Look for the 'beehive' houses that stand in the desert on this route.

● **To Damascus** Karnak has four buses (0700-1830). The fare is S£50, or S£65 with aircon. It's S£30 with local buses for the two-hour trip.

Train Homs station is two km south of the town centre. There are two trains daily to Damascus (S£48/30/25 1st cl/2nd cl/stu). Both, however, leave in the early morning (0340 and 0455) and take two hours.

PALMYRA (TADMOR) تدمر

Syria's greatest tourist attraction is also one of its more remote. Known to the Syrians as Tadmor ('the City of Dates'), the oasis town of Palmyra ('City of Palms') lies some 160km east of Homs and 230km from Damascus in the midst of the vast Syrian Desert. It's one of the most rewarding places to visit on this route through the Near East – the site of the ruins of a famous ancient city that combines picturesque Graeco-Roman architecture with a harsh, undulating desert landscape.

One should aim to spend at least a couple of days in Palmyra as there is so much to see. The best time to view the ruins is late afternoon when the few tour buses that do come here have disappeared and it's cooler. As dusk falls, climb a small hill by the ruins to see the changing effects of the light on the ancient city, and then sit back to watch the local children using the ancient Palmyric columns as goal-posts.

Orientation and services   (Palmyra ☎ area code 034)

There are no banks in Palmyra. Stock up on S£ before you arrive, or bring dollars in cash to exchange on the black market.

The modern town lies to the north-east of the ruins, separated by a roundabout which joins the ancient ruins to the new town. Nearly everything a traveller could want is either on the roundabout, or very nearby. This is the Syrian approximation of a tourist ghetto: the **GPO and phone office** (0800-1400 except Fridays) and **archaeological museum** are all near the roundabout, while the hotels, restaurants and bus offices are on the street that runs to the east. The **tourist office**, just to the north of the Zenobia Hotel, proffers an informative pamphlet.

❑ Palmyra's rise and fall

Palmyra grew in prominence during the Roman period. Having conquered the rest of Syria in 63BC, Pompey decided not to bother marching his troops through the desert to Palmyra. Instead the town became a kind of buffer, separating the Roman and Persian Empires.

This favoured treatment brought Palmyra its own rewards: in AD130 Hadrian declared Palmyra a free town, allowing Palmyrenes self government, and in 217 Rome went even further and granted the city the status of Roman colony, exempting its citizens from paying taxes and ensuring that their rights were on a par with those of Rome. The Palmyrenes renamed the city Palmyra Hadriana in gratitude.

Throughout the Roman era Palmyra grew fat on the passing caravans that travelled between Rome's dominions and the mighty empires of the East. Evidence of Palmyrene trade has been found in such far-flung places as the Persian Gulf and Newcastle-upon-Tyne in England. Petra's demise in the second century was Palmyra's fortune, as more and more trading routes through the region came under Palmyrene control. The city reached its apogee in the third century. Firstly, Rome granted the Palmyrene King Odenathus control over all the Roman forces in the region, following his rescue of the Roman Emperor Valerian from Persian kidnappers. Then, following Odenathus' assassination in 266AD, his beautiful wife Zenobia assumed the throne in place of their infant son and set about expanding the Palmyrene kingdom. Within five years Syria, Egypt and Asia Minor (up to and including Ankara) had fallen under her command. The mints of Alexandria were franking coins with her image on them, and Zenobia had taken to calling herself Augusta, the Roman imperial title.

This was too much for Rome to bear and Emperor Aurelian retaliated. By AD272 Rome had defeated her troops at Antioch and Emesa (Homs), and was harrying them back to Palmyra. The city fell soon after, and Zenobia was captured as she tried to flee. Bound in golden chains and borne off to Rome, she spent the rest of her days as a prisoner in Italy. The following year after yet another rebellion Roman troops poured in to crush the city. Thereafter it never regained its former power. The Abbassids ignored it, and an earthquake in 1089 toppled most of the buildings. Throughout the next 400 years Palmyra was largely abandoned.

It wasn't until 1751 that Palmyra was rediscovered by two Englishmen, Dawkins and Wood, who recognised that the walls of a small Bedouin village were actually part of Palmyra's Temple of Bel. In 1924 excavations began in earnest to discover just what lay beneath the desert sands, and ever since then the 'Bride of the Desert' has been slowly restored to her former radiance.

Where to stay

The buses pull up at the main roundabout, where the owner of the *Citadel Hotel* فندق القلعة (☎ 910537) will usually be waiting for you (S£150-200pp upstairs, S£100 in an airless basement dorm). Their motto is 'clean, comfortable and safe', all of which is very true, although they do operate an annoying 10pm curfew which puts some people off. Most of those who do stay away head for the *New Tourist Hotel* فندق السواح الجديد (☎ 910333),

whose manager, Sammy, is something of a celebrity. To some his idio-
syncrasies are charming but to others he's an irritating individual whose
bottomless teapot cannot compensate for his manner. Whatever you feel
about him, one thing you will hate is the muezzin bellowing through your
window at 4am from the minaret next door.

To the north of the roundabout is the *Afqa Hotel* فندق الأفق (☎ 220386).
Although it is owned by one Waleed Shleed, it is his larger than life son
who really runs the hotel. Camping trips and even fishing expeditions can
be arranged here. The rooms are OK, although the showers are temperamental and some of the beds are awful – the young Simeon the Stylite
would feel right at home sleeping here. It is absolutely vital that you bargain: it is possible to pay as little as S£75 pp, although some poor souls
have ended up paying as much as US$25.

The top hotel in the modern town is the *Palmyran Villa* (☎ 910156),
catering mainly for tour groups. It has some lovely rooms (US$58/70/80,
sgl/dbl/tpl) but try to get one on the top floor or your view will be
obstructed by the neighbouring buildings.

There is also the delightful *Hotel Zenobia* فندق زنوبية an elegant 1920's
building situated on the edge of the ruins, (from where it scavenges material for some of its lobby furniture). Prices here are similar to the
Palmyran Villa.

Where to eat

It won't take you long to realise why this place is called the City of Dates;
there is a whole row of shops on the edge of the ruins near the roundabout
that deal in nothing else. The sellers are persistent, the dates delicious.

Supplement your diet of dates by visiting the string of restaurants on
the main tourist drag. Most advertise student discounts, although ISIC
cards are not usually necessary. Currently the pick of the bunch is the
Traditional Palmyra Restaurant. Their food is very good, although the
repetitive aural diet of Boney M may drive you from the restaurant sooner than you would have wished.

Those in need of beer should drop into the *English Pub* in the basement of the Palmyran Villa, but it's S£100 a bottle. For S£200 you can
feast on the all-you-can-eat breakfast in the fourth floor restaurant.

Temple of Bel معبد بيل

(0830-1600 except Tuesday; S£200, S£25 students). To the east of the
Colonnaded Street stands a temple dedicated to the ancient god Bel, possibly the Baal of Baalbek fame. A dedicatory inscription tells us that the
present temple was constructed in AD45, although it is likely that there
was a temple here long before then.

It was the Arabs who built the 15m high walls that enclose the site and
hide the temple's original monumental entrance. You can get a better
impression of this entrance from within the complex, where the three cer-

emonial gates can still be seen. The ramp that rises to the podium ahead of the modern entrance was probably the passageway for the sacrificial animals, since an altar used to stand on this podium. The temple itself used to house the statue of the god Bel, and was once highly-decorated and fitted with brass. Some of the decorations survive to this day.

The Colonnaded Street

Stretching some 750m from the doorstep of the Temple of Bel to the threshold of the **Funerary Temple** (a third-century tomb and temple) is the Grand Colonnade. This street performed a dual role in ancient Palmyra, being both a religious processional way and the main shopping arcade. The shops that lined the street have long since disappeared, although some of their signs still rest above the doorways, giving details of the name of the shopkeeper as well as the nature of his store. Behind and amongst these stores are the remains of several important buildings.

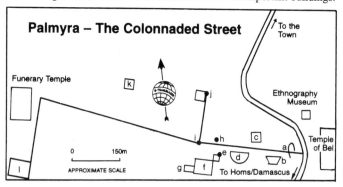

Palmyra – The Colonnaded Street

a) Monumental Arch

b) Nabo Temple Nabo was a Babylonian god, which suggests that there may have been a significant Mesopotamian or Babylonian population in the town. It is similar in layout, if not in scale, to the Temple of Bel.

c) Diocletian's Baths You will see little that is bath-like in the stones that lie scattered here today. The signpost states that these ruins were the baths of Zenobia. The signpost is wrong.

d) Theatre Unlike Diocletian's baths, this theatre is at least in a fairly good condition, although only a third of the seats remain.

e) Senate House

f) Agora A public meeting place that differed little in function from the Roman forum. A door in the west wall leads to the Banqueting Hall.

g) Banqueting Hall Where public dignitaries would adjourn after their meetings in the Agora.

h) Nymphaeum Ruined.

i) Tetrapylon Four kiosks of four Aswan granite pillars set in the middle of the street that mark a crossroads in the colonnade. Only one of the pillars left standing is original, and the statues that were placed on the plinths have disappeared. The colonnade kinks here. The road to the west passes rubble-strewn sand that was once the residential quarters of Palmyra, whilst to the north a path leads to the Temple of Baal Shamin.

j) Temple of Baal Shamin Halfway between the Hotel Zenobia and the tetrapylon stands this temple dedicated to the Phoenician god of rains and storms, who was appropriated by the Palmyrenes for their own worship.

k) Byzantine church

l) Camp of Diocletian After the funerary temple the street turns 90 degrees to the south, where it finishes at this small village, built for the Roman troops stationed here after the Palmyrene rebellion of AD273.

Tombs

The Palmyrene beliefs about death and the afterlife were very similar to those of the ancient Egyptians: both buried their dead to the west of the city, and both believed that the tombs were houses for the deceased's spirit and as such should be made as comfortable as possible. Palmyra's necropolis contains over 300 of these tombs. The earliest are the tower tombs from the second century BC. Following the Romans' arrival in Syria the fashion for tombs went underground, and many subterranean graves were dug at this time.

Today most tombs are little more than dark, empty caves redolent of urine but a stroll down the valley with a torch can still reveal some surprises, including one tomb that contains three skulls.

The Tombs of Elahbel and the Three Brothers Two of the better-preserved tombs are kept under lock and key. Viewing them involves quite a convoluted process, although they are worth the hassle. These two tombs are opened four times a day; the opening times are displayed by the entrance to the museum. First you must buy a ticket from the museum (S£100, S£25stu) and then find a taxi and a guide (approximately S£100 for each; try to get a group together to split the cost) to take you there.

The tower **Tomb of Elahbel** was originally built in AD103 for four brothers whose portraits decorate the interior walls. The tomb is a pleasing mixture of architectural styles; the tower is a Palmyrene design, but it has Greek fluted columns decorated with Corinthian capitals.

On entering you will notice how the tomb resembles a filing cabinet for the deceased. On each of the four floors there are nine recesses, and each recess could hold nine corpses, one on top of the other. This makes a grand total of 324 bodies in one tomb! Profit was the motive: the more bodies the tomb could hold, the more money the owners could make by renting tomb-space out to people who could not afford to build their own.

The underground **Tomb of the Three Brothers** (AD160) lies to the south-west of Palmyra, a few km past the dried-up sulphur spring. According to the Palmyric inscription above the door it was built for three siblings Male, Saadai and Naamain. They each have a funerary bed inside, under which the body was probably housed. Lifelike funerary statues surmount these beds, although they have all been decapitated – perhaps by robbers, or maybe at the hands of the iconoclasts. On the wall of the tomb a large fresco depicts the deceased, carried away to heaven by winged Victories.

Fakhreddine Castle
The most conspicuous building in the whole of Palmyra is not Roman or Greek influenced but Islamic. The mighty Fakhreddine Castle was probably built some time in the 13th century by the Mamlukes but it is named after the 17th-century Lebanese Emir whose rule stretched over much of modern-day Syria (see p181). The castle is surrounded by a moat traversed by a fairly shaky bridge. It costs nothing to enter, although there is little inside that will hold your attention, and you'll soon be gazing over the parapets to enjoy the desert landscape below.

Archaeological Museum
(0800-1300; 1400-1600 winter, 1600-1800 summer; closed Tuesday; S£200, S£25 students). The ground floor of the museum describes the history of Palmyra, from the flints of Neolithic man through to the glorious days of the second and third centuries AD. There is also a display on the Palmyric language, and two dead Palmyrenes reclining behind glass.

Museum of Popular Culture
(0830-1430, closed Tuesday; S£100, S£10 students). No tourist town in Syria would be complete without an ethnographic museum, where mannequins are arranged to portray scenes of traditional Arab life. Palmyra is no different. Their museum is in the former Ottoman Governor's Residence next to the Temple of Bel. The exhibition is labelled in English but the building, which was used by the French as a prison after the Ottomans left, is more interesting than the museum.

Moving on
Try to book your tickets out of Palmyra the day before you wish to leave. The Karnak office is by the roundabout. They have plenty of buses going via Palmyra to Damascus (S£90) but most begin at Deir el-Zur and are full by the time they reach here. Tickets for Pullman buses to Damascus (S£100) can be bought from the Restaurant of Spring. The cheapest way to reach Damascus, however, is to catch a microbus to Homs (S£50) from the station to the south of the main drag, and take a local bus from there (S£30).

Damascus
دمشق

... the oldest metropolis on earth, the one city in the world that has kept its name and held its place and looked serenely on while the Kingdoms and Empires of four thousand years have risen to life, enjoyed their little season of pride and pomp, and then vanished and been forgotten! – **Mark Twain** *The Innocents Abroad*

Twain was only half right. Damascus is indeed very ancient: Aramaean settlers arrived here 50 centuries ago and today it is the world's oldest, continually inhabited city. But Damascus has never looked 'serenely' on anything, preferring instead to take a very active role in the affairs of the Near East. It has been the seat of many empires down the ages and has played a crucial role in the development of both Christianity and Islam.

Damascus is a cosmopolitan metropolis. People from all parts of Africa and Arabia – Algerians, Iranians, Ethiopians, Somalis, Sudanese – mingle amongst 2.5 million Damascenes, giving the city an international air which belies the fact that there are so few Western tourists here. It is the most exotic, least Western capital you'll visit on this route. Of all the cities in the Near East, Syria's capital has had the greatest success in stemming the flow of Western culture that has engulfed so many other parts of the region. Step into parts of the old city and you feel as if you've stepped back in time: the women are in full purdah, the men are in full cry in the ancient souk, and the relentless drone of traffic has been reduced to an insignificant hum.

It's enchanting. As the Syrian-produced *Damascus Tourist Guide* enthuses: 'It has been named the beauty-spot of the world, the calyx among flowers, a moon-halo on earth, and many other names from paradise.' Quite so.

HISTORY

Prior to becoming the seat of an empire, Damascus had to play the reluctant host to a procession of invaders. All the usual suspects were involved: the Egyptians under Pharaoh Thutmose III, David's Israelites, the Assyrians, Babylonians and Persians – the roll-call is a familiar one. Even the Nabataeans nabbed it for a while from 85BC, before the Romans in turn took the town endowing it with the status of Roman Colony.

But let us leap forward to the seventh century. Damascus was by this time a Byzantine bishopric, and one that was besieged by Muslims. It was six months before the Muslims gained control but once they did

Damascus got the empire it deserved. The Ommayads (AD651-750) were powerful, ambitious and cultured, and by establishing their capital in Damascus the city became the centre of the Islamic world.

Even after the Abbassids removed the caliphate to Baghdad eighty-nine years later, Damascus still enjoyed considerable power. In 1154 Nehruddin took the city. He was succeeded by Saladin who made it the centre of his Ayyubid Empire. Religious authority remained with Baghdad but in all secular matters the Ayyubids ruled. The Mamluke slaves who followed them into power spent the next three centuries building Damascus as an industrial centre, and repairing the damage caused by two devastating Mongol invasions.

Throughout the Ottoman era the city earned a reputation for being a hotbed of political activity. Unhappy at being part of somebody else's empire, the citizens of Damascus continually rebelled against Turkish rule, and in one bloody 16th-century episode a third of the population was slaughtered by the Ottomans following a failed coup. The frustrations of living under Turkish rule often manifested itself in religious bloodletting too, culminating in the destruction of the entire Christian quarter by the Muslim population in 1860.

Fortunes changed little over the next century, even after the Turks had been chased out by the Arab Revolt in 1916. Now it was the French who took their turn to lord it over the city, which twice involved subjecting it to aerial bombardment following attempted coups. Syrian persistence finally won the day in 1946 when Damascus was declared the capital of the newly-independent Republic of Syria.

ORIENTATION

Although little more than a dark brown stream of sludge these days, the Barada still bisects the city and most of the important buildings are located on its banks: the river runs alongside the Old City's north wall, under the monument on Martyrs' Square (ساحة الشهداء) and follows the main Sh al-Kuwatli St (شارع القوتلي) where the Ministry of Tourism and the National Museum are located. The main embassy enclave of al-Muhajirin (المهاجرين) is to the north of the Barada, west of the New City.

LOCAL TRANSPORT

Except for a few bus and railway stations, everything is within easy walking distance of Martyrs' Square. For these transport terminals you need to catch the following white microbuses:

To Yarmouk Sq ساحة اليرموك (for the southern local bus station and the train station): S£5 from the bus station behind the phone office.

To Abbasine Sq ساحة العباسين (for local buses to eastern and northern destinations): S£5 from al-Ittihad St near the fruit and vegetable market. The

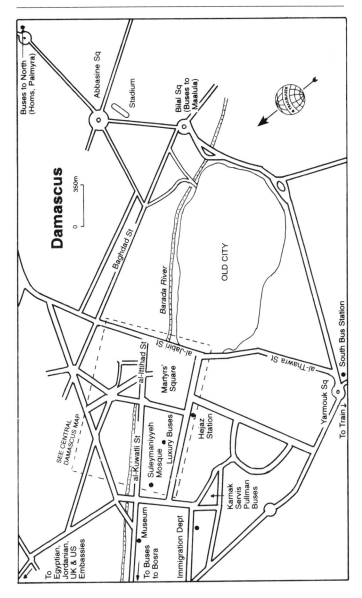

Damascus

0   350m

Buses to North (Homs, Palmyra)

Abbasine Sq

Stadium

Bilal Sq (Buses to Maalula)

Baghdad St

Barada River

OLD CITY

al-Jabiri St

al-Ittihad St

Martyrs' Square

al-Thawra St

South Bus Station

Yarmouk Sq

To Train

al-Kuwatli St

Suleymaniyyeh Mosque

Luxury Buses

Hejaz Station

Karnak Servis Pullman Buses

SEE CENTRAL DAMASCUS MAP

Museum

Immigration Dept

To Buses to Bosra

To Egyptian, Jordanian, UK & US Embassies

bus station is a ten-minute walk north of Abbasine Sq. To catch a microbus from this bus station to the centre of town, cross over the road and wait by the whitewashed wall.

To Bilal Sq ساحة بلال (for buses to Maalula). Catch the Abbasine Sq bus, and walk south down Annasirah St.

To the airport Bus (S£5) from outside Kinda Hotel on Al-Ittihad St.

SERVICES (Damascus ☎ **area code** 011)

● **Bookshops** Damascus has a paltry selection of reading material to offer the English speaker. The **Librairie Universelle** has some English-language texts, and outside **Chachati** on Shukri al-Kuwatli St a boy sells a few second-hand English books (see the Central Damascus map, p145). There is also a small bookstore at the **Cham Palace**.

● **Changing money** The easiest legal place to change money is in the small Bank of Syria office opposite the Hejaz Station (محطة الحجاز) where for some reason they forego all bureaucracy and just hand over the cash. For illegal transactions, all around Martyrs' Sq and in the main souk you will be pestered by touts wanting to indulge in a little pecuniary naughtiness. Just take care. **AMEX** is in the Sudan Airways Building, Fardos Balkis St (0900-1330, 1700-2000) – see the Central Damascus map, p145. They cannot change money here, although you can have your mail delivered to this address (PO Box 1373).

● **Post** The GPO (0800-2000 daily except on Friday when it closes at 1300) is to the north of the Hejaz Railway Station on al-Jabiri St. For Poste Restante, bring your passport. The parcel office is round the corner.

● **Laundry** There is a launderette next to the al-Haramain Hotel, which many say is good value.

● **Photography** Off Port Said St is a small paved road full of photo stores and camera shops. Check expiry dates if you're buying film; there is a lot of very old film stocked in Damascus.

● **Telephone** The 24-hour telephone office is on al-Nasr Ave, to the east of the Hejaz station. These days foreigners are encouraged to use the phonecard phones; if you don't, be prepared to wait for an hour or two to

---

❏ **Embassies**
* **Australia** (☎ 6660238) al-Farabi St, al-Mazzeh
* **Canada** (☎ 2236851) Fayez Mansur St, al-Mazzeh
* **Egypt** (☎ 3332932) Abu Rumanah St, al-Muhajirin; **visa**: 0900-1100 Sun-Thu, one photo, S£725, collect 1400 same day.
* **Jordan** (☎ 3334642) Abu Rumanah St, al-Muhajirin; **visa**: 0900-1400 Sun-Thu, one photo, same-day process, costs: Aus free, Can S£1300, UK S£900, US S£1100.Note that the staff here are adept at ripping off the unwary.
* **UK** (☎ 3712561/2/3) Muhammad Kord'Ali St, al-Muhajirin
* **USA** (☎ 3332814/15) Ata al-Ayouby St, al-Muhajirin

be connected via the operator. For local calls, the rusty orange phone boxes outside the GPO actually work.

● **Tourist information** The main tourist office is on 29 May St near al-Azmeh Sq ساحة العزمه. There is a smaller branch in a side road to the east of the Ministry of Tourism Building, which is situated on Shukri al-Kuwatli St. Both branches are open from 0800-1900, closed Fridays.

● **Visa extensions and re-entry permits** For extensions ranging from 15 days to 1 month go to the **Immigration Dept** (0800-1400) on Filastin St (شارع فلسطين) one block west of the main bus station (see map, p141). The process takes one day and costs S£25. Three photos are required. For any other visa requirements, visit the **Immigration Office** opposite the Grand Ghaze Hotel (see Central Damascus map, p145). If you have a Lebanese visa, a re-entry permit enabling you to come back to Syria is available from here. It costs S£10, no photos are required, and the whole procedure takes only about 45 minutes.

> ❑ **The Damascene bath scene**
> If you're beginning to smell like a camel you'll be pleased to know that the Damascene bath scene is alive and splashing. Prices are usually printed by the entrance; as a foreigner, expect to pay about S£200 for the works.
>
> There are some wonderful baths in the Old City. The most famous is the 11th-century **Hammam Nehruddin** (حمام نور الدين). One peek inside the sumptuous interior and you'll want to strip naked then and there, but be warned: German tour groups regularly poke their lenses round the door to snap away at the palatial surroundings, which can be a bit disconcerting if you happen to be wearing only a revealing towelette at the time. Remember to smile. This bath has women-only times; ask at the door for details.
>
> Another historical bath is the **al-Malik Azzaher Hammam** near the Madrassa of Baybars. Unfortunately, their staff range from the unfriendly to the over-friendly, with no one in between. A better bet is round the corner at the **Hammam al-Selsleh** (حمام السلسلة), to the north of the Grand Mosque. The masseuse/washer here is very thorough, and will scrub down parts of your body that even you didn't know you had.
>
> There is also a women-only bath, **Hammam Keimarieh** (حمام الخيمرية), in a side street opposite the Madrassa of al-Fattiyeh. It has no sign, so look out for a curtain draped across a doorway. According to one recent foreign visitor there wasn't much bathing going on when she visited, although there were a couple of women steaming vegetables in the sauna.

WHERE TO STAY

Budget hotels

In a vine-covered alley off al-Ittihad St are a number of stylish residences, built in traditional Damascene fashion with an open central courtyard. If it wasn't for the modern appliances you could believe that you've been transported back 400 years. The *al-Haramain* فندق الحرمين [1] (☎ 2229487

☎ 2319489) is the ace in the pack, and has become a fixture on the travellers' circuit. Clean, quiet and cheap (S£150/200/325 for dorm/sgl/dbl),
it also has a useful 'travellers' tips' book for you to peruse. The only
downside is the state of the old metal beds – 'like being shot in the hip'
said one guest after an uncomfortable night. Nearby the **al-Rabie** [2] (☎
2218373), and round the corner the **al-Saadeh** [3] (☎ 218373), both offer
similar accommodation but without the charm of the Haramain.

If these are full, search amongst the warren of buildings surrounding
Martyrs' Square. Beware: many buildings say 'Hotel' on the outside,
whereas 'brothel' is what you find on the inside. Avoid a sticky situation
by staying at one of the following: the friendly **Zaid Hotel** فندق زايد [4] (☎
2229875) is the cheapest at S£100pp, but here you may have to contend
with not one but millions of uninvited bedfellows: bed bugs.

Nearby, the **al-Ahram** فندق الاهرام [5] (☎ 2217626) on al-Nasr St is OK,
although it is not unknown for the manager to agree to one price (usually about S£250pp), and then try for another when you pay your bill. The
rooms are big, the en suite sink small, and the beds hard. Avoid the noisy
front rooms if possible.

Just west of Martyrs' Sq is the immaculate **Grand Ghaze** فندق غزة الكبير
[6] (☎ 2214581). A lot of effort has obviously gone into the decor, with
matching curtains draped over every available opening (S£375 dbl with
claustrophobic shower). The **Zahraa** فندق الزهران [7] (☎ 2225375), which is
up on the fifth floor of a high-rise building near the square, is adequate if
the others are full.

Medium and top-range hotels

The **Amal** فندق الأمل [8] (☎ 2215880) has been highly recommended by a
number of people, although many have made the same complaint too: that
the rooms directly above the al-Arabi Restaurant are far too noisy. Rooms
are US$15/22/25 sgl/dbl/tpl, all en suite. For a little more peace check out
the **Hamra Hotel** [9] (☎ 217742), on Furat St behind the GPO.

The top place in town is the **Cham Palace** [10] (☎ 232300), next to
al-Azmeh Square. It even has a cinema incorporated into one wing.
Rooms are US$210/240 sgl/dbl plus 10% tax.

WHERE TO EAT

Central Damascus

There is a fine array of food hidden amidst the dust and diesel of downtown Damascus. All around Martyrs' Square are a number of brightly-lit
restaurants, replete with mirrors and uniformed staff. Some, such as **al-
Arabi Restaurant** [e], are OK, but be careful as rip-offs are a speciality
of many. On the north side of the square you'll find a fruit and veg market, and nearby are some cheap chicken and shwaarma joints.

A Damascene speciality is the Syrian burger (S£15): a lump of meat, (the origin of which is probably best left undiscovered), garnished with an egg, chilli sauce and other bits and pieces. The *juice bar* [f] near the Hejaz Station on al-Barudi St شارع البارودي serves them, as does the one on al-Ittihad St [f]. Also near the station are a couple of other cheap places [g], including one which specialises in that dubious Damascus' delicacy: sheep's testicles.

For those who are literally fed up with Arabian fare, there are a number of palatable Western alternatives. On the fourth floor of the *Ala'a Tower* [h] is a restaurant where the pizzas (S£125) are almost as good as the view, and there are a couple more places west of the Cham Palace Hotel on Maysalun St: *Pizza Hat* (sic) and *Roma Pizza* [i]. Try Roma's S£110 Super Supreme Pizza.

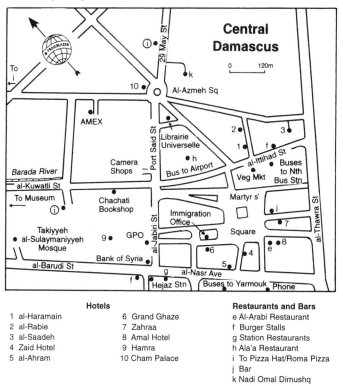

Hotels		Restaurants and Bars
1 al-Haramain	6 Grand Ghaze	e Al-Arabi Restaurant
2 al-Rabie	7 Zahraa	f Burger Stalls
3 al-Saadeh	8 Amal Hotel	g Station Restaurants
4 Zaid Hotel	9 Hamra	h Ala'a Restaurant
5 al-Ahram	10 Cham Palace	i To Pizza Hat/Roma Pizza
		j Bar
		k Nadi Omal Dimushq

Old City

There are a couple of convenient snack stalls in the Old City that provide tasty sustenance for the weary sightseer. If you like felafel you'll be cock-a-hoop at the extraordinary size of those on offer on شارع الخيمرية al-Keimarieh St ([a] on Old City map opposite). For S£25 you could be in felafel heaven. Also on al-Keimarieh St is an excellent *café* [b]. Every evening at 5pm a story-teller recites a tale (in Arabic, of course) to the Syrian throng, who sit motionless and puff on nargileh looking a little bored. Unfortunately, tour groups have also discovered this cafe but it's still a good spot to chill out.

On Straight St is a wonderful *Pizza Bakery* [c], where for as little as S£4 you can indulge in mouth-watering Syrian pizza.

Finally, for something completely different head for the *Ommayad Palace Restaurant* [d]. It is a little kitsch – from the ridiculously-attired minstrel strumming on the aoud to the midget staff who scuttle around between the tables – but you'll experience no other restaurant like it on this route through the Near East. There's a S£700 all-you-can-eat buffet, or it's S£350 for lunch.

NIGHTLIFE

Damascus has three main watering-holes. The *Australian Embassy* holds a regular Thursday evening session, and rumour has it that other embassies may follow suit. On Martyrs' Square above the *Siyaha Hotel* [j] is a gloomy little den full of contemplative Algerians smoking nargileh. And lastly, there's the *Nadi Omal Dimashq* [k] (Working Men's Club) next to the al-Majid Hotel off 29 May St. A beer here is only S£45, and they have outdoor seating, too.

WHAT TO SEE

Old City

Whilst Damascus lacks the glorious temples of Jerusalem, the imperial monuments of ancient Istanbul and the hurly-burly of Islamic Cairo, it also lacks the tourist hordes; and for that simple reason a walk through the medieval alleyways of the Old City can be magical.

The walls of the city and many of the buildings within them were built by the Mamlukes, although some of the city gates are Roman. Of the other buildings, most are Ayyubid or Ottoman. Despite determined destruction by the Mongols and French over the years the Old City has lost none of its beauty.

The Ommayad Mosque المسجد الأموي

(Closed Fri at noon during prayer-times; S£10). One of the attractions of this mosque is its lack of austerity. After Israel's Dome of the Rock, this

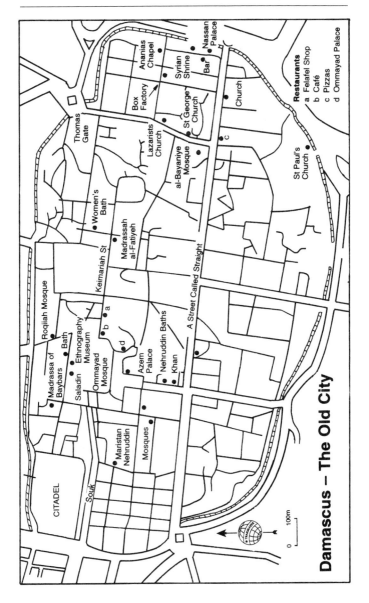

Damascus – The Old City

Ananias Chapel
Nassan Palace
Syrian Shrine
Bar
Box Factory
St George Church
Church
Thomas Gate
Lazarists Church
al-Bayaniye Mosque
St Paul's Church
Women's Bath
Madrassah al-Fatiyeh
Keimariah St
A Street Called Straight
Roqiiah Mosque
Bath
Ethnography Museum
Madrassa of Baybars
Saladin
Ommayad Mosque
Azem Palace
Nehruddin Baths
Khan
Maristan Nehruddin
Mosques
CITADEL
Souk

Restaurants
a Felafel Shop
b Café
c Pizzas
d Ommayad Palace

0   100m

was the first great mosque of Islam, built in AD705 by the Ommayad Caliph al-Walid as a celebration of Islam's victories in the Near East. The toil and craftsmanship that went into its construction are obvious in every carefully-crafted mosaic and panel. It is said that al-Walid used only Byzantine artists, for at that time they were better than any Muslim craftsman.

Like many religious sites, the grounds of the mosque have seen a number of temples through the years. The Aramaean god, Haddad, had his temple here first (ninth century BC) who was later identified by the Romans with their own god, Jupiter. You can see the ruins of this Roman Temple of Jupiter between the mosque and Souk al-Hamidiyeh St; this building was in turn converted by the Byzantines into a church dedicated to John the Baptist. Finally, the Ommayads destroyed the church but kept the saint's head for luck. (Supposedly discovered in a crypt during the construction of the mosque, **John the Baptist's head** is now housed in a small marble structure inside). Despite fire (1893) and earthquake, the Ommayad Mosque continues to serve as a centre for worship to this day.

For most visitors, the highlights are the gorgeous golden mosaics surrounding the courtyard that shimmer in the sunlight during the afternoon. Although they follow the essential iconoclastic laws of Islam (ie there are no human figures) the work is undoubtedly that of Byzantine craftsmen. The scenes are believed to depict fantastical versions of Damascus; their version of the Barada River is preferable to the real thing.

Of the three structures that stand in the courtyard, only the octagonal building, the treasury, dates back to the Ommayad Dynasty, and may even be Byzantine in origin. Its original purpose is unknown.

Entering the mosque, one is immediately struck by the sense of space and lack of clutter. It is also very cool, very tranquil, and the soft carpets underfoot are very comfy – a combination that may well induce you to do as the locals do: sit down, relax, and fall asleep.

Saladin's Tomb قبر صلاح الدين

Your ticket to the Ommayad Mosque also entitles you to visit the red-domed mausoleum of Saladin, Islam's greatest leader during the Crusader invasions. It is an indication of the indifference the Arabs feel towards Saladin (who was a Kurd) that last century's restoration was not financed from their pockets but by the German Emperor Kaiser Wilhelm II. The original mausoleum, which dates back to 1193 and the Ayyubid Dynasty, had fallen into a sad state of disrepair prior to the Kaiser's intervention.

Azem Palace قصر عازم

(0800-1600, closed Tues; S£200,S£25 students). Hidden amongst the jumble of terraced buildings to the south of the Ommayad Mosque is the Ottoman pasha's residence, Azem Palace. Built in 1749 by Assad Pasha al-Azem, it was subsequently used by all the Syrian pashas until the fall of the Ottoman Empire and was later used by Syria's man-who-would-be-king, the Arab revolutionary Faisal (see p29), as his palace.

The black and white building surrounds a central courtyard. As was common, the palace was split into two sections; one part was for receiving visitors, the other housing private living quarters. Within the buildings is yet another **Museum of Popular Tradition**, although this one is better than most. Don't miss the Islamic art collection either, which includes a grain of rice on which is written six lines of poetry, and an eggshell which has an entire chapter from the Koran on it. Amongst the rooms open to the public are the labyrinthine baths and the room used by King Faisal during his brief reign.

Chapel of Ananias كنيسة الاتانياس

(0900-1700; donations welcome). Reputedly the former home of Ananias, a Damascene Christian who, on God's orders, blessed Saul and restored his sight to him (Acts 9), the chapel is now maintained by Franciscan monks. A room to the right contains scenes from the life of Paul (as Saul was later known) with explanations in French only.

St Paul's Chapel كنيسة سانت باولس

This chapel marks the spot where Paul was lowered on a basket to escape from the Jews, but there's little to see. The easiest way to find it is to walk out of the Old City through Bab Sharqi, turn right and continue for five minutes. The entrance to the chapel is round the back, inside the Old City.

❏ **The life of St Paul**

St Paul's contribution to the history of the Middle East was immense, to Christianity vital. With Roman citizenship (he was born in Tarsus in modern-day Turkey) and Greek as his mother tongue he was able to spread the word to Greece and Rome, which eventually led to the conversion of the Roman and the Byzantine empires. He was also the first apostle to attempt to convert Gentiles as well as the Jews, ensuring both the survival and the growth of Christianity.

It all started when this former tentmaker 'saw the light' on the way to Damascus, cAD33, where he was about to indulge his penchant for persecuting Christians. Indeed the light he saw was so strong that he was blinded, and had to spend some time recuperating in a house on 'a Street called Straight'. There he was visited by Ananias, who blessed him and restored his sight. Paul so enraged the Jewish population of Damascus after his conversion that he had to escape from their clutches by being lowered outside the city walls in a basket.

His next 25 years were spent touring round the Near East, preaching, praying, and writing his Epistles of advice and admonishment to the Corinthians, Ephesians and many others. As a result Christianity swept through the area but his work made him many enemies. In AD57 he was arrested in Jerusalem by the Romans and sent to Rome. His Roman citizenship did not save him and he was executed on Emperor Nero's orders in AD60.

The Mausoleum of Lady Roqiiah ضريح السيدة روقية

This mausoleum of the great granddaughter of Mohammed is the only Shi'ite monument in Damascus' Old City, and unlike any other Islamic building here. It's fascinating, with an amazingly over-the-top gilt and marble interior which is matched by the excessive reactions of the faithful who weep and wail at the tomb, throwing veils and scarves over the cenotaph and pushing money through the surrounding metal grill. Many have made a special pilgrimage from Iran. Needless to say, photographs are strictly forbidden, shoes must be removed, and women should be covered from head to toe before entering. Robes are provided.

Maristan Nehruddin نور الدين مريمي

(0830-1400, closed Tues; S£100, S£10 students). Despite the cruel appearance of some of the implements on display here, this building was not a place of torture but a hospital. When it was opened by Nehruddin in 1154 it was the most advanced in the region. Not only were the patients subject to the best medical care – including music to help them forget their ills – but on leaving they were given clothes and money to help them on their way. Amongst the implements on display are a selection of teeth-pulling pliers and circumcision scissors (both of which bring tears to the eyes just to look at), as well as a supply of natural remedies such as lizard's skin (supposedly an aphrodisiac). There's also a small collection of lucky talismans; superstition still played an important part in the healing process in those days. Labels are in French and Arabic only.

Other sights in the Old City

A couple of madrassas stand opposite each other near the Azzaher Hammam. The **Madrassa and Mausoleum of Baybars** مدرسة البيبارس , the Mamluke's most successful sultan, is dated by a plaque on the front to 1277, whilst the **Madrassa and Mausoleum of Sultan al-Adel Ayyubid**, Saladin's brother, is dated 1222. It is possible to see both tombs, although a little baksheesh may be necessary.

Down in the Christian quarter are a number of churches representing almost all of the different denominations. There is also **Nassan Palace** (قصر نعسان), a stately home with a small, elaborately-decorated courtyard. A couple of inlay factories stand nearby. Finally, in the north-west corner of the city stands the **Citadel**, an Ayyubid construction which was heavily restored by the Mamlukes. Unfortunately, it has been closed to the public for a number of years.

The National Museum المتحف الوطني

(0900-1600 winter, 0900-1800 summer; closed Tues, and Fri between 1115-1300; S£200, S£25 students; see map on p141 for location). Unless your French is very good it is worth hiring a guide for this museum which contains Syria's best collection of archaeological finds and national treasures. The monumental entrance to the museum originally stood as the main gateway of Qasr al-Hair al-Gharbi, a castle in the Syrian Desert near Palmyra. Inside the building almost every era of Syria's past is represented: the prehistoric skeleton of a two-year old infant found in a cave in north-west Syria, a reconstructed underground Palmyrene tomb, and a reconstructed Ottoman room. There is also a contemporary arts section, which isn't very good but does at least offer the chance to see pictures that do not portray President Assad.

Takiyyeh al-Sulaymaniyyeh Mosque مسجد اتقيا • السليمانية
This mosque is yet another example of the genius of Sinan, the architect whose graceful buildings adorn Istanbul. Built in 1554 using alternate layers of black and white stone, it has lost little of its charm down the centuries despite the incorporation of an **Army Museum** in its grounds and a craft market in the old caravanserai next door.

Excursions from Damascus
Quneitraالقنيطرة This town, 35km from Damascus and the capital of the Golan Heights region, marks the northernmost point captured by the Israelis during the Six Day War of 1967. It was devastated during the fighting, and today it is little more than a ghost town. The Syrian government is still sensitive about the incident, and consequently a permit is required from the office near Mansour St (near the British embassy). The process should only take ten minutes; bring your passport.

A microbus leaves from near the Karnak Bus Station, costing S£20 for the one-hour trip.

Maalula معلوله, 27km from Damascus, has neither historical significance nor any building of particular interest although the way the village sprawls vertically up one side of the valley is extremely photogenic (see opposite p97). Instead, tour buses come to this quiet Christian enclave to hear the locals, for Maalula is one of only three villages in Syria where Aramaic, a Semitic language and the mother tongue of Jesus, is spoken.

There are also two convents of note: the Convent of St Sergius houses a small monastery with a tiny Byzantine church, and the Convent of St Thekla offers wonderful views of the valley from the cliffs nearby.

You may feel, however, that all this is not compensation enough for the haemorrhoid-inducing hour-long bus ride but it is pleasantly peaceful after Damascus. To get here, take a bus from Bilal Sq (S£10). Check when the last bus from Maalula leaves (usually about 1700), or you could be stranded here with only the ghastly five-star Safir Hotel to sleep in.

MOVING ON
Buses There are many bus stations in Damascus, each serving different destinations with different classes of buses. The main terminus, to the

west of the Hejaz station, is used by Karnak buses, servis taxis, and Pullman buses. Local buses heading north, and east to Palmyra, leave from the station to the north of the Abbasine Stadium. Local buses to Dera'a, and occasionally Bosra, use the station near al-Yarmouk Sq. There are also a couple of 'luxury-bus' stations, as marked on the map.

● **To Bosra and Dera'a**   Buses to these two destinations leave from Yarmuk Sq. The fare to Dera'a is S£30. There are very few buses to Bosra (S£40). Luxury buses to Bosra leave from under the President's Bridge on al-Kuwatli St, west of the museum, for S£45 (six buses per day).

● **To Lebanon**   Karnak operate two buses to Beirut, at 0730 and 1530, for S£125. The trip takes approximately four hours. The servis taxis from here charge S£200. Luxury buses also ply the route, beginning from the station near the national museum. The fare is also S£200.

> ❏ **Train – The Hejaz Railway**   If you take only one train journey in the whole of the Levant, this should be it. Closed for many years, the Jordan and Syrian governments recently agreed to reopen the historic Hejaz rail link between Damascus and Amman. Like every other train leaving Damascus, the Hejaz train currently stops a few km out of town at Kaddam. It is hoped that it will run to the Ottoman Hejaz station one day, and you can buy tickets from here.
>
> The train departs just once a week, on Sunday at 0700. There is only one class (S£160). It is painfully slow: the trip takes ten hours, delays permitting!

South Syria

BOSRA بصرة الشام

Most people know of Bosra as the site of a huge citadel-cum-theatre, the venue of Syria's biggest arts festival. But although the citadel is Bosra's icing, one should not miss the cake itself: the village is a fascinating array of tumbledown basalt cottages, many incorporating pieces of Roman ruins in their structure.

Bosra's quaintly-dilapidated state belies a glorious past. It first flourished under the Nabataeans and was later the capital of the Roman province of Arabia (AD106), 'Nova Trajana Bostra'. It then became the centre of a Byzantine diocese, and following the Muslim conversion it was an important pit-stop on the Haj route. Pilgrims would come here to see the village where a Nestorian monk told Mohammed that he would be a prophet. The Mongols subsequently destroyed much of the city in 1261, and as neighbouring Dera'a grew in size and popularity, Bosra declined.

There is a rumour that the authorities are going to drive the villagers out of Bosra, just as they did at the Crac des Chevaliers. Since much of

Bosra's charm is derived from the fact that this is a 'living-museum', where day-to-day life continues amongst the ruins, this would be a great shame. Visit now, just in case the authorities go ahead with their plan.

Where to stay

Amazingly, it is possible to sleep inside the Citadel. At the back of the *citadel's café* there is a typical 'Bedouin-style' lounge, where for S£125 (after haggling) you can unroll your sleeping bag, or use the blankets provided. There is nothing to stop you using the café's kitchen either. It may not be the most comfortable place in Syria, but where else do you have the chance to sleep inside a real Roman theatre?

The Citadel

The bus drops you off by the centrepiece of Bosra, the marvellously-preserved citadel. The 15,000-capacity theatre that occupies the centre was built by the Romans during the second century AD, but the defensive walls that surround it are Muslim. The Ommayads were the first to build fortifications, the Abbassids extended them, the Fatimids dug the moat and the Ayyubids built the nine surrounding towers to house their troops. These defences were good enough to repel two attempted invasions during the Crusades, but fared less well when the Mongols arrived in 1261.

Today the theatre has been restored to much of its former size and splendour, although originally the stage was covered with marble and sheltered by a wooden roof. The defensive towers are mostly closed off, although there are two museums and a café in those that are open.

The village

This lies north-west of the citadel's entrance. It is built amongst a diverse collection of ruins. These include a **Nabataean Gate**, formerly part of the palace of the last Nabataean king, Rabbel II; Roman ruins such as a **Colonnaded Street**, **baths** and a **Nymphaeum**; a Byzantine **cathedral** which was, in fact, the prototype for Justinian's Aya Sofya in Istanbul and a fourth-century **monastery**, where Mohammed met his prophetic Nestorian; and two mosques, the **Mosque of Fatimah** and the **Mosque of Omar**. This last mosque is said to be one of the three oldest mosques in the Islamic world, and indeed inscriptions on the pillars date it to about AD720; most of what you see, however, is about 500 years younger.

Moving on

A bus from here to Dera'a costs S£25 (last bus 1500) and takes 90 minutes. The last bus to Damascus is at 1730.

DERA'A درعا

Syria's southern border town was built to remind us that travelling isn't always fun, although your time in Dera'a will probably not be as bad as

Lawrence of Arabia's, who suffered an unpleasant encounter here with a lusty Turkish Bey and a bullwhip. There's little to do except spend your last few Syrian pounds on shwaarma and give a farewell hug to the government agent who may have been tailing you since Aleppo.

The bus station lies a S£5 taxi-ride away from the town centre. To catch the bus into town (S£2), cross over the main street to the bus stop.

If you wish to stay there are a two squalid hotels on the main street. The **al-Ahram** has a manager who speaks a little English; the manager of the **al-Salaam**, further down on the opposite side of the road, speaks none. Threaten to go to the al-Salaam, and the boss of the al-Ahram will soon drop to a reasonable price – and it probably works the other way round too. Both will charge S£150 for B&B (that's bed and bugs, not breakfast). For **transport to Jordan**, see p184.

❏ **Other attractions in Syria**
This country strains under the weight of ancient sites, there's so much to see.
   Much of what we know about Syria's distant past has been gleaned from the 15,000 clay tablets found at Ebla, on the Aleppo-Hama road 50km south of Aleppo. These stele date back to the third millennium BC, are written in Sumerian, and even include dictionaries of other tongues.
   Other ancient sites include: Ain Dara, a second millennium BC Hittite temple that supplied many of the basalt statues in the Aleppo museum; Ras Shamra (ancient Ugarit) where a small stele was discovered, on which was written the first alphabet (now on display in the Damascus museum); Doura Europos, a Graeco/Roman settlement on the Euphrates; and Mari, the remains of an important Mesopotamian city which also lies on the Euphrates.
   Don't overlook the Mediterranean coast, either. Lattakia is Syria's main port, and the ideal base to explore Ugarit (above) and other sites. South from here is Tartus, near the Lebanese border, surrounded by attractive fishing villages.

THE BORDER – SYRIA AND LEBANON

● **Syria to Lebanon** Before leaving Syria ensure you have a visa that allows you to return (see p143). Coaches and servis taxis leave from most major towns; a servis takes less time to be checked through at the border.
● **Lebanon to Syria** It is possible to turn up at this border without a visa for Syria and still be permitted to cross, but only after a lengthy wait (five to six hours) while border staff contact Damascus. There does not seem to be any hard and fast rule about who gets a visa at the border: some get nothing, some receive three-day transit visas whereas others get the full fifteen-day tourist visas. Increase your own chances by bringing a letter of recommendation from your embassy with you.

For the foreseeable future, the **Syria/Israel-Palestine border** is closed.

PART 5: LEBANON

Facts about the country

Pity the nation that is full of beliefs and empty of religion **Khalil Gibran** *The Garden of the Prophet*

Lebanon has some of the most dramatic scenery anywhere in the world; they say you can go skiing in the mountains in the morning and then cool off in the gentle waters of the Mediterranean in the afternoon. It also has towns as ancient as any in Syria, an example of Corinthian architecture at Baalbek that more than equals the splendour of Turkey's Ephesus, and the southern ports of Sidon and Tyre which feature more frequently in the Bible than most places in Israel. Visitors will also find the food delicious, the travelling cheap and the Lebanese people as wonderfully warm and generous as their Syrian neighbours. Unfortunately, 17 years of brutal

---

❏ **Country ratings – Lebanon**

● **Highlights** The temple at Baalbek and Lebanon's crazy capital, Beirut, are both 'must sees'. For an unusual get-away-from-it-all retreat, consider, too, the mountain village of Becharré, where the air is pure and the hiking invigorating.

● **Expense ✔✔✔✔** Possible US$10-15 per day but more temptations to spend, especially in Beirut.

● **Value for money ✔✔** Accommodation, alcohol and food are the three main expenses for travellers.

● **English communication ✔✔** You'll often have more success using French than English, especially along the coast. French street names still used in Beirut.

● **Getting around ✔✔✔✔** Although the transport network was fairly shattered, all the big cities are connected by servis taxis or buses. It is only in the Kadisha Valley that you'll probably have to resort to hitch-hiking.

● **Travellers' scene ✔** A fairly traveller-free zone at the moment.

● **Visible history ✔✔✔** The evidence of Lebanon's recent history is everywhere. Much of this rubble hides more ancient ruins, particularly in Beirut. Despite this, there is plenty to occupy the historian. Check out Baalbek, Byblos and the Dog River for the highlights.

● **Woman alone ✔✔✔** This is a male-dominated culture but, like Syria, the attention tends to be friendly and non-threatening.

● **Good food ✔✔✔✔** Vies with Turkey for the honour of producing the best quality food in the region. Street food – Lebanese pizzas, felafels and kebabs – second to none.

● **Vegetarian friendly ✔✔✔✔**

war has left Lebanon with a huge image problem, and very few tourists come to experience these treasures. A glance at the postcards sold by the Beirut street vendors gives a good indication of how much the country has suffered; produced in the early 1970s, they depict pothole-free boulevards with gleaming whitewashed high-rise buildings and lush green palm trees. It's a cruel mockery of the shattered downtown area that confronts today's visitor.

Nevertheless, this is a fascinating opportunity to see a country in transition. Bomb-damaged buildings now rub cornices with shiny new structures as Lebanon undergoes a huge rejuvenation process. Much of the infrastructure is in a state of disrepair – and that part which has been mended is still unreliable – but this all makes for a wild ride, and an unpredictable, unforgettable visit.

Modern Lebanon

Before it hit the self-destruct button, Lebanon was *the* place to be in the Near East. With Israel in a state of turmoil, Lebanon was where businessmen and holidaymakers alike came to enjoy the balmy waters of the eastern Mediterranean. It was rich, beautiful and glamorous. As a poignant reminder of these halcyon days, Pepe's Fishing Club, the seaside restaurant in Byblos, is decorated with pictures of its former clients: David Niven, Michael Caine, Peter Sellers, Brigitte Bardot – all the jet-setters of the era came to Beirut for their holidays.

And then, of course, it disintegrated. So what exactly has 17 years of violence actually achieved? Parliament is still divided on religious grounds, with an equal number of Christians and Muslims sharing the power. The Syrians continue to maintain a large presence in Lebanon, where they are resented by the Lebanese who consider them an occupying force rather than peace keepers; and fighting still persists in the very south between Hizbollah and Israel, where as recently as April 1996 Israel launched 'Operation Grapes of Wrath', bombing Beirut and South Lebanon for 16 days.

On the plus side, the country does appear to be enjoying a greater degree of stability than at any other time in the last 20 years. Israel's bombing campaigns seem to have united the country in a way that no peace treaty ever could, and while the weapons of war have not been destroyed, just cached away, both Christians and Muslims agree that they have too much to lose to resume hostilities. Hizbollah still enjoys huge grass-roots support, a popularity earned by their extensive social welfare activities such as building new hospitals and funding schools. Much of the credit for this transformation is due to Elias Hrawi and Rafik Hariri, both still in office, and both important instruments in helping Lebanon find peace and prosperity.

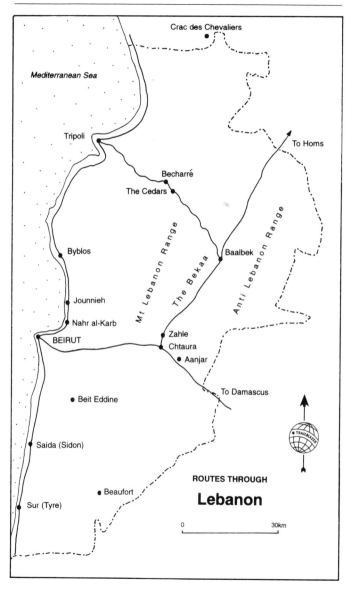

Crac des Chevaliers

Mediterranean Sea

To Homs

Tripoli

Becharré

The Cedars

Mt Lebanon Range

The Bekaa

Anti Lebanon Range

Byblos

Baalbek

Jounnieh

Nahr al-Karb

BEIRUT

Zahle

Chtaura

Aanjar

To Damascus

Beit Eddine

Saida (Sidon)

Beaufort

Sur (Tyre)

ROUTES THROUGH

Lebanon

0   30km

GEOGRAPHICAL BACKGROUND

Lebanon is a tiny, mountainous country. At just over 10,000 square km it is about a third of the size of Portugal, and crammed into this space are two parallel mountain ranges running north to south – the Lebanon and Anti-Lebanon ranges – separated by the Bekaa Valley. The waters of the Mediterranean lap the western shore, Syria lies to the west and north, whilst the southern border remains a bone of contention with Israel and the two countries are currently separated by a UN buffer zone.

RELIGION

Although no accurate census has been taken for some time, the largest religious group is now believed to be the Shi'ite Muslims, of which the majority in Lebanon are the poor and under privileged.

The Mt Lebanon Range is the homeland of the Maronite Christians, a branch of Roman Catholicism that fled persecution in Syria. There are also a large number of Druze (see p308) in the Shouf Mountains, and Sunni Muslims in Tripoli and the north.

❏ **Practical information – Lebanon**

● **Visa** Usually valid for 15 days

● **Currency** Lebanese Pound (LE). The US dollar is accepted everywhere too, and in many hotels that is all they will accept. US$1=1550LE. UK£1=2580LE

● **Banks** Lebanon is the best place to buy **foreign currency**, in particular US dollars and Syrian pounds (where the rate for the latter is equivalent to the black-market rate in Damascus). Be very careful however: there are lots of fake US$100 bills floating around the country. Most banks refuse to change money, and instead you'll be sent to one of the high street exchange booths. These places seem to remain open nearly all the time. Cash is usually changed without charge, although there is a US$2-5 commission on travellers' cheques. **Credit cards** are accepted in many of the shops and better hotels. The Credit du Liban allows you to withdraw money on your Visa card, for which they charge US$5 commission.

● **Time** GMT + 2 (GMT + 3 in summer)

● **Electricity** 110/220 volts AC, 50 Hz. Intermittent!

● **Post** The postal service is still struggling to find its feet after the war. There are two post offices in Beirut and one in Tripoli that have a fairly good reputation but the others are distinctly unreliable.

● **Telephone** There is currently no state telephone service, although an office near the GPO in Beirut is opening soon. The rates per minute here are: 5000LE for Australia, and 4000LE for UK, USA and Canada. To make a local call, ask any shopkeeper or hotel; it usually costs about 1000LE for a short call.

● **Warning** Everywhere you go you will encounter roadblocks belonging either to the government, Hizbollah or the UN. Most of the time the soldiers will smile sweetly and wave you through but you should always carry your passport with you in case they need to see ID.

LOCAL TRANSPORT

The buses are up and running once more, although at present they serve the more popular routes between the major cities only. This means there is still a big demand for Lebanon's ubiquitous mode of transport, the servis taxi. These shared taxis operate both within the major cities and between them. You'll find them a cheap way to get around – the only trouble is, they are indistinguishable from the more expensive private taxis. To find out if the car is a servis taxi, shove your head through the window (making sure it's open first) and shout 'servis?'. Once inside, immediately proffer the correct fare to prevent arguments later on. (See p161 for information on fares in Beirut.)

Hitching is also easy in Lebanon, although the first car that stops will usually be a servis taxi anyway.

❏ **Route through Lebanon**
Because Lebanon is so small we have not followed a particular route through the country. Many travellers use Beirut as a base and make excursions from there.

Beirut
بيروت

Paradoxically, it is one of the most precarious places to visit, and yet in a great many ways it is one of the most pleasant. The visitor prepared to risk the hazards of civil strife will be enriched by the experience **Traveller's Guide to the Middle East, 1980**

Beirut is a delicious cocktail: take the heady exoticism of the Orient, add the frenetic pace of New York, a dash of Rio's glamour, a sprinkling of Los Angeles' materialism and mix with liberal amounts of Parisian style. It's the perfect destination for any traveller who has overdosed on ancient ruins, for this is one city that definitely does not dwell on the past. After the best part of fifty years spent fighting over religion, the citizens have reverted to worshipping at the altar of Mammon. Instead of mosques, mausoleums and monasteries this city has clubs, casinos and conspicuous consumption.

At the moment, of course, it is still a bit of a mess – not so much a shoreline of chic as a riviera of rubble. But Beirut is anything but a ghost town. The downtown area trembles with the roar of construction companies rebuilding the 'Paris of the East', while Hamra is a cacophony of car horns and street vendors. And this all goes on against a backdrop of neon-lit devastation. It's a fascinating metropolis, one which is both poignant and uplifting, tragic and hopeful. Don't miss it.

HISTORY

Beirut's rich past has previously lain hidden under the pavements of the modern metropolis, and the recent war has at least given historians a chance to uncover a little more before the concrete returns again. Starting out as an unimportant Phoenician fishing village, the town first came to prominence under the Romans. For 700 years the city flourished as the home of a famous Roman law school which also became renowned for the hedonistic lifestyle of its citizens. It is a reputation that Beirutis still go to great lengths to maintain today.

A huge earthquake in AD551 put an end to this Roman holiday. Of the few survivors, most were swept away by an enormous tidal wave that arrived a few minutes later. Roman Beirut never recovered. Throughout the subsequent invasions by the Arabs (AD632), Crusaders (1110) and Mamlukes (1291) it remained a relatively insignificant settlement, and it was not until the latter half of the Ottoman era that the city began to revive. As the Ottoman grasp on the Levant weakened, so other colonial powers began to seize control, with Beirut falling first to Mohammed Ali's Egyptians in 1832 (see p305) and then into British hands (1841). Foreign consulates began to open in the city and in 1866 the Syrian Protestant College (now the American University of Beirut – AUB) was founded, ensuring that Beirut was once again a centre of education and research in the Middle East.

Recognising Beirut's pre-eminence in Lebanon, the French made it the capital of their Mandate State in 1920. This was the beginning of an extraordinarily prosperous time for the city. The Gulf States viewed Beirut as a safer place than Israel to terminate their oil pipelines to the west, and this attracted an enormous amount of investment and commerce to the area. These were the halcyon days, where the East and the West would meet, get rich, and party till dawn. It was a melting pot of cultures, a hygienic, sanitised Orient for the Westerner and a den of Western-style immorality for the Arab.

Unfortunately, not everybody got their share of the spoils and a wide 'Belt of Misery' formed in the southern suburbs, home to a large Shi'ite community. Disaffected, they would turn their resentment into direct action during the war. The traumas suffered by Beirut during the 'events' (as they now call the war) have been well-documented, with the capital divided along a Green Line separating the Christians from the Muslims. The Israelis and Syrians both occupied the city for a while and various UN forces stepped in to try to calm the situation at different times.

(**Opposite**) **Top**: Along Beirut's Green Line the scars of battle are only too obvious. **Bottom**: The mosaic collection at Beit Eddine (see p169) contains some of the finest examples of the Byzantine art.

Today, much of Beirut resembles a building site as all evidence of fighting is torn down to make way for a gleaming new metropolis.

ORIENTATION

The city of Beirut is built on a promontory that juts out into the waters of the Mediterranean. The city is still very much divided by the Green Line that used to separate East and West Beirut during the war. Today most of this line is the Beirut Central District (BCD), the former downtown area that is undergoing the most intensive rebuilding programme. To the west is Hamra (الحمرة), the main shopping and hotel centre, and Raouche (روشة), an upmarket residential area where apartments cost upwards of two million dollars. You will also find the Pigeon Rocks here, where the Phoenicians are said to have kept their carrier pigeons.

East of the old Green Line lies the port district of al-Sahfi (الصحفي), home to a few budget hotels. South of Sahfi is the residential suburb of Ashrafieh (الشرفية), a quieter alternative to Hamra that largely escaped the ravages of the war. Even further east is Dora (الدورة), seldom visited by travellers except when a servis taxi north is required.

Coming from Syria, you will probably arrive at the bus station of Cola (كولا), south of Hamra; see the Beirut map on p164 for details.

LOCAL TRANSPORT

Beirut is the only city in Lebanon that has a local **bus service**. For Cola Station, buses leave from outside the tourist office and also from the Corniche (both 250LE). After Cola they continue to the National Museum ('Madhaf' المتحف – for 250LE), from where you can catch a bus to Dora (250LE), or to the airport (500LE).

Servis taxis are everywhere (see p159 for how to use one). The fare is a set 1000LE, although if you are travelling to Dora it rises to 1500LE.

Standard taxis are an expensive option in Beirut, and you have to haggle furiously to get a fair price. The gaps in the average taxi driver's knowledge of the area are quite astounding too, and you will often end up driving around in circles, asking passers-by for directions. It can all be very infuriating.

SERVICES   (Beirut ☎ area code 01)

● **Baths** The only bath here is on Rue Sheikh Elias Gasparo, and it's a little run down and seedy.
● **Bookshops** Beirut rivals Jerusalem as the finest place to buy reading

---

(**Opposite**) The six surviving pillars of Baalbek's Temple of Jupiter (see p177) are each over 22m tall.

material in the region. Possibly the best second hand store on this route through the Near East is the **Help Bookshop** on Rue Jeanne D'Arc, one of a number of bookstores in the area. It has been selling books to AUB students for about 35 years now, and the prices are usually low. The **Librairie du Liban** on Rue Hamra has the best selection of new books.

● **Car rental** The tourist office has brochures on car rental companies. Prices start at about US$35 per day.

● **Changing money** There are plenty of money-changers on Rue Hamra (شارع الحمرة), although it is imperative to ascertain the market rate and shop around for the best deal before you exchange. Be very careful when checking your money, too; it is not unknown for dealers to substitute a (worthless) foreign note amongst your change.

If you're arriving at Cola, the Karnak office can change money (cash only) but the rate is slightly lower than in town. The **AMEX** office is at the Gefinor Centre Block 'A', Clemenceau St PO Box 115865.

● **Post** Send mail from the main GPO (Mon-Thu 0800-1400, Fri 0800-1100, Sat 0800-1300) on Rue Riad el-Solh or from the AUB only (although the office on Rue Makdissi is said to be reliable). The main GPO also deals with Poste Restante, which is held in a shoebox at the back of the building.

● **Photography** Beirut is a good safe place to buy film, and most brands (except Fuji) are stocked here. There are a number of camera shops along Rue Hamra, some of which also do repairs.

● **Telephone** For international calls, try the **Beirut Book Fair**; their charges are often the lowest in town and there is no minimum call time. Alternatively, there is a phone office in the car park opposite the tourist office but there's a minimum three-minute charge here.

● **Tourist Information** The tourist offices in Lebanon are all much the same: staffed by polite and friendly English-speakers, and full of maps and leaflets from the 1970s. This one, on Rue Banque du Liban, is no different and open Mon-Fri 0900-1400, Sat 0900-1200.

● **Tours** A number of fledgling tour agencies have recently set up in Hamra offering, for about US$40 per day, 'trouble free' excursions to various destinations in Lebanon. Since most of the places they offer trips to are easy to reach by public transport anyway you're unlikely to encounter 'trouble' if you travel independently. Their guides, however, are usually

---

❑ **Embassies**

It is a good idea to check with your embassy on the current situation in parts of the Lebanon. You may also wish to register your arrival in the country with them.

● **Australia** (☎ 347080) 463 Rue Bliss, Hamra
● **Canada** (☎ 342112) Coolrite Bldg, 434 Jal el-Dib Highway
● **UK** (☎ 403640) Rabieh, No 8 St
● **USA** (☎ 402200) Aouncar, facing the Municipality

very knowledgeable and they have been recommended by some. Currently, Tania Travel is the market leader (☎ 219906).

● **Travel agencies** There are few agencies on Rue Hamra but Beirut is not the cheapest city to fly from (eg Beirut-London US$330 o/w). It's cheaper to fly out of Israel or Turkey.

● **Visa extensions** Your first port of call when extending your visa should be the **Sureté des Etrangers** (0900-1300 Mon-Fri) just down from the National Museum on Ave Abdallah Yafi.

WHERE TO STAY

Budget hotels

Whilst Hamra is once more bursting with hotels, budget travellers are forced to rummage amongst the ruins to the east of the Green Line to find a bed for the night. Some cheaper options have sprouted from the rubble here, most catering to foreign Arab workers or dispossessed locals made homeless by the war. In these places nearly all the guests and staff are male, and whilst I have yet to hear any disturbing reports, the atmosphere could be a little intimidating for women travelling alone.

The first place to try is the Druze-run *Tallal's New Hotel* (☎ 446520) فندق طلال الجديد in al-Sahfi (see the main Beirut map on p164). You can't miss it – the building next door has collapsed. You will see little of the manager here, and it is his woolly-hatted assistant, Khaled, who really runs the show. Use of the kitchen is free, and whilst the rooms and location are nothing special, there is always a very welcoming atmosphere (5000/15,000LE sgl/dbl).

There are a number of similarly-priced places in the area, although only Tallal's and the *al-Rahib* (☎ 447297) down the hill have signs in English – ask at Tallal's for directions to the others.

Apart from its location, just a one-minute walk away from the Corniche and a couple from Hamra, the *al-Halla Hotel* [1] (☎ 386246) has little to boast about; there is barely enough room to swing a shwaarma in some of the rooms, and the reception is furnished with a pride of soccer-mad Lebanese men permanently ensconced in front of the television. However, at only LE7000 for a dorm bed (12,000LE for a single room) you can't really complain. There is no sign on the front of this building, but look for one reading 'Wash-me Cars'; the hotel is in the next building on the second floor, reached by the stairs at the back.

Right in Hamra, the *San Loranzo* فندق سانت لورينزو [2] (☎ 348604) has been spruced up and is now quite pleasant. Singles/doubles are US$13/21; add another US$3 for en suite rooms.

Nearby is the *Hotel Moonlight* [3] (☎ 352308). Whilst a single room is US$20 here, a double at US$25 is better value, and triples at US$28 are a bargain.

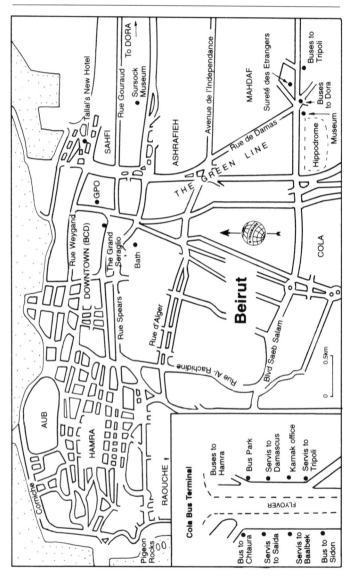

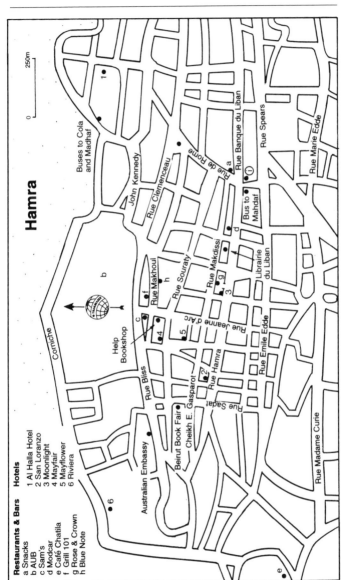

Hamra

Restaurants & Bars
a Snacks
b AUB
c Sam's
d Modcar
e Café Chatila
f Grill 101
g Rose & Crown
h Blue Note

Hotels
1 Al Halla Hotel
2 San Loranzo
3 Moonlight
4 Mayfair
5 Mayflower
6 Riviera

Buses to Cola and Madhaf

Bus to Mandaf

Rue Banque du Liban

Rue Spears

Rue Marie Edde

Rue de Rome

Rue Clemenceau

John Kennedy

Corniche

Rue Makhoul

Rue Souraty

Rue Makdissi

Librairie du Liban

Rue Jeanne d'Arc

Rue Hamra

Rue Emile Edde

Rue Bliss

Help Bookshop

Rue Sadat

Cheikh E. Gasparot

Beirut Book Fair

Australian Embassy

Rue Madame Curie

0   250m

Moderately-priced hotels

The *Mayfair Residence* [4] (☎ 340050) is one of the choicest hotels in this price bracket. For US$50 per night you get a large, spacious room with satellite TV and en suite shower/bath. Nearby is the *Mayflower Hotel* [5] (☎ 340680/1), one of the very few hotels that remained open throughout the entire war. Formerly the Australian embassy, if the large rooms aren't enough to entice you here, the English-style pub – the Duke of Wellington – almost certainly will.

Down on the Corniche, the *Riviera Hotel* [6] (☎ 602273) is encrusted with civil war history. Next door was the former site of the US embassy where a suicide bomber blew 63 people away, and the hotel itself is where Terry Waite enjoyed his last night of creature comforts before being chained to a radiator for the next five years. It remains a good hotel with single rooms for 256,000LE, doubles for 304,000LE; try to get a seaside view if possible .

WHERE TO EAT

There are two small *food stalls* [a] opposite the tourist office that are very popular with the good citizens of Beirut, who pause here just long enough to grumble about the state of the nation and wolf down their meal before they rush off to work. One stall specialises in scrumptious Lebanese pizza (750-2000LE) whilst the other majors in delicious sandwiches.

If you're in the vicinity of the AUB check out the *AUB refectory* [b], which serves cheap, subsidised food (daytime only). Back outside in the real world, look for Sam's Pool Hall opposite the main AUB entrance; next door is an anonymous *burger-joint* [c], where a burger and chips costs 4500LE. If your image is more important to you than any nutritional considerations then the coolest place to be seen drinking expresso is the *Modcar Café* [d] on Rue Hamra. Beware though: this place is expensive.

A former favourite with the intelligentsia is *Café Chatila* [e] near the Luna Funpark. It's still the best place to go and discuss the philosophies of Kant, or maybe just sit and write postcards.

For a bit of a feast, the *Grill 101* [f] on Rue Makhoul offers a great US$14 platter including beef, chicken and shrimp. The beer is only US$3 here too. Ice cream freaks will be pleased to hear that *Baskin & Robbins* have a branch in Raouche near the Pigeon Rocks.

If you are stuck in al-Sahfi looking for a snack, check out *al-Makhlouf* opposite the al-Rahib Hotel – they do some great hot sandwiches here.

NIGHTLIFE

Beirut has always been renowned for its night-life – it's as much a part of the tourist trail as any ruin. Most of the better nightclubs are situated in

Jounnieh, although with an entrance charge of up to US$30 they can be prohibitively expensive. In Beirut nearly all the clubs are strip-joints. If the sign outside says 'Super Club', then you can be sure that inside some poor girl is getting her kit off. An exception is *BO18* in Hash Tabet which is currently *the* place to go. Fads change however; ask at the AUB for where the latest 'in' places are.

Despite the paucity of decent clubs in Hamra, there are still some respectable watering-holes. The *Duke of Wellington* [5] (part of the Mayflower Hotel) claims to be the oldest pub in the Middle East. It used to trade under the name 'The Pickwick Bar', and for many years was run by Jackie Mann (another famous hostage). The current owner's efforts to recreate an authentic English Pub even extend to holding a darts night on a Wednesday; all it needs now is warm beer and ridiculous licensing hours. Another English-style place is the *Rose and Crown* [g], where you can even get fish and chips.

If this all sounds a little dull, the *Texas Lone Star* (opposite the main entrance to the AUB) and *Henry J Beans* (Raouche) are both very lively, catering mainly to AUB students and Beirut's burgeoning ex-pat community.

Finally, for something a little more sophisticated, the *Blue Note* [h] (Rue Makhoul, Hamra) has a jazz band every night. It's probably a little too pretentious for most travellers but if you do go, watch out for the various extras they whack on your bill at the end.

WHAT TO SEE

A walk along the Green Line

The Green Line is a one-mile wide swathe of land stretching from the foothills of the Shouf Mountains in the south all the way to the Mediterranean shore. This line defined the border between Christian East and Muslim West Beirut, and as such saw much of the worst fighting.

Beirut now markets itself as a Phoenix rising from the ashes of civil war and whilst the Phoenix is undoubtedly apt since a new building seems to spring up somewhere every week, the ashes themselves have a macabre fascination for many visitors. Although it is only natural to be curious, don't forget that many thousands lost their lives in the areas you will be visiting so you should be sensitive to the feelings of the locals and ask permission before you point your camera at people or their homes.

A good place to begin a tour of the Green Line is outside the **National Museum** (Madhaf), which was once the only official crossing point between the two sides. The authorities had cemented the museum's treasures into the basement to protect them, but not before many had been vandalised by soldiers using the building as an impromptu barracks. The

---

❑ Hostage-taking

The kidnapping of foreign nationals was one of the more effective tactics deployed by the militias during the war. Even though the kidnappers' demands were seldom met, the taking of a Western hostage was always a newsworthy event and brought their cause into the public eye.

Kidnapping was nothing new in Lebanon. It had been practised for centuries, and during the early stages of the war 2691 Muslims were taken by their Christian enemies in just one night. But with the snatching of foreigners the practice reached a new level of refinement. In July 1982 David Dodge, acting president of the AUB, was the first to go. Although he was subsequently released many who were to follow were not so lucky. Neither were the kidnappers very particular about who was taken: journalists, priests, charity workers, special envoys of the Archbishop of Canterbury – all were fair game. Many were held by Hizbollah extremists whose demands, issued on Iranian orders, were to have Shi'ite terrorists held in a prison in Kuwait (the Dawa 17) set free. The Iranians were behind many of the kidnappings, a fact that came to light during the Irangate affair when it was disclosed that Col Oliver North had authorised the delivery of arms to Iran in return for the release of American hostages.

In the end the hostage crisis resolved itself. The Iraqi invasion of Kuwait in 1991 allowed the Dawa 17 to escape and most of the hostages – including Terry Anderson, who at seven years had been held captive the longest – were set free. By June 1992, with the release of two Germans, all hostages had been released.

---

museum remains closed to the public as restoration of these exhibits continues. It may open in late 1997. From here head towards the coast along **Rue de Damas**, where the bullet-spattered facades and uncleared rubble attest to the heavy fighting that went on along the Line. Soon you'll pass under a flyover, where the two sides used to return the bodies of murdered hostages to their families.

You are now treading on the mud of the **Beirut Centre of Development** (BCD) where Solidere, the company charged with the task of rebuilding the city, is focusing much of its attention. The large building to the west is the **Grand Seraglio**, a former Ottoman barracks that's undergoing renovation. In the centre of the BCD wasteland stands the **Martyr's Statue**, originally a tribute to those who died fighting the Ottoman Turks in 1915 but now a poignant memorial to more recent events: pockmarked by bullets from celebrating gunmen or maybe just from bored snipers in search of target practice, it now stands alone, a mute witness to the relentless devastation of the previous decade.

The American University of Beirut (AUB)

The AUB also witnessed its fair share of murders and kidnappings during the war, but today it once more provides a peaceful green haven from the Hamra crowds. Founded in 1866 by missionary, Daniel Bliss, as the Syrian Protestant College, the AUB has always been a centre for educational excellence, and in the past has tutored many a Middle-Eastern leader. (Unfortunately, if the spelling in the men's toilets is anything to go by, educational standards today appear to have slipped: 'Death to Turkey, mascara of the innocents!' proclaims the graffiti). Within the grounds is a small archaeological museum, and the university is a good place to find out about local events from the students.

Sursock Museum متحف سرسوك

(0900-1700 daily; free). This mansion is the centre for contemporary art in Beirut, although some visitors prefer the building to its contents. Unless you have a particular interest in Middle-Eastern modern art it's not really worth a special trip, although you may consider incorporating a visit into a stroll around genteel Ashrafieh.

Hippodrome سباق الخيل

Hidden behind the high stone wall that runs along Ave Abdallah Yafi is a huge racecourse, and every Sunday the local population gathers for the weekly races just as they did throughout the war. For US$3 (US$10 for a 1st class ticket) you can join them. The fun begins at 10am.

Dog River (Nahr al-Karb) نهر الكلب

So called after a statue of a dog that was said to stand up and bark at the approach of an enemy, the Nahr al-Karb today sets the northern boundary for Greater Beirut. Even without this canine version of an early-warning system invaders would still find it difficult to scale the sheer cliffs and cross the valley, and each success was recorded on a stone tablet placed on the river-bank. Ramses II started the trend, Nebuchadnezzar II (the only one to have a tablet on the north bank) followed suit, and today 17 such stele exist covering all the major invasions, including the Greek, Roman and Napoleonic forays. The last stele was laid in 1946 by President Beshara al-Koury, with a prayer for an end to foreign invaders in Lebanon.

To get to the river, take a servis from Dora along the Beirut-Tripoli Highway as far as the small overpass near the signs to 'Happy Valley'.

Five km to the east is the source of the Dog River at the **Jaita Grotto** مغارة جعيتا (16,000LE summer only), consisting of two caves, one of which can be visited by boat only, and over six km of passages.

Excursion to Beit Eddine بيت الدين

(0830-1700, closed Mondays; 2000LE). For an excellent day out prepare a picnic, head off to the Shouf Mountains (servis taxi 3500LE from Cola) and visit the nineteenth-century palace at Beit Eddine. Built for Emir Bechir el-Chehabi II, a man renowned for being a fair and independent leader, this palace gives a good indication of how luxurious life could be for an emir in Ottoman Lebanon. After Bechir was summoned by his masters to Constantinople in 1840 the palace fell into disuse, but was reopened in 1943 when it became the summer residence of the Lebanese president. The ashes of Bechir were brought back from Constantinople and buried here soon after.

The building is deceptively large and split into three sections. A scale model in the guest rooms by the first courtyard gives a clue to the palace's complexity, and 'Follow me' signs help you negotiate the maze of rooms. The first courtyard is flanked on the right-hand side by the guest rooms, which today hold a small collection of costumes and the armoury.

The second section of the palace is reached by way of the Tumbling Stairs (so called after a ram, escaping an imminent future as a kebab, butted a foreign dignitary down the steps during an official function). Most of the rooms surrounding this courtyard are locked but a guard will gladly accept a small fee to open them for you. Don't miss the cedar Damascene ceilings, intricate marvels of the woodcarver's art. The stables house a large mosaic exhibition, many of which were taken from a fifth-century Byzantine church at Jiyyeh.

The best of the palace is saved until last, however: the third section was the private quarters of the emir, and is by far the most sumptuous part of the building.

Jounnieh (جونيه) and Harrissa

A short servis-taxi ride from Dora (2000LE) brings you to the night-club centre of Jounnieh. This place boomed during the 1980s as people fled Beirut. Many of the bars and discos here stayed open throughout the troubles, proving that Beirutis never let *anything* come between them and a good night on the town. There is a cheapish (US$15 per night) hotel, the *St Joseph's*, if you can't face going back to Beirut after a heavy night.

Jounnieh is also Beirut's main port, from which the ferry to Cyprus is said to be about to recommence sailings.

From Jounnieh you can take the **telepherique** cablecar (0930-sunset summer, 0930-1230 winter, closed Mon; 6000LE return, 3500LE one-way) up to the **Church of Our Lady of Harrissa**, from where there are unparalleled views of the city and kiosks selling naff souvenirs.

MOVING ON

See the Beirut map on p164 for a plan of the **Cola Bus and Servis Terminal** showing where to catch servis taxis and buses at this confusing terminal. Information you receive from the drivers there is often contradictory. Cola is the largest of the three transport terminals in the city.

Karnak buses leave to Damascus at 0700 and 1530 for 7000LE. You may prefer to take a servis taxi, however, for it's less of a wait at the border. For Homs and Aleppo there are 10 buses per day. The cost is 11,000LE. Buses to Saida (1hr) leave frequently and cost 1000LE-

1750LE depending on the class of the bus. There are also two buses to Chtaura (for Baalbek) including one at 1330 (2000LE, 1hr 30min). Servis prices include: Baalbek 8000LE, Beit Eddine 3000LE (1hr), Chtaura 5000LE, Saida 2000LE (1hr), Tripoli 4000LE, Damascus S£300 (3hours), Homs S£300, Aleppo S£500. Note that servis taxi drivers on routes into Syria prefer to be paid in S£.

From the museum buses leave every thirty minutes for Tripoli (2000LE, 1hr 30min) and Jbail (1500LE, 45min). For servis taxis to these destinations you need to go to Dora in the east of the city. Prices by servis are: Tripoli 4000LE, Byblos 3000LE, Jounnieh 2000LE (20min).

North Lebanon

JBAIL (BYBLOS) بايلوس

The small town of Byblos claims to be the oldest continually inhabited site in the world, a claim the citizens of Damascus and Jericho would probably dispute. Whilst this may or may not be true, there is no doubting the importance this village has had in helping historians piece together Lebanon's ancient past.

Visitors today will find evidence of this long history inside the old bronze-age city walls. Almost every era is represented here in some form. Entrance to the site is via the **Crusader Castle** (0800-sunset; 4000LE, 1000LE unofficial student price), built after they had conquered the city in 1108AD; the town was already over 6000 years old even then!

Climbing the south-east tower one can see the various archaeological exhibits laid out below. In particular look for: the compressed floors of several simple **Neolithic fishing huts**, at 7000 years old the most ancient of all the ruins you can visit on this Near East route; the **Temple of the Obelisks**, dating from when the city used to trade with the Middle Kingdom pharaohs from Egypt (c2000BC); and a small, reconstructed **Roman theatre**, with perfect miniature porticoes adorning the walls.

In the town itself is an astonishingly overpriced **Wax Museum** (0900-1800; 5000LE), an appalling hotchpotch of legend and history unconvincingly recreated in wax. Not worth the money, except to laugh at the attempt to provide Adonis with chest hair. The **Church of St John** nearby dates back to 1215 and the Crusaders, and is usually open for you to have a look inside.

Although there is a reasonable *camp-site* موقع الكامب 7km to the north (☎ 09-940322), most travellers make Byblos a daytrip from Beirut (1000LE, 45min) or Tripoli (1500-2000LE, 45min).

TRIPOLI طرابلس

Known to the Arabic world as Tarablus al-Sham (Tripoli of Syria), to distinguish it from the other one in Libya, Tripoli today is an interesting town built around some fine Mamluke architecture and topped off by an imposing Crusader castle. It was founded in c800BC by the Phoenicians and was originally called Athar. The town became an important 'neutral' venue for assemblies between the three Phoenician kingdoms of Tyre, Sidon and Arwad, and was renamed Tripoli (Three Cities) after it was divided into three districts, each one occupied by traders from each of the three kingdoms. The city flourished throughout this period. Subsequent occupations by the Seleucids and Romans introduced new architectural styles but the same huge sixth-century earthquake that destroyed Beirut also flattened Tripoli. Thus the Old City buildings left standing today are mainly the work of the Crusaders who arrived in 1110, and the Mamlukes who invaded 200 years later.

For much of the war Tripoli, traditionally a Sunni Muslim stronghold, was occupied by the Syrians. Today the city is still very much Syrian in flavour, retaining close ties with its neighbours 30km to the north. You should try to give yourself at least two days here if you can – it takes at least one to look round the sites of the Old City.

Orientation and services
(Tripoli ☎ area code 06)
On either side of the roundabout with a large 'Allah' sculpture in the centre are the **post office** and **tourist office**.

To **change money** visit any of the booths near the clock tower. As in Beirut, it is imperative you shop around to find the best rate and check your money carefully.

Where to stay
There are a number of decent hotels clustered around the Ottoman clock tower in the centre of town, the best of which is undoubtedly the **al-Koura Hotel** [1] فندق الخورة near the Air France office. Run by a polite, French-speaking family, they charge 7000LE for a bed in a four-bed dormitory (12,000/16,000LE sgl/dbl), which includes steaming-hot showers and that rarest of budget-hotel perks, toilet roll. There are cheaper places in town – the **Hotel al-Ahram** [2] فندق الاهرام opposite the Becharré servis station has dorm beds for 6000LE – but you get much more for your money at the al-Koura.

Moving up the price scale, (though not necessarily with a commensurate rise in quality), there's the **Palace Hotel** [3] (☎ 432257) on Rue Abdud Hanid Karame. Some rooms (US$10/20 sgl/dbl) can be a little gloomy here, and for the same price you can find much smarter accommodation 200 metres further up at the **Hotel al-Tall** [4] (☎ 628407). Both these places are reluctant to accept Lebanese currency.

Where to eat

The many cheap cafés around Place Gamal Abdel Nasser are perfectly acceptable, and most of the standard Lebanese fare can be enjoyed here. With its predominantly Sunni Muslim population, Tripoli is also the best place to rot your teeth on baklava.

Old City

Tripoli undoubtedly has the best preserved Old City in the whole of Lebanon. Although it did not completely escape the ravages of recent events – the 14th century **Hammam 'Izz al-Din** حمام عز الدين, for example, is now little more than a warehouse for rubble – enough of the Old City has survived to retain its distinctive medieval atmosphere.

Most of the buildings date back to the Mamlukes but, as was typical of the time, a lot of the material they used was scavenged from earlier structures. Look for the Byzantine pillar over the entrance to the **Khan el-Khayyatin** خان الخياطين as an example of this early recycling programme.

The tourist office provides a complete list of the Old City buildings. Highlights include the **Hammam al-Jadid** الحمام الجديد (ask in the shops opposite for the key to this beautifully preserved bath), the 15th-century **madrassas** near the Great Mosque, the **Great Mosque** الجامع الكبير itself (currently undergoing restoration) and the **Taynal Mosque** مسجد تاينال at

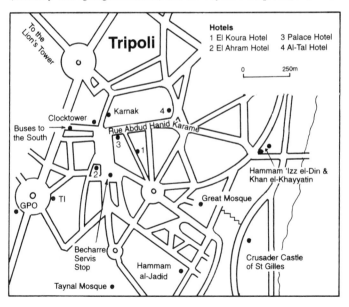

the southern end of town. The inscription over the doorway of this last building tells of its construction in 1336 by Saif el-Din Taynal. It was built around the nave of a 13th-century church, of which traces remain.

Finally, don't miss the **Hammam al-Nouri** حمام النوري, where the local populace still comes to scrub off the grime, much as it has done for the last 600 years.

Crusader Castle of St Gilles

(0800-1700 everyday; 2000LE, no reduction) Standing aloof atop Mt Pilgrim, this 12th-century citadel was built during the First Crusade by Raymond of St Gilles with a little help from his Byzantine allies. It was intended to be used both in defence of the new realm and as a launch pad for attacks on the port and adjoining town. Throughout the centuries it has been partly destroyed, modified, and reassembled by various owners, with each leaving his mark; the inscription above the Frankish gateway is of the fourteenth-century Mamluke Sultan Sha'ban and gives details of the military budget, whilst above the first door is the familiar inscription of Süleyman the Magnificent who carried out the castle's first restoration.

It later became an Ottoman prison, and during the recent civil war the banqueting hall was used as the headquarters of a Sunni militia. Considering its turbulent history it remains remarkably well preserved; one can spend hours walking among its corridors and courtyards, and admiring the excellent views it affords over the city.

The harbour

An important and bustling port during Ottoman times, the harbour area of al-Mina is today a pleasant place to relax and watch the local fisherman. (You may even be able to get one of them to take you to some of the islands). Near the harbour is the **Lion's Tower,** (برج الأسد) an elaborately-sculpted watch-tower and originally one of four built by the Mamlukes. Today it stands isolated save for the rubble of a second tower nearby.

Moving on

Karnak bus tickets can be bought at Transtour near the clock-tower. Destinations include Homs, Aleppo and Damascus, each costing S£250.

Buses for destinations in Lebanon leave from Rue Abdud Hanid Karame, where tickets to Beirut can be bought from the Ahdab Bus Office for LE1500-2000. (On the journey, look out for the Arabian Museilha fortress, perched on a rocky pinnacle 20km outside Tripoli). They will happily drop you off in Byblos, too, but you'll probably be charged the full Beirut fare. Servis taxis leave from the same street – fares include: Syria 3500LE, Byblos 3000LE, Beirut 5000LE. For servis taxis to Becharré (5000LE), head down Rue Sheikh Mohammed Hoysain; the station is on the left past the small park.

BECHARRE (بيجاري) AND THE KADISHA VALLEY

The Kadisha (Holy) Valley is Lebanon's beauty spot: a deep groove in the Mt Lebanon Range along which runs a twisting mountain road that leads eventually to the Maronite village of Becharré and the Arz al-Rabb (The Cedars of our Lord) at the summit. This valley is one place where the cliché about travelling being better than arriving certainly holds true. The drive up is truly breathtaking with ancient monasteries, seemingly held aloft by little more than prayer, clinging precariously to the sheer valley walls.

The area has been a Christian stronghold since 650AD when Syrian monks, followers of St Maron, fled to the mountains to avoid persecution at home. Through the centuries the valley has been home to many of the powerful Maronite families, such as the Gemayels and the Franjehs, and has witnessed some of the most bitter acts of rivalry between them. In the past this rivalry took the form of building bigger churches than their neighbours – that is why Becharré alone has three – but during the civil war this feuding manifested itself in violent inter-Maronite blood-letting.

Today the Kadisha is once more a peaceful haven, with the sound of church bells replacing the gunfire, and no sound fiercer than the rushing of the nearby waterfalls.

Exploring the valley can be awkward if you do not have your own transport. Hitching is difficult with infrequent traffic, while the local taxi-drivers view foreigners as a limitless source of money and charge accordingly. But any effort to fully discover the region will be rewarded with some gorgeous perspectives of the gorge and its surroundings.

Where to stay

Officially there are two hotels in Becharré: the Venezuelan-run *Palace Hotel* (فندق القصر ☎ 06-671460), where a room costs US$25/30 for a single/double; or the *Hotel Chbat*, where for US$70/80 you get a room at the best hotel in the valley. A sauna, health club and panoramic restaurant are the features here.

Unofficially, however, there is a third and considerably cheaper option. Continue down the main street past the Palace Hotel and you soon come to the green-shuttered windows of the *Hotel Rahme* فندق رامي. Closed for business for a while now, the owner and his family are still in residence, and with typical Lebanese hospitality are currently allowing backpackers to stay in their disused hotel. They even leave toilet roll and a towel outside your room! Whilst they make no charge for all of this don't forget to leave a tip, and make sure you have a contingency plan before you arrive in case the hotel has finally shut down.

The Cedars الأرز

These are the mighty cedars of the Bible, used in the construction of Solomon's Temple in Jerusalem and the temple at Baalbek. Today the area is one big disappointment, consisting of a tawdry overpriced ski resort (winter only, pass and ski hire US$10 each per day), a few kitsch souvenir stalls and a clump of cedars barely large enough to fill the frame on your photos. But the two-hour walk to get there is great, with stunning views of both the valley and Lebanon's highest mountain, Qornet el-Sauda (3090m), on the way.

The Kadisha Grotto was still closed at the time of writing, but take this road for a more scenic walk. If you'd rather hitch, walk for 100m past the army checkpoint at the top of the town and wait by the signpost that says 'Cedars 7km, Grotto Kadicha 5km'. Taxis are extortionate: US$20 for the 15-minute trip.

Gibran Museum

(0900-1700 everyday except Mon. 3000LE adults, 2000LE student)
Lebanon's most famous cultural export, Gibran Khalil Gibran (1895-1931) spent only the first twelve years of his life in Becharré before his family moved to Boston. But today his body rests, as he wished, beneath the roots of a cedar tree in the former convent at Mar Sarkis. Famous for his rather gloomy view of mankind, and in particular an abhorrence of man's inherent greed (he'd obviously spent too long in the company of Becharré's taxi drivers), his reputation is founded on a number of sublime poetical works. He's is best known for *The Prophet*, published in 1923.

The museum displays paintings and books collected together after his death, as well as a reconstruction of his New York apartment: a sparsely-furnished room with his waistcoat still hanging from the door, and a simple tapestry of Jesus on the wall.

The museum is 100m from Becharré past the Virgin's Waterfall. Above it is a Phoenician tomb dating from about 750BC, and nearby is the Grotto de Lourdes (closed).

Other sights in the Kadisha

The cave outside the **Monastery of St Antoine** (دير سانت انتوني) is known as the Grotto of the Mad and still contains the leg-irons with which the lunatics used to be restrained. It also houses a collection of Christian relics, including pieces of the 'True Cross'.

Over the Bridge from Becharré is the neon-lit **House of St Charbel** (بيت سانت جاربيل) at Bkaa Kafra, Lebanon's highest village. You may also wish to visit the villages of **Ehden** (عدن) and **Amyoun** . This last village is surrounded by Roman and Byzantine temples, evidence of earlier civilisations in the Kadisha.

Moving on

Servis taxis leave from the main square near Gibran's birthplace. You will be very fortunate to find a taxi to Beirut – everything seems to go to Tripoli (5000LE if the taxi is full, more if you leave in the afternoon when there are usually fewer passengers). The taxi drivers here are, almost without exception, a scheming bunch of crooks who will try anything to get both your custom and your money. Take care.

BAALBEK AND THE BEKAA VALLEY

Dividing the Lebanon and Anti-Lebanon ranges, the Bekaa Valley سهل البقاع is a pretty area of green meadows flanked by distant snowy peaks. Known in ancient times as Coele ('Hollow') Syria, this sparsely-populated trough has played an important part in the area's commercial history and used to be a busy north-south caravan route. In recent times agriculture has been the main industry, producing two intoxicating crops: Lebanese Black, a high quality dope (so I'm informed) that financed many a militia during the war; and also some very fine wines produced in the Bekaa's many vineyards.

The area's reputation for marvellous hospitality and worry-free travel has been besmirched by the civil war. It was (and remains) a Hizbollah stronghold, with the former army barracks at Baalbek their wartime HQ. Even today the British Embassy still advises against visiting the area. Although this may be a little over-cautious, it is wise to find out the latest situation from locals and fellow travellers before setting out.

A servis from Chtaura to Baalbek is 3000LE (1hr).

Where to stay

Baalbek The preferred budget option for Baalbek is the *Hotel Shams* (فندق الشمس) ☎ 08-770990). From the taxi rank follow the main road into town and it's 100 metres down on your left. Owned by the son of the dentist who plies his trade next door (and who probably supplies the hotel with its dreadful 1970s magazine collection), they charge the standard US$5 for the privilege of a night in one of their lofty iron beds. Around the next corner is a cheaper, scummier alternative (dorm beds 7000LE), although this should be used as an overflow option only. It appears to have no name, just a *'Pension'* sign outside.

The *Hotel Palmyra* فندق البلمير (☎ 08-370230) like the Baron Hotel in Aleppo, smacks of faded grandeur. Creaking under the weight of 120 years of history and dust, it's a melancholy place these days. Luminaries such as Charles De Gaulle, Louis Napoleon and Kaiser Wilhelm II have spent time between the sheets here. It still has a marvellous rooftop terrace, where guests can sip on G&T and gaze at the sun going down behind Mt Lebanon. Prices are US$30/45 for singles/doubles.

Chtaura The *Hotel Khater* (فندق الخاطر ☎ 08-840133) will, with a little tenacious haggling, offer you a cosy little room for US$5 per person. The hotel is on your left as you head from the junction towards Beirut. Electricity here, as elsewhere in the Bekaa, is intermittent.

Chtaura شتورة

This village lies at an important cross-roads in the Bekaa: to the north is Baalbek, the south leads to Beaufort Castle, and the Beirut-Damascus road runs west to east. The village itself has very little to offer, but the ruins of **Aanjar** (عينجار , 0900-1700 everyday; free) lie just 10km along the road to Damascus. These are the best remains of an Ommayad city (660-750AD) in Lebanon, although exactly what a city as extensive as this (containing over 600 shops and a palace) was doing here is still a mystery. The city planners obviously borrowed heavily from the Romans, with two main streets dividing the town into four quarters. To get there, take a servis (1500LE) and ask the driver to drop you at the Aanjar turn off, from where it's a twenty-minute walk. A taxi to the site from Chtaura will cost you US$5.

The restaurant village of **Zahle** (زحلة), 10km north of Chtaura, stretches up the hillside in a way that is reminiscent of Maalula in Syria. The restaurants and cafés by the river are renowned throughout Lebanon; call in here for lunch if you can.

Baalbek بعلبك

A race of gods or of giants must have inhabited Baalbec many a century ago. Men like the men of our day could hardly rear such temples like these. **Mark Twain** *The Innocents Abroad*

The Roman temples at Baalbek are the highlight of any trip to Lebanon, and the one tourist attraction that you will definitely not have to yourself. The tourist hordes arrive by the coach-load (usually Lebanese tourists), and the postcard-sellers and camel-drivers have more in common with the overpopulated attractions of Egypt than the deserted sights of Lebanon. Don't let this put you off, however; Baalbek is truly awesome.

The Temples of Jupiter and Bacchus/Astarte (0830-1630 everyday; 4000LE) Like the Ommayad Mosque in Damascus and many other sacred places in the Near East, Baalbek has witnessed a number of temples through the years. The Roman temple you see today was built over an earlier Phoenician temple dedicated to Baal (God of Thunder and War), and the Greeks also worshipped at the site, renaming the town Heliopolis (City of the Sun).

Construction of the Roman temple began in 16BC and was completed in 60AD. It was designed as a display of Roman might for the trading caravans that passed down the Coele-Syria. The Byzantine Emperor Constantine, whilst condemning the worship of pagan gods, could not avoid being seduced by the temple's colossal size and beauty and converted part of it into a church. The Arabs decided on a more pragmatic use for the masonry, however, and surrounded the area with high walls, turning the place into a fortress. Two Mongol invasions and a few earthquakes (the last in 1759 which knocked down three more of the great pillars, leaving only six standing) ensured that the archaeologists would have their work cut out restoring the temple, which they have been doing, on and off, since 1848.

The main temple stands on a huge substructure made of granite hewn from the nearby quarry. It is split into four sections. The **Propylaea** (porch) is the first of these. The columns here, as elsewhere in the temple, are made of granite from the quarries at Aswan in Egypt. The second section, the **Hexagonal Courtyard**, lies through the central door in the Propylaea. This area was converted into a church by the Byzantines; you can still make out the odd cross scratched into the stone.

The third courtyard is also the largest. The surrounding wall of the **Courtyard of the Altars** is carved with niches which used to house the statues of gods and local dignitaries. The zealous Christians subsequently smashed every statue (about 240 in total), but you can still see some intricate carving on the niches themselves – in the southern wall look for Medusa surrounded by dragons and vampires. Another Byzantine church stood in the centre of this courtyard but nothing remains now except a few foundation stones. In its place are reconstructions of two pagan altars. The larger one was used for religious ceremonies, and the second supported the statue of Jupiter. Either side of these are two pools for ritual purification.

The temple itself is reached via the steps to the west. The six huge columns – at 22m high they vie with those at Karnak (Luxor) to be the tallest in the world – once numbered 54. The Byzantines removed most of them for their own purposes, and eight were shipped off to Constantinople to be incorporated into the Aya Sofya.

The Temple of Bacchus/Venus This is even more impressive, despite the fact that experts are still unsure as to whether the site is dedicated to Jupiter's consort, Venus, or, as the decorations would suggest, Bacchus, the god of drinking and pleasure. Completed in 220AD and dubbed 'The Small Temple' because of its larger neighbour, it would still dwarf the Acropolis in Athens. The stone walls are alive with scenes of nature (birds, vines and dancing figures) all in a wonderful state of preservation. The Mamluke tower on the south-eastern corner looks ridiculously out of place amongst such Corinthian beauty.

Leaving the site via an underground passage through the substructure originally used for storage, you arrive at a second **Temple of Venus**, a small circular set of ruins near the entrance. Those whose lust for Roman ruins has still not been sated can visit the foundations of the **Temple of Mercury** nearby, and even the quarries to the south-west of the town from where they originally brought the stone for the temple's foundations. The largest rock ever to have been quarried by man, the **Stone of the Pregnant Woman** (حجر الحبلى), still lies there.

Moving on

Chtaura lies on the old Beirut-Damascus Highway, which during Ottoman times was used to divide the country between the Maronites to the north and the Druze to the south. If you wish to continue to Damascus, fares are 6000LE (S£200) from Chtaura, or 8000LE from Baalbek.

South Lebanon

The twin ports of Sur and Saida (Tyre and Sidon) today slumber innocuously in the warmth of the Mediterranean sun, a sleep interrupted only by the occasional raucous Hizbollah demonstration and the ear piercing scream of Israeli jets whistling by. Yet their history is a turbulent one stretching back six thousand years, during which time both ports witnessed periods of such enormous prosperity that they earned frequent condemnations in the Bible for their greed and materialism. Both cities owed their success to the murex snails found along the shore, from which they extracted the precious royal dye, Tyrian purple ('Phoenician' is Greek for purple). Later they diversified, mass-producing and exporting glass as well. Their greatest legacy, however, is the Phoenician alphabet, a phonetic derivative of Egyptian hieroglyphics and the forerunner of our Roman system.

Today there are enough remains of the cities' colourful past to make a visit worthwhile, and you'll probably be well-treated by curious locals eager to meet the only foreigner in town who doesn't work for the UN.

For accommodation, there's nothing under US$80 in Sur. There's only one hotel in Saida but at least it's cheap.

SAIDA (SIDON) صيدا

Named after the eldest son of Canaan (one of Noah's grandsons) Sidon usually reaped the benefits of co-operating with the coast's numerous conquerors. In particular this included the Persians, to whom they supplied both boats and sailors to use in the battles against the Egyptians. This Persian era proved very prosperous as new trading routes were opened to the east, but culminated in tragedy, with 40,000 Sidonians choosing to commit suicide rather than face the approaching forces of another Persian king, Artaxerxes III (344BC). The two castles left standing today are the handiwork of the Crusaders who captured Sidon in 1111 and held it until Saladin drove them out in 1187. They returned briefly for four years in 1287. Thereafter the town declined, until Emir Fakhreddine Ma'an (1572-1634) – Lebanon's most independent-minded emir whose rule encompassed the whole of modern-day Lebanon and much of Syria – restored some of its glory during the 17th century. It remained the main port for Damascus throughout the Ottoman era until superseded by Beirut in the last century.

Where to stay

The *Orient Hotel* (فندق الشرق) may be a little grotty but it's only 7000LE for a bed in a dorm (20,000/22,000LE sgl/dbl). From the bus station head towards the shopping area; at the end of the road is the Shamaa Pharmacy. Turn left here, and continue for about 100m; the hotel is the first yellow building on your right.

Where to eat

The *Abou Ramy Falafel Sandwich* opposite the castle serves the best felafel in town according to the locals, while next to the castle the *Rest House* is beautiful. At 2500LE for a soft drink, however, don't come here unless you have cash to splash.

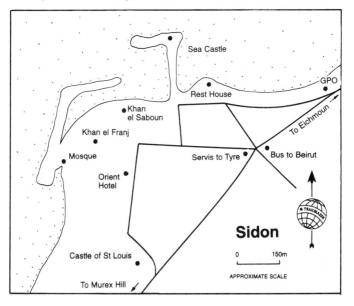

What to see

The **Sea Castle** (0830-1600 daily; 2000LE) was built during the 13th century by the Crusading Knights of St John of the Hospital of Jerusalem in order to protect the harbour. Today little remains except two towers: the right-hand one was a small church, and the left one (which you can climb) was the meeting hall. The site was evacuated in 1291, and suffered a great deal of damage when the British bombed it in 1941.

The **Castle of St Louis** inland has unfortunately suffered similar ruin, and there is very little left that was probably not subsequently rebuilt by the Arabs. The Israelis used it as their base in 1982. To the south is **Murex Hill** (تل موريكس), which is a Phoenician rubbish dump made from the discarded shells of the murex snail. A cemetery now occupies one side of it. The **Great Mosque** was, in fact, once a church built by the same Crusaders who constructed the Sea Castle. To find it, head through the souk from the centre of town. It's on the west side, by the coast.

Echmoun Temple

(0830-1630 daily; free). You may be very underwhelmed by the overgrown ruins of Echmoun since most of the better parts were removed to the Topkapi Archaeological Museum in Istanbul, but their historical importance far outweighs any aesthetic shortcomings. The ruins are Phoenician, dating from the sixth century BC when the city was under Persian rule. Indeed, the Persians probably financed the temple to ensure loyalty from Sidon.

Echmoun was the patron god of the city. According to legend he was a good-looking lad from Beirut, who killed himself to avoid the attentions of the goddess Astarte (it is her throne you see in the front of the podium). She then reincarnated him as the god of healing.

To reach the temple catch a servis (1000LE) back towards Beirut until you come to a fairground on your right. Take the road that runs by the side of this fair, turn left at the end and follow the road along a river lined with orange groves. After about twenty minutes you'll see the gate on your left.

Moving on

A servis taxi between Sur and Saida costs 750LE.

SUR (TYRE) صور

O Tyr, you have said "I am perfect in beauty". Your borders are in the heart of the seas; your builders made perfect your beauty **Ezekiel 27:1-3**

It's difficult to imagine that the fishing village of Sur, tucked away on the south coast of Lebanon, was once the mighty Tyre of the Bible, whose influence spread over the whole of the Mediterranean and beyond; a city whose sailors circumnavigated Africa, whose citizens founded Carthage and whose merchants traded with places as exotic and far-flung as Wales. Yet for 300 years, during the period known as the Hegemony of Tyre, the town reigned supreme as *the* port of the Mediterranean, even eclipsing its former colonial rulers at Sidon. The city reached its epoch under King Hiram (970-936BC), who opened up a trade route through to the Red Sea by establishing trade links with King David in Jerusalem. Hiram also supplied the cedars for David's son Solomon to build his temple.

The city also proved to be more resilient than its coastal neighbours. Nebuchadnezzar had to besiege Tyre for 13 years before it finally fell, as Ezekiel had predicted, in 585BC; and even Alexander the Great was kept waiting for seven months before he captured the city. In order to storm the city the Greeks built a bridge (as Tyre was then an island off the coast). That causeway has since silted over, joining the island to the mainland permanently, paving the way – literally – for subsequent invasions by the Romans, Arabs, Crusaders, Mamlukes and Turks.

Today Tyre is a Hizbollah stronghold (there are posters of the Ayatollah everywhere) and as such has been a regular target for bombing campaigns by Israel. The most recent was in April 1996, when Israeli jets flew missions against the port every day for over two weeks.

Hotels in Sur are expensive: US$80 per night or more. Most travellers day trip from Saida or even Beirut.

What to see

The ruins that remain today are Roman rather than Phoenician. By the coast in the centre of Tyre is the old **Roman Way** to the port (0800-1700 everyday; 1000LE) including giant Tyrian columns and unusual geometric mosaics lining the path. About a kilometre inland is the main site, including a huge **hippodrome** and **necropolis**. The overgrown necropolis still has many of the Roman sarcophagi in place, complete with inscriptions. It's a good place to practise your Latin.

Moving on

The buses and taxis both drop you off by the main roundabout. Buses to Beirut are between 1250-1750LE. A servis to Tyre from the opposite side of the roundabout costs 3000LE.

❏ **Other attractions in Lebanon**
It may be minute, but this country has an enormous amount to offer the visitor. As you'd expect from a country that borders Syria and Israel, the whole area is rich in religious and historical sites.

In the south of Lebanon is the ancient village of Cana, the same Cana where Jesus turned the water into wine, (John 2:1-11). There is also the ancient castle at Beaufort, a fine example of a Crusader fortress. Unfortunately it is currently still occupied by the Israelis. The taxi drivers in the area will probably refuse to drive you near it, so at present you'll just have to make do with a distant glimpse.

GETTING FROM LEBANON TO JORDAN

Since there's no border between Lebanon and Jordan and the border between Lebanon and Israel remains firmly closed (as is the Syria-Israel border), you'll need to return to Syria to continue to Jordan.

The border – Lebanon and Syria
See p154 for information on this crossing.

The border – Syria and Jordan
● **Syria to Jordan** The Dera'a-Ramtha border is a popular smuggling route, so don't be surprised if the servis driver asks you to hide a box of cigarettes in your luggage. Indeed, use this as a bargaining tool when haggling over the servis fare (and make sure the number of cigarettes he gives you doesn't exceed the duty free quota).

The servis from Dera'a to Ramtha (S£125) takes approximately two hours. Buses from Ramtha to Irbid leave frequently, and cost 100fils for the 20-minute trip. Try to complete the crossing in the morning, otherwise you may have to wait a while in Irbid for your connection to Amman.

You can buy your Jordanian visa at the border (no photos required). Prices are as follows: Australians free, Canadians JD31, British JD23, US citizens JD15. There is also a bank for foreign exchange at the border. It stays open until about 2200 and will accept travellers' cheques; the rates are reasonably competitive.

● **Jordan to Syria** There's a bus from Ramtha to the border for 70fils, but from there the guards will insist you take the first car that comes along. This is, more often than not, a servis taxi, which will charge you the same as if you started in Ramtha (JD2). The Jordanian departure tax at this border is JD4.

See p198 in the Amman section for the timetable for the **Hejaz Railway** from Amman to Damascus.

PART 6: JORDAN

Facts about the country

Too arid for agriculture, barren of oil, overburdened by Palestinian refugees and dependent on Western aid for its survival, Jordan looks like a ticking time bomb ready to go off. Bearing this in mind, you might think that it would be wise to take advantage of their modern transport network and travel from one end of the country to the other without stopping, or even opening the windows. But you'd be wrong.

Jordan is the eye of a storm, a small oasis of calm surrounded on all four sides by a maelstrom of turbulent nations. It may have no oil but it does have that one commodity which, in this region at least, is just as precious: peace. It's probably the least exotic, sanest country on this route. But that's not to say it's boring; any country that contains both the majestic scenery of Wadi Rum and the mind-blowing, spellbinding glory of Petra could never be described as dull. What it does mean is that travelling through Jordan is easy and comfortable, and this combination of

❑ **Country ratings – Jordan**

● **Highlights** Without Petra, Jordan's fragile tourist industry would all but disappear. Petra is not the only attraction, however. Wadi Rum, Kerak (which is ignored, surprisingly, by the majority of travellers) and Aqaba (which you can't help but visit) are all worth spending a little time in.

● **Expense** ✔✔✔ Jordan is not as expensive as many travellers make out. Even Petra's entrance fee – at JD25 (2 days) the single biggest expense for most visitors to Jordan – represents reasonable value for money.

● **Value for money** ✔✔✔ See above

● **English communication** ✔✔✔✔ A surprisingly large proportion of Jordanian and Palestinian nationals speak English.

● **Getting around** ✔✔✔ Public transport along the King's Highway is notoriously bad but it's fine along the Desert Highway.

● **Travellers' scene** ✔✔✔ Mainly in Petra.

● **Visible history** ✔✔✔✔ All along the King's Highway

● **Woman alone** ✔✔✔✔ Attention from Jordanian men is mostly harmless. If you're hitching along the King's Highway do so with a companion.

● **Good food** ✔✔ Not exactly varied but most of the food is well-prepared. Chicken is a main ingredient in most dishes, and half a roast chicken is a very popular and cheap Jordanian speciality. Look out for the ice-creams in Aqaba too (only 100 fils!).

● **Vegetarian friendly** ✔✔

Oriental excitement and Western convenience is quite appealing, particularly to those who've recently suffered the tribulations of travelling through the neighbouring territories.

Modern Jordan

The stability of the monarchy is one reason why Jordan has witnessed less upheaval than the other countries in the Near East. The first king, Abdullah, ruled for fully 30 years before he was gunned down by a Palestinian refugee in Jerusalem in 1952. His son Talal was considered mentally unfit for the job (which might be thought a positive advantage in some of the countries around here) and so Abdullah's grandson, Hussein, ascended to the Jordanian throne where he still sits today. Just two kings in seventy-five years, a remarkable record anywhere in the world and even more so in the troubled Near East.

The longevity of King Hussein's reign can be put down to his success as negotiator and diplomat. He has had to use these skills on plenty of occasions. Firstly, after taking the West Bank in 1948, Jordan became the country with the largest refugee population in the world: approximately three million at the last count. In an effort at appeasement, Hussein offered Jordanian citizenship to all of them in 1960, an offer which most accepted. Then in 1974 Hussein recognised the PLO as the sole representative of the Palestinian people, and in doing so renounced all claims to the West Bank and Jerusalem. This was a necessary step to take, since Jordan's sour relations with the PLO were beginning to cloud its relationships with neighbours Syria and Lebanon. And then finally, in the Gulf War of 1991, King Hussein managed to both support Iraq – their biggest trading partner – and at the same time comply with the UN sanctions. By such tact and diplomacy has Hussein managed to stay on the throne.

Although Jordan today is one of the few countries which keeps on good terms with all its neighbours, it still has a number of domestic problems. Riots over food prices (as recently as August 1996), unemployment running at 30% and a faltering economy – barren of oil and overburdened by refugees – means that the country, while outwardly serene, continues to have plenty to worry about at home.

GEOGRAPHICAL BACKGROUND

Jordan is two main roads and an awful lot of desert. The roads – the Desert and King's Highways – run parallel to each other north to south. To the west lies the Jordan Valley, part of the Rift Valley that begins in Africa, continues under the Red Sea to emerge at Aqaba, and then heads north to peter out in Lebanon. To the east of the country lies the North Arabian Desert, which Jordan shares with Iraq, Syria and Saudi Arabia.

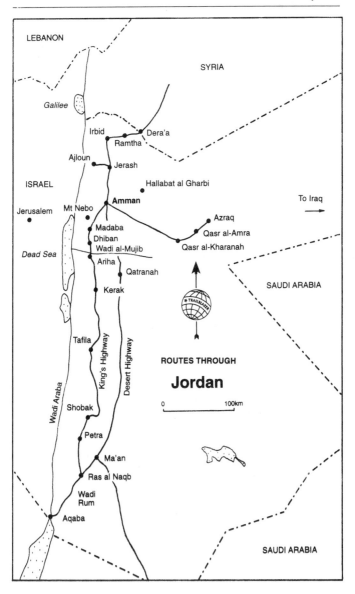

LEBANON

SYRIA

Galilee

Irbid
Dera'a
Ramtha

Ajloun
Jerash

ISRAEL
Hallabat al Gharbi

Jerusalem
Mt Nebo
Amman
To Iraq

Madaba
Azraq
Dhiban
Qasr al-Amra
Dead Sea
Wadi al-Mujib
Qasr al-Kharanah
Ariha
Qatranah

Kerak
SAUDI ARABIA

Tafila

Wadi Araba
King's Highway
Desert Highway

ROUTES THROUGH

Jordan

0   100km

Shobak

Petra

Ma'an

Ras al Naqb
Wadi
Rum
Aqaba

SAUDI ARABIA

RELIGION

Like the weather, Jordan's population is largely Sunni (95%). Most of the rest are Christian, belonging mainly to the Greek Orthodox church. Baha'is, Druze and Shi'ites also have tiny populations here. Incidentally, the 'Hashemite' of the country's full name (the Hashemite Kingdom of Jordan) refers to Mohammed's grandfather Hashem, from whom the Jordanian royal house claims direct descent.

LOCAL TRANSPORT

Jordan has both private buses and servis taxis. There is also a national bus company, Jett, but their services are expensive and limited to four buses per day to Aqaba and one to Petra. Travelling down the King's Highway by public transport can be a time consuming and frustrating affair, and on some stretches it is impossible. Hitching (fairly easy in Jordan) is the only option on these stretches.

❏ **Routes through Jordan**
This chapter follows the historic King's Highway through the country. Public transport along this route is notoriously bad so details of transport connections along the Desert Highway are also given.

North Jordan

IRBID أربد

This rather unlovely sprawling industrial town, 140km north of Amman and 30km from the Syrian border, is Jordan's third largest city and home to almost 300,000 of its citizens. Apart from two museums at the university there is little to keep the traveller here and for the majority the Irbid experience amounts to little more than a short pause at the new bus terminal, two km south of the city.

Occasionally, however, circumstance and an erratic bus schedule conspire to delay the unwitting traveller in the city overnight. If this happens to you, catch a cab to the **Abu Baker Hotel** فندق ابو بكر (☎ 242695). Prices start at JD2 for a dorm bed, JD3/5 sgl/dbl; the fare here should be about 400 fils, or 80 fils by servis but be warned: Irbid's taxi drivers are a mendacious bunch of villains who will try anything to squeeze every last fil out of you. Abu Baker's curmudgeonly manager requests that you try to avoid arriving in the afternoon, for he likes to take a nap then. As with many hotels in Jordan, single female travellers are not allowed to use the dormitory, and have to rent a whole room for themselves instead.

From the new bus station the Hijazi bus company runs a regular service to Amman (820 fils; first bus 0600, last one 1600; 2hrs). A cheaper alternative is to take one of the private buses for 500 fils. Minibuses to Ramtha الرمثة leave when full (100 fils for the 20min trip) and to Jerash (290 fils; one hour journey).

JERASH الجرش

(0800-1900, 0800-1700 during Ramadan; closed Friday; JD2). The ruins at Jerash, 50km north of Amman, vie with Ephesus as the best preserved example of a Roman city you'll see on this route through the Near East.

Like Amman, Jerash was part of the Roman trading confederation known as the Decapolis, and it continued to be important during the Byzantine era as a regional centre for Christianity; archaeologists have uncovered the remains of fifteen Byzantine churches amongst the ruins. It remained a vital, wealthy city until the Persian invasion of AD614 brought it to its knees. With the arrival of Islam soon afterwards Jerash and its churches were largely abandoned, and for over one thousand years the ruins lay forgotten and buried in the undergrowth. Then in 1806 a German traveller, Ulrich Seetzen, rediscovered the town and at the beginning of this century excavations began in earnest.

Orientation   (Jerash ☎ **area code** 04)

Jerash is bisected by a river. As in Roman times, the majority of Jerash's 15,000 inhabitants today live on the east side, now also the location of the bus station. The entrance to the Roman site is five minutes south of the town, on the west side back towards Amman. These ruins were once the administrative and commercial centre of the city.

The ruins of Jerash

Apart from **Hadrian's Arch**, which you can see in the distance to the south, most of the ruins are to the north of the **Southern Gate** by the entrance. Jerash was a large town. The largest of Jerash's three theatres, the **Southern Theatre**, up the hill on your left as you pass through the southern gate, could hold 6000 people.

The layout of the town is fairly simple. At the centre is the **Oval Plaza** or **Forum**, the circumference of which is partly lined by two rows of reconstructed Ionic columns. As with Constantinople and Ephesus, the forum was the centre of town: market place, civic centre and law court all rolled into one.

North from here is the semi-colonnaded **Cardo**, the old Roman main street which stretches for 600 metres to the **Northern Gate**. The shifting land has caused the paving stones to rise and become uneven, and 700 years of chariots, horses and barrows have all left their mark on the slabs; but such wear and tear has done little to diminish the street's grandeur. A few metres north of the forum one finds a major road junction marked by a **Tetrapylon** – four plinths on which statues used to stand. The road that runs through the tetrapylon perpendicular to the Cardo is known as the **Decumanus**, which originally headed east to the **Eastern Baths**, next to the bus station.

Flanking the Cardo on either side are the main public buildings. The first building we come to on the left after the forum is the **Cathedral**. Next door is the **Nymphaeum**, the city's fountain which probably had some religious function too in its day. The edifice has two rows of seven niches, which formerly housed busts of the city's noblemen and gods. These busts and the roof which used to cover the fountain have gone the same way as the tetrapylon's statues.

Further north and still on the left, opposite yet another church and preceded by yet another processional stairway, stands the second-century **Temple of Artemis.** Dedicated to the city's patron goddess, this was the largest building in the Roman town and remains one of the more imposing ruins today, even though many of its columns were subsequently scavenged and used in other buildings by the Byzantines and Arabs.

Before you leave the ruins, check out the small museum to the east of the Forum which, amongst all the Byzantine and Roman paraphernalia, contains artefacts dating back to the Neolithic era.

Getting to Jerash

It takes only a couple of hours to look over the ruins, and because there is no accommodation in town this is a daytrip from either Irbid or Amman. The 45-minute trip in a large bus from here to the Abdali bus station in Amman costs 350 fils.

Amman
عمان

If it weren't for the amphitheatre and the remains of a Roman citadel atop Jabal Qala'a, one would probably guess Amman to be about seventy or eighty years old at the most. The dreary downtown scenery – ugly, concrete housing dumped alongside faceless high-rise buildings – reveals little of the capital's ancient past. But excavations tell us that this city actually dates back to the Bronze Age, and these modern monstrosities are just new carbuncles sprouting on the face of a venerable 5000-year-old pensioner.

> ❏ *And David gathered all the people together, and went to Ammon Rabbath, and fought against it, and took it...and he brought forth the people that were therein...and made them pass through the brick-kiln.* - **Samuel 12:26**

Known in the Bible as Ammon-Rabbath, the city was the capital of the Ammonites, a Semitic people who had migrated westwards from the deserts of Mesopotamia. Relations between the Ammonites and their fellow Mesopotamian migrants the Israelites were often strained, until Israel's King David captured Ammon-Rabbath in about 1000BC and disposed of the Ammonites accordingly.

The city stagnated for a while after this until it was rebuilt by the Ptolemites who renamed it Philadelphia. Further confirmation of the city's growing importance was bestowed by the Romans, who seized control of the city in AD106 and considered it a worthy inclusion into the Decapolis (see Jerash, above).

But after this Amman went into hibernation. Until the end of WWI the town was little more than an insignificant village on the Hejaz route. It was awoken from this slumber only in 1921 by King Abdullah, who announced that Amman was to be the capital of his new Transjordan state. As the city grew in stature, so it grew in size: by 1991, thanks mainly to a huge influx of Palestinian refugees, the population topped 1.5 million.

With a population this big it is not surprising that Amman has spilled over its original borders and oozed onto each of the surrounding seven hills. These hills are steep and walking in Amman is strenuous. Nor is there that much to see in the capital; most travellers stop only briefly before making their way to the more romantic splendours of Petra, Damascus and Jerusalem. But it is a friendly place, and a well-organised, efficient metropolis. You may not be thrilled here, but at least your stay should be comfortable and relatively hassle free.

ORIENTATION

The city is built on seven hills, so the Roman soldiers who were garrisoned here must have felt very much at home. Squashed at the foot of these hills is the downtown area المركز التجاري بعمان, the liveliest quarter of the city where most of the shops, banks, restaurants and hotels are to be found. Unfortunately, this means that everything else is uphill from here. Of the seven hills, the embassy quarter on Jabal Amman (جبل عمان) is perhaps the most important to the traveller. The main road that climbs Jabal Amman from downtown is punctuated by seven numbered junctions, called circles. Most addresses on this hill give the nearest circle number rather than the road name. This is just as well, for there are few street signs in Jordan.

Of the other hills, Jabal Qala'a (جبل القلعة), to the north of the centre, is the home of the citadel, and to the west lies Jabal al-Luwaybida and the main Abdali bus station محطة سيارات العبدلي . A second bus terminus, Wahadat (الوحدات), lies to the south of the downtown area.

LOCAL TRANSPORT

The servis taxi is the most convenient and cheapest way of travelling in Amman. Unlike other servis taxis, Amman's behave just like buses: they are numbered and follow a set route. The places to catch these taxis are shown on the map on p195; attempting to catch one en route can be difficult as they are usually full. Do not be put off by the large queues waiting for your servis; they usually shrink rapidly. The fare is a standard 70 or 80 fils, although if you hand over 100 fils don't be surprised if the change is not forthcoming. Here are a few of the more useful services:

- **Servis 3**: from downtown to fourth circle.
- **Servises 6/7**: downtown to Abdali bus station
- **Servis 27**: downtown to Wahadat bus station

To get to the **airport**, catch a bus from Abdali. The journey takes about one hour and costs 750 fils.

Private taxis are everywhere in Amman and they are good value, provided you can get the driver to switch on the meter. As a guide, from downtown to the fourth circle is about 500 fils.

(**Opposite**) The first of Petra's glorious façades, the Khazneh (see p208).

SERVICES   (Amman ☎ **area code** 06)

● **Bookshops** Amman has disappointingly little to offer the English-speaking bookworm. The Intercontinental Hotel has probably the widest choice, with an excellent Middle Eastern selection, but it's not cheap.

● **Car hire** The **Yahala** office is the cheapest place to hire a car in Amman. Prices start at JD20 per day for a Skoda.

● **Changing money** It is worth doing a little window shopping amongst the small exchange counters in downtown Amman. The banks usually offer a higher rate but they also charge a hefty JD2 commission on travellers' cheques. The branch of **AMEX** in Amman is a long way out of town. The address is: International Traders, Shemeisani-Abdel Hamid Sharaf, PO Box 408, zip code 11118. This office does not change money.

● **Post** You will find the main GPO on Basman St (شارع بسمان). It is open between 0800-1900 every day. Poste Restante is a small wooden box in front of the last counter from the entrance. The parcel office is near the telephone exchange, on the hill behind Basman St.

● **Laundry** Near the telephone office is a small shop that takes in washing for about JD2 per load.

● **Telecommunications** The telephone office is up the hill behind the main GPO. It is open until 2300 every day, although it closes during the afternoon during Ramadan. Surrounding the office are a number of private telephone offices. They charge a slightly higher rate but do not have a minimum three-minute charge and many stay open all night.

● **Tourist information** The only official tourist office in Amman is the Department of Tourism and Antiquities on al-Muttanabi St, just up from the Third Circle. It has a few maps and handouts, and a small computer screen that you can play around with; trying to obtain any useful information, however, is a little too tricky.

● **Travel agencies** You will have no trouble finding a travel agent in Amman (there are many on King Hussein St) although once again it is important to shop around. If you have a visa for Lebanon but not Syria, buy a flight to Beirut (approx JD40), then try to get into Syria from there (see p154). For Europe, America and Australia the cheapest option is to catch a flight to Turkey (approx JD80) and buy your ticket in Istanbul.

● **Visa extensions** Visas can be extended to three months at the **Moh Hajireen Police Station** (مركز شرطة المهاجرين); servis taxi 35 will drop you nearby, or it's a 30-minute walk from the post office (250 fils in a taxi). The officials here are very helpful, the process takes only five minutes and it costs nothing. It is open 0800-1400 every day except Friday, 1000-1300 during Ramadan.

(Opposite) The tradition amongst Bedouin women of tattooing the face is far less common these days.

❏ **Embassies and consulates**
• **Australia** (☎ 673246) Above Fourth Circle, Jabal Amman
• **Canada** (☎ 666124) Shmeisani
• **Egypt** (☎ 605202) Qurtubah St, Fourth Circle, Jabal Amman (sixth street on right after Fourth Circle). **Visa**: get here early, as it gets very busy. Mon-Thu, Sat 0900-1100. One photo, collect 1500 same day. JD12 (JD15 multiple entry).
• **Lebanon** (☎ 641381) Second Circle, Jabal Amman. **Visa**: Mon-Thu, Sat 0830-1100. One photo, collect same day at 1330, JD14.
• **Syria** (☎ 641076) Haza al-Majali, Third Circle, Jabal Amman. **Visa**: Unless you are a resident in Jordan you will *not* be able to obtain a visa here (see travel agents on p193). Mon-Thu, Sat 0900-1100.
• **UK** (☎ 823100) Abdoun
• **US** (☎ 820101) Abdoun

WHERE TO STAY

Budget hotels

Although downtown Amman is teeming with accommodation, most of these are pretty lousy. Travellers thus tend to stay at the same reliable places that have catered to their needs for years. Chief amongst these is the *Cliff Hotel* [1] فندق كليف (☎ 624273) down an alleyway off Basman St, where a bed in a dorm upstairs is JD3, (JD5 sgl, JD8 dbl). The rooms are nothing special, and probably the main reason to stay here is the manager, a wheezy old encyclopaedia of local knowledge who dispenses information and phlegm with equal aplomb. In the next alleyway is the *Vinecia* [2] فندق فينيسيا (☎638895), the Cliff's main rival and a better deal. Rooms are JD1 cheaper here, beginning at JD2 for a bed in their 'five-star' dormitory (so called because that is what you can see through the hole in the ceiling). Use of the kitchen is free but, like the Cliff, they rather cheekily charge JD0.5 for a shower.

Continuing down towards the King Hussein Mosque, the *Riad* [3] فندق الرياض (☎ 624260) (or the Riyadh, Riyad or Ryad depending on which sign you see) is unaccustomed to dealing with Westerners. This is not a criticism, however, for they spare no effort to make everyone feel welcome and at JD3 for a bed, including use of the kitchen, it's a very good deal indeed. Double rooms are JD8; there are no singles.

Right by the King Hussein Mosque is the *Zahraan Hotel* [4] (☎ 625473). The main feature of this establishment is the compulsory 4:30 am wake-up call to prayer provided by the muezzin from the adjoining minaret. Although it does have the twin saving graces of an ever-cheerful manager and a cheap price (JD1.5 per person, and free showers, too) that holy racket ensures that this place is really only for the devout, the destitute, or the deaf. Nearby, the quieter *Vienna Hotel* [5] (☎ 658994) will, with a little bargaining, offer you a similar price.

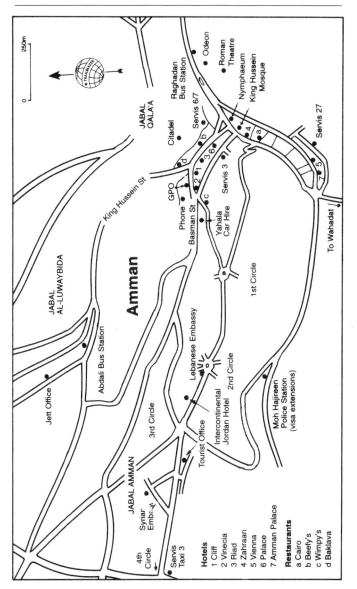

250m

Amman

JABAL
QALA'A

JABAL
AL-LUWAYBIDA

King Hussein St

Odeon
Roman
Theatre
Nymphaeum
King Hussein Mosque
Raghadan
Bus Station
Servis 6/7
Servis 27
Citadel
Servis 3
GPO
Phone
Basman St
Yahala
Car Hire
1st Circle
To Wahadat

Abdali Bus Station

Jett Office

3rd Circle

Lebanese Embassy

Intercontinental
Jordan Hotel
2nd Circle

Moh Hajireen
Police Station
(visa extensions)

Tourist Office

JABAL AMMAN

Syrian
Embassy

4th
Circle

Servis
Taxi 3

Hotels
1 Cliff
2 Vinecia
3 Riad
4 Zahraan
5 Vienna
6 Palace
7 Amman Palace

Restaurants
a Cairo
b Beefy's
c Wimpy's
d Baklava

At the top end of this price range is the one-star *Palace Hotel* [6] (☎ 624326). This place deserves inclusion, if only to mention the absurd decor of plasterboard Corinthian-style pillars and capitals. The staff can be a bit surly, however, not what you would expect from a hotel charging JD8 for a single, JD15 per double.

Moderately-priced hotels

The *Dove Hotel* فندق الحمام (☎ 697601/2) is conveniently located next to the Egyptian Embassy, five minutes up from the Fourth Circle. It's an attractive place, and each room has a mini-bar, TV and air-con. There's also an Irish Pub in the basement, and a stuffed monkey at reception. Prices start at JD21.5 single, JD26 double.

The *Amman Palace* [7] (☎ 646169) is the vast, spacious establishment next to Saviour's Church, catering almost exclusively for visiting Middle-Eastern businessmen, (even the mini-bars in the rooms are non-alcoholic). The tariff here is similar to the Dove's.

WHERE TO EAT

The first place to look for cheap grub in Amman is the alleyway opposite the Vinecia Hotel. Each café here specialises in a different snack and for about JD1.5 one can feast on a banquet of roast chicken, salad and hoummus. During Ramadan this place is also a visual feast as famished locals arrive in force at dusk, spilling out onto the surrounding pavements in their enthusiasm to break their fast. If the jostling crowds prove too much, one can indulge in the same fare in the *Cairo Restaurant* [a] behind the King Hussein Mosque.

For something a little less alien to the Western palate. *Beefy's* [b] is a fast food joint near to the al-Hussein Cinema, where for JD0.5 you can pick up a burger and fries. There is also a branch of *Wimpy* [c] on Basman St, opposite the post office, and up near the First Circle the *Diplomat* does take-away pizzas that are certain to get your salivary juices flowing. For a few dinars more, at the Hotel Inter-Continental there is an Indian Restaurant, *Bdeiwi*, which claims to be the only curry house in the city. Their murg tandoori (JD5) is particularly fine, although according to some reports it can cause bad '*hawa*' (wind).

A good way to round off any meal is to visit one of the baklava/sweet shops, *Habibah*, *el-Quds* or *Jabri* [d], situated where King Hussein St joins King Faisal St.

With so little to see and do in Amman many travellers cultivate a drinking problem just to kill time. There are a couple of dimly-lit drinking dens in the alleyways around the Cliff Hotel which serve the big bottles of Henninger beer for JD1, and in the basement of the Dove there is Amman's own *Irish Pub*. It's not a very authentic version – they didn't even serve Guinness when I last visited.

WHAT TO SEE

Citadel complex

Impressively situated on the summit of Jabal Qala'a, this is the highlight of Amman. The **Archaeological Museum** is the first place to visit here; it's not brilliant but it does have some artefacts which date back 8000 years to the very beginning of Amman's existence.

In front of the museum is a small sixth-century **Byzantine Basilica** and to the south are the scattered remains of a **Roman Temple** dedicated to Hercules. It requires considerable mental effort and some archaeological knowledge to be able to imagine, from the heaps of rubble left today, how either of these constructions must have originally looked. The **Citadel**, which cowers round the back of the museum, is in a better state of repair. Dating back to the Ommayad era it has a cruciform shape, although archaeologists are still puzzled as to who built it and why.

Roman ruins

From Jabal Qala'a you can get a good view over the capital and its other main attraction, the second-century 6000-seater **Roman theatre**, resembling a giant snail half-buried in the side of Jabal al-Taj. Also here are the **Museum of Traditional Jewels and Costumes** and the **Folklore Museum**. Admission to the theatre is free, although there is a cover charge of 250 fils for each of the two museums.

By the entrance to the theatre are the remains of a **colonnaded street** and the **city forum**; a little to the north-east is the **odeon**, a miniature version of the theatre but, unfortunately, this is closed to the public. Yet another Roman relic, the **nymphaeum** (النيفايوم (الهبيل, a public fountain-cum-consecrated shrine, stands to the north of the King Hussein Mosque on Quraysh St.

Desert castles

One of the more curious sets of ruins in Jordan is the collection of castles lying to the east of Amman. Most of them were built during the Ommayad Dynasty and were used by the caliphs as hunting lodges. Sadly the game they used to hunt – bear, deer, boar, gazelle – have been wiped out, and the lodges have deteriorated as a result. Don't be misled by the term 'castle' either; most resemble little more than large houses.

All but two of the castles lie on a tarmac loop east of Amman and can be seen in one day. The easiest way to visit them is to hire a car (see under 'Services' above) which, if there are enough of you to split the cost, can be reasonably cheap.

It is also possible to visit most of them by using public transport and/or hitching. Begin by taking a bus to **Hammamat Ma'in** حمامات ماعين – a hot spring that has become something of a tourist destination in its own right. From there you can catch a bus to the ruined castle at **Hallabat**

al-Gharbi حلبة الغربي (entry free). From here, wait by the main road for the
bus to Azraq (الأزرق), the main town and oasis in the Eastern Desert. Like
the Hallabat al-Gharbi, this fourth-century castle is not Ommayad but
Roman in origin. After the Ommayads had left, it fell into disrepair until
TE Lawrence briefly used it as his regional HQ. Entrance is free, but the
caretaker expects a tip.

The best castle lies on Highway 40, the southern half of the loop.
Qasr al-Amra (قصر العمرة) has some wonderful frescoes including a picture of a naked woman bathing, most surprising for a castle built under
the puritanical Ommayads.

About 20km further towards Amman you reach Qasr al-Kharranah
(قصر الخرانة), possibly the only Ommayad castle that was built for battle
rather than hunting. From here, catch a bus back to Amman.

MOVING ON

Bus
There are three main bus stations in Amman. **Abdali bus station**, on
Jabal al-Luwaybida, serves destinations to the north and west. Buses
leave frequently to Jerash (270 fils in a small bus, 350 fils in a large one)
and Irbid (500 fils in a small bus). There are also buses to the King
Hussein Bridge on the Israeli border (JD1, 1hr). Servis taxis ply all of
these routes; their station is just below the bus terminus.

Up the hill from Abdali is the **Jett bus station** and a couple of Jett
ticket offices. You can catch a bus to Jerusalem from here (0630, JD6.5),
Damascus (0700 and 1330, JD4.5), Petra (0630, JD5.5) and Aqaba (four
buses, JD4).

Buses to southern destinations leave from the **Wahadat bus station**.
Buses to the start of the King's Highway at Madaba cost 170 fils
(45mins). Other prices include: Kerak 600 fils; Aqaba JD2.5; Petra JD2.
This is also the servis taxi station for southern destinations. Prices per
person: Kerak JD1; Aqaba JD3.5; Petra JD5.

Train
Services on the Hejaz Railway (see p152) to Damascus leave every
Monday at 0800, and arrive, all being well, at 1700 the same day. The fare
is JD2.5. Take servis 17 from the Raghadan interchange (تقاطع رغدان) to
Mahata (المحطة), or a taxi from downtown for 700 fils.

The King's Highway

The historic King's Highway stretches from Amman in the north to Ras al-Naqb, 40km south of Petra. Believed to have been the main road which linked the three ancient kingdoms of Moab, Edom and Ammon during Biblical times (c1100BC), the King's Highway remained the main north-south thoroughfare until the Desert Highway was built parallel to it earlier this century.

It's hardly surprising then, that most of Jordan's historical sights line this ancient road. Unfortunately, public transport is non-existent in places; you may have to hitch for some of the way or travel via the Desert Highway and Ma'an.

MADABA مأدبا

Madaba, a smallish town lying 30km to the south of Amman, is famous for some splendid Byzantine mosaics discovered here towards the end of the last century. The Old Testament Book of Joshua (13:9) tells us that 'Medeba' used to lie on the border between the kingdoms of Moab and Ammon. Not a great deal is known about the Moabs but they must have been an earthy lot; one of their deities was the God of Dung, whom they worshipped by baring their buttocks to the altar.

Madaba prospered under the Romans, and thrived as a bishopric under the Byzantines. Although most of the Byzantine churches were destroyed by the Persians in 614AD, and those which remained were subsequently razed to the ground by an eighth-century earthquake, the splendid mosaics that decorated the church floors did survive. Even the iconoclasts, who replaced the pictures of humans and animals with blank squares, could not fully disguise the original artistry of these mosaics.

Yet they remained entombed under the earthquake's rubble for over a thousand years, avoiding the attentions of both Ulrich Seetzen (who discovered Jerash) and Johann Burkhardt (Petra, Abu Simbel) who both passed through. They were eventually discovered by the 19th-century Christians who came to resettle the town.

Where to stay

There is only one place to stay in Madaba. *Lulu's Pension* (فندق لولو ☎ 8543678) charges JD10 per person, which may seem a lot but is only a fair reflection of the quality of the place. The rooms are spotless, the lounge pleasant and sunny, and the breakfast (included in the price) huge. One suspects that bargaining is not out of the question here either.

What to see

The pride of Madaba has to be the **mosaic map of Palestine**, which will be familiar to anybody coming from Jerusalem where posters of it abound in the souvenir shops. The mosaic was once much larger, covering an area 25m by 5m, and was made from over two million squares of stone (*tesserae*). Today it is housed in the 19th-century Greek Orthodox **Church of St George** كنيسة سانت جورج (0830-1800 Mon-Thu and Sat, 1030 -1800 Fri and Sun; a JD1 entrance fee may soon be introduced). The map, which dates back to cAD560, describes an area from Egypt to the Phoenician cities of Tyre and Sidon. In the centre is the walled city of Jerusalem, with the original Byzantine Church of the Holy Sepulchre rising above the other buildings.

There are many other mosaics here; the tourist office (0930-1400, closed Tues) in the archaeological park opposite the Church of St George has details of them. You should try not to miss the **Apostle's Church** كنيسة أبوستل which contains a number of mosaics from all over town, and the **Church of the Virgin** كنيست العذرا، where a beautiful geometric mosaic, renovated during the Ommayad era, can be seen. There is also a small **museum** (0900-1700, closed Tues) tucked away to the south of the Latin Convent on top of the hill.

Mt Nebo جبل نيبو

The final resting place of Moses at Mt Nebo is a ten-minute servis taxi ride from Madaba. After leading the Israelites on their 40-year exodus from Egypt, God called 120-year old Moses up to the summit of Mt Nebo to see the Promised Land, Israel, that lay just over the Jordan River:

> ❏ *And the Lord said unto him, 'This is the land which I sware unto Abraham, unto Isaac, unto Jacob, saying, I will give it unto thy seed: I have caused thee to see it with thine eyes, but thou shalt not go over thither'. So Moses the servant of the Lord died there in the land of Moab...*
> **Deuteronomy 34:1-5**

In the fourth century the Byzantines built a church on what they claimed to be the site of Moses' tomb (even though Deuteronomy 34:6 states that 'no man knoweth of his sepulchre unto this day'). As with Madaba, however, it is not the church that pulls in the crowds – that has long since gone – but the church's mosaic floor of lions, elephants and spotted camel-like animals. The mosaic is housed in what is now a Franciscan-owned building; their monastery lies nearby.

To get to Mt Nebo, take a servis from outside the Jordan Bank in Madaba to Fasilliyeh الفيصلية (100 fils). From there it's a stiff five-km walk to the summit. Not only is the church's mosaic stunning, but the view from the summit over the Promised Land is, by heavenly appointment, pretty good too.

Moving on

The bus station in Madaba is just off the King's Highway at the foot of the hill. Buses run frequently to Dhiban (30 minute trip, 200 fils).

WADI AL-MUJIB وادي الموجيب

This high, handsome Wadi is believed to have marked the border between the Biblical kingdoms of Ammon and Moab. It is over one km deep and the views from the twisting King's Highway which crosses it are spectacular. Approaching from the north, buses run as far as Dhiban ذيبان from where you must hitch, *inshallah*, to the Wadi. On the other side, the nearest town with a transport connection is four km away at Ariha أريحا, where you can catch a bus to Kerak (one hour journey, 250 fils).

KERAK الكرك

The main feature of the hilltop town of Kerak, 65km south of Madaba, is the crumbling Crusader castle – the Crac de Moabites – perched on a precipice to the south of the town.

Orientation and services

Arriving at the bus station on the east side you can see the beginnings of the castle walls, lining the edge of the hill to the south. To get to the entrance of the castle from the bus station walk up the hill behind. Most of the hotels and tourist restaurants are by the castle entrance. The **banks** and **post office** are to the north of the castle in the centre of town, by the statue of Saladin.

Where to stay

There are worse places than Kerak to spend a night, and worse places than the *Rum Hotel* فندق الرام (☎ 351351) in which to spend it. It is not unknown for the Rum's proprietor, Mahdi, to come hurtling out on to the streets to welcome weary, rucksack-laden travellers into his hotel, and although he tries for JD6 per person (with a 500 fils shower charge) it shouldn't be too much of a problem to beat him down to JD3-4. Much of the hotel was still under construction when I stayed but the parts that have been completed are pleasant, with firmly-upholstered beds hidden under crisp white linen. It's situated just 100m to the east of the castle entrance.

Opposite the castle entrance, aptly enough, is the *Castle Hotel*. This place and the nearby *Tower Hotel* are owned by the same chap: the former caters for the riffraff (JD3.5 for a grimy room), the latter is more exclusive (JD7 for a room and breakfast).

Right by the castle is the government-controlled *Rest House* (☎ 351148), the best place in town. It, too, is ridiculously overpriced at JD26/37 for a single/double but every room comes with a mini-bar, TV, shower and a wondrous view of the valley.

Where to eat

If you've looked around the Crac and are feeling peckish, be warned: the restaurateurs near the entrance are a mercenary band of brigands who charge up to three times the normal price for their wares. The Fed'a Restaurant is particularly culpable. To reduce your chances of being ripped off, head down the main street to the centre of town, where there are a couple of cheap eating places near the statue of Saladin. The hoummus here is the best, and at only 50 calories per tub you'll still be able to squeeze into your jalabiyyeh afterwards.

Crac de Moabites المتحف المؤابي

(0800-1800 daily, closed Tues; JD1). The fortress was built in 1132 on the orders of King Baldwin I of Jerusalem. It was just one link in a chain of fortifications that stretched from Aqaba to Kerak and from there up to Syria and Turkey. They were designed to protect the newly-established Kingdom of Jerusalem from the tribes that lived to the east of the River Jordan, an area known as Oultre Jordain to the Crusaders.

Towards the end of the 12th century the castle became the residence of Reynald de Chatillon, who had successfully courted Stephanie, the widow of the castle's previous owner. M de Chatillon was the most barbaric knight of the famously brutal First Crusade: when he wasn't throwing Muslim prisoners off the parapets and into the moat below, he was attacking the caravans that passed by on the King's Highway. Unfortunately for him, one of these caravans contained Saladin's sister. Saladin responded by launching an attack on the Crusaders' kingdom which did not finish until Jerusalem was captured six years later, in 1187. Reynald was amongst the 1000 prisoners taken during the capture of Jerusalem; he had the privilege of being beheaded by Saladin soon after. Although his widow Stephanie held out in the fortress for another year, she was eventually starved out by Saladin's troops.

Visiting the castle Despite the best efforts of the Mamluke Sultan Baybars to restore the fortifications, the castle today is in a fairly poor state of preservation. The decaying battlements are overgrown with tufts of wiry grass, the underground tunnels are damp, dank and mossy, and it is difficult to envisage how the fortress must have looked in its heyday. The small **museum**, which used to be the barracks during Mamluke times, now houses a number of displays on recent archaeological excavations as well as a tribute to Gertrude Bell, archaeologist and contemporary of Lawrence of Arabia.

To enter the museum you may need to find the guard with the key; once you have found him, don't let him escape until he has unlocked the gate to the underground rooms across the way. A torch is essential. Down here is a huge **vaulted hall** measuring over 150m in length. This was possibly used as a storage room, or perhaps as stables. From this hall a secret tunnel begins, passing under the town and out to the fields from the side of the hill. Today that tunnel is blocked but you can see the entrance as you approach Kerak from the north. It was last used as a bomb shelter in 1991, when Saddam Hussein was launching missiles over Jordan and into Israel.

Moving on

Unsurprisingly, Kerak's buses do not run to a fixed timetable but operate on a leave-when-full basis. There are no direct buses to Petra; you must go via Ma'an (JD0.5) and catch another bus or servis from there. If you are determined to travel down the King's Highway to Petra, then catch a bus to Tafila الطفيلة (500 fils) and hitch from there.

Tafila can boast of a Crusader castle too, but this is fairly decrepit and closed to the public. If you are hitching from Tafila to Petra call in at **Shobak**, a Crusader castle which pre-dates Kerak by 20 years. If you're heading north to Wadi al-Mujib and Madaba, buses will take you as far as Ariha; otherwise, simply avoid all this hassle and travel via the Desert Highway (Amman 700 fils, Aqaba 1750 fils).

PETRA البترا

Petra, meaning 'Rock' in Classical Greek, was the sumptuous capital of the Nabataeans, a fairly obscure Arab tribe who settled in the area in the sixth century BC. As they prospered so Petra grew in both size and perfection, and the buildings they erected are spellbinding testimonies to their success. Today the interiors of these buildings are empty, shadowy hollows, unremarkable save for the Impressionists' palette of coloured striations on the stone. But it is the exterior of these buildings – exquisite façades, deliberately sculpted on an enormous scale out of the solid rock to impress on visitors the might and majesty of the Nabataean kingdom – that draws tourists in their thousands to Petra.

There are over 800 tombs, temples, homes and other buildings in Petra. One could spend weeks here but most people find two days give enough time to visit the major buildings and capture the essence of this splendid forgotten city.

History

Excavations reveal that a prehistoric settlement had existed in Wadi Moussa in about 7000BC, a birth date to rival Byblos and Jericho for antiquity. By the time the Nabataeans arrived the Wadi was part of the Edomite kingdom, although the Nabataeans met with little opposition as they settled down to live off the caravan routes that passed through the area. Initially they robbed the caravans but later they learned that it was a lot more profitable, and a lot less risky, to extort a levy from the traveller in return for guarantees of protection through Nabataean-held lands.

The Nabataeans also discovered a talent for commerce and their capital, Petra, became a huge clearing house for the goods that were being transported through the region, mainly frankincense and myrrh from East Africa and Arabia.

By the second century BC the Nabataeans controlled most of the trade that flowed through the region, and Petra became even more beautiful as a result. But no kingdom at this time, however wealthy and isolated, could resist the might of Rome; in AD106 Petra became part of the new Roman province of Arabia. It maintained a certain degree of independence after this but an earthquake in 551 finally shattered the city and broke the resolve of its residents. Thereafter, although the Crusaders built two castles in the vicinity and the Mamluke Sultan Baybars and his forces passed through, Petra seems to have lain largely undisturbed for over a thousand years.

Then in 1812 the explorer Burkhardt (who was to go on and discover Abu Simbel the following year) heard local Bedouin talking about some half-forgotten ruins buried beneath the sand in Wadi Moussa. Excited by the possibility of discovering the fabled capital of the Nabataeans but frightened by his Bedouin guides who were extremely suspicious of foreigners, he managed to engineer an excuse for the visit later described in his book, *Travels in Syria and the Holy Land*.

> ❏ '.... I therefore pretended to have made a vow to slaughter a goat in honour of Haroun, whose tomb I knew was situated at the extremity of the Valley, and by this stratagem I thought I should have the means of seeing the valley in my way to the tomb.'
> **Burkhardt Travels in Syria and the Holy Land**

It was to be another one hundred years before the site was fully excavated but today archaeologists and tourists alike can – and do – descend on the 'rose-red' city in huge numbers to marvel at the magnificent sandstone legacy of the Nabataeans.

Orientation and services – Wadi Moussa وادي موسى
The entrance to Petra is about a ten-minute walk downhill from Wadi Moussa, the village where most of the accommodation and amenities can be found. There is a (useless) **tourist office** near the entrance to Petra as well as a small **post office**. The roundabout is the centre of the action in Wadi Moussa: the **banks**, restaurants and buses are all here.

Where to stay
With lots of hotels and little co-operation between them, Wadi Moussa is a good place to flex those bargaining muscles.

A new place has opened in town – so new that it has yet to be formally named, although it may eventually trade under the name *Hubbly Bubbly* فنق النرجيلة – but it's already doing well. Located near the mosque, its popularity is down to two factors: the exertions of its manager, a young man of boundless energy who is there to greet every new arrival as they step off the bus with charm and chai; and beds in a four-bed dorm that can be bargained down to JD1.5 each.

For a little more comfort, however, try *al-Twaissi* الواسي (☎03-336923) another new hotel near the main roundabout. With good views over the valley, a lounge/games room, kitchen, and beds starting at JD2 for a mattress on the roof, (JD3/6/12 dorm/sgl/dbl), this place is all set to become the travellers' favourite. You can also get a massage here, although it could be rather more thorough than you might wish. They also show *Indiana Jones and the Last Crusade* every evening, although this is hardly an original idea; Hotel Mussa Spring has been doing it for years

Travellers agree that the showers at the *Hotel Mussa Spring* فندق ربيع موسى are unsurpassed in the entire Middle East, and the rooms here are fine (JD4pp). But it's a one-hour hike up the hill from Petra, and even though they provide lifts there and back, it's a bit inconvenient. This criticism – nice hotel, shame about the location – can also be levelled at the *al-Anbat* (☎ 03-336275), just a little further down from the Mussa Spring. It offers a similar deal (JD4 for a bed, JD12 half-board; lift to Petra included) but with the added bonus of a superb panoramic restaurant.

The last place in this category is the *Orient Hotel* (☎ 03-337020). Don't be dissuaded from staying here just because the reception area is made from goat hair, for their simple and pleasant rooms are far more tastefully decorated (JD5pp in a double or triple).

A popular alternative to staying in a hotel is to sleep in the Petra caves themselves. It's cold, dark and, of course, illegal.

Where to eat

There are a number of small general stores and greengrocers near the roundabout, where one can pick up the ingredients necessary to prepare a packed-lunch for Petra. If you forget to do this the night before, there is an early-morning *bakery* down the hill towards Petra which opens at about 5am.

Down near the entrance to Petra are two fast-food joints. The *Papazzi*, which a few people have raved about, and *Petraburger*, which does a fair impersonation of a Western junk food shack.

The *Treasury*, back in the centre of town, turns out some marvellous food; their spicy chicken (JD2) is the best in Jordan. Make sure you ascertain the price of everything before buying, however, or the bill may come to rather more than you'd expected. Over the road is a cheaper alternative.

Visiting Petra

(0600-1700 daily; JD20 for 1 day, JD25 for 2 days, JD30 for 3). The seemingly exorbitant entrance fees at Petra are causing many travellers to take direct action by sneaking in without paying. Managers in the cheaper hotels suggest ways of avoiding the fees but this is getting harder all the time. Guards carry out spot-checks in the site, and there is rumoured to be a JD50 fine for those caught without a ticket (although ejection from the site is the more likely penalty). Although JD20 *is* a lot to ask for one day's admission, JD25 for two is reasonable and JD30 more of a bargain: after all, this is the most fabulous site in the Middle East. When paying, you will be asked to sign the ticket to prevent you selling it on to someone else later. You will also receive a free map; although it looks as if it was drawn by a four-year-old with crayons, it is actually quite accurate.

It is a good idea to equip yourself with a good supply of food and water before entering the site, for the restaurants and cafés in Petra are expensive.

There are plenty of ways to get around Petra. Posted round the site and in the tourist office are lists of rates for hiring a camel, horse or calèche (horse-drawn carriage). Use these rates as the upper limits when bargaining.

The Siq

Part of the attraction of Petra is its dramatic location amongst the cliffs to the east of Wadi Araba. To reach the main city one must first pass along the Siq, a narrow corridor cutting through these sandstone cliffs. The corridor was not created by water but rather by tectonic forces that rent this single mass of stone asunder; you can see that the patterns in the rock on one side of the corridor are duplicated on the other side.

Just before the Siq are a number of tombs. The **Snake Tomb**, on your left opposite the tower-shaped **Djinn Blocks**, is most 'un-Nabataean': no

❑ The Nabataeans

Originally hailing from the southern deserts of Arabia, the Nabataeans were a tribe of wandering herders steeped in the nomadic traditions of pasturing, pirating, pillaging and plundering. Their peregrinations eventually took them northwards to the Kingdom of Edom; there they forsook their rootless existence for more permanent settlements at Petra and the surrounding area. Edom at this time was a land suffering from wave after wave of marauding invaders, and the Nabataeans' survival in those early days depended on their ability to know which regional power to back, which one to bribe and which to fight. Their intuition appeared faultless; not only did they survive in this hostile land but they grew wealthy too by controlling the caravan routes that passed through the area.

Every year the Nabataeans would hold a vast trade fair out of town, during which time the wives, children and valuables were transported to the top of a naturally-fortified hill for protection. It was during one of these trade fairs in 312BC that Athenaeus, a Greek general who had served under Alexander, attacked Petra, slaughtered the women and looted the city. On discovering the atrocity the Nabataeans pursued the attackers and wreaked their revenge, killing all but fifty of Athenaeus' men.

Although they were not large enough to build and maintain an empire themselves, by 83BC their influence had extended over a vast area, from Damascus to Medain Salih in Saudi Arabia, and from the Suez through to Wadi Sirhan (on the Jordan-Saudi Arabian border).

It seems that the enormous wealth they eventually amassed had a civilising effect on these former nomads. By the start of the first millennium AD the Nabataeans were enjoying a reputation as one of the more culturally-advanced societies in the region, a society where women were respected as equals, slavery was all but forbidden and policies were decided according to the laws of democracy. Soon Nabataean rulers were fraternising with royalty from the neighbouring lands; Herod Antipas (son of Herod the Great) was married to a Nabataean princess for a while.

As new trade routes via the sea were discovered and the old camel paths declined in popularity, so the Nabataeans' fortunes dwindled. The last king, Rabbel II, moved the capital to Bosra to be nearer the new commercial centre of Palmyra but his people were already beginning to disperse and seek their fortunes elsewhere. Eventually the Nabataean kingdom was absorbed into the vast Roman territory, Provincia Arabia.

glorious facade on the outside, just twelve graves and a small relief of two snakes attacking a dog on the inside. The **Obelisk Tomb** on the other hand – just below the Snake Tomb and easily recognisable by the four obelisks carved into the cliff face – gives a better indication of things to come. Those fluent in Ancient Greek or Nabataean will be able to read the inscription on the cliff opposite, which explains that the Obelisk Tomb was built for the family of Abdmouk, during the reign of the Nabataean King Malichus in the first century AD. Below the Obelisk Tomb is the **Triclinium**, a room containing three benches, which was originally used for feasts.

The beginning of the Siq is marked by a **Triumphal Arch**. The arch itself crumbled away last century, and only the sides remain. Originally the Siq was paved along its 1200m length; a few patches of the paving remain, on a higher level than the rest of the path.

The overbearing walls of the Siq humble many into silence, the only sound being the passing of an occasional calèche. As you near the end of the Siq, however, you become aware of a murmuring crescendo – a cumulative intake of breath as visitors get their first view of the Khazneh.

The Khazneh الكهازني

You emerge from the Siq's twilight world at the brilliant Khazneh, the most recognisable façade in the whole of Petra thanks to its starring role in Steven Spielberg's *Indiana Jones and the Last Crusade*.

According to legend, the sandstone urn which sits above the Khazneh was placed there by an Egyptian pharaoh and contains a vast hoard of ancient treasures. This explains both why this building is called the Khazneh ('Treasury'), and why the urn is somewhat battered – down the years the local Bedouin have frequently taken pot shots at it in the hope that treasures will come cascading down. It also explains why Burkhardt and other early visitors received a frosty reception from their Bedouin hosts, who thought that they had come to claim the treasure for themselves.

Little is known about the Khazneh. It is believed that it was built sometime during the reign of Aretos III (86-62BC), and the figures of the gods carved into the wall, most of whom are associated with death, suggest that it was a tomb, or possibly an Egyptian-style mortuary temple (see p285) where the late king was worshipped. The capitals and friezes, thanks to the surrounding cliffs that protect it on every side, are in such a good state of preservation that they appear to have been carved yesterday. Try to be here to view it at about 10am, when the building is bathed in sunlight.

The Outer Siq

The Siq continues to the right of the Khazneh where it is called, somewhat confusingly, the Outer Siq. Four more tombs line the western side. These wonderful façades deserve better titles than the prosaic ones they have been given: **Nos 67, 68, 69** and **70**. Opposite are several other tombs: look out for **No 825**, a family tomb containing over 18 graves; and the **Tomb of Uneishu**, (formerly No 813), which was re-christened after an inscription naming Uneishu as the owner was found on a stone inside.

Jabal al-Madbah جبل المادبة

In between tomb Nos 69 and 70 a stairway leads up the side of Jabal al-Madbah. After 30 minutes of puffing and panting you arrive at the **High Place of Sacrifice**. It's certainly high (1035m above sea level) and was the site of numerous animal sacrifices to the two main Nabataean gods, Dushara and al-Uzza. Today two seven-metre obelisks representing these two gods stand on a flattened terrace a little way to the south.

Past the obelisks a path runs down the Wadi Farasa on the western side of the hill. The water channels carved into the cliff-face are part of the Nabataean's elaborate cistern system, which ensured the city was well supplied with water and prevented flooding. About half way down the hill the channels culminate in the **Lion Monument**. Water used to gush from the lion's mouth and into a basin beneath but unfortunately the head has disappeared and the water has dried up. These channels have become blocked over time, so Petra is once more at the mercy of the weather. In 1991 many sightseers had to be rescued from Petra after a particularly heavy downpour.

Below this near the foot of the hill is the **Garden Temple**, a relatively simple structure with two free-standing columns and two engaged pillars adorning the façade.

A little further down you come to the **Roman Soldier Tomb**, so called because of the headless, legless soldier in the centre of the façade. Despite this, the architectural style is Nabataean and not Roman, and most experts date it to the pre-Roman first century AD. The **Triclinium**, opposite, is unusual for Petra in that a lot more work has gone into the interior, which is decorated with pillars and cornices, than the plain exterior.

Below these two is the elegant **Renaissance Tomb** and the **Broken Pediment Tomb**. After this a path to the right neatly brings you back to the Outer Siq.

Amphitheatre and Royal Tombs

It seems strange that an amphitheatre, a place of entertainment and fun, has been built on what was once a graveyard. Indeed the theatre has actually been built over some of Nabataean tombs, and you can see their sliced forms when you wander amongst the theatre's aisles. This 7000-seater theatre is Nabataean in origin, although it looks distinctly Roman in style. It was built between 27BC and 4AD.

On the al-Khubtha cliff-face opposite the theatre are the **Royal Tombs**, so-called because many believe that such majestic constructions could only belong to Nabataean royalty. The **Urn Tomb** – on the far right as you face them – is named after the small urn that sits atop the façade. The actual burial chamber is carved high up near the top of the façade, above the main room between the two central pillars.

Next door stands the **Silk Tomb**, so called because of the myriad of colours streaking the interior walls which are supposed to resemble silk. Continuing round you come to the badly-eroded **Corinthian Tomb**, a more squat, less elegant version of the Khazneh which is actually

Nabataean and not Roman in origin. Further north is the vast **Palace Tomb**, so big (approximately 50m wide and a similar size high), that it actually extends beyond the cliff face. Again this monument is in rather a poor state of repair, although it is probably one of the youngest of the tombs; estimates suggest that it was built during the reign of Rabbel II (AD70-106), the last Nabataean king.

The **Tomb of Sextus Florentinus**, a little way to the north of the Palace Tomb, has also been badly eroded. This tomb *is* Roman in origin: Sextus Florentinus was the Roman governor of Arabia soon after that provinces' inception in AD106, and the tomb was erected in AD130. It is a pleasing mixture of the two architectural styles. To the north-east is the pretty **Carmine Facade**, whose purpose is unknown.

The Colonnaded Street

Opposite the Royal Tombs the Outer Siq turns fairly sharply to the west. This is the main thoroughfare of the city. Underneath the street archaeologists discovered the remains of a Nabataean settlement dating back to the fourth century BC, the oldest buildings found in Petra. The street that now stands on top of these houses, however, with its columns and archways, is undoubtedly Roman.

At the end of the street, on the left-hand side, stands **Qasr al-Bint Far'oun** ('The Palace of the Pharaoh's Daughter'). This is a first-century temple, the largest and most important in Petra. We still do not know to whom it was dedicated but a marble hand, part of a statue which would have stood about six metres tall, was found in the Holy of Holies at the back of the temple. Behind the temple and up the steps is a small **museum**.

To the right of the street, the forest of stunted columns standing on a raised platform is the **Temple of the Winged Lions**. A **Byzantine Church** lies nearby, housing possibly the world's oldest Byzantine mosaic (still undergoing restoration). Back down on the road there's another **museum**, which explains in greater detail the history of Petra and the Nabataeans.

The Monastery (الدير (موناستيري)

Continue along the Wadi. After passing the **Lion's Tomb** you reach, 45 minutes later, **al-Deir (the Monastery)** the biggest monument in Petra, probably used originally as a banqueting hall and mortuary temple.

A peek inside the Monastery is worthwhile, for the walls are beautifully coloured. Petra is often called the 'Rose-Red city' after the poem by Rev JW Burgon but this does Petra an injustice, for the rock from which the city has been sculpted is a thousand different colours. The name 'Monastery' refers to its Byzantine use during the fifth and sixth centuries, when it was converted into a church and the interior was adorned with crosses. Don't miss the chance to give yourself vertigo by climbing up the steps to the left of the building, which lead eventually to the urn on top of al-Deir. The view from here is truly spectacular.

Other hikes and scrambles around Petra

For the best view over Petra and the surrounding area it is necessary to climb **Umm al-Biyara**, a stiff and scary two-hour scramble. This is the most likely site of the 'secure-place', where the Nabataean men stored their wives, children and valuables when they left town. Another climb, this time up **al-Habis** (the hill behind Qasr al-Bint), brings you to the remains of a Crusader fortress.

For those with more time and energy, the five-hour trek up **Mt Hor** to **Aaron's Tomb** and the **Snake Monument** is well worth it. This is one of the more dangerous expeditions, however, and taking a guide is compulsory. The path begins to the south of Qasr al-Bint.

Away from Petra altogether, if you are staying at the Mussa Spring Hotel you may wish to visit the whitewashed, triple-domed building of **Ain Mussa**, where Moses, towards the end of the Exodus, was reputed to have struck with a rod the rock from where 'water gushed forth' for his dehydrated Israelites.

Moving on

Buses leave from the main roundabout. There is now a daily bus to Wadi Rum (JD2.5, 2hrs) leaving at 0630. Miss this and you'll have to catch a bus to Ma'an for 400-500 fils and try to hitch from there.

If you wish to go to Kerak and you don't mind missing the King's Highway, go to Ma'an. The last bus to Ma'an from Petra leaves at 1300 (30 mins).

Other fares include: Aqaba, three morning buses, JD2.5; Amman, three morning buses, JD2 (or take a servis for JD3). There is also one Jett bus per day to Amman (1500, JD8).

South Jordan

MA'AN معان

At some time or another most travellers will find themselves in Ma'an, the administrative capital of the region and a major transport hub.

Very few tourists stray beyond the confines of the bus station; if you do you are likely to receive puzzled looks from the locals and the police may even invite you into their station to enquire about the wisdom of staying in Ma'an. After a short while here you may well be asking yourself the same question. If you do get stranded, there is the *al-Gezzira Hottel* (sic) فندق الجزيرة about one km from the bus station along Abdullah el B al Hussein St, the road that runs between the mosque and the bus terminus. The hotel is probably the best thing about the town but that isn't saying very much. It's JD3 for a dorm bed, or JD10 for a room to yourself.

Thankfully, it is not too difficult to escape Ma'an. The two-hour trip to Aqaba costs a mere 750 fils, and it is only 400 fils to Petra, (500 fils by servis taxi). Buses to Amman are JD1.5. Try to leave early: by 1600 many of the buses have stopped running.

WADI RUM وادي رعم

Lawrence spent little time in 'Rumm' but that has not stopped Jordan's tourist authority from naming every well, spring and palace in the vicinity after him. But no matter, for visitors do not come to Rum to seek evidence of the WWI hero. Instead, they come to see the gorgeous scenery that so impressed Lawrence and continues to captivate the legions of tourists who have followed in his wake.

> ❑*Thinking of this, we wheeled into the avenue of Rumm, still gorgeous in sunset colour; the cliffs as red as the clouds in the west, like them in scale and in the level bar they raised against the sky. Again we felt how Rumm inhibited excitement by its serene beauty. Such whelming greatness dwarfed us, stripped off the cloak of laughter in which we had ridden over the jocund flats.* **TE Lawrence** *Seven Pillars of Wisdom*

The land here is not stereotypical desertscape, for there is little sand and no dunes. Instead, Rum's countenance has been defined by bald cliffs of ochre and rust; these monolithic high-rises are separated by vast, gravel valleys which perform the role of avenues through this desert city. It's an empty, bleak vista, but one which very few visitors ever grow tired of seeing.

Try to spend at least one night at Wadi Rum if you can, in order to witness the changing effects of the light. The best time to be here is just before dusk: during the day the colours are muted and dull but as the searing sun wearies and dips behind the horizon the red cliffs come alive and scream out against the vivid blue sky. This is the perfect time to scramble up the nearest hill to view the glory of the desert stretching out below. Keep your ears open too, for you might just hear something that you rarely hear in this part of the world: silence.

Orientation and where to stay

There is an entrance fee of JD1, which you pay as soon as you arrive at the small government office. If you wish to bring in a car it is JD5 extra.

Next door is the ***Rest House***, the only official accommodation in Rum. It is JD2.5 to sleep on the roof, or you can stay in one of the small two-man tents behind the Rest House for JD3pp. Otherwise you can sleep on the desert floor, (bring a sleeping bag as it can get very, very cold) or befriend a Bedouin who lives in one of the tents scattered throughout the area. The Bedouin near the entrance charge for their hospitality, although if you get off the beaten track you may be fortunate enough to find one who doesn't. Bring as much food as you can before arriving in Wadi Rum: the government-run Rest House is overpriced.

Visiting Wadi Rum

There are a number of landmarks dotted throughout the desert, although only the **Nabataean Temple** (1km) and the **Spring of Lawrence** (7km) are within easy walking distance of the entrance. Inside the Rest House is a printed tariff which lists how much it would cost to travel to the other sites by camel or four-wheel drive. These prices should be used as the upper limit when bargaining, as you can get a better price by haggling with the Bedouin direct. (For instance, the official price for a 4WD to the Rock Bridge is JD31, yet it is possible to bargain this down to around JD12 if you talk to the Bedouin at their village near the Rest House).

Most of the sights, the **Bridge** and **Sunset** viewpoint excepted, are nothing special, and it is the journey through the desert to get there that is the most enjoyable part. It is possible to organise a three/four day expedition to Aqaba by camel for about JD15 per day. If there are more than four of you, however, it is necessary to hire an extra camel to carry all the provisions.

Moving on

The new direct bus service from Wadi Rum to Petra and Aqaba is very unreliable, and you may find yourself hitching to the Desert Highway and continuing your journey from there. The bus to Aqaba (JD1) leaves at 0700, and to Petra (JD1.5) at 0900. For those who wish to spend only a day here, it is possible to hire a taxi from Aqaba which will wait for you and collect you at dusk (JD20).

AQABA العتبة

Aqaba is Jordan's Red Sea riviera, an easy-going resort where Jordanians and foreigners alike can come to sit in the sand, soak in the sun, and indulge in all-manner of aquatic activities. While it cannot compete with its neighbour, Eilat, in terms of hedonism or glamour, it compensates by being a lot less crowded and a whole lot more friendly.

Aqaba is worth 6000 square km of Jordanian desert. That is how much land the Jordanians ceded to Saudi Arabia in 1965, in return for which the Saudis, who had disputed Jordan's ownership of the town ever since the British arbitrarily drew the border in 1925, gave up their claims to Aqaba. They also handed over another 12km of Red Sea coastline into the bargain. And it appears the Jordanians got a good deal, for Aqaba is not only of vital military and commercial importance – without it Jordan would be landlocked – but it can also boast a lengthy history too. According to the Bible, Solomon built a fleet of trading vessels in the harbour; later it became a major stopping-point on the main Roman Road from Damascus to Egypt; the Crusaders built a castle on nearby Pharaoh's Island and the Mamlukes did likewise on the mainland; and 400-years worth of Ottoman troops topped up their tan here, before they were finally driven out by Lawrence and Prince Faisal in 1917.

Although most treat Aqaba as a mere transit point, pausing only as long as the bus schedules and ferry timetables will allow, the relaxed atmosphere and balmy climate reward the traveller who can afford to linger longer.

Orientation and services   (Aqaba ☎ area code 03)

Aqaba is a very compact town. Apart from the ferry terminal seven km to the south everything is within easy walking distance of the centre. The **GPO**, **telephone office** and a very good **exchange centre** are all north of the main square. South of the main square along the Corniche there's the Mamluke fort, which today houses a small archaeological **museum** and the **tourist office**.

To get to the ferry terminal, catch one of the minibuses which leave from outside the museum on the Corniche. The fare is 250 fils.

Where to stay

● **Budget hotels** Save for the caves of Petra and the desert floor of Wadi Rum, Aqaba has the cheapest accommodation in Jordan. Most travellers head for the cluster of three hotels which do battle nightly with each other for the pleasure of your company (and money).

The *Petra Hotel* [1] فندق البترا (☎ 313746) is the best of these; warm and cosy in winter, light and airy in summer, clean and comfortable all year round. It's JD2/4/6 for dorm/sgl/dbl. Don't be alarmed by the parrots on sale out front; they're only a nuisance if you get the room directly above them. At the *Jordan Flower* [2] (☎ 314377), rooms are comparable but unfortunately they have no dorm (JD4 sgl, JD5 dbl). On the other side of the Petra Hotel is the *Jerusalem Hotel* [3] – dingy, and definitely the third choice.

The *Qasr el-Nil* [4] فندق قصر النيل (☎ 315177) sits to the north of the park. The taciturn manager is actually a most helpful fellow but unfortunately your sleep may be disturbed either by the old iron beds that squeak at every twitch, or by the nearby mosque whose muezzin is only too audible from here. Nevertheless, at JD1.5 for a bed in a two-bedded room it's still a sound choice.

The *Red Sea Hotel* [5] (☎ 312156) is another favourite; their rooms (JD5/7sgl/dbl) are large and come with showers and fans. Next door the

Nairoukh Hotel [5] (☎ 312984), and the *Nairoukh II* round the corner do not offer such good terms.

● **Moderately-priced hotels** The Corniche is lined with middle-bracket hotels, and as supply often exceeds demand some good deals can be had with a little determined haggling. The *Crystal Hotel* (الكريستال) فندق البلورة [6] had only just opened when I visited, and in order to try to attract custom they were offering rooms for JD24 single and JD36 double – all en suite and with TV and minibar.

Where to eat
There are dozens of tourist restaurants down on the Corniche, with prices hiked for the clientele who seem to know no better. The *Syrian Palace* [a] merits a mention, for the food is superior and the menu diverse. Nearby, the *Ali Baba* [b] remains the most popular eatery in town, and with some justification; nobody ever seems to come away disappointed after eating here.

By the old parking lot near to the Kerak bus station there are several cheap chicken places where it's a dinar for dinner. For JD1 you get half a bird, roasted and seasoned, and garnished with onions and lemon. Most agreeable.

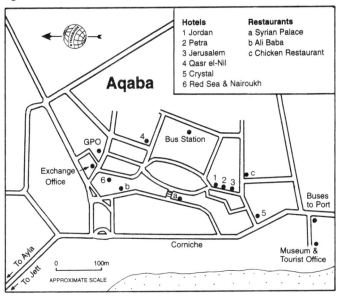

Hotels	Restaurants
1 Jordan	a Syrian Palace
2 Petra	b Ali Baba
3 Jerusalem	c Chicken Restaurant
4 Qasr el-Nil	
5 Crystal	
6 Red Sea & Nairoukh	

Aqaba

What to see

To the south of the town between the Corniche and the sea stands a small **Mamluke fort**. Built on the orders of the penultimate Mamluke ruler Qansuh al-Ghouri in the fourteenth century, it has rarely been called upon in a defensive capacity, and more often than not in the past it has functioned as a rest house for pilgrims travelling down to Mecca. The **Archaeological Museum** (0800-1300, 1500-1700, closed Tues; JD1) next door displays some of the findings from the excavations carried out in the town. Many of the artefacts here were found at **Ayla**, the old city a little way to the north of Aqaba's town centre. Digging continues here but you are free to wander around the site.

If you're sated with history there's always the **beach**. Large tracts of the shore are owned by Aqaba's big hotels, who charge JD3 for the privilege of sitting on their sand. There's a free beach about 20 minutes north of the city but it is a little more unkempt and polluted than the others.

Diving courses are available in Aqaba but wait until the Sinai, where it's cheaper and the underwater scenery is more dramatic.

Moving on

There is one early morning bus to Wadi Rum (JD1). The departure time is approximately 0700. If you miss this, catch a bus from the station to the Wadi Rum turn-off (JD0.5) on the Desert Highway, and hitch from there. Other destinations include Petra (JD2.5, 0630 and 0830; take a bus to Ma'an if you miss these) and Amman (JD3). To cross into Israel from Aqaba, take a servis from the centre (JD1). For Nuweiba ferries see p217.

❑ **Other attractions in Jordan**

Although most of the main sights in Jordan have been covered in this chapter, there are a few minor attractions for those with a little more time.

The Arab castle at Ajloun was the Islamic answer to the Crusader fortresses built in the valley. It is a pleasant day-trip from Amman, as is Herod the Great's fortress at Machaerus, 50km south of Madaba. It is also possible to visit the Dead Sea from Amman.

BORDER CROSSINGS

The rules concerning this border crossing change frequently, so always check with other travellers about the latest situation.

● **Jordan to Israel/Palestine** The border is open from 0800-2400 everyday but avoid crossing on a Saturday when everything in Israel is closed. If you are heading to Syria/Lebanon after Israel, it is imperative that you **do not have your passport stamped** at this border. The only certain way to do this is to cross via the Allenby Bridge; a bus from Amman's Abdali bus station is JD1.5. On arriving, complete the Jordanian exit formalities, and ask them to put their exit stamp on your yellow departure card. There is a JD4 departure tax (not applicable if you've been in Jordan less than 24 hours). It is then another JD1.5 to go across the 10m-long girder bridge in the Jett bus, which leaves every 30 minutes. At the Israeli border, again ask passport control to stamp a **separate piece of paper** rather than your passport. There is an exchange counter by the exit. Rates are 10% below those in Jerusalem, with an appalling rate for the Jordanian Dinar. You have two choices to get to Jerusalem: a servis for NIS26, or a bus to Jericho (NIS5.5) from where there's a NIS5 servis to Jerusalem.

● **Israel/Palestine to Jordan** It *is* possible to re-use your original Jordan visa to go back into Jordan provided you did not receive Jordanian exit stamps in your passport when you crossed to Israel. At both the Allenby Bridge and the Eilat-Aqaba crossing the Jordanians will stamp a piece of paper that allows you to spend 15 more days in Jordan, regardless of how long you were there before. The only problem is this: according to your passport you have one 15-day Jordanian visa, but the entry and exit stamps suggest that you have spent longer than 15 days in Jordan. The Syrians will assume that you've been to Israel, and turn you back. Avoid this problem by extending your Jordanian visa in Amman (see p193).

There is a departure tax from Israel. Crossing via the Allenby Bridge will cost a whopping NIS85. From Eilat NIS49.5. This border is open from 0630 to 2000 (1800 on Friday and Saturday). Servis taxis charge a ridiculous JD4 for the 7km trip from Aqaba.

● **Jordan to Egypt** There are two ways of crossing the 65 km from Aqaba to Egypt's Nuweiba. The first is by a fast catamaran, the Turbo Cat, where you can snuggle into airline-style seats for the 50-minute trip (US$27, 1100 daily). On arriving, you should be in time to catch the bus straight to Dahab. The alternative is to take the overcrowded large ferry, the Santa Catherina, (US$19 +200fils; allegedly 1100 daily, 3hr crossing). You'll probably have to stay in Nuweiba/Tarabim overnight.

If you are buying your ticket from a travel agent in Aqaba (usually the fast ferry only) you should be able to pay in JD's but be careful about the exchange rate they are using. At the port it's dollars only – a bank there will exchange for you. If you plan to return to Jordan later on, buy a one-year open return ticket on the fast ferry (US$41) – it's the cheapest way.

In Aqaba, a bus to the ferry terminal from the museum costs 250fils (JD1 in a taxi). At the port the ticket office is upstairs in the departure hall, but you must go downstairs to pay your JD6 departure tax. Try to arrive an hour before departure. On board your passports are taken from you; if you need a visa it can be arranged here or at the port in Nuweiba.

● **Egypt to Jordan** Egyptian taxes make tickets expensive: the slow boat from Nuweiba is US$32, the Turbo Cat (departs 4pm) costs US$42 (both include departure tax). Tickets are bought from the white building 200m south of the port. Payment is in US$ only; there are three banks in town.

PART 7: ISRAEL AND PALESTINE

Facts about the country

Israel boasts a long history and a short temper. Whether they're discussing the status of Jerusalem, the rights of Palestinians or how much hoummus should be poured onto a felafel, the denizens of this troubled land never seem to agree with one another. All this discord leads to a very acrimonious, noisy atmosphere, and at times a very unfriendly one too.

For many travellers these unpleasant aspects override all others, and few consider Israel to be their Promised Land. Nevertheless there are some treats in store for those with the patience of Joab, the dedication of a pilgrim, and the wealth of Solomon (Israel is not that cheap). Within its narrow borders lies Jericho, arguably the world's oldest, continuously-inhabited town; the Dead Sea, undoubtedly the world's lowest point; and Jerusalem, almost certainly the world's holiest city. Add to this all the conveniences of a modern developed world state where 80% of the people speak English, not to mention some delicious food, good weather, and all those Biblical places which you probably first heard about whilst still in the cradle (or manger), and you have a country that demands – volubly – a little of your time. Arguably.

Modern Israel

After the giant steps towards peace that were made following the Gulf War of 1991, it appears that once more Israel is slipping back into the dark days of the 1980s when the country was in the grip of the Palestinian Intifada. The turning point came in 1995 when prime minister Yitzhak Rabin was gunned down by a Jewish extremist upset at the concessions that he had made to the Palestinians and their allies. It was a devastating blow to the peace process. Rabin was the man who had negotiated with Yasser Arafat and helped to create a new Palestinian state, and who had successfully ended 46 years of hostilities with Jordan.

But although Rabin's killer appears to have been working alone, there can be no doubt that he was not the only Israeli to believe that Rabin had sacrificed too much Israeli territory in his quest for peace. The mood of the Israeli people had changed. Rabin's successor, Yitzhak Shamir, endeavoured to continue the peace process but in May 1996 he surprisingly lost the election to the hard-liner, Binjamin Netinyahu. Netinyahu's promise to adopt a tougher approach to the peace process proved very popular with the Israeli people, who felt that his predecessors had been too generous and weak in negotiations. Whether Netinyahu's election victory is the rock on which the peace process founders remains to be seen. The omens do not appear to be good: in October 1996 the fragility of the peace was cruelly exposed when seventy people died in riots following the opening of a Jewish tunnel underneath the al-Aqsa Mosque. In an attempt to put the peace process back on course Netinyahu, King Hussein of Jordan and Yasser Arafat were all flown over to Washington to meet President Clinton. Little progress was made, however, and the situation in Israel has remained tense ever since.

GEOGRAPHICAL BACKGROUND

Sandwiched between the Mediterranean and the River Jordan, Israel is a land of great diversity. Although much of the south is desert, the north is home to the fertile Plain of Sharon that skirts the Mediterranean coast, and running parallel to that are a series of fertile hills and valleys that stretch right across the country.

❏ **Country ratings – Israel and Palestine**

● **Highlights** Jerusalem is, of course, the main reason for visiting the country and the Old City is the main reason for visiting Jerusalem. The Temple Mount, Western Wall and Holy Sepulchre are the major sights of the Old City, whilst to the east is the Mount of Olives, another sacred Christian and Jewish site. Those interested in seeing more of the Holy Land are spoilt for choice; Bethlehem, Nazareth, Lake Gallilee and Jericho are all nearby.

● **Expense $$$$$**

● **Value for money ✔✔** Compared with the rest of the Near East, the prices charged seem extortionate but by Western standards they are fair. In most cases, be prepared to pay Western prices for goods and services. That way you will occasionally be pleasantly surprised, rather than sorely aggrieved.

● **English communication ✔✔✔** Nearly everybody in Israel speaks some English, so, although the official language of Israel is Hebrew, you should have no trouble making yourself understood.

● **Getting around ✔✔✔✔** (0 on Shabbat, see p223) Often entails a ride on an Egged bus (expensive but convenient) or hitching (cheap but not easy).

● **Travellers' scene ✔✔✔✔** In Jerusalem, Eilat, and Tel Aviv you will have no trouble finding fellow travellers, most of whom are working.

● **Visible history ✔✔✔** Jerusalem (of course), Jericho and Jaffa have numerous ruins for the history buff.

● **Woman alone ✔✔✔** Lots of attention as usual but if you swear at these perpetrators in English, at least most of them will be able to understand you.

● **Good food ✔✔✔✔✔** Great food, from cheap Near Eastern fare (refillable felafels and shishlik, the Israeli kebab) to exquisite international cuisine if you can afford it. Israeli fruit (especially their oranges and grapes) is cheap and delicious. Don't forget to try the home-grown wine, either.

● **Vegetarian friendly ✔✔✔✔**

RELIGION

Over 80% of the country is now Jewish. About 15% are Muslims, whilst the Christians account for only 3% of their Holy Land's population.

LOCAL TRANSPORT

Compared to other countries on this route, travelling in Israel is expensive. Egged is the national bus service, and although their network is extensive and their services reliable, they aren't that cheap. Students get a discount of 10% on fares. Palestinian buses are much cheaper but their network is restricted to Arab destinations only.

There are not many other forms of public transport in Israel. A train service runs from Haifa to Tel Aviv, then on to Jerusalem, but it's infrequent and the stations are out of town. The sherut – Israel's answer to the servis taxi – is another option but again they provide a limited service only.

Hitching is a possibility but don't be surprised if a car pulls up, then speeds off when they realise you're not an Israeli soldier on leave.

❑ **Practical information – Israel and Palestine**

● **Visas** Most nationalities (including citizens of Australia, Canada, UK and USA) do not require a visa.

● **Currency** New Israeli Shekel (NIS), divided into 100 agorot. US$1=3.5, UK£1=5.86. No black market.

● **Banks** You will have little trouble finding places to change your money day or night here (except on Shabbat), although it is crucial that you shop around to find the best exchange rate since they can vary enormously. Two commission-free places are the **post office** and **Changepoint**; the latter has branches in Tel Aviv and Jerusalem. Credit cards are readily acceptable, and every bank will be able to sort out money transfers. **AMEX** has an office in each of the major towns.

● **Time** GMT + 2 (+ 3 April to August)

● **Electricity** 220 Volts AC, 50Hz

● **Post** The postal system is reliable, fast and surprisingly cheap.

● **Telephone** Most of the government-run telephone exchanges have closed down and been replaced by private companies. The best of these is **Solan Express**, which has offices in Jerusalem, Tel Aviv and Tiberias. Rates are a third cheaper at night, and cheaper still at weekends. Rates per minute at Solan are: Europe NIS6.80; USA and Canada NIS6.00; Australia NIS9.30. Alternatively, there is the phonecard. A 20-unit card, which lasts about three minutes to Europe, costs NIS13.

● **Warnings** i) Travellers must have a very flexible itinerary when visiting Israel as certain areas – particularly the West Bank, Jericho and the Gaza strip – can be suddenly closed off without notice.

ii) On a more mundane level, be careful when strolling around town; jaywalking attracts a hefty fine. The Israeli police are not known for their leniency towards foreigners.

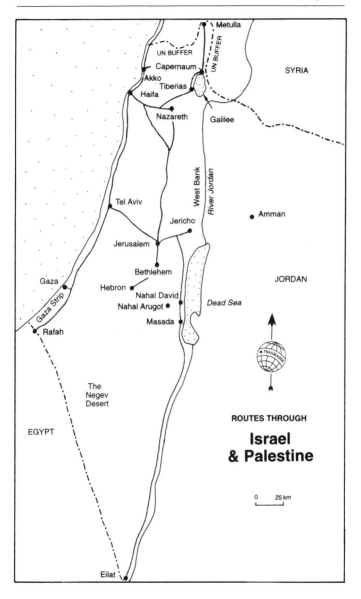

Metulla

UN BUFFER

UN BUFFER

SYRIA

Capernaum

Akko

Tiberias

Haifa

Nazareth

Galilee

West Bank

River Jordan

Amman

Tel Aviv

Jericho

Jerusalem

Bethlehem

Gaza

Hebron

Nahal David

Gaza Strip

Nahal Arugot

Dead Sea

JORDAN

Masada

Rafah

★ TRAILBLAZER

EGYPT

The
Negev
Desert

ROUTES THROUGH

Israel
& Palestine

0   25 km

Eilat

❑ **Routes through Israel and Palestine**
As with Lebanon, we have not followed a particular route through this country.
Since the distances between major sights are not great many travellers base them-
selves in one place, usually Jerusalem, and make day-trips from there.

ACCOMMODATION

The competition between hostels is fierce, and touts are employed to
hijack tourists as they alight from the bus. Unlike other countries on our
route, however, room prices in Israel are usually fixed and haggling often
leads to nothing but rejection (and possibly ejection too). Rates double
over Christmas as the mass invasion of 'pilgrims' occurs, and they are a
little higher in summer as well. (It is, however, possible to sleep out on
the roof of many hostels in summer which is a cheaper option). In some
of the better hotels you can avoid VAT by paying for your room in US
dollars.

While the hostels are usually good, some of the guests leave a lot to
be desired. Jerusalem in particular attracts more than its fair share of odd-
balls. Many are just over-enthusiastic evangelists, although it's not
unusual to find a prophet or even deity in the bunk bed above you. The
last time I was in Jerusalem a kindly, fragile old lady interrupted my dinner to show me her stigmata scars, which put me right off my shwaarma.
If similar misfortunes happen to you, just smile and consider it part of the
Israeli experience.

Jerusalem

*....Jerusalem was a squalid town, which every Semitic religion had made holy.
Christians and Mohammedans came there on pilgrimages to the shrines of its past,
and some Jews looked to it for the political future of their race. These united forces of
the past and the future were so strong that the city almost failed to have a present.*
Lawrence of Arabia – *Seven Pillars of Wisdom*

Derived from the Hebrew 'Yerushalayim' – which translates, ironically
enough, as the 'City of Peace' – it is difficult to think of another city that
has been invaded, besieged, captured, burnt, pillaged and destroyed quite
as frequently as Jerusalem.

It is the religious significance of the place that is behind most of these
catastrophes. When the world was still considered flat, early cartogra-
phers drew Jerusalem as the centre of the universe; everything else as a
mere satellite. Everybody wanted to own the world's most important city.

Even today it remains the spiritual centre for over a third of the planet's population. Little surprise, therefore, that this metropolis of about 600,000 souls is the main reason people come to Israel. Despite the exorbitant expense, occasional unfriendly local, cackling herds of tourists and the edgy, intense atmosphere, it is an unusual traveller indeed who has no desire to visit.

HISTORY

David's Jerusalem

It could be argued that the tempestuous 3000 years suffered by the Holy City have, as their cause, one single, fateful act: the arrival of the Ark of the Covenant, following David's capture of Jerusalem from the Jebusites, in 1000BC. This Ark, a chest containing the Ten Commandments as presented to Moses by God on Mt Sinai, ensured that Jerusalem became both the political and spiritual home of the Jews. David's son Solomon built an enormously ostentatious temple to house the Ark.

Unfortunately for the Jews, this shameless display of wealth attracted many covetous tribes, and for the next 1000 years the Jews spent most of their time fighting them off. The Assyrians raised a siege for four years from c710BC; Nebuchadnezzar's Babylonians were more successful, capturing (and flattening) Jerusalem in 586BC; after the Jews returned 48 years later to rebuild their city, the Greeks came along (331BC); the Jews snatched it back in the Maccabaean Revolt, but then the Romans arrived in 63BC to take it away yet again. After two unsuccessful revolts (in AD66-70, and again in the Bar Kochba rebellion of AD132) the Romans decided that the only way to crush Jewish insurgency was to flatten the city, build a Roman pagan town, Aelia Capitolina, on the ruins and bar the Jews from entering altogether.

Byzantine Jerusalem and the Islamic invasion

Ever since, Jerusalem has been the subject of a tussle between the three major religions. The Christians were the first to claim it, after the Byzantines had inherited it from the Romans. The city of Christ's death and resurrection became a major place of pilgrimage for the Byzantines, after Emperor Constantine's mother, the sprightly 72-year old Helena, built the Church of the Holy Sepulchre on the supposed crucifixion site.

> ❑ **Shabbat**
> Shabbat is the Jewish Sabbath, which begins every Friday at dusk and continues until dusk on Saturday evening. Many Jewish towns grind to a virtual standstill on Shabbat. All the shops, banks and restaurants close, many tourist sites are shut down and the inter-city bus service is suspended. This could have important consequences for your trip – plan your schedule to allow for it.

The Muslims were next. By the beginning of the seventh century the Byzantines' grip on the Near East was coming to an end, and their resistance had been severely weakened by a Persian invasion in AD614. The Islamic invasion 24 years later thus proved to be a relatively simple affair.

The beautiful Old City that you see today was beginning to take shape. Graceful Islamic architecture now jostled for space with Byzantine buildings. The Muslims were fair to their old Christian enemies; in return for a swift capitulation, they allowed Christian pilgrims to continue visiting their holy city. Just to remind everyone that they were now in charge, however, they built the Dome of the Rock and the al-Aqsa Mosque on the site of the old Jewish temples of Solomon and Herod.

The Crusades

This period of tolerance did not last. The Fatimid Caliph al-Hakim (996-1013; see p308) destroyed the religious harmony and revived the tradition of Christian persecution. The Seljuk Turks followed suit (1071), barring pilgrims from entering the city.

On 7th June 1099 the knights of the First Crusade arrived at the Gates of Jerusalem. Legend has it that one of the Crusading priests dreamt that if they all marched around the city walls barefoot three times, the city would be theirs. This they did; five days later, with their shoes back on, they entered the city. In just two days 40,000 Muslim men, women and children were slaughtered. Godfrey de Bouillon was pronounced the first ruler of the Kingdom of Jerusalem in 1099, and the next year, on Christmas Day, his brother Baldwin was crowned King of Jerusalem (a title his brother had always refused).

Saladin finally ousted them 87 years later, returning the city to a level of religious tolerance last seen two centuries before. The Mamlukes who followed him into power enhanced the beauty of Jerusalem with their own distinctive architectural style, and the Ottomans rebuilt the walls and maintained the Islamic shrines in the city.

1918-67

Following WWI, Jerusalem came under British control. It was a temporary solution only. The city had become a major bone of contention between the Arabs and immigrant Jews. Consequently, with Arab-Israeli tensions rising towards the end of the Mandate, the UN decided to split Jerusalem between the two sides. The Palestinians never received their share, however. As the British withdrew in 1948, the Jordanians invaded and appropriated East Jerusalem. Nineteen years later it was reunited under Israeli rule following the Six Day War of 1967.

Jerusalem today

The future status of Jerusalem remains at the forefront of the peace process. The latest proposal is to re-establish Jerusalem as an international city independent of any nation but few believe that the Israelis will accept this idea. And so the squabbles continue. Palestinian anger was inflamed when the Israelis opened a tunnel underneath the al-Aqsa Mosque in September 1996, provoking widespread rioting throughout the West Bank and violent demonstrations in Jerusalem.

It seems that whatever status Jerusalem is finally given, it is sure that the arguments over the City of Peace will continue for a long time yet.

ORIENTATION

The Old City stands in the east of the city. Heading west away from Jaffa Gate is Jaffa Road, which bisects the New City on its way to the Central Bus Station (CBS). Almost everything of interest in the New City, save the museums, lies near the Jaffa Road. To the east of the Old City are the holy Mount Scopus and the Mount of Olives.

LOCAL TRANSPORT

Jerusalem has an extensive bus network. Fares are a standard NIS3.30 however far you travel, although if you plan to be here a while you can purchase 25 tickets for the price of 20. Useful services include:

● **Bus No 1**: Wailing Wall from the Central Bus Stn (CBS)
● **Buses Nos 13/20**: Jaffa Gate from CBS
● **Buses Nos 23/27**: Damascus Gate from CBS.
● **Bus No 99** is a special tourist bus which travels on a continuous loop around the major attractions of Jerusalem. Passengers buy a one-day pass (NIS15) which allows them to embark and alight wherever they wish.

SERVICES   (Jerusalem ☎ area code 02)

● **Bookshops** The bookstore chain **Steimatzkys** has a branch at 39 Jaffa Road and another at 9 King George St in the Old City. The best second-hand bookstore is **Mavin's** on Agrippa St.
● **Changing Money** The post office on Ben Yehuda changes money, including travellers' cheques, without charging commission. There is a branch of **Changepoint** at 2 Ben Yehuda St, and a branch of **AMEX** at 40 Jaffa Road (PO Box 31094). The smaller exchange counters dotted around the city tend to offer a lower rate.
● **Post** The main post office is at 23 Jaffa Road (0700-1900 Sun-Thu, 0700-1200 Fri, Sat closed). Post Restante is at counter No 1.

❏ *The Traveller*
Seek out a copy of *The Traveller*, a free, monthly publication produced by travellers for travellers. Most of the bigger hostels have a stock in reception. The pages are crammed full of info from job hunting to nightlife.

❏ **Embassies**
• **UK** (☎ 828281)19 Nashashibi St, Sheikh Jarra Tower House
• **USA** (☎ 253288) 16 Agron St

● **Launderette** The *Bird of The Soul* (Tzipor Hanafesh) at 10 Rivlin St is actually a café with three washing machines. Sit in the nude, drink expresso and watch your smalls spin round (NIS7 wash, NIS7 dry, NIS1 washing powder).

● **Telephone** There is a branch of Solan on Luntz Street off Ben Yehuda.

● **Tourist Information** There are plenty of tourist offices in Jerusalem. Probably the best and most conveniently located is the one beneath David's Tower in the Old City (0830-1545 Sun-Thu, 0830-1245 Fri, Sat closed). A newly-refurbished office near the Jaffa Gate is opening soon.

● **Tours** Ask at the tourist office about their free tours, which they run every Saturday. It's a fulfilling way to spend a Shabbat morning. There are also a number of private companies offering a better quality service for a fee. My favourite is **Zion Walking Tours** (☎ 287866), opposite the entrance to David's Tower.

● **Travel agents** Charter flights operate to London, Paris, Amsterdam, Munich or Frankfurt and prices are comparable with those from Istanbul (ie about US$150 to London). Prices for scheduled flights are regulated by the government, so vary little from agency to agency. Try not to pay for your flight in shekels: you lose out by doing so. The agency at 31 Jaffa Road has been recommended.

● **Work** Most of the larger hostels have notice boards with the latest work opportunities, but remember that most of the jobs are cash-in-hand and illegal, so heed the warning on p48. For Moshav or Kibbutzim work, visit **Project 67** (☎ 5230140) at 94 Ben Yehuda St.

WHERE TO STAY

Budget hotels

It's no wonder many travellers seem to spend their entire time confined to the hostel, when many of the larger establishments offer so much more than just a bed. The *Palms Hostel* [1] (☎ 273189; NIS11/16/50 roof/dorm/dbl), situated across from the Damascus Gate at 6 Hanevi'im St, is a case in point. This place appears to have everything: kitchen, TV, video, job information, travel agency and Moustache, a very large cat. Like many other hostels in Jerusalem, however, it can suffer from a somewhat stagnant atmosphere caused by too many long-term residents. One Old City hostel, the *New Swedish* [2 on Old City map, p229] at 29 David St (☎ 894124) has tried to combat this problem by imposing a two-week maximum stay. It is a pleasant, if rather cramped, hostel with two large dormitories (NIS12-15pp) and one double (NIS60). Facilities include free tea and coffee, free lockers, the use of the kitchen and TV, and a bathroom so clean you could eat your dinner off the floor.

On Souk Khan el-Zeit is that perennial travellers' favourite, the *Tabasco Hotel* [3] (☎ 283461; NIS10/11 dorm, NIS40 dbl). The air in some of the rooms is thick with the odour of travellers' socks but the new dormitory is fresher. The bar downstairs is very popular thanks to two happy hours. Eating your dinner off these floors is definitely not recommended. Further down is the *Hashimi* [4] (☎ 284410; NIS15 dorm), a more respectable and quieter establishment.

Pick of the Old City for many people, however, is on Aqabat Darwish. The *Black Horse Hostel* [5] (☎ 276011) at No 28, ranks as one of the best hostels in the Near East. Set in a peaceful quarter off the Via Dolorosa, their pleasant courtyard is a great place to relax and forget the hurly burly outside. A bed in one of the cavernous cellars is NIS15, or NIS10 for a mattress on the floor. A double room costs NIS50.

In contrast, if it's hurly burly you're looking for, the *Capital Hostel* [6] (☎ 251918; NIS20 dorm) is located next to the Q Bar and above the Underground night club on Yoel Solomon St. It's very lively, and catering mainly for a young crowd. You can't miss it – look for the stream of soapsuds that cascades down the steps and on to the street below from their washing machine.

Medium and top-range hotels

There are a couple of wonderful mid-range places that describe themselves as hostels but look and act like three-star hotels. Established in 1863, the *Austrian Hospice* [7] (☎ 271463; US$10/42 dorm/dbl with breakfast) on the Via Dolorosa is the oldest pilgrims' hostel in Israel. The building is as clean as a hospital, as tranquil as a convent and has the austere presence of an Austrian Consulate; not surprising, really, as it has been all of these at some stage in its history. From its roof it offers a view over the Old City that will make your jaw drop.

In the New City, blessed is he or she who stays at the *Jerusalem International YMCA 3 Arches Hotel* [8] (☎ 257111). It is, quite simply, the most beautiful YMCA in the world. Swimming pool, gym, 150ft bell tower, international-class restaurant and an auditorium which holds regular folklore performances – it appears to have everything. The price, however, reflects this: US$90/110/140 sgl/dbl/tpl.

Finally, over the road from the YMCA is *David's Hotel* [9], the best hotel in Israel. Since its inception in 1931 David's Hotel has maintained a glamorous reputation, and a flick through the guest book confirms that this is the place to hang out if you are either a) rich, b) famous or c) an autograph hunter. Prices start at US$156/172 sgl/dbl.

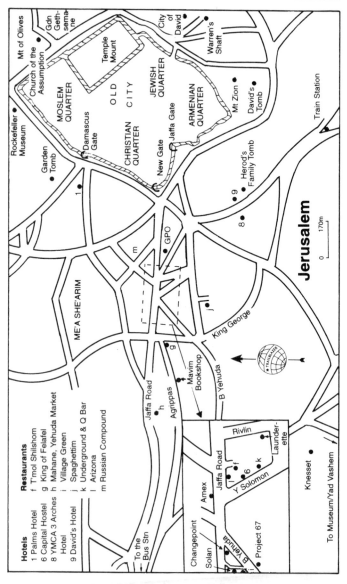

Jerusalem

0   170m

Hotels
1 Palms Hotel
6 Capital Hostel
8 YMCA 3 Arches Hotel
9 David's Hotel

Restaurants
f T'mol Shilshom
g King of Felafel
h Mahane, Yehuda Market
i Village Green
j Spaghettim
k Underground & Q Bar
l Arizona
m Russian Compound

Mt of Olives
Gdn Gethsemane
City of David
Warren's Shaft
Church of the Assumption
Temple Mount
Rockefeller Museum
MOSLEM QUARTER
OLD CITY
JEWISH QUARTER
ARMENIAN QUARTER
Garden Tomb
Damascus Gate
CHRISTIAN QUARTER
New Gate
Jaffa Gate
Mt Zion
David's Tomb
Herod's Family Tomb
Train Station
ME'A SHE'ARIM
GPO
King George
Jaffa Road
Agrippas
Mavim Bookshop
B Yehuda
Rivlin
Launderette
Amex
Jaffa Road
Y Solomon
Knesset
Changepoint
Solan
B Yehuda
Project 67
To the Bus Stn
To Museum/Yad Vashem

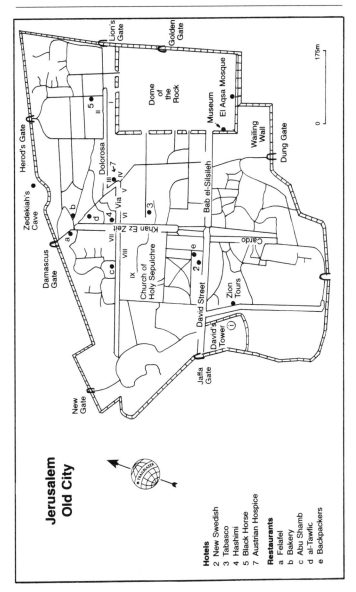

**Jerusalem
Old City**

Hotels
2 New Swedish
3 Tabasco
4 Hashimi
5 Black Horse
7 Austrian Hospice

Restaurants
a Felafel
b Bakery
c Abu Shamb
d al-Tawfic
e Backpackers

Lion's Gate
Golden Gate
Herod's Gate
Dome of the Rock
Museum
El Aqsa Mosque
Wailing Wall
Dung Gate
Zedekiah's Cave
Damascus Gate
Dolorosa
Via
Khan Ez Zeit
Bab el-Silsileh
Cardo
Church of Holy Sepulchre
David Street
Zion Tours
David's Tower
Jaffa Gate
New Gate

175m
0

WHERE TO EAT

The Old City
You'll be pleased to know that the land of milk and honey now has a more extensive menu, and there is no better place to sample Israeli fare than Jerusalem. The best place to find cheap snacks is just inside Damascus Gate, where a multitude gather to sample the Holy Land's cheapest felafel (NIS2) [a]. On the opposite side is a 200-year old Ottoman *bakery* [b], that not only makes all 'manna' of breads, but also the most mouth watering egg-topped pizzas imaginable (NIS4). The bakery is unmarked: just look for their bright green door.

Staying within the confines of Süleyman's Walls, the pizzas at *Abu Shanab* [c] (from NIS8) are very, very scrumptious. This explains why this place is always very, very busy, despite the lack of alcohol on the premises. The small *al-Tawfic* [d] restaurant on el-Wad Rd, while not approaching the standards of Abu Shanab, does some pretty good meals too. In contrast, the food at the *Backpackers* [e] on Aftimus St is nothing to get excited about but it does hold a very cheap happy hour and shows movies every night.

West Jerusalem
One of the coolest establishments to munch on muffin is *Tmol Shilshom* [f], down a little alley off Jaffa Road behind Yoel Solomon St. Come here during the day to enjoy their snacks and peruse their book collection. Food for the stomach, and food for thought.

The best felafel (NIS4) can be found at the *King of Felafel* [g], on the corner of Agrippas and King George.

For those who are cooking for themselves, the famous *Mahane Yehuda Market* [h], between Jaffa Road and Agrippas St is the place to stock up on provisions. Take your camera, too.

West Jerusalem is also a rich hunting-ground for those wishing to spend a little extra and enjoy a slap-up food-fest. The *Village Green* [i] at 8 Ben Yehuda St is a vegetarian, eco-friendly café where a snack will cost around NIS17. *Spaghettim* [j] on Rabbi Akiva St is, unsurprisingly, a pasta joint. It is also one of the few non-kosher restaurants in the city, where you can pig out on piggy until your feet turn to trotters. Prices again start at around NIS17.

Finally, for those who have just returned from the pub and are suffering from an attack of the midnight munchies, there are two *bakers* up from the Palms Hostel near Damascus Gate that stay open until very late.

NIGHTLIFE

There are plenty of places in Jerusalem where you can sit with a quiet beer and discuss the current Israeli-Palestinian situation – or do as everybody else does and just drink until you're ill. The **_Underground_** [k] on Yoel Solomon St currently has a 'travellers only' happy twenty minutes where the beer is **free**! (although it costs NIS5 to enter); in true Cinderella fashion, at midnight this place turns into a night-club-cum-meat-market. Conversation is out of the question at the **_Q-Bar_** [k], just up from the Underground. Dancing to Gloria Gaynor, however, isn't.

On the other side of Jaffa Road is the **_Russian Compound_** [m], home to a number of upmarket bars and restaurants. If you wish to sink an over-priced bottle of wine to the accompaniment of light jazz, this is the place. You're expected to leave a tip in these places, as the staff are not paid.

In the Old City, the best place to wet your whistle is at the **_Tabasco_** [3], which has stolen a march on its rivals by holding two happy hours every evening.

THE OLD CITY

If Jerusalem is a simmering cauldron of religious and racial tension and a melting-pot of cultures, ideas and beliefs, then the Old City is the flame which keeps those passions bubbling. With over 25,000 people of almost every religious persuasion crammed into an area no bigger than one square mile, it's little wonder that the atmosphere can get a little intense here at times. The City Walls, which once kept invaders at bay, now serve only to keep the seething tension bottled up inside.

The Old City is divided into four quarters. The biggest, the **Muslim Quarter** in the north-east, is a largely residential area that contains the Temple Mount, most of the Via Dolorosa and some stunning Mamluke architecture.

The **Armenian Quarter**, the smallest of the four, lies to the south-west; like the **Christian Quarter** to the north of it, this area is more ecclesiastical than residential, and the buildings are mainly monasteries and churches.

The fourth area is the **Jewish Quarter** to the south-east, which until 1967 belonged to Jordan. Before they fled the Jordanians were careful to destroy many of the buildings; much is still under reconstruction today.

One can find something of interest in almost every building and street in the Old City, so the following is merely a guide to the highlights.

Tower of David Museum
(1000-1600 Sun-Thu, 1000-1400 Fri-Sat; NIS20, NIS15 students). This is an excellent place to begin a tour of the Old City. Despite its name, it's actually the restored citadel of the Crusaders, which was built over the levelled palace of Herod the Great. Two of the towers from Herod's time remain. The 'Tower of David' is a misnomer dating back to the Byzantine era, when it was assumed that the palace was King David's and not Herod's. The building itself is nothing special but it is the history of

Jerusalem – a pro-Zionist regurgitation, organised into chronological order and festooned with various lights, holograms and other interactive wizardry – that is the main attraction. From Sunday to Friday at 11am there is a free guided tour around the museum, although there is really no need for one as everything is so well presented. There is also a sound and light show most evenings, and a 'Murder Mystery Extravaganza' every Saturday at 9pm.

The Ramparts
(0900-1600 Sat-Thu, -1400Fri; NIS8, NIS4 students. Tickets valid for two days). Süleyman the Magnificent's greatest contribution to Jerusalem offers visitors incomparable views over the Old City. The walls are split into two walkable sections: one stretches from Jaffa Gate to Lion Gate, the other section begins at the Jaffa Moat (south of the Tower of David) and finishes at the Zion Gate. There is also a ticket office at the Damascus Gate; notice the crenellated walls above, which are designed to resemble the helmets of the Ottoman soldiers.

Consider buying the NIS12 combination ticket. This includes entrance into the **Ophel Archaeological Garden** near the Dung Gate where archaeologist Benjamin Mazar has uncovered layer after layer of Jerusalem's history, and the **Roman Plaza** by Damascus Gate.

The Temple Mount
(Opening times vary according to Islamic calendar but generally 0830-1130, 1230-1500; 0800-1000 only during Ramadan; NIS22, NIS12 students). The ticket kiosk is on your right as you enter through the Chain Gate (at the end of Bab el-Silsila). Tickets include entrance into the al-Aqsa Mosque, the Dome of the Rock and the small Islamic Museum in the south-west corner. Modest dress and undemonstrative behaviour is of the utmost importance here.

When wandering around the grounds, don't stray too far; the authorities are very anxious about terrorists and will arrest anyone who meanders into a prohibited area.

The Dome of the Rock
The summit of the mount shelters under the Dome of the Rock, where it emerges as a single grey lump from the temple floor. This delightful mosque, completed in AD691 (the oldest in the Islamic world), has recently been restored to its original Ommayad splendour.

The elaborate artistry of the interior forms a neat juxtaposition with the rock's simplicity. Take time to contemplate the craftsmanship of the dome itself. Outside, the eye-catching roof is made of copper and covered in 80kg of 24-carat gold leaf, while the interior is lined with intricate mosaics produced by eighth-century Syrian Christians, the finest mosaicists at the time whose work we have already seen on the Ommayad

---

❏ **Temple Mount – sacred to three faiths**

The contrast between the hullabaloo of the Old City and the refreshing tranquillity within the fortified walls of the Temple Mount is striking. This reverential hush is hardly surprising, however, given that the hill, Mount Moriah, is sacred to each of the three faiths:

• **Judaism** The Jews were the first here. According to Jewish tradition, Mt Moriah is reputedly the spot where Abraham prepared his son Isaac for a sacrifice to God (Genesis 22). King David bought the hill in 997BC from a Jebusite man in order to build a temple, a project that was eventually completed by his son Solomon (960BC). The temple formed the focal point of the Jewish faith until Nebuchadnezzar destroyed the entire city in 587BC. Ezra built a second temple – a much less spectacular affair – in 535BC, and five hundred years later Herod, seeking approval from his Jewish subjects (not to mention his Jewish wife), extended Ezra's effort to match the original glory of Solomon's design.

• **Christianity** Many well-known episodes in the life of Jesus took place near Herod's Temple: His parents found Him praying here as a young boy (Luke 2:41-51), the Devil set Him upon the highest point of the Temple to tempt Him with worldly goods (Matthew 4:5), and it was here that He lost His temper, upsetting the tables of the moneylenders and evicting them from the grounds (Matthew 21:12-17). Jesus predicted the temple's complete destruction, so that 'there shall not be left here one stone upon another, that shall not be thrown down' (Matthew 24:1-2). His prophecy was fulfilled to the letter by the Romans in 70AD.

• **Islam** Today the Mount has neither church nor synagogue upon it but instead two glorious mosques. The Mohammedan's reverence for the site is based around the 17th sure (chapter) of the Koran, which concerns a 'night-flight' taken by the Prophet Mohammed to a 'furthermost place'. From there he ascended to heaven to receive God's commands. This furthermost place – Masjid al-Aqsa – was interpreted by the Ommayads as Jerusalem, and Mohammed is believed to have begun his ascension to heaven that night from Mt Moriah.

---

mosque in Damascus. One of these Syrian mosaics credits the Abbassid Caliph al-Mamun with the mosque's construction. This is a paltry deceit. Not only was al-Mamun a liar – he had merely effaced the name of the original creator, the Ommayad Caliph Abdul Malik ibn Marwan, and inserted his own – but he was also an incompetent one, for he forgot to alter the dates when changing the names.

About a dozen steps lead down beneath the rock to the Well of Souls, where Elijah is believed to have prayed. Back upstairs, a three-metre high cylinder is said to contain hairs from Prophet Mohammed's beard. His footprint is on the rock nearby; he appears to have been at least a size 15.

Al-Aqsa Mosque The larger, black copper-domed building to the south is the al-Aqsa Mosque. It has been argued that this temple was originally a Byzantine basilica, and its symmetrical design, open porch and huge supporting columns certainly lend credence to this theory. Most people, however, now credit its construction to the Ommayads four centuries later. Although the exterior is less striking than the glistening dome of its neighbour, just as much money and skill has been lavished on al-Aqsa's construction: the paintwork on the ceiling is a gift from Egypt's King Farouk, the columns were donated by Mussolini and the carpets are high-quality Persian. These recent amendments were necessary following earthquakes that destroyed the original mosque soon after its inception.

It was in this mosque that the Jordanian King Abdullah was assassinated in 1951. The traumas have not ended there: a Christian fanatic tried to set fire to it in 1979 and destroyed the original minbar donated by Saladin, and on 8th October 1990 an Israeli soldier opened fire with a machine-gun in the mosque. The clothes of his victims form a gruesome opening display in the **Islamic Museum**, to the west of al-Aqsa.

The Western Wall
(Open 24 hours, free. Modest dress; no smoking and photography on Shabbat and Jewish festivals.). The Western Wall was originally part of the retaining wall of Herod's Temple. It's the only surviving remnant of the sacred Jewish temple which was torn down by the Romans in 70AD.

The temple shared some similarities with the pharaonic temples of Egypt (see p281), with a section – the Holy of Holies – forbidden to all except the high priests. Following the temple's destruction, the Jews avoided unwittingly setting foot in this sacred area by ignoring Mount Moriah altogether. Instead they congregated at the Wall to bemoan the loss of their holiest shrine. This action gave the Wall the Gentile name, the Wailing Wall. To this day Jews are forbidden by the chief Rabbi from venturing up to the Temple Mount; instead, they pray to the Mount through the Western Wall.

The Wall is organised like a traditional synagogue, with women on the right hand side, men on the left. Prayers are written on pieces of paper and inserted into the gaps in the stones by the faithful. Men are allowed to visit the Wall as long as they cover their head; cardboard yarmulkes are provided for this purpose. Women must be covered up, and clothing too is provided here.

The Church of the Holy Sepulchre
This is Christianity's holiest site, the location of the Christ's Crucifixion, His internment in the tomb and His Resurrection (Matthew 27:33-66 and 28:1-9). It was designated as such by Constantine's mother, Helena, during her pilgrimage in AD326; the cave where she is reputed to have found the True Cross is situated in the east of the church.

Save for a few Byzantine capitals in the courtyard, however, her church did not survive the Persian invasion in 614AD and another built in its place was devastated by Caliph al-Hakim in 1009. The current building dates from the Crusades in the 12th century. Many famous

❑ The Stations of the Cross

The 14 Stations which lie along the Via Dolorosa from St Stephen's Gate to (and inside) the Church of the Holy Sepulchre traditionally mark the last 14 major events in the life of Christ. They begin with the venue of His trial (**Station I**) and end with the Crucifixion and Resurrection (**Stations X to XV** in the Holy Sepulchre). The positions of these stations have little historical foundation and the traditional route has changed many times over the years. Nevertheless, it is still an act of devotion for many to walk the Via Dolorosa; every Friday at 3pm Franciscan monks march along this route, usually followed by a sweating mass of devotees, cross-bearers, hawkers and hangers-on.

I) Christ's Trial. The first station is now inside the courtyard of the el-Omariyeh College to the east of Ecce Homo Arch.

II) The Churches of the Condemnation and Flagellation. These Franciscan chapels mark the spot where Jesus was condemned to death and beaten by His persecutors. Barabbas is set free, and Pontius Pilate, the Roman governor at the time, washes his hands of the whole affair (Matthew 27:15-26).

III) After passing under the Ecce Homo Arch the Via Dolorosa merges with the main north-south el-Wad Rd for a few metres. Turn left at the junction. Next to the entrance of the imposing Armenian Catholic Patriarchate Hospice is a Polish chapel, the spot where Jesus first fell under the weight of the cross.

IV) This is also in the wall of the Armenian Hospice and marks the place where Jesus caught sight of His weeping mother, Mary.

V) The Via Dolorosa heads west once more; take the first turning on the right. Next to a brown door is a plaque marking the site where Roman soldiers ordered Simon the Cyrene to help Jesus with the cross (Matthew 27:32).

VI) A church has been built next to the spot where Veronica was supposed to have wiped Jesus' face with a cloth.

VII) Opposite the end of the Via Dolorosa on Suq Khan el-Zeit one finds a light brown door where Jesus stumbled for a second time.

VIII) Opposite a large souvenir shop is the place where Jesus met a group of wailing women and told them to 'weep not for me, but weep for yourselves, and for your children' (Luke 23:27-31).

IX) Back on to Suq Khan el-Zeit, turn right, and climb the steps on the right towards the Coptic Church. At the end of the alley on the right is a well, used in Byzantine times to quench the thirst of Helena's workers who were building the Sepulchre. The pillar at the entrance, on which a red cross has been painted, is where Jesus fell for a third time. The gate opposite Helena's Well should be open, allowing you to walk through the Ethiopian Monastery and into the Holy Sepulchre for the last five stations.

X to XIV) Just inside the entrance to the Church of the Holy Sepulchre is the marble Stone of the Unction, where Jesus' body was supposedly anointed before His burial. Up the stairs to your right is Calvary and two chapels. The first is Franciscan, and houses both **Station X**, where Jesus was stripped of His garments, and **Station XI**, where He was nailed to the cross. Next door is the Greek **Station XII** where His cross is supposed to have stood, and next to that is the site where Jesus was taken down (**Station XIII**). Now go down the stairs and round the ugly but necessary 19th-century supporting wall. Opposite the large Greek Orthodox Chapel is **Christ's Tomb (Station XIV)**, donated by Alexander of Russia in 1810.

knights, including Godfrey and King Baldwin (the Kingdom of Jerusalem's first two rulers) are buried inside.

Unfortunately, the feelings of visitors today are caught somewhere between reverence and revulsion. What upsets most is the petty squabbling between the different churches over who owns what in the building. The crux of the argument is this: a 19th-century Ottoman decree states that whichever church repaired a section of the building could claim that section as their own. It was hoped that this decree would stop the churches fighting over ownership. Unfortunately, it has only lead to further disputes, with each church now fighting for the right to restore each section. As a result, nothing gets repaired at all. This is why a couple of the chapels and corridors are still covered in soot from the fire of 1809, and why the ladder resting against the Church's exterior has stood there for decades, still waiting to be used in the restoration of the crumbling façade. It's enough to make you blaspheme.

So is this the actual Hill of Calvary where Jesus died and was resurrected? Maybe. The excessive zeal with which the early Christians defended the site prove that they certainly believed it to be, and it is true that the hill on which the church stands used to lie, like Calvary, outside the city walls. But it is impossible to know for sure, and it seems that the churches here are less interested in finding out the truth, and more concerned with bickering.

For a description of the Stations of the Cross within the Church see p235.

The Cardo
Down in the Jewish quarter underneath Habad St is an excavation of the Roman/Byzantine Cardo, the main thoroughfare of Aelia Capitolina. There is little to see now except for a few souvenir shops and a couple of unremarkable pillars.

EAST JERUSALEM
Mount of Olives
This hill, to the east of Lion's Gate, was the venue of many crucial events leading up to the condemnation of Christ. A number of churches have been built on the hill to commemorate these events.

The best and most important of these churches stand at the foot of the hill: the **Church of the Assumption and Grotto** is the next to the colourful **Church of all Nations** and the **Garden of Gethsemane**, where Jesus was reputedly arrested (Matthew 26:48-56).

The path in between these two winds up the hill to the summit, where you can look out across the Kidron Valley and over the Old City. Many of the churches on the mount are open to the public with no entry charge, although once you're inside some of the priests adopt rather high pressure selling techniques to get you to buy one of their kitsch souvenirs. On the slopes beneath the summit is the world's oldest and largest Jewish cemetery. According to Jewish tradition, on the Day of Judgement those buried in this cemetery will be the first to be resurrected.

Zedekiah's cave – King Solomon's Quarries
(0900-1700; NIS2, NIS1 students). It is possible that Solomon excavated these caves originally to use the stone for his temple, although they are better known nowadays as the possible escape route of Zedekiah following the destruction of the First Temple by Nebuchadnazzar. There is little to see here now other than a cave. The entrance is to the north of Damascus Gate, outside the Old City.

Garden Tomb
(0830-1230, 1430-1730 Mon-Sat; free). If you were a little disillusioned by the cynicism and brusque manner of the priests at the Church of the Holy Sepulchre, a visit to the Garden Tomb could be just the tonic. Lying to the north-west of Damascus Gate, this cave is a worthy rival to the Holy Sepulchre's claim to be the site of Jesus' Crucifixion.

The Garden Tomb's case is strong: it lies outside the city walls near to a Roman road (crucifixions used to take place by the side of the road) and Jesus was crucified on the Hill of Calvary, or Golgotha, which means 'skull' - and the most obvious landmark of the hill is the rocky outcrop that does, from a distance, resemble the human cranium.

Whatever the arguments, today it represents a little piece of rural England in the heart of the Middle East – it was bought by the English Protestant Church from the Ottoman Turks – and it offers a tranquil escape from the Old City.

Mt Zion and the City of David
To the south-east of the Old City lies the original c1000BC City of David (0900-1700; free). The excavations are extensive and continue to this day; so far the original Jebusite town, David's castle and a host of other buildings have been discovered. You are free to wander around these, though there is little to hold the average traveller's attention for long.

Also on the mount is the **Cenacle of Coenaculum**, a possible site of the Last Supper (Matthew 26:26-35). The Cenacle is not the main hall, but the small chamber at the back behind the door. Behind the Cenacle is the **Tomb of David**, the **David Museum** and Jerusalem's first **Holocaust Museum**.

Hezekiah's Aqueduct
Possibly the main reason why the Assyrians were foiled in their attempt to capture the city during their four-year siege, the aqueduct was built on the orders of King Hezekiah to provide Jerusalem with a secret source of water. A popular activity is to wade from one end of the tunnel to the

other – a distance of some 500m. If you decide to join in, wear suitable clothing (shorts), and bring a torch (flashlight). **Warren's Shaft**, an earlier aqueduct that now houses a small museum, lies near the entrance. To reach them, leave the Old City via the Dung Gate, turn left and then first right – it's downhill nearly all the way. The tunnel is signposted.

WEST JERUSALEM

Yad Vashem – the Holocaust Museum
(0900-1700 Sun-Thu, -1400 Fri; free). A must. Whilst the criticisms levelled against the museum – that it has been used by pro-Zionists to promote and excuse subsequent Jewish atrocities – may seem fair, it is nevertheless a moving and absorbing tribute to the victims of the Nazi Holocaust. The museum is set in a pine forest and is split into many different sections; the free map provided at the entrance should ensure that you do not miss any of them. From Sunday to Wednesday there is a guided tour of the site, beginning at 10am. Catch bus Nos 18 or 20 from the Central Bus Station to get here.

Alongside the displays recounting the history of the Holocaust are a number of memorials to the victims. The children's memorial – one flame in a mirrored hall, with the names of the victims echoing in the background – is particularly moving.

Israel Museum
(1000-1700 Sun/Mon/Wed/Thu, -2200 Tue, -1400 Fri, -1600 Sat; NIS22, NIS15 students. Includes entry into Rockefeller Museum). This is one of the better museums in the Near East. What it lacks in substance it makes up for in style. It is well laid-out and every exhibit is labelled clearly and precisely. The bulk of the main building and the nearby sculpture gardens are taken up with the Israeli National Art collection, a curious pot-pourri of styles where the curators have apparently attempted to buy one work from every famous Western artist.

Pride of place in the museum goes to the **Dead Sea Scrolls**, housed in a special room called the Shrine of the Book. Amongst them are the oldest surviving Biblical texts (second century BC), and an account of the Bar Kochba revolt of AD132.

To get to the museum, catch bus 17 from Yad Vashem, or number 9 from King George St.

Knesset
Just over the road from the museum is the **Knesset**, Israel's parliament. The procedures and structure are based on the original Jewish parliament from the Second Temple Period. Occasionally it holds open sessions when the public can view proceedings. On Sundays and Thursdays you can join the free tour around the building; just bring your passport.

Mea She'arim

Although not officially a tourist attraction, this Jewish 'ghetto' to the north of Jaffa Road entices many curious foreigners, who come to observe the behaviour and customs of the fanatically Orthodox inhabitants. If it weren't for the incessant drone of the traffic, a stroll in these streets could make you feel as if you'd stepped back in time a couple of hundred years. Unfortunately, the residents do not take too kindly to having sightseers snooping around; avoid causing offence by being very discreet when taking photos, and being as polite and obsequious as possible. Whilst it is unnecessary to adopt the 18th-century costumes of the locals, one should still follow the unofficial dress code here: long skirts and sleeves for the women, long trousers for the men.

To get here, walk to the junction of Jaffa Rd and King George V St and then head north along the latter to Nathan Strauss; Mea She'arim is the compound on your right after HaNevi'im.

BETHLEHEM

The birthplace of Jesus, 11km from Jerusalem, is inevitably disappointing. No one would expect to see a small wooden stable with oxen lowing around a manger full of hay but the big ugly car park and the two kitsch chapels offend one's susceptibilities. Bethlehem is little more than a Jerusalem suburb now, and one governed by the same 'Order of the Unholy Mercenaries' as Jerusalem's Church of the Holy Sepulchre.

The **Church of the Nativity** is the focal point of the town. It was originally a Byzantine structure which was built on the most probable spot of Jesus' birth. Nearby is the **Milk Grotto Chapel**, where the family hid from Herod before escaping to Egypt, and **Rachel's Tomb**, one of the holiest sites in Judaism where the wife of Jacob is interred.

There are a number of places to stay in Bethlehem and you shouldn't have a problem finding accommodation except, like Mary and Joseph, at Christmas. The *Franciscan Convent Pension* near the Milk Grotto has dorm beds for NIS22 – the cheapest in town.

Many people try to hike to Bethlehem, though the three-hour walk is not particularly scenic and Bethlehem is rather an anti-climax. But if you are in perambulatory mood – and assuming there is no bright star to guide you – then head along the Hebron Road past the railway station and the Greek Monastery. Bethlehem will appear on the horizon.

MOVING ON

For Bethlehem buses you need to visit the **Arab Bus Station** to the north of Damascus Gate on Hazanhanim. Fares are about NIS1.5. There are also sheruts that leave from the car park opposite Damascus Gate. The fare to Bethlehem is NIS3, to Jericho NIS5. The following is a brief

summary of the buses that depart from the **Central Bus Station**.
Remember, there is nothing on Saturday (except after 1800 between
major cities) and nothing on Friday after about 3pm.

	Bus No	Price (stu)	Frequency	Journey
Airport	945/947	15.50 (14)	every 20mins, 0630-2030	45mins
Tiberias	961/963	30 (27)	2 per hr, 0650-2030	1hr
Haifa	940/945/947	28.50 (25.50)	every 20mins, 0600-2030	2hrs
Tel Aviv	405	14 (12.50)	every 15mins, 0550-2200	1hr
Masada only	486	27 (24)	4 buses, morning only	4hrs
Eilat/Masada	444	44 (40)	5 per day 0700-1700	2hrs

Northern Israel

TIBERIAS

This is a good place to visit if you're sick of looking at ruins. Apart from
a few unimpressive stones in the Archaeological Gardens by the Moriah
Plaza, most of the history of Tiberias has been smothered by the prome-
nades, arcades and shopping malls of the new Tiberias Resort.

And there is a lot to smother. Tiberias has a lengthy and turbulent history. The town was founded by Herod the Great's son, Herod Antipas, in
about 20AD, and was named after the Roman Emperor Tiberias.
Following the Bar Kochba revolt it became one of Judaism's four holy
cities and many Jewish philosophers and rabbis subsequently settled in
the area. It was returned to the Jews – following tenures by the Crusaders,
Saladin and the Mamlukes – in 1562 by the Ottomans, who presented it
to the influential Jewish leader Don Joseph Nussi as a gift for his loyalty.
Save for a few years in the 18th century, when Galilee was an independent fiefdom of the Arab Sheikh Daher el-Omar, it has remained in
Jewish hands.

Although it is not the place to come looking for evidence of the past,
it is a good place to savour the serenity of Lake Galilee, and a convenient
base for exploring both the lake and the nearby Golan Heights.

Orientation and services   (Tiberias ☎ area code 06)
Tiberias is on the south-western side of Lake Galilee. The suburbs sprawl
up the hill but the tourist centre is concentrated into a one square km area
next to the lake. The **post office**, (0800-1230, 1530-1800 on Sun-Thu,
0800-1130 on Fri, 0800-1300 on Wed), currently undergoing renovation,
is on the junction of HaYarden and Elhadeff. You can **exchange money**
here, or at the 24-hour automatic change machine on Ha Bannim. The
regional tourist office (0830-1600 Sun-Thu, 0830-1200 on Fri) is in the
middle of the Archaeological Garden .

Most of the hotels can hire out bikes to their guests for about NIS35 per day, and you can have a very pleasant day cycling by the lake. Cars, boats, horses, yachts and even donkeys are also available to rent.

Where to stay

Offering a wide variety of clean and well-furnished rooms, the *Nahum Hostel* [1] (☎ 721505) is the best place to stay in Tiberias. Starting at NIS20 for a dorm bed and NIS80 for a double (NIS25/100 dorm/dbl in summer) each room boasts a fridge, central heating, air-con, and some now even have TV. Summer barbecues are held at their MTV-equipped rooftop bar.

There are two of similarly-priced rivals nearby: the *Aviv* [2] (tel 720007) has the hardest working touts at the bus station but its location by a busy junction may well put some people off; the *Maman* [3] (☎ 792986), just up the hill from the Nahum, is perfectly acceptable but lacks the atmosphere of its neighbour.

There's also the stylish *Scottish Guesthouse* [4] (☎ 723769), formerly a hospice established by a Scottish Missionary in 1855. The hostel has some lovely sprawling gardens in which to relax. Rooms cost US$45/70 for a single/double with breakfast; in the summer they also have dorm beds for US$6 per night – the best value in Tiberias.

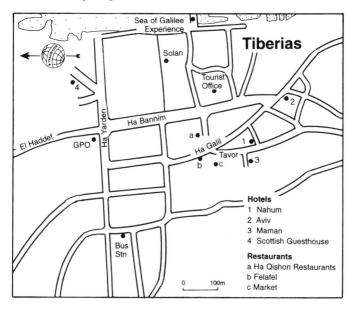

Tiberias

Hotels
1 Nahum
2 Aviv
3 Maman
4 Scottish Guesthouse

Restaurants
a Ha Qishon Restaurants
b Felafel
c Market

Where to eat

If you want to splash out in Tiberias, there are plenty of restaurants eager to separate you from your money on Ha Qishon [a]. The local speciality is St Peter's fish, and most restaurants have their own way of cooking and serving it. In most cases, however, the result is the same: bland and bony.

If you wish to eat cheaply you have just these two options: the numerous small snack bars on Ha Galil where a refillable felafel is NIS6 [b], or the food market behind Tavor St.

Tours of Northern Israel

Most of the better hostels and a few travel agents offer tours that give visitors a chance to view the major sites of the surrounding area. These tours start at about US$30 for the day, food included.

The **Mount of the Beatitudes** is the top sight. Three important episodes in the ministry of Jesus occurred here: the Sermon on the Mount (Matthew 5-7), the Miracle of the Loaves and Fishes (Luke 9:10-17) and the post-Resurrection appearance of Jesus to the disciples (Matthew 28:16-20). Three churches now stand in celebration of these events.

Other attractions in the area include: the Crusaders' **Castle of Nimrod**; **Quneitra**, part of the UN buffer zone; **Capernaum**, where Jesus' ministry began (a hideous chapel now sits on the remains of the synagogue); and, finally, the **Good Fence at Metulla**, an Israeli medical outpost which cares for both Israeli and Lebanese citizens. You can get a good view of Beaufort Castle in Lebanon from here.

Lake Galilee

On the edge of Lake Galilee is a small lakeside promenade with a few overpriced restaurants and a pier. One of the features of this pier is the **Galilee Experience** which, with only 27 projectors and 36 minutes to play with, attempts to bring alive the 4000-year history of Lake Galilee. For only US$6, there are worse ways to spend 36 minutes.

Moving on

Every 50 minutes there are buses to Nazareth (Nos 331 and 431, NIS14, NIS12.70 for students) and Haifa (Nos 331 and 431, NIS17/15.5). Buses to Tel Aviv (No 830, NIS25/22.5) leave every 30 minutes.

NAZARETH

'Can something good really come out of Nazareth', asked Nathaniel on being told where Jesus lived (John 1:46). Even today the town is not very attractive but Nazareth has the largest Arab population in Israel (60,000) and a number of churches and shrines which mark the sacred Christian sites of this, the home town of Mary and Joseph. It is also one of the very few towns in this book with a predominantly Christian population, and as such the Sabbath falls on Sunday here, not Saturday.

Orientation and services   (Nazareth ☎ **area code** 06)
The town of Nazareth is split into two. Do not get off at Illit Nazareth, for
this is the industrial part of town and lies a few km from the centre.
Instead, look for the conical roof of the Basilica as you speed down St
Paul VI St (a petrol station stands opposite) and jump off there. The **post
office**, hotels, **tourist office** (0830-1700 Mon-Fri, 0830-1400 Sat) and a
bank are all nearby.

Where to stay
There is really only one budget place to stay in town: the *Sisters of
Nazareth Convent* (NIS22 in dorm, US$22/30 sgl/dbl) on Casa Nova St,
opposite the Basilica of the Annunciation. The sisters are a French order
who arrived here in 1850. Beneath their convent are some ruins discovered in 1884. Records suggest that they could be the foundations of the
Byzantine Church of Nutrition, built on the site where Jesus reputedly
spent much of his youth. Most of the ruins seem to date from the
Crusades, however.

Even without the archaeological interest the convent is still the place
to spend a night, for it is immaculately clean, has a large lounge and
kitchen and a pleasant courtyard. It does have a 9pm curfew but there is
little to do in Nazareth after that time anyway. The building is virtually
anonymous; look out for the tiny red and white sign, 'Religeuses de
Nazareth', and ring the doorbell.

If you are looking for something to eat, there are a number of restaurants, a bakery and a few baklava shops on Paul VI St.

What to see
The most important stop on the tourist itinerary is the Franciscan **Basilica
of the Annunciation** (c0830-1800, one-hour break for lunch, closed during services; free entry), said to mark the site where the angel Gabriel
announced to Mary that she was to bear God's child (Luke 1:26-28). The
basilica you see today was built in 1969 to replace an earlier church from
the 18th century.

Before entering, look at the elaborate main portal. On the left-hand
side Adam, Abraham and David are carved into the frame, on the right are
the twelve disciples. The door itself shows scenes from the life of Christ.

Inside, the church is split into two levels. The lower floor contains the
remains of earlier churches – Byzantine, Crusader – built on the site,
whilst the modern upper level houses a collection of paintings and
mosaics donated by Christian organisations all over the world.

From the upper level you can walk to the **Church of St Joseph**, reputedly built on the site of Joseph's carpentry shop. This simple church,
which is almost completely overshadowed by its grand neighbour, is also
a twentieth-century building.

Other sacred Christian sites are dotted throughout Nazareth. These include the **Convent of Mary's Fear**, from where Mary watched as the citizens of Nazareth attempted to cast Jesus off a cliff (Luke 4:29-30); **Mary's Well** and **St Gabriel's Church** near the top of Nazareth hill, where Orthodox Greeks believe the Annunciation took place; the **School of Jesus the Adolescent** with the accompanying basilica to the north-west, and a **Greek Catholic Church**, supposedly built on the site of the synagogue where Jesus taught.

Moving on

There is no bus station in Nazareth, so buses stop in the main street near the turn off for the Basilica. There are a couple of small ticket offices here. Bus numbers and prices are as follows: Haifa (Nos 431 and 331, NIS14, NIS12.70 students), Tiberias (No 431, NIS14/12.70), Tel Aviv (Nos 823 and 824, NIS27/24.30).

HAIFA

Haifa is a fairly attractive industrial town at the northern end of Israel's Mediterranean coast. Not usually regarded as a tourist destination, Haifa does, nevertheless, have some pleasant beaches and a few historical towns nearby. Its most important landmark, however, and one which completely dominates the city centre, is the Shrine of the Bab, the head-quarters of the Baha'i faith.

Like their Lebanese neighbours to the north, Haifa was originally a Phoenician trading port, and the docks are still busy today, with many travellers arriving here in order to catch a ferry (see p247) to one of the Mediterranean islands.

Orientation and services   (Haifa ☎ area code 04)

Haifa stretches from the summit of Mt Carmel (the affluent and chic quar-ter of the city) down to the Mediterranean shore and the port. The **GPO**, a **tourist office** (as in many cities in Israel, there are two competing offi-cial tourist organisations) and the **banks** are about halfway down the hill in the town centre. By the port is the train station; and about 10 minutes to the west there's the concrete bus terminus. The main focus for visitors is Ben Gurion Boulevard, which runs from the coast to the gardens in front of the Shrine of the Bab.

The easiest way to ascend the hill is on the Carmelit, an underground railway travelling between Gan Hu Em at the summit and Paris Square. The stop for the town centre is Hanevi'im. The fare is NIS3.30.

Where to stay

Haifa's selection of budget hotels is limited. Nearly everybody ends up at the *Bethel Hostel* (☎ 521110), at 40 HaGefen, which is a tad expensive at NIS30 for a dorm bed. There's a picnic area, snack bar and even a small

basketball court. They do, however, operate an infuriating lock-out policy between 0900 and 1700. To get here, walk up Ben Gurion Boulevard
and turn right at the top; the hostel is on your right after about 100m.

Up amongst the big hotels on the summit of Mt Carmel is the diminu-
tive **Beth Shalom** (US$44/66/84 sgl/dbl/tpl). It's very pleasant, but they
impose a strict three-night minimum stay, and it is unlikely that one
would wish to commit oneself to Haifa for that long.

Where to eat

There is an anonymous **felafel stall** [a] at the junction of Allenby and
Endor which is terrific value. A felafel with unlimited salad is just NIS6,
or NIS4 for a small one. At the corner of Hagyfen and Ben Gurion is a
kebab house [b], where their NIS7 shwaarma is enough to satisfy even
the keenest of appetites.

At the top of Mt Carmel, the **Bank** offers that rarest of Israeli fare, a
bacon sandwich (NIS21.90).

The Shrine of the Bab

Dominating the city of Haifa and standing amidst some splendidly man-
icured lawns, the golden-domed Shrine of the Bab houses the body of the
Martyr-Herald of the Baha'i faith, Baha'u'llah. Executed in Iran in 1850
for his religious teachings, the Bab's remains were brought here some 50

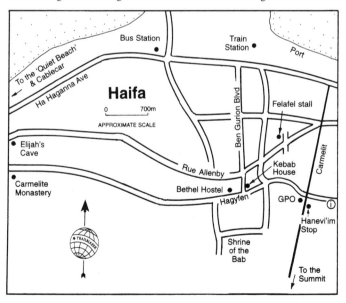

years later and interred in the shrine by Abdu'l-Baha, the son and successor of Baha'u'llah. The shrine is open to visitors from 0900-1200, and the gardens remain open until 5pm (free admission).

Nearby are other important Baha'i buildings, including the Universal House of Justice, (the large, white house behind the Shrine of the Bab), and the International Baha'i Archives, containing the relics of the Baha'i faith. Unfortunately, both are closed to the general public.

To reach the shrine of the Bab, catch the 22 bus from Blvd Ben Gurion, and get off by the Sculpture Garden.

Cablecar

(1000-2100 Sun-Thu, 0900-1400 Fri, 1000-1800 Sat). A relaxing way to spend a few hours is to head to the 'Quiet Beach' (see map), top up your tan, and then ride the cablecar over the city to the summit of Mt Carmel. While you ascend a recorded commentary points out the few highlights of Haifa below. Bus No 2 to Bat Galim will drop you at the beach.

Carmelite monastery

This monastery lies at the western end of Rue Allenby. The Carmelites are a 12th-century order, founded by European Crusaders who wished to emulate the simple, uncluttered lifestyle of the prophet Elijah. The grounds have been used as the site of a hermitage ever since then, although the current monastery was built only in the last century. Below the monastery is a cave once used by the prophet; follow the path which leads down the hill from the monastery.

Museums

Much of Haifa's past now sits behind glass in the city's many museums. The tourist office has handouts detailing the opening hours and prices. The best two are the interactive **Technion** at the Institute of Technology, and the **Haifa Museum**, which is actually three museums in one (ancient and modern art, music and ethnology). While none of the museums are worth rescheduling an itinerary to go and see, they are useful time-fillers if you have an afternoon to kill, and many are also open on Shabbat.

Akko (Acre)

The site of the Crusaders' last stand in the Near East, Acre is an easy and diverting daytrip, 18km from Haifa. The Crusaders first took the city in 1100, and remained within the city walls for almost two centuries. It was not an unbroken tenure: for four years (1187-91) the city was held by Saladin, and was only recaptured following a two-year siege during which 80,000 Crusaders died. The Europeans were finally ousted by the Mamlukes under al-Ashraf Khalil in 1291.

As well as many Crusader buildings, Akko also has an extremely photogenic harbour and a small bazaar. To reach Akko from Haifa, catch bus Nos 251/271 from Haifa Central, or a sherut from David St.

Moving on

Buses There are buses to Tel Aviv (Nos 900,901 and 921; NIS17, NIS15.50 for students) every 15-20 minutes from 0535 until 2300. For Nazareth, Arab Bus No 331 (NIS14/12.70) leaves every 20 minutes (inc Shabbat). For Jerusalem (Nos 940/945/947; NIS28/25.50) buses depart every 30 minutes from 0540-2000.

Ferries There are several agencies, the best of which, **Mano Seaways** (☎ 8667666), can be found at 2 Palmer Gate. Piraeus (US$96 low season, deck class), Rhodes (US$90) and Limassol (US$58) are the three main destinations for the once-a-week ferry. Ask for a student discount – you may be entitled to a reduction of up to 20%. To reach the ferry terminal, take the large blue bridge next to the railway station.

CAESAREA

Caesarea, 40km south of Haifa, was the capital of Roman Judea following the destruction of Jerusalem during the Bar Kochba Revolt in AD132. The city was founded by Herod in 22BC. Ever the diplomat, Herod named it after the Roman Emperor Augustus Caesar, and it remained the capital of Judea for over 600 years. The port that Herod constructed here was so architecturally advanced that, until divers recently began to bring evidence to the surface, its very existence had been in doubt.

Caesarea stretches for four km along the shore. A massive lighthouse and two enormous breakwaters were the most visible of the harbour's structures, although you'll see little evidence of them today. Indeed, compared to some of the other Roman ruins on this trip Caesarea is a mite disappointing. An amphitheatre, the remains of a walled Crusader town and a fifth-century Synagogue are the highlights.

To get here take one of the Tel Aviv buses from Haifa Central, alight at the Caesarea turn-off and walk or hitch for four km to the site.

TEL AVIV AND JAFFA

Tel Aviv's port, Jaffa, is the oldest working harbour in the world, possibly founded by and named after Noah's son Japhet in c1750BC. Fittingly, its history is a colourful one, and down the centuries Jaffa has had its fair share of unwelcome visitors. Some have been devious – the New Kingdom Pharaoh Tuthmose III conquered the city by smuggling his troops into the town inside large storage jars (c1468BC) – whilst others have just been destructive: Napoleon wreaked such havoc here in 1799 that only a quarter of the population survived. Jaffa also features in the Bible. Hiram delivered the cedars for Solomon's Temple to Jaffa (2 Chronicles 2:16), it was Jonah's last stop before meeting the whale (Jonah 1-4), and St Peter raised Dorcas from the dead here (Acts 9:36-40).

Throughout the 20th century the town has been plagued by some of the worst Arab-Jewish hostilities, and today Jaffa is overshadowed by its younger, brasher brother to the north.

Tel Aviv is a 20th-century invention, originally founded as a small Jewish settlement by the residents of Jaffa. Even in the 1920s the population was still less than 1000 but increased immigration and the construction of a new port north of Jaffa has sent this figure spiralling to nearly 1.8 million today. This population explosion has forced the town to carry out some pretty hurried construction work in order to accommodate these people; many buildings seem to have been erected with little consideration for harmony or composition. But ugly as it is, Tel Aviv is still the commercial, cultural and entertainment capital of Israel, and probably the most modern of all the cities on this route.

Local transport
The bus is really the only way to travel in Tel Aviv. Fares are a standard NIS3.30. Below are some of the most useful routes:
● Bus No 4: Central Bus Station (CBS) to Allenby St/Ben Yehuda and vice versa
● Bus No 44: CBS to train station and vv
● Bus No 46: CBS to Jaffa and vv
● Bus No 27: CBS to the university and vv
● Bus No 222: Frischman St to the airport and vv
● Bus No 10: Allenby/Ben Yehuda to Jaffa and vv
● Bus No 25: Allenby St to the University and vv

Orientation and services
(Tel Aviv ☎ area code 03)
The **tourist office** (0900-1700 Sun-Thurs, and 0900-1300 on Friday) is next to platform 630 at the Central Bus Station. The main **GPO** and **phone office** is on Mikveh Y'Israel St (0700-1800 Sun-Thu, 0700-1200 Fri); the small phone office at counter 10 is open until 2200. To change money, the commission free **Changepoint** company have an office at 96 Hayarkon, and there is a branch of **AMEX** 100m further north (112 Hayarkon, PO Box 3292). There is a good **launderette** below the Josef Hostel, while the Saskiah Hostel on Ben Yehuda doubles up as a travel agency called the **Travel Centre,** and also has a **Kibbutz Centre**. Further up Ben Yehuda, (at No 36) is a specialist travellers' shop, **Maslool**, stock-

---

❏ **Embassies**
• **Australia** (☎ 250451) 37 Shaul Hamelech Blvd
• **Canada** (☎ 228122) 220 Hayarkon St
• **Egypt** (☎ 5465151) 54 Basel St. Visa: open 0900-11 Sun-Thu; 1 photo, pick up 1pm same day. See Eilat section for prices.
• **UK** (☎ 5100166) 192 Hayarkon St
• **US** (☎ 5174388) 71 Hayarkon St

ing everything from rucksacks to hiking boots, currency converters to universal plugs. Tel Aviv, or more precisely the 14th floor of the Shalom Tower on Herzl St, is also the place to come if you need to extend your **visa** (0800-1200 Sun-Thu. Also 1600-1900 Sun-Wed). A three-month extension costs NIS100; one passport photograph is required.

Where to stay
Tel Aviv suffers from plagues of travellers who are **S**tuck in a **H**ostel in **I**srael **T**rying to **S**ave. Being underpaid and overworked in a foreign country is few people's idea of fun and, unfortunately, the hostels can become depressing places because of them. The following are some of the better ones:

The ***Josef Hostel*** [1] (☎ 5282308) is currently the cheapest in town, with dorm beds for just NIS18 on their covered roof. It's owned by the same guy as ***The Office*** [2] (☎ 5289984) but it's a more laid-back, long-haired alternative. The Office charges NIS25 per night (dorms only), which includes a breakfast of jam and toast. It boasts a TV lounge, fully-equipped kitchen and, best of all, a huge bar open long hours.

Down by the beach the ***Sea and Sun Hostel*** [3] (☎ 5173313; NIS19/45 dorm/private room) at 62 Hayarkon St is a quieter alternative, probably because many prospective punters are put off by the lengthy lists of rules pinned everywhere. It is the best hostel to come to if you wish to work in Tel Aviv – construction companies often call in at the hostel if they need more hands that day.

Further north along Ben Yehuda and nestling amongst the big hotels are the ***Gordon Hostel*** [4] (☎ 5229870), and behind it, the ***No 1 Hostel*** (☎ 5237807). The former has a good roof top bar and a laundry service; I was also impressed by the friendly atmosphere here – a rarity in Israel. Prices for both are NIS25/27 rooftop/dorm. As with seemingly every hostel in Tel Aviv however, these hostels have a lock-out period between 11am and 2pm when guests are forbidden to enter. This applies also to the ***White House*** [5] on 19 Hanevi, a recently renovated place charging NIS25 per night for a dorm bed.

On Ben Yehuda are a couple more recommendations: the ***Travellers' Hostel*** [6] (☎ 5272108) at number 47, where the staff are very amiable, and the ***Saskiah*** [7] (☎ 5280955) at number 18, a smaller and more cosy alternative. Room rates for both begin with a roof bed for NIS22, although there are cheaper weekly and monthly rates. Watch your stuff in the Saskiah: there has been a spate of thefts recently.

Where to eat
Many of the hostels also provide some of the best value meals; the ***Office*** is particularly recommended for its junk food menu.

In a side road off King George St is a large felafel stand, where a refillable felafel costs just NIS6. For something a little different, check out *Eternity* [a] at 60 Ben Yehuda. This place serves macrobiotic vegan food; try their tofu cream pies (NIS4.5) or vegetarian hot dogs (NIS10). For self-caterers, the *Carmel Market* [b] to the west of Rue Allenby is a must. Nearby in the Yemenite quarter a number of more upmarket restaurants have sprung up; *Shaul's Inn*, particularly, serves up some tantalisingly tasty treats.

Nightlife

The bar scene is thriving in Tel Aviv where the concept of happy hour has been taken to even more tempting dimensions. At the *Leprechaun* [c] on Hayarden St they actually serve, between five and six in the evening, a free meal with your drink! Turn up early as the food supply is not inexhaustible. Another travellers' fave is the *Buzz Stop*, on the beach to the south of the Dolphinarium. This is the best place to come and watch Jaffa's orange sun melt into the sea.

Beers [d], at 16 Allenby St, advertises itself as a real 'English Bar', and has a selection of over 30 different beers. However, *Mulligan's* [e], appropriately nicknamed 'Hooligans' by its regulars, has a more authentic English Pub atmosphere. It's for anybody whose conversational skills do not stretch beyond 'What are you staring at!' or 'Did you just spill my pint?'

Old Jaffa

Taking a stroll southwards along the beach from Tel Aviv to Jaffa's twee Old Quarter is probably the highlight of Israel's Mediterranean coast. Follow the coastal road and you'll eventually reach the **Old Ottoman Clock-tower**. On your left is the flea market, and on the right a path winds its way up to the Old Quarter.

There is an interesting exhibition of Jaffa's **Archaeological Excavations** (0900-2300 Sat-Thu, 0900-1400 Fri; free) in the Old Quarter beneath the main Kedumim Square at the top of the hill. Beyond this there's a warren of artists' galleries, cafés and restaurants. The large church to the north of Kedumim is **St Peter's**, established by Franciscan monks and now used as the Vatican Embassy. Napoleon spent the night here in 1799 after invading the town.

❏ Andromeda's Rock

Greek legend has it that Queen Cassiopeia once declared her daughter Andromeda to be more beautiful than a mermaid. The god of the sea, Poseidon, was miffed by this slight against his mermaids, and sent a monster to Jaffa as punishment. To appease Poseidon, Andromeda was tied to a rock which you can still see in the middle of Jaffa's harbour, as a sacrificial offering to the monster. The story has a happy ending, however, for Andromeda was rescued by Perseus on his winged steed.

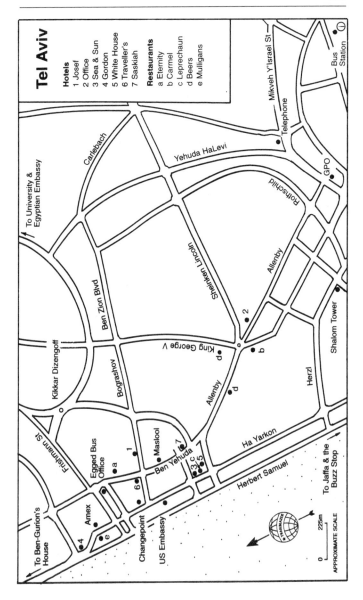

Tel Aviv

Hotels
1 Josef
2 Office
3 Sea & Sun
4 Gordon
5 White House
6 Traveller's
7 Saskiah

Restaurants
a Eternity
b Carmel
c Leprechaun
d Beers
e Mulligans

Sights in Tel Aviv

Tel Aviv's attractions are nearly all to do with Jewish history, and as such may not be of great interest to Gentiles. On David Ben Gurion Blvd there is the former **House of David Ben Gurion**, Israel's first prime minister (0800-1500 Sun/Tue/Wed/Thu, 0800-1700 Mon, 0800-1300 Fri). Behind the house is an exhibition of his life and work.

Out at Tel Aviv University is the exhaustive **Museum of the Diaspora** (1000-1400 Sun-Thu, 0900-1400 Fri; NIS22, NIS16 students), and 1km to the south there's Tel Aviv's main **Museum Complex** (NIS14, NIS10 students). Back in the centre of town, the Shalom Tower has a laughable **Wax Museum**, and an **observatory** (1000-1730 Sun-Thu, 1000-1330 Fri; NIS6, NIS5 students) on the top floor, from where the panorama can be pretty spectacular on a clear day.

By far the most popular attraction, however, is the **beach**. This strip of white sand can get incredibly crowded on Jewish holidays and Shabbat. While the sand is beautiful and the sea is fairly clean and warm, the unwanted attentions of the salivating Israeli male towards the scantily-clad Western female can prove a little irksome sometimes. You should also watch out for the currents in the sea.

Moving on

The most useful buses and their prices (full fare/students) are as follows:

	Bus No	Price	Frequency
Jerusalem	405	14/12.50	every 15mins
Rafah		27/24.30	0900 only
Nazareth		27/24.30	every hour
Tiberias	830	25/22.50	every 30mins
Eilat		46/41.40	every hour

Southern Israel

JERUSALEM TO EILAT – THE DEAD SEA

The Dead Sea is the lowest point on earth, lying 400m below sea level. Along its 80-km shoreline are tourist highlights such as the nature reserves of Ein Gedi, the Dead Sea resorts dotted along the shore, and Masada – the site of Herod's mountain-top retreat and the scene of one of the biggest mass suicides ever. The latter is now a major place of pilgrimage for all Jews; Gentile tourists, too, flock there.

The Dead Sea coast does have its down side: the roads often flood in winter, the choice of accommodation and places to eat is small – thus prices are high – and the transport connections are inconvenient.

Consequently, this is one place where taking an organised tour is not such a bad idea. Most of the hostels in Jerusalem organise daytrips to see the sunrise at Masada, as well as many of the regions other attractions. Whilst the time spent at the sites on these tours may be minimal, at only NIS50 it is the cheapest way to explore the region.

Where to stay

There are *youth hostels* at both Masada (☎ 057-584349) and Ein Gedi (☎ 057-584167) with the same price structure: US$14.50, or US$15.50 for non-members. If this is too expensive there is a concrete shelter by the entrance to the Masada hostel where you can sleep rough, and the hostel will allow you to use their lockers (NIS4) and eat in their restaurant (NIS29 for dinner).

Masada

(0630-1530; NIS13, NIS9.80 youth). A tiring pre-dawn scramble up to the ruins of Herod the Great's hilltop retreat at Masada rewards you with the spectacle of the sun rising over a shimmering Dead Sea. The vista is pleasant enough but a straw poll amongst my fellow climbers declared it inferior to Mt Sinai's spectacular morning panorama. Follow the Snake Path for 45 minutes to reach the top.

Once the sun has risen, however, there is more to see on the hill itself. Herod began work on his palace here in 43BC, after Jerusalem had fallen briefly to the Parthians, an empire to the north of Persia. Whether he stayed much in his palace is doubtful, and the excellent natural defences of Masada were utilised fully only by the Jews only following the first anti-Roman revolt of 66AD. The fort became a safe haven for those who wished to escape the fighting, and continued to offer sanctuary to the revolutionaries four years after Rome had retaken the rest of the country.

Eventually, in AD73, the Romans arrived to storm the hill. The inhabitants, 967 of them according to the historian Josephus, chose suicide over Roman rule. Ten men were chosen to kill all the others before killing themselves, and the place was torched by the last man alive. Although there is some doubt as to this tale's validity, this small episode in Jewish history has become an important symbol for the Jewish struggle for independence, and their fight against foreign oppression.

Herod's palatial residence is now rather less impressive; some of the buildings are little more than small piles of crumbling mud brick, and it's all rather disappointing. The line painted around many of the 'walls' show where the original remains finished and the restoration began. There are two maps to help you determine what you are looking at, and it is also possible to hire a set of 'Easyguide' headphones.

If you're not too bothered about seeing the sun rise, there is a cable car (beginning at 0830) but the price is as steep as the climb up the path: NIS27/17.80/14 (adult/student/youth) one way, NIS38/23.80/20 return.

Ein Gedi Reserve

(0800-1600; NIS9.50, NIS5.50youth). Officially called Nahal David, this is one of the better wildlife reserves in the region, offering a welcome escape from the endless diet of ancient ruins and holy sites. Try to avoid coming after 10am, when the many areas of the park are too crowded. The free map handed out at the entrance is good, although the estimated walking times are for snails. Read the map and pamphlet carefully before setting off, for it contains route guides and tips on how to be an eco-friendly trekker.

There is plenty of wildlife here. You should have little trouble seeing **ibex**, which crowd around the entrance looking for food, and the playful **rock hyraxes** which have made the park their own. The authorities, with typical Israeli concern for the tourist, have also released a dozen **leopards** into the park (latest score: tourists mauled to death by leopards, 2, leopards mauled to death by tourists, 0). Signs advise you not to wander off by yourself, particularly if you smell of cat food. In fact, it's very unlikely you will see any leopards and consider yourself lucky if you do – provided you're a safe distance away, of course.

By Ein Gedi is **Nahal Arugot Reserve**, which usually attracts fewer tourists. The entrance is to the south of Nahal David, about 3km back from the Dead Sea along the Arugot Canyon. The entrance ticket to Nahal David is valid for both parks.

Just one km to the south by the car park is a free place to **float on the Dead Sea** (an interesting sensation because the high concentration of salt stops you from sinking low in the water). Facilities here include a café, shop and showers, essential for anyone who has been into the water.

Moving on

The same buses serve both Masada and Ein Gedi. The following is the bus schedule for Masada, which is 25 minutes to the south of Ein Gedi. To catch the bus in Ein Gedi, allow for the 25 minute time adjustment and wait at the stop in front of the petrol station. Bus Nos 384/385 (NIS9.80) run between Ein Gedi and Masada. Bus Nos 444/486 take you to Jerusalem (NIS27/24 adults/students; 1hr 45min). It is imperative that you book in advance. There are nine buses per day, with three on Friday (last Friday bus 1515) and none on Saturday. There are four buses per day to Eilat and three on Friday (NIS37/34; last Friday bus 1515).

EILAT

Eilat is Israel's Red Sea resort, attracting millions of European sun-seekers each year. Whilst the year-round sunshine and luxuriant necklace of golden sand ensure that these package tourists usually go home satisfied, the overland traveller, spoilt by the charming resorts of the Sinai and Turkey, may well find Eilat a bit of an overpriced, concrete hole.

Orientation and services

(Eilat ☎ area code 07)

The bus station is about twenty minutes up the hill from the beach. The road to the west of the station, Sederot HaTemarim, leads down to the airport; further on you'll find the marina and lagoon where most of the better hotels are gathered. To the south the beach stretches as far as the eye can see, sweeping past the main Eilat port, a free campsite, a couple of 'mini-resorts' and finally into the Sinai and Egypt.

The **tourist office** is behind Burger King on Derekh Yotam. The **GPO** (0800-1230, 1600-1830 Sun-Thu; 0800-1300 Wed) is at the back of the Red Canyon Center. Down the road in the Shalom Tower is the **Express International Telephone**, currently the cheapest place to phone from. The GPO also offers a phone service. The **Egyptian Consulate** lies to the west of the bus station in the suburb of Tzofit on Neshev St. It's open 0900-1100 for visas, collect 1230-1300 same day (one photo, NIS60 to most nationalities, NIS40 to US, Danish, Finnish and German citizens).

Apart from the attractions to the south of the town on the main Eilat-Taba road, the town is fairly compact and you have no need of public transport. Bus No 15 plies the route to Taba (NIS4 if travelling all the way to Taba, NIS2.40 to anywhere along the way).

Where to stay

Throughout the year a number of budget travellers take up residence on the beach to the south of the port, where a ***camp-site*** has been established.

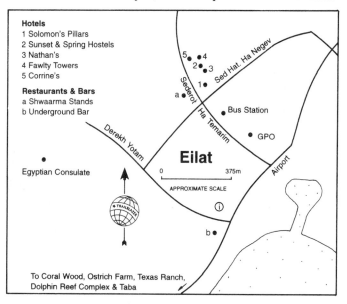

Hotels
1 Solomon's Pillars
2 Sunset & Spring Hostels
3 Nathan's
4 Fawlty Towers
5 Corrine's

Restaurants & Bars
a Shwaarma Stands
b Underground Bar

Egyptian Consulate

Sederot Ha Temarim

Sed Hat Ha Negev

Derekh Yotam

Bus Station

GPO

Airport

Eilat

0   375m

APPROXIMATE SCALE

TRAILBLAZER

To Coral Wood, Ostrich Farm, Texas Ranch,
Dolphin Reef Complex & Taba

There is no charge, and the site has toilet and (intermittent) shower facilities. It is possible to sleep here without a tent but watch your stuff: leaving your gear unattended on the beach is extremely risky.

Those who don't want sand in their pyjamas should head to the hostels across Sed Hativat HaNegev from the bus station. The cheapest here is **Solomon's Pillars** [1] (☎ 376280), charging NIS18 for a dorm bed and communal use of the kitchen, pool table and telly. It's a bit messy, but you get what you pay for: very little. For a few shekels more there's much nicer accommodation across the wasteland behind Solomon's, including the **Sunset** and **Spring Hostels** [2] (☎ 374660 for the Spring; NIS25 dorm with breakfast, NIS100 dbl). Next door to the Spring is the popular **Nathan's** [3] (☎ 376572; NIS20dorm, NIS40pp private) and on the same block **Fawlty Towers** [4] which charges NIS20 for a night in one of their huge 16-bed dormitories. Finally in this area, **Corrine's** [5] (☎ 371472) is a new place with eight double-bedded chalets for NIS40pp, and a dormitory down in the cellar for NIS20. As with almost every hostel here, a kitchen is available for you to use, and they offer free tea and coffee too.

Down near the beach, the **International Youth Hostel** [6] (☎ 370088) is a beautiful place but it's US$15.50 for a dorm bed. Full of school kids, it boasts a TV lounge, disco, café and launderette.

For those eating on a tight budget, on Sederot HaTemerim there are a couple of small bakeries, felafel and shwaarma stands [a]. The **Underground Bar** [b] on Derekh Harava was offering free meals the last time I visited but don't expect haute cuisine.

Sights in Eilat

From **pedallos** (1hr, NIS50) and **kayaks** (1hr, NIS40), to **water-skiing** (10mins, NIS50) and **parasailing** (10mins, NIS90), there are plenty of ways of making a splash in the Red Sea. You can even catch a ride on an **Inflatable Banana** (10mins, NIS20).

Most of the other attractions in Eilat line the main coastal road to Taba. At the **Dolphin Reef Complex** it's possible to swim with one of these friendly, finned fellows for a mere NIS124 (0900-1700). Further south is **Coral World** (NIS49 including electronic guide, Sat-Thu 0830-1630, Fri 0830-1500), an underwater observatory that offers you the chance to see the underwater world, without going underwater. Or you can take the **Yellow Submarine** (NIS194 for the 35min tour, including entry into Coral World), or the glass-bottomed **Jules Verne Explorer** (about US$17 for two hours) which sails around the gulf over the coral.

Away from the sea there's an **Ostrich Farm** (☎ 373213; open 0900-1400 Mon-Sat, NIS5) and even a **Texas Ranch** (☎ 376663, NIS8), built as a film set but now used as a base for horse and camel riding.

(**Opposite**) The Dome of the Rock in Jerusalem (see p232) is covered with over 80kg of gold leaf.

> **❏ Palestinian territories**
> Yet another candidate for the title 'Oldest City in the World', **Jericho**'s claims
> are stronger than most. Now part of the new Palestinian autonomous region on
> the West Bank, the city is believed to have been founded around 7000BC.
> Although there is some doubt about this, few argue with the claim that it is the
> world's lowest town, lying some 250m below Sea Level. It's a pretty place, and
> although there is little here that will captivate it is the most accessible of the
> Palestinian towns. For something a little different, consider visiting the other
> Palestinian territories on the **Gaza** and the **West Bank**. The boundaries of the
> West Bank vary according to whom you speak but include towns as far west as
> **Hebron** and Bethlehem. A visit to some of the refugee camps is not for the faint-
> hearted, however: amenities, including the water supply, are unreliable, and the
> atmosphere can be very tense.

Moving on

It is important to book your bus out of Eilat at least a day before you wish
to travel. To the Jordanian border take bus No 16 (every 15 mins from
Central Bus Station, NIS4). To Taba: No 15, every 20 mins, NIS4.

THE BORDER – ISRAEL AND EGYPT

Do **not** cross here if you plan to go on to Syria or Lebanon: your passport
will be stamped

● **Israel to Egypt** There are two Israel/Egypt border crossings. The first
and most popular is the **Eilat-Taba crossing**. It is vital that you set out
early from Eilat. Bus No 15 runs every 15-20mins to the border for NIS4.
At the border there is a departure tax of NIS49.50. The last Taba-Nuweiba
bus leaves at 3pm. Miss this and you have two options: catch a servis, the
cost of which trebles after 3pm; or stay in Taba's only hotel, the Hilton.

The second border post is in the **Gaza**. If you are taking a bus from
Tel Aviv or Jerusalem to Cairo then this is the border crossing you will
use. The Rafah border charges a steep NIS83.50 departure tax, plus E£7
Egyptian entry tax. There is always a lot of waiting around at this border,
especially as the Egyptians insist that the bus has a police escort across
the Sinai. The whole journey takes about 11 hours.

● **Egypt to Israel** A bus from Dahab to Taba (E£10) departs at 1030, calling at Nuweiba at midday. From Suez a bus departs at 1500 (E£25). The
departure tax is a stiff E£17. Tickets straight from Cairo to Tel Aviv (via
Rafah) cost as little as E£100 plus departure tax. If you plan to return to
Cairo, it's cheaper to buy a return ticket (E£136). There are plenty of travel agents in Cairo that sell these tickets: try the East Delta Bus Company
behind Ramses Station or Travco in the Sheraton Hotel.

(Opposite) Top: Church of All Nations stands in the Garden of Gethsemane in Jerusalem (see p236). **Bottom:** Heads must be covered at the Western Wall (see p234).

PART 8: EGYPT

Facts about the country

Egypt has a dual personality. On the one hand there is the Egypt of the tourist brochure: azure skies, picturesque Nile villages and austere pharaonic temples. The flip side, however, is somewhat different: a distressing mélange of filth, noise and squalor. Right beside the ancient temples are streets that teem with life and vitality. They also teem with donkeys, taxis, camels, kids, potholes, cinemas, felafels, and fruit and vegetables. The country will always be renowned for its breathtaking historical attractions but it's much more than a museum piece, preserved behind glass and left to gather dust.

Egypt is indeed a suitable place to begin a trip through the Near East. This was, after all, where recorded history started. But those coming to the end of their travels in this region will find Egypt a very appropriate finale as well. The Persians, Alexander the Great, the Ottomans and the French under Napoleon all charged through the Middle East on their way to Egypt, their ultimate destination. And after you've seen the majesty of its temples, wallowed in the atmosphere of its medieval souks and gazed at the breathtaking treasures of its ancient rulers, you too will probably consider this dazzling country to be a fitting end to your Near Eastern expedition.

Modern Egypt
Egypt was one of the last countries in the area to become fully independent, and until the overthrow of King Farouk (Fuad's son and the last of the Mohammed Ali dynasty) the country had not had a home-grown ruler for almost 2000 years.

Gamel Abdel Nasser was the man who led the coup to depose the king in 1952. This charismatic general was revered by his people, and for the first few years in office the gods seemed to smile on him too. In 1956 he nationalised the Suez Canal to help pay for the Aswan Dam. The previous owners, Britain and France, invaded the Sinai to force Nasser to back down but he refused to capitulate. Eventually, the UN forced the European powers to withdraw and Nasser was fêted as a hero.

The Egyptians' love affair with their general continued up to his death in 1970. This was despite a very patchy record. He led the country into defeat twice against Israel (in 1956 during the Suez crisis and again in

1967) and at home his socialist reforms suffocated the economy during the 1960s. Yet on each occasion he was forgiven.

His successor, Anwar Sadat, was less popular. The people never forgave him for negotiating with the Israelis at Camp David in 1979. Although the benefits were manifold – the Sinai was handed back, the economy improved and the border between the two countries was opened – Sadat never enjoyed the popularity of his predecessor. On 6th October 1981 he was gunned down by disgruntled Islamic extremists.

Sadat's successor was Hosni Mubarak, who still holds power. It has always been a precarious position but like other Middle Eastern leaders he has found the best way to survive is by performing a delicate juggling act. By playing one superpower against the other he managed to receive aid from both, and by balancing these two with his Arab partners he has been able to maintain Egypt's position as the most influential Arab state in the Near East.

The main threat to Mubarak's power today comes from within: Islamic extremists fighting for a more fundamentalist Egypt have already made a number of attempts on the president's life, and have deliberately targeted foreigners (see the warning on p260) in their campaign to destroy the economy and bring about revolution. It is a terrorist problem that Mubarak has yet to solve.

❏ **Country ratings – Egypt**

● **Highlights** Egypt has a wide variety of attractions; the key is to sample them in moderation. It is all too easy to see too many temples, catch too much sun, or enjoy oneself a little too much in the Sinai. Whilst the pharaonic ruins are the most spectacular sights in Egypt, and the Sinai and Siwa are idyllic paradises, one should also allow some time in which to fully appreciate the chaos of Cairo, far and away the most exciting city in Africa.

● **Expense $$** (Sinai **$$$**)

● **Value for money ✔✔✔** The Sinai is a little more expensive but, overall and despite the recent price increases, Egypt is still a cheap country to travel through.

● **English spoken ✔✔✔** One can usually find somebody who speaks a little English, and those who don't will often help you find somebody who does.

● **Getting around ✔✔✔** Much of this route is well serviced by buses and trains but in the Sinai the trains are non-existent and the buses both less frequent and more expensive. Be sure of the bus timetable in the Sinai before setting off.

● **Traveller's scene ✔✔✔✔** Just about everywhere, although especially at Dahab, Cairo and the Siwa Oasis.

● **Visible history ✔✔✔✔** Egypt's strongest suit. The desert sands are great preservers, as the thousands of pharaonic ruins testify.

● **Woman alone ✔✔✔** A lot of hassle but rarely dangerous

● **Good food ✔✔✔** Street food deserves a five-star rating, particularly fuul sandwiches (only 25pstr), ice cream cornettos (E£1) and the splendid fruit cocktails (E£1).

● **Vegetarian friendly ✔✔✔**

GEOGRAPHICAL BACKGROUND

Although Egypt is just under one million square km in size, 90% of the population live along the Nile, the south-north artery that splits the near-featureless Egyptian Desert. Most of the other 10% live on the Red (or Med) Sea coasts, or in one of the oases that fleck the Sahara west of the Nile. Separating Egypt from Israel is the Sinai, a large barren peninsula.

RELIGION

Egypt has a large Sunni Muslim population and a small but significant number of Shi'ites. It is also the world centre for Coptic Christianity, a sect which is closely related to the Greek Orthodox Church. Copts account for approximately 10% of the entire population in Egypt.

❑ **Practical information – Egypt**

● **Visas** If you enter Egypt on a Sinai-only permit you can still try to buy a one-month Egyptian visa at Sharm el-Sheikh airport or the ferry terminal at Nuweiba. Everyone, however, must **register** with the police within 15 days (see p262).

● **Currency** Egyptian pounds (E£), divided into 100 piastres. No black market. US$1=E£3.39, UK£1=E£5.69

● **Banks** The Egyptian pound is now fully exchangeable and the black market is all but extinct. Most of the banks do not charge commission for changing travellers' cheques, just a small stamp duty of about 80pstr. Business hours are usually 0830-1400, Sunday to Thursday, although in some of the bigger cities they stay open longer and work all seven days. During Ramadan, banks open only in the morning.

● **Time** GMT+2 (+3 from 01May to 01Sep)

● **Electricity** 220 volts AC, 50Hz

● **Post** The postal system, while still chronically slow, has become a little more reliable in recent years. Everything gets to its destination eventually; just don't attempt to send anything that has a sell-by date.

● **Telephone** Almost every town has a telephone exchange where international calls can be made. Calls are about 25% cheaper after 8pm. Standard charges for three minutes are: Europe E£21; USA E£24; Australia E£31. For local calls, it is easier to use the hotel phone than attempt to find a phone box that works.

● **Warnings** i)The Muslim Brotherhood, Egypt's fanatical terrorist group, is attempting to hurt the government by damaging the economy, and the bedrock of the economy is tourism. This has led to some wicked atrocities against tourists through the years, and as a result certain areas are off limits, especially south of Cairo to Qena. You will usually be put back on the train if you attempt to disembark in this area.

ii) The biggest complaint travellers make about Egypt concerns the relentless hassle that they've suffered at the hands of over-persistent locals trying to sell goods and services. There is very little you can do to avoid it short of staying in your hotel room all day. When you do encounter somebody being awkward be patient but firm; if you give in to all their demands it makes it more difficult for travellers who follow in your footsteps.

LOCAL TRANSPORT

Train

When travelling up and down the Nile, take the train. There are two
tourist trains, consisting only of first and second-class air-conditioned
carriages, that depart every day between Aswan and Cairo. When buying
tickets, unless you specify against it, the E£20 dinner will be included.

There are also six **third-class trains** (or second-class with no air-con)
that ply the Nile route. These trains are crowded, filthy and very, very
slow, and as such are deemed to be too arduous for the average foreigner. Nevertheless, if you have the time a short journey can be fun and a
good way to meet the locals and their livestock. It is difficult to buy the
tickets in advance for these trains so it's a case of turning up and jump-
ing onto the next one. The timetable for 'non-tourist' trains leaving from
Cairo can be found on p311.

Bus and servis taxi

Egypt's bus service is very good, and the servis taxi flourishes as well
here as in other parts of the Middle East.

Stand anywhere in Cairo (preferably on a pavement), and with every
passing second you'll hear some vehicle somewhere trumpeting out a
horn voluntary. It seems that for all forms of road transport a working

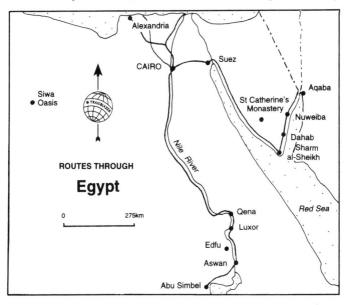

❑ **Route through Egypt**
This route through Egypt begins in the barren wastes of the Sinai, joins the Nile at Aswan and heads north to Cairo via Luxor and Edfu.

horn is of far greater value than working brakes. Strewn along the hard shoulders of this country from Abu Simbel to Alexandria, Siwa to the Sinai are the wrecks of vehicles that obviously hadn't had their horns adequately re-tuned before they set out.

Servis taxis – tip The front seat in servis taxis seats three. Avoid it as you'll often land up next to the driver, the most uncomfortable spot.

❑ **Registering your visa**
Every tourist to Egypt must register their presence in the country within 15 days of arriving. This can be done at any police station, or at the Mogamma building in Cairo. If you're arriving from Jordan, the police station in Dahab is a good place to register as the process takes only two minutes. The fine for registering after the 15 days is E£28.40. At the Mogamma building it is also possible to extend the visa to six months (E£11.10 plus one photo), or change a single-entry visa to multiple-entry (E£13.75).

ACCOMMODATION

Egypt has a wide variety of accommodation, from the super-cheap flea pit to five-star luxury. Whatever type you choose, the golden rule is the same: haggle! The number of touts that surround you as soon as you arrive is an indication of how desperate the hotels are for your custom; a little friendly bargaining can reap rich rewards. It is OK to follow one of these touts but you should be aware that they do not stand at the train stations all day for free; if you follow one back to their hotel, their commission comes from your pocket in the form of a higher room rate.

The Sinai

سيناء

One visit to the Sinai will show you why this peninsula was referred to as 'the wilderness' in the Bible: it is a bleak, uncompromising land. The sandstone cliffs have a harsh beauty all their own, however, and anybody who enjoyed the desert scenery of Wadi Rum will be similarly enthralled by the Sinai. This 'wilderness' is supposedly where Moses and his band of Israelites arrived at the beginning of their 40-year search for the Promised Land. It is hardly surprising, therefore, that the main historical site in the Sinai is biblical: Jabal Moussa (Mt Sinai), where Moses is believed to have received the Ten Commandments on stone tablets, attracts thousands of pilgrims throughout the year.

The Sinai also has miles of unspoilt coastline, and the clear aquamarine waters of the Red Sea that lap against the shore ensure that the beach resorts prove just as popular as God's holy mountain. Amongst them is up-market Sharm el-Sheikh, laid-back Tarabim and, most popular of all, Dahab, the ultimate travellers' centre.

NUWEIBA نويبيه

Nuweiba is a town split into three distinct parts, of which the somnolent **port area** is probably the first you'll encounter. There are a number of banks here, a few over-priced hotels, a resident dolphin and very little else except for a lot of people hanging around and a few goats grazing on the litter. If you arrive here late at night take a taxi for the seven km to **Tarabim** (طارابين E£10), Nuweiba's seaside resort, which lies somewhere between calm and comatose. Accommodation is in beach huts, which are similar in price (E£5pp) and quality to those in Dahab. The beach is not hidden under restaurants as at Dahab but the coast here is far from immaculate. The other drawbacks are that the nearest bank is a 40-minute walk away at the Helnan Village Resort (cash dollars can be changed at the shops in Tarabim), and most things, particularly food, are more expensive. You can save money by walking two km and buying your groceries from the small collection of shops that form the third area of Nuweiba, which laughably calls itself **Nuweiba City**.

Alternatively, escape altogether on one of the buses that career along the main road to Dahab (E£6), departing at 0700 and 1500. Note that servis taxis also ply these routes but their price depends on when you wish to travel – fares treble after the last bus has departed.

DAHAB ذهب

You'll probably hear about Dahab ('Golden') long before you reach the Sinai. At the bus station, it appears no different from any other Egyptian seaside town, being both scruffy and deserted. But the Dahab of travelling legend is in the 'Bedouin village' a couple of km north along the coast (E£1 by pick-up truck). This 'village' is *the* travellers' hangout in the Middle East, a hedonistic play ground for the travel-weary Westerner.

Opinions about Dahab are mixed. Some argue that a stay here isn't 'real travelling' (whatever that is), and walk on by. Others, addicted to the intoxicating mix of beads, body-painting and Bob Marley, put down roots and stay forever. Still others have every intention of leaving tomorrow but never seem to get round to it. It's not the place to come if you're bored with Bob or dread dreadlocks but neither do you have to smoke dope or enrol on a diving course to be allowed in. Dahab is just a very relaxed resort and an ideal spot to recuperate from the exertions of travel.

Orientation and information

In the 'town' is the bus stop, **post office**, **telephone exchange** and a **police station** where you can register your visa. The **tourist police** have an office in the courtyard of the Holiday Village. There is a **bank** in town too, as well as a small branch of the **Cairo Bank** in the Bedouin village.

In the village itself you will be bugged by camel drivers, who charge about E£10 per hour for the privilege of sitting on one of these choleric beasts. With a group it is possible to organise a trek overnight into the desert – count on about E£50pp per day. Horse-riding, pedallos, buggy bikes and windsurfing are some of the other activities available.

Where to stay

On one side of the Dahab road is the accommodation. For the majority this means a small, airless cell, where the only decorations are the smeared corpses of mosquitoes on the walls and the only furniture is a Rizla-thin mattress on the concrete floor. These cells are organised into camps, many of which are virtually indistinguishable except for their name. Currently the cheapest is the *Caravan Camp* معسكر الكزفان (E£2.50) to the south of the town. This place does have its faults: privacy in the straw huts is minimal, but it's not bad. Most of the other camps charge about E£4-5, including *Muhammad Ali's* محمد علي, still the most popular thanks to recommendations in other guidebooks.

For a little more (E£10/15 sgl/dbl) the *Green Valley* الوادي الأخضر huts are a great leap up in quality, and their restaurant has become a travellers' favourite too. Highly recommended.

What to do in Dahab

In Dahab there are three main activities: dining, diving and drug-taking. For dining, opposite the hotels on the seaward side of the road is a string of wooden-shack restaurants. These places are more like lounges than restaurants, and many travellers spend their entire day lying around them, playing backgammon, swishing the flies off the food and listening to the cacophony of three restaurants playing their stereos simultaneously.

At least the flies have good taste in Dahab, for some of the food is delicious. The pancakes at the **Blue Hole Café** are divine, the **Caravan Club** has some heavenly specials, and **Tota's**, further south, is superb.

Diving in Dahab is very cheap, and some of the underwater scenery is truly breathtaking. A beginner's five-day PADI course is about US$280 including certificate. Arguably the best diving-school is **Fantasea** (☎ 062-640043); **Club Red** (☎ 062-640380) has also been recommended. The best spot to dive is the Blue Hole, seven km north of Dahab, a coral well that plunges 70m down into the gloomy depths.

And then there's the drugs. Just one word of warning for those who are tempted. Although it isn't too difficult to obtain the drug of your choice, Dahab is not exempt from Egyptian law – all drugs are illegal, and occasionally the authorities arrest some foreigner to make an example of him/her. If you should happen to be the unlucky one you'll probably end up in a small, airless concrete cell, where the only decorations are the smeared corpses of mosquitos on the walls...only this time you'll be sharing with 20 or so sweaty Egyptians who'll probably hog the mattress.

Moving on
Other than the odd servis taxi to Cairo (E£30) from the village, to leave Dahab you must return to the bus station in town. The bus to St Catherine's departs at 0930 (E£10, two hours), although most prefer to hire a taxi for about E£80 per cab, which will wait at the bottom of Mt Sinai overnight and bring you back to Dahab in the morning.

When crossing by bus from the Sinai to 'mainland' Egypt catch a bus to Suez and then catch another one on from there; this is cheaper than catching a 'through' bus direct to your next destination.

MT SINAI AND ST CATHERINE'S MONASTERY

After the beaches, the most popular place to visit in the area is Mt Sinai (Jabal Moussa) and St Catherine's Monastery below it. Each night a crowd of travellers struggles 2300m up the Mt Sinai to freeze on the summit in anticipation of a dramatic sunrise. The spectacle rarely disappoints.

Orientation
The bus from Dahab drops you at **al-Milga** (جبل سيناء، الميلجا), four km from the monastery. Al-Milga has a police station, GPO, 24-hour telephone office, a couple of banks and a few restaurants and shops. To get to the monastery, take a taxi (E£4pp in a full taxi). Half way between al-Milga and the monastery is a roundabout and the very pricey *St Catherine Tourist Village*. If you are going to walk from the bus to the monastery,

ask the driver to drop you off here before al-Milga. It is possible to stay in the *Monastery Hostel* (☎ 470343) near the entrance. Bed, breakfast and dinner is E£35 in a dorm (E£40pp dbl). If you're staying the night on Mt Sinai, leave your luggage at the hostel (E£1), and just have dinner here (E£5-7). The shop has batteries and film and provisions for the hike.

Climbing Mt Sinai • جبل سيناء

Remember to take a torch and wrap up really well, especially in winter. It's a fairly straightforward two-hour ascent along the **Camel Path**, and there is only one place where you may get lost. Near the summit and just beyond a teahouse is a narrow passage between two rocks; after this the path splits – take the path to the left, where the steps to the summit are hidden behind two small buildings. (The path straight ahead leads to the **Steps of Repentance** that go back down to the monastery). At the summit you'll find a 20th-century church, two kiosks that sell provisions and hire out blankets (E£2.50), and one that also hires out mattresses (E£5). Beneath one of the shops is a small 'grave', the warmest place to sleep. On the way down, take the Steps of Repentance. There are nearly 4000 of them in total, and all laid by one monk. The chapel you pass marks the spot where the prophet Elijah heard the voice of God.

> ❏ *And mount Sinai was altogether on a smoke, because the Lord descended upon it in fire: and the smoke thereof ascended as the smoke of a furnace, and the whole mountain quaked greatly....and the Lord called Moses up to the top of the mount; and Moses went up.* **Exodus 19:18-20**

St Catherine's Monastery دير سانت كاترين

(0900-1200, closed Fri and Sun; modest dress, no shorts, free entry). At the foot of Mt Sinai stands a small 4th-century chapel, built at the behest of Constantine's mother, Helena. It reputedly marks the spot where the angel appeared to Moses 'in a flame of fire out of the midst of a bush', instructing him to return to Egypt to lead the Israelites from oppression (Exodus 3). Today this chapel is surrounded by a monastery, built during the reign of Justinian. Originally called the Monastery of the Transfiguration, in the 11th century it underwent a name change after the body of St Catherine, an Alexandrian martyr, was discovered in a perfect state of preservation on a nearby mountain. The monks brought the corpse back to the monastery to give her the burial she deserved.

Apart from the burning-bush chapel (closed to the public), the monastery also houses the oldest unrestored basilica still in use (AD542). Its survival is thanks in part to the monastery's fortress-like construction and in part to the guarantees of protection it enjoyed from both religious and secular leaders. You can see copies of both the Prophet Mohammed's and Napoleon's guarantees at the entrance (being illiterate, Mohammed signed his with a handprint).

Today just 25 monks guard the monastery's priceless treasures, including a vast library (closed to the public) of over 6000 valuable books and manuscripts. Many of the monastery's icons can be viewed, however. Located in the narthex (entrance) of the basilica, they have survived the destructive efforts of the iconoclasts and thus have a rarity value beyond price. Separating this gallery and the ostentatious Greek Orthodox-style basilica are a pair of beautifully-fashioned doors of Lebanese cedar.

As you leave the monastery you may be accosted by an old monk. This fellow will ask for baksheesh, in return for which you will receive a private viewing of his bones. (He's got the key to the Ossiary, where the skulls of all St Catherine's monks are stored).

Moving on
The Suez bus leaves from al-Milga at 0600 and costs E£25, so you may wish to take a servis taxi (E£35) from here instead. If you're going on to Aswan, arrive in Suez early as the Suez-Aswan bus leaves at 1030.

SUEZ السويس

Most travellers at some point in their travels find themselves drinking chai at the Suez Bus Terminus. The city will never feature on many postcards – it was heavily damaged during the Sinai War and the rebuilding was a little hurried – but it is a friendly and functional place. It is located at the southern end of the 200km Suez Canal. If you have time to kill between buses, you could go to the port area to watch the boats.

If you get stuck in Suez for the night there are several cheap hotels. Walk through the back of the bus station, turn left and walk along the road as far as the main street (Sharia as-Salaam). Turn right and continue for 10 minutes until you reach the White House Hotel. The road beside this hotel contains a number of cheapies, the best value being the *Mecca Hotel* فندق مكة(☎ 062-223626; E£4/7.5 sgl/dbl) four blocks along the road.

Moving on
The bus and servis stations are conveniently situated opposite each other. Buses leave to Aswan at 1030 (E£32), taking 16 hours. For Cairo, use a servis taxi for E£4.50 – they leave very regularly, and take two hours.

❏ **Duty free earner**
Duty-free stores have been established in all the major cities which sell alcohol and cigarettes for less than half the normal retail price. Consequently, many travellers are paid by locals to buy alcohol and cigarettes for them. A free bike for the day is the minimum you can expect, and some travellers have reported collecting over E£50. The duty-free limit is three bottles of spirits and three boxes of cigarettes. You can visit the stores only once, and it is best that you do so at the beginning of your holiday in Egypt (otherwise customs officials at the border may enquire as to the whereabouts of your purchases).

The Nile
النيل

For many, the Nile, the country's life-supporting artery, is where one finds the real Egypt. This was the home of the pharaohs, and all the way from Cairo to Aswan you'll be encountering magnificent testaments to their power and wealth. To take a trip north along the Nile is to journey back through time. The temples around Aswan and Edfu are the youngest on the Nile and date from the Ptolemaic era, the Greek rulers who maintained the pharaonic tradition; Luxor was the capital of the New and Middle Kingdoms, predating the Ptolemaic era by 1200 years; whilst from Cairo you can visit the most ancient pharaonic sites of all (more than 5000 years old) at the Old Kingdom necropolis at Giza and Saqqara.

To make the most of your time on the Nile you need to understand why and for whom these tombs and temples were built. A basic overview is given on p281 and p285 but for more information on the life and times of the Ancient Egyptians, *The Penguin Guide to Ancient Egypt* by WJ Murnane (Penguin Books) is highly recommended.

ASWAN أسوان

Geographically speaking, Aswan lies some 576 miles south of Cairo. To most, however, the frenetic pace of the capital seems a million miles away. Aswan is both pretty and pretty laid-back, a border town imbued with the relaxed attitude of the Nubian settlers who arrived here in the wake of Lake Nasser. It is an ideal stepping stone between dozy Dahab and chaotic Cairo. There are attractions aplenty, including temples nearby that will satisfy the cravings of the keenest pharaophile. But many travellers never bother, preferring instead to spend their time playing backgammon in cafés, drifting down the Nile on feluccas or admiring the Nile view through the bottom of a bottle of Stella.

And what a beautiful view it is. All along the Nile a green ribbon of fertile land separates the river from the desert but it stops before it reaches Aswan. Hereafter golden sand and blue (ish) water now clash directly in a vivid collision of colour. The lush green palm trees on the riverbank and the pink granite cliffs beyond all add to this radiant prospect.

The focus of activity today is the East Bank. In ancient times, however, Elephantine Island was the major settlement. This island, lying in the centre of the Nile across from the Cataract Hotel, was the capital of the first *nome* (administrative district) and the centre of the cult of the ram-headed god, Khnum. Then called Yebu ('Elephant' after the giant boulders, like the backs of elephants that lie half-submerged in the Nile

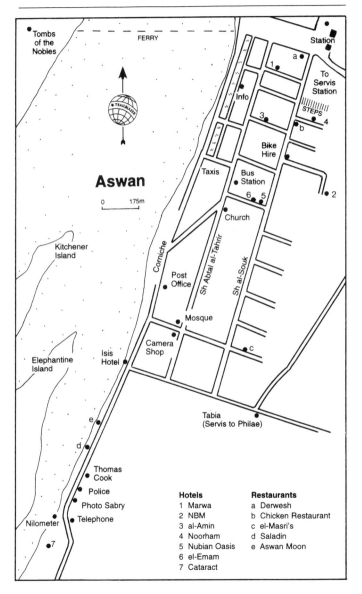

Tombs
of the
Nobles

FERRY

Station

a

1

To
Servis
Station

Info

STEPS

3

b

4

Bike
Hire

Taxis

Bus
Station

2

Aswan

0   175m

6   5

Church

Kitchener
Island

Corniche

Post
Office

Sh Abtal al-Tahrir

Sh al-Souk

Mosque

Elephantine
Island

Isis
Hotel

Camera
Shop

c

Tabia
(Servis to Philae)

e

d

Thomas
Cook

Police

Photo Sabry

Nilometer

Telephone

7

Hotels
1 Marwa
2 NBM
3 al-Amin
4 Noorham
5 Nubian Oasis
6 el-Emam
7 Cataract

Restaurants
a Derwesh
b Chicken Restaurant
c el-Masri's
d Saladin
e Aswan Moon

along its shore), Elephantine was the border town and gateway to Africa. Aswan still lies at the crossroads between Arabia and Africa today; the influence of both can be seen in the goods on sale in the famous souk, the centrepiece of this historic city.

Orientation and services   (Aswan ☎ area code 097)

You should have no trouble finding your way around Aswan, since the main city is little more than three roads running south from the station parallel to the Nile. Immediately south of the station is the market street, Sharia al-Souk شارع السوق ; one block further west is Sharia Abtal al-Tahrir شعبة التحرير; finally there is the Corniche الكورنيش, where most of the banks and top-range hotels are located.

Near the train station is a **tourist booth**. There is also an office near the Abu Simbel Hotel. The **post office** and **telephone office** are both on the Corniche, while **AMEX** have their office in the New Cataract Hotel.

Where to stay

At the northern end of Sharia al-Souk, the first hotel you come to is the best budget place. The **Marwa** [1] فندق مروة (☎ 310620; E£5/8/10 dorm/sgl dbl, all with breakfast) is one of two main travellers' hangouts in Aswan, with good clean rooms and piping hot showers. Though the Marwa is a much better place it's not as popular as the **New Bob Marley** [2] (NBM) فندق بوب مارلي الجديد which charges the same and is to the left of the souk a little further on. Back towards the station and down a little side street there's the **al-Amin Hotel** [3]فندق الأمين(☎ 314189). This place is nearly always deserted: stay in the dormitory (E£5) and you'll often end up with the whole room to yourself. The manager is a particularly decent fellow, and if you can ignore the bathrooms – so small that you have to put your leg in the toilet when showering – then it's fine.

A couple of blocks before the NBM (but streets ahead in terms of quality) is the **Noorhan** [4] (☎ 316069; E£10/12 sgl/dbl, plus E£3 for en suite). This hotel has its fans but the **Nubian Oasis** فندق واحة النوبة [5] (☎ 312126) is better value and more agreeable, with a lovely sunny lounge/reception area and clean air-conditioned rooms (E£10/15 sgl/dbl).

Since the Nubian Oasis opened the **el-Emam** [6] (☎ 310439) next door has been completely overshadowed, and is now so desperate for custom that you may, with a little haggling, get a room for as little as E£3.50pp.

The top hotel in Aswan is still the **Cataract** [7]فندق كاتراكت (☎ 323222), a favourite haunt of Agatha Christie. To watch the feluccas from this hotel's veranda whilst feasting on knickerbocker glory is to enjoy one of life's great pleasures. Unfortunately, nirvana now has its price and there is a minimum charge of E£15. The hotel itself is not without charm; rooms start at US$110 but you should pay the extra US$40 for the river view.

Where to eat

The street stalls in Aswan try to charge E£0.50 for felafel or fuul. You have to haggle to get the going rate of E£0.25.

Next to the teahouses opposite the train station stands a lovely little *café* (the sign is in Arabic only) serving delicious Egyptian pizza. The *Derwesh* [a] next door does some tasty chicken meals, but if chicken's your choice head down the *souk*, where half a roast bird with bread and salad is a mere E£4 [b]. Further on still is *el-Masri's* [c], (not el-Basri's nearby), which does a great all-inclusive three-course meal for E£15-20.

Along the Corniche and away from the souk are a number of floating restaurants: *Saladin's* [d] is the cheapest, while *Aswan Moon* [e] is the most popular, and the best place to arrange a trip with felucca owners.

Aswan's West Bank

While nowhere near as impressive as the treasure trove on Luxor's West Bank, crossing the Nile at Aswan still makes for a rewarding daytrip. After alighting from the ferry (E£1, 25pstr to the locals) that leaves from opposite the train station you're faced with a warren of caves in the hill ahead: the **Tombs of the Nobles** مقابر النبلاء (0700-1700,-1600 winter; E£6, E£3 students). As the name suggests, these were built for Aswan's minor royalty during the Old and Middle Kingdoms, thus pre-dating the Valley of the Kings by as much as 800 years. The pick, **Sarenput II**'s tomb (1800BC), contains an image of the mummified prince sculpted out of the rock and a small granite offering table with food carved onto its surface. The sixth dynasty father-and-son tomb of **Mekhu and Sabni** (2300BC) nearby is Aswan's oldest. At the top of the hill the **Kubbet al-Hawa** (Tomb of the Winds) affords the best view of the Nile.

A path from round behind the hill brings you, after 30 minutes of struggling across the desert sands, to the sixth-century **Monastery of St Simeon** دير سانت سيمون. (Alternatively, go by camel for E£5-10. If you do, ask to see the tip of an obelisk lying on the desert floor to the west of the path). From a distance the monastery (0800-1600; E£6, E£3 students) resembles a fortress and one of its main roles was to protect the monks from the infidel. It was finally abandoned in the 13th century. It is wonderful to walk amongst the ruins and you can still see scraps of colourful Coptic art on some of the mud-brick walls and cornices.

From here you can go south-east back towards the Nile and the **Mausoleum of Aga Khan** ضريح الأغا خان, (0900-1600, free entry). The Aga Sultan Mohammed Shah (1887-1957) was the leader of the Ismali branch of Islam who followed in the footsteps of the pharaohs by choosing the West Bank as his final resting place. Each day a red rose is still placed on his sarcophagus by his wife, just as he requested.

There is no ferry from here to Elephantine, just a lot of feluccas hanging around to exploit the captive market. Expect to pay about E£4.

Elephantine Island جزيرة الفيلة

To get to this island from the East Bank, take the river crossing near the nilometer (see below) for 25pstr. The island played a major part in early pharaonic religion and was the centre of the cult of Khnum, the ram-headed god. There are a number of places of interest scattered hereabouts.

The **Aswan Museum** (0830-1800, -1700 winter; E£5, E£2.50 students) is a compact and informative little place. In the back garden of the museum was found a mummified sheep, possibly worshipped as Khnum in pharaonic times. On the south of the island are the ruins of **Khnum Temple**. Nearby is a **Nilometer** which, along with its partner on the East Bank, was used to gauge the height of the Nile. From this measurement the governors of Aswan could predict the height of the annual flood, and thus calculate the abundance of that year's harvest. They would then set the year's taxes according to this estimate. A few small villages still exist on Elephantine too. They're very photogenic but, sadly, the villagers view tourists as little more than automated baksheesh dispensers.

Kitchener's Island جزيرة الطباخين

(E£5). Anybody in search of tranquillity should come to this island garden. A keen botanist, General Kitchener was given this island towards the latter half of the last century so he could indulge his passion. The island is also home to many exotic birds that are just as eye-catching as the plants. You may wish to incorporate a visit here into an afternoon cruise on one of Aswan's feluccas (about E£10 per hour – haggle fiercely).

The Temple of Philae معبد فيلي

(0700-1600 winter, -1700 summer; E£6, E£3 students; E£33 sound and light show). Philae lies nine km south of Aswan near the old British Dam; catch a servis from beneath the mosque at Tabia الطابية to the barrage (50 pstr, ask for 'Sahari') from where you can walk to the boats. The boat prices are posted by the ticket booth, 100m back from the launch: it costs a lot more per person if there are less than eight of you. Unfortunately the boatmen on the launch are a malicious bunch, refusing to allow single travellers to join a group of eight and insisting that they hire a boat for

---

❑ **Cleopatra and the Roman Empire (200BC-330AD)**
The end of Ptolemite rule in Egypt was the third and final stage in the Roman conquest of the Near East. Cleopatra VII was the last Ptolemite ruler and indeed the last pharaoh. By a combination of feminine guile (which included bearing Julius Caesar's child) and political nous she had managed to keep the latter at bay for almost 20 years. But by backing Mark Anthony in his power struggle against the Roman Emperor Octavius she picked a loser, and their combined forces were defeated at Actium in 31BC. Weighing up the options: death by suicide, or something altogether messier at the hands of Octavius, she chose the former. And so, with one bite from an asp, 3000 years of pharaonic rule was brought to an end.

themselves. The solution is simple: wait by the ticket booth and form a group of eight there and then head down to the boats.

Like Abu Simbel (see below), this is another temple that avoided an underwater future only through the efforts of UNESCO. Indeed, the original Aswan Barrage was already subjecting Philae to seasonal flooding, and visitors often had to view the partially-submerged complex by boat. In 1964 the temple was relocated to the nearby island of Agilka, which had been landscaped to resemble the temple's original home on Philae.

This temple marks the spot where Isis was supposed to have found Osiris' heart, (see p281). As such it was an important destination for early Egyptian pilgrims. Construction of the complex initially started in the Ptolemaic period, although the temple was added to and altered over the course of the next 800 years. In AD550 Justinian terminated all pagan activities, allowing Christians to move in and deface the building.

The basic layout of Philae is typical of pharaonic temples. Alighting from the boat you are faced by a large **Processional Courtyard**; at the end is a huge **Pylon** (the monumental entrance gate you see before you) and beyond is the smaller **Second Courtyard** and the **Hypostyle Hall** (the columned hall, common to nearly all temples, the exact purpose of which is still unknown). Beside this is the **Mamissi,** the divine birth-room. All pharaohs were believed to be reincarnations of the god Horus; within the mamissi the pharaoh would perform the rituals which symbolised this re-birth from god to king. A relief of Horus rising up from the marsh (his traditional home) decorates the back wall. Finally, at the back of the temple is the **Holy of Holies**, this time dedicated to Isis.

In detail, however, Philae is radically different. Look, for instance, at the two colonnades that flank the processional courtyard; every column on the western one is surmounted by a different capital, whilst behind the unfinished eastern one some small temples have been built, including one dedicated to Imhotep, the Old Kingdom architect responsible for the Step Pyramid.

Excursion to Abu Simbel أبو سنبل

(E£21, E£12 students)**.** Unfortunately, the taxi-drivers who ply the route to Abu Simbel insist on travelling in convoy (E£25pp, 4 hours), so the Abu Simbel experience can become a suffocating game of sardines played with approximately 2000 video-wielding tourists. Avoid this by taking the local bus (E£26 return, dep 0800 and 1600, rtn 1400 and 0700).

After spending centuries buried beneath the desert sands the temples were discovered in 1813 by the explorer Burkhardt. They are, however, as much a testament to the miracle of modern technology as they are to the skill and vision of the ancient architects. For, though difficult to believe, these gigantic temples were actually shifted some 270 metres in 1966, and the 'cliff ' they stand in today is entirely man-made.

The relocation was ordered as the rising waters of the newly-formed Lake Nasser threatened to engulf their original home. For over two years an international team of workers carved up the temples into blocks weighing up to 30 tonnes, and then reassembled the entire lot at the new site. The project was successful, and the giant statues of Ramses II and Nefertari today gaze over the Lake – in much the same way that they must have stared over the Nile centuries ago – without fear of getting their feet wet.

The temples The **main temple** is the handiwork of Ramses II (1279-1212BC), the most prolific builder of all the New Kingdom pharaohs and the longest-reigning – 67 years on the throne. It is his image you can see in quadruplicate on the temple facade, sitting 20m tall in the sunshine, with more realistically-sized versions of his family gathered around his knees. The entrance is between the middle two Ramses. It is guarded above by a relief of Ra Harakhty, the falcon-headed God of the Sun. The entrance has been vandalised by Napoleon's troops, who had a penchant for scrawling their names on ancient temples.

The design of this temple is very simple, and rather untypical. Inside is an eight-pillared hall decorated with reliefs of the Battle of Kadesh (see p22). These include some gory post-victory scenes: Ramses' men torturing the prisoners, others counting the severed hands of the dead. The rooms leading off to the side are for storage, whilst at the back is the Holy of Holies (see p281) still containing the four gods (including Ramses II himself) to whom the temple is dedicated. Such was the precision with which the temple was re-built that the sun's rays still reach back here twice a year, just as they used to in Ramses' day, on 22nd February and 22nd October. The **smaller temple** on the right is dedicated to the cow-headed goddess of joy, Hathor, but it is Ramses II's wife Nefertari who is the more predominant; she appears twice on the facade.

The small door between the two temples leads into the heart of the 'man-made mountain'. Viewing the hollow mountain gives you a good idea of how complex the re-location project was. Make sure you see this at the end of your visit rather than the beginning, otherwise it becomes difficult to see the temples as anything other than a wholly-modern construction, more suited to the desert of Las Vegas than the sands of Nubia.

Aswan's other attractions

Tours to Abu Simbel usually also take in Sadd al-Ali, the **Aswan High Dam** (اسوان، السد العالي)(E£3, no concessions). Whilst its vital statistics are undoubtedly impressive – 1km thick at the base, 111m high and over 17 times as large as the Great Pyramid at Giza – the physical reality is a bit of a concrete eyesore, and by standing on top of the dam you get little idea of its vastness. A better view of the dam is from the temples of **Kalabsha** (الكلابشة), **Kertassi and Beit al-Wali**, all rescued from the watery grasp of Lake Nasser by international co-operation. Whilst Kalabsha and Beit al-Wali are both worth viewing, particularly for their fine reliefs, Kertassi was only partially rescued and just a few blocks remain.

Three km south of Aswan lies the **Unfinished Obelisk** المسلة الغير منتهية (E£5, E£2.50 students), which, if it hadn't developed a flaw while still in the quarry, would be by far the largest obelisk in the world: at an estimated 1000 tonnes it is over twice the size of Hatshepsut's at Karnak. On the way is a **Fatimid Cemetery** المقبرة الفاطمية, which includes the tomb of Mohammed's granddaughter, Sayyida Zeinab. (Curiously, she also has a mausoleum outside Damascus).

Moving on

● **Train** Tourist trains from Aswan to Luxor (4hrs 30mins) currently depart at 0545 (E£20/13 in 1st/2nd class, E£13/9 1st/2nd class student) and 1800 (E£22/14 in 1st/2nd class , E£15/11 1st/2nd class student)

● **Bus** Buses leave every hour to Luxor (E£6.50), from 0530 to 1430. The ride takes four hours.

● **Servis** The servis station is a ten-minute walk east of the railway lines. It is E£8 to Luxor, E£4 to Edfu (two hrs), although in practice these figures are often revised upwards for tourists.

❑ **Felucca trips**

A visit to Upper Egypt would not be complete without a leisurely excursion on a felucca. While many are content with an afternoon's sailing, it has become almost *de rigueur* amongst certain travellers to take a three-day trip to Edfu which costs about E£50 all in. Often the felucca captains will drop you at the village before Edfu; determine your final destination before you agree to take the trip.

Whilst it would be difficult to recommend specific captains – there are, for example, at least four who call themselves 'Bob Marley' – I do urge you to be extremely careful when arranging a tour. Follow these guidelines: firstly, ask other travellers for their recommendations; inspect the boat to see if it looks river-worthy; try to meet your fellow passengers before you agree on joining them; make absolutely certain that both you and the captain are in agreement over the itinerary, and what is – and is not – included in the price; and ensure you buy adequate supplies for the journey. Other than that, just enjoy yourself – it is a lovely way to travel.

EDFU إيدفو

According to pharaonic tradition it was at Edfu that Horus finally gained victory over his uncle Seth (see p281), and the gigantic Ptolemaic temple that dominates the city is dedicated to the victor.

To reach the temple from the servis station, go south along the river to the first major junction. Turn right, and continue past the police station until you reach the roundabout with the fountain in the middle: the temple is straight ahead. The bus station is 100m to your right.

The Temple of Horus

(0600-1800, 0700-1600 winter; E£10, E£5 students). Although work began in 237BC, because of the unstable political climate that existed throughout the Ptolemaic era the work was continually interrupted. It was finally completed 180 years later in 50BC.

Having bought your ticket at the booth, walk south along the entire length of the temple to the entrance, past reliefs depicting the battle between Horus and Seth (the latter, for some reason, disguised as a hippo). At the end there's a courtyard in front of the **Pylon**, decorated with some rather stale renderings of Ptolemy VIII defeating his enemies.

The temple's layout is fairly standard: courtyard, pylon, courtyard, hypostyle hall (in this instance, two hypostyle halls), and Holy of Holies. Thus, moving between the two statues of Horus (portrayed, as always, as a falcon) one reaches the second courtyard. The scenes on the back of the pylon show the 'Festival of the Beautiful Meeting' (see p281) between Horus and Hathor; the latter has his temple at Dendera, 50km north of Luxor. Passing through two colossal **Hypostyle Halls** you get to the **Holy of Holies**, surrounded on three sides by small chapels. It's a good idea to bring a torch to Edfu for the pharaonic technique of reducing the light towards the back of the temple – to increase the mystery surrounding the Holy of Holies – is particularly effective here, and many of the small chambers and storage rooms can really only be appreciated with a torch.

Where to stay

Those wishing to spend a night in Edfu have two options. The **Dralsum** فندق درلسم(☎ 701727) is located just a few metres from the temple near the mini tourist market. Your arrival at reception will probably cause a flurry of activity and leave the owner flustered; he's obviously not used to Westerners staying here. The rooms are OK but a bit overpriced (E£12 dbl, no sgls). Alternatively, ask directions to get to **el-Madina** فندق المدينة , near the bus station, where the manager offers 'good rooms, hot showers and fun!'. I can't guarantee the last, but the showers were hot and the rooms adequate when I visited. It's very good value too: E£6 per room, and an extra E£3 for a huge breakfast.

Moving on

The most convenient mode of transport for Edfu is the servis taxi; the station is by the bridge on the western bank of the Nile. The trip to Luxor costs E£4.50 (2hrs 30mins). If every last piastre is precious to you, buses to Luxor (E£3.75) leave from the bus station in the centre of town. Occasionally, buses to Edfu drop off passengers on the east side of the Nile, from where a servis taxi takes you across the bridge for 25pstr.

There is little point in travelling by train to and from Edfu. The station is inconveniently located on the east side of the Nile.

LUXOR الأقصر

In 1886 Thomas Cook chose Luxor, a medium-sized town in Upper Egypt, as the destination for his pioneering package-tour group. What drew Mr Cook and his tourists here was the plethora of New Kingdom delights that lie scattered on both sides of the Nile. Many of these treasures were discovered by Napoleon's team of intellectuals, the 'savants', who studied the area and sent reports of their discoveries back home to a fascinated Europe. In doing so they sparked off an interest in Ancient Egypt that led to the package-tours of Thomas Cook, and which eventually blossomed into the tourist boom of today.

The boundaries of Luxor encompass the ancient cities of Thebes – the capital of Egypt for most of the Middle and New Kingdoms – and Karnak, where the most glorious pharaonic temple of them all was built. Thebes was the political and religious centre of a New Kingdom Empire that conquered most of the Near East, and as such was adorned with the most wonderful buildings. The sheer scale of these buildings is impressive enough; imagine, then, how they must have looked in their original condition, with all the gold, silver and marble glinting in the sunlight. One can only surmise that the pharaohs lived in similar splendour. They certainly chose to die in style, and their opulent tombs, once piled high with treasures, are the chief attractions of Luxor's West Bank.

While the West Bank continues to glorify the ancient dead, the bustling city on the east side remains very much alive. The economy here is fuelled almost totally by tourism, and although the hassle this causes can sometimes be a little overwhelming – it begins the moment you arrive in Luxor with hotel touts bombarding you with offers of accommodation – it does mean that almost everything in Luxor is conveniently geared towards the foreigner. No Egyptian city has had more practice at catering for the tourist – or indeed more practice at ripping them off.

Orientation and services

(Luxor ☎ area code 095)

Luxor is a slender town hugging the east bank of the Nile. The train station is fairly central. The road ahead, Sharia al-Mahatta شارع المحطة, leads to Luxor Temple. North along the Corniche is Luxor Museum, and Karnak Temple, to the south lies the town centre and most of the budget hotels. Unfortunately, road names are largely ignored in Luxor.

The banks, post office and tourist office are all conveniently huddled around Luxor Temple. The **GPO** is at the end of Sharia al-Mahatta on the left. The **telephone office**, open 24 hours, is to the right of the temple on Sharia al-Karnak, while the **tourist office** is open 0800-2000 every day and is round the corner from the post office. Further south along the Corniche are **AMEX** and **Thomas Cook**, opposite each other by the entrance to the Winter Palace. The **police station** lies past the Novotel to the south of the city.

Local transport

Luxor is small enough to walk everywhere, although the baking heat may tempt you to catch a calèche (horse-drawn carriage) to some places. If you do hire one, consider the horse and don't overfill the carriage.

Where to stay

● **Budget hotels** Anybody who finds the noise and fumes of Luxor a little too overpowering should stay in the tranquil *Queen's Hotel* (فندق الملكة (كوينز) ☎ 384835) on the West Bank (see map, p287). The owner, El-Hag Ali Hassan Khalefa, is a shaky old boy with a wonderful smile and a warm heart. His hotel is similarly charming. The decor, from the souvenir Eiffel Tower adorning the lounge table to the plastic apple tree in reception, are endearingly naff; the hotel, although a little ramshackle, is cool and clean, while the rooftop terrace affords lovely views of sunset over Medinat Habu, the perfect place to sip a mint tea. And all this for E£10pp! Next door, the *Habou Hotel* (☎ 372677) is not quite so good good but charges double the price. To get here, cross the river on the local or car ferries, then catch a van (25pstr) from the dock to Medinat Habu.

The hotels on the East Bank are a truly curious collection. The *Sherif* شريف [1] (☎ 370757) is probably the most normal of them all, if you ignore the combination of Bob Marley posters and fake Louis XV furniture in reception. The manager, a decent sort of fellow, is not as pushy about selling his West Bank tours as many of the others in this price range, and backpackers have responded by turning up here in ever-greater numbers (E£6pp, plus E£1 for breakfast).

The *Ibis* [2] (☎ 376505) is run by three men who call each other Ahmed, and although the hotel has some very pleasant rooms (E£5pp) and the showers, though temperamental, are warm, it is unfortunately devoid of both custom and atmosphere. Three blocks further down at the *Moon Valley*وادي القمر[3] (☎ 375710) things start getting *really* surreal. It is owned by a chap who's convinced he's Michael Jackson, and the many photos displayed show him in various MJ poses. It's a nice enough place (E£10/20/30 sgl/dbl/tpl), but it's a little disconcerting having Mr Jackson stare down at you from every wall while the manager practises his moon-walk downstairs.

Maintaining the bizarre nature of Luxor's hotel situation is the *Everest Hotel* فندق ايفريست[4] (☎ 370017), over-priced (E£10sgl, E£15/20 dbl) but very popular ; the *Oasis Hotel* فندق الواحة[5] which is a great value place (E£8sgl, E£16 dbl, inc shower and breakfast) that's nearly always ignored; and the *Venus Hotel* [6] (☎ 382625), recommended by so many and yet, to be frank, quite appalling (although the price, E£4 per person, may account for some of the enthusiasm about this place). To be fair to the Everest it does feature a rooftop terrace and a washing machine, and the many travellers it attracts seem to be happy. Back near the station, the

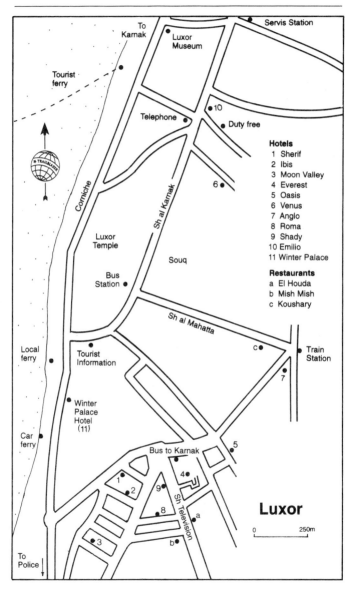

Hotels
1 Sherif
2 Ibis
3 Moon Valley
4 Everest
5 Oasis
6 Venus
7 Anglo
8 Roma
9 Shady
10 Emilio
11 Winter Palace

Restaurants
a El Houda
b Mish Mish
c Koushary

To Karnak

Servis Station

Luxor Museum

Tourist ferry

Telephone

● 10

● Duty free

Sh al Karnak

Comiche

6 ●

Luxor Temple

Souq

Bus Station ●

Sh al Mahatta

Local ferry ●

Tourist Information

c ●

Train Station

7 ●

Winter Palace Hotel (11) ●

Car ferry ●

Bus to Karnak

5 ●

1 ●

2 ●

4 ●

9 ●

8 ●

a ●

Sh Television

3 ●

b ●

To Police

Luxor

0   250m

Anglo [7] (☎ 381679) is a slight return to normality, despite the Swiss mountain scenes and Virgin Mary icons that decorate every floor. The Coptic owner, Mr Faz, is a lovely fellow, and his hotel boasts a washing machine and a small garden. Every room has a fan too, essential in this weather. The rooms (E£8 for a poky single, E£15 dbl, E£20dbl with bath, E£25 tpl). are cleaned daily. Bargain here to get a good, hearty breakfast included in the price.

Finally, back down near Sharia Television (شارع التلفزيون) is the *Roma Hotel* [8] (E£4pp). Features here include Bob Marley decor, an Essex girl called Sharon who's married to the owner, and a large rat that visits every Tuesday. Strange indeed.

● **Medium and top-range hotels** The *Shady Hotel* [9] (☎ 374859) may not have an apt name but it is not a bad deal and a dip in their pool is most pleasant. Don't be put off by the price-list behind reception that asks for US$38 for a double room: instead, confront the receptionist politely and haggle; the real price is closer to E£45. The *Emilio* [10] (☎ 376666) also has a pool, although you could drown amongst the waves of tour groups that stay here. The basic room charges are US$30/45 sgl/dbl, but taxes increase the final price significantly.

At the top end is the glorious *Winter Palace* [11] (☎ 380422). Whilst the old wing continues to charge exorbitant prices, the new wing is a lot more reasonable (US$75 per room). It is, however, a lot less romantic.

Where to eat
The *el-Houda* [a] ranks as many people's favourite. This restaurant serves some wonderful food with satellite TV to watch. Opposite is *Mish-Mish* [b], and their pizzas, from just E£3.50, are good value (tell them to go easy on the pepper). For those who prefer something more Egyptian, there is a great *Koushary* [c] shop on Sh al-Mahatta, and plenty of cheap felafel stands and chicken stalls on the small road to the north.

Luxor Temple معبد الاقصر
(0600-2200 summer, -2100 winter; E£10, E£5 students). Try to visit this temple in the early evening; the entry fee is then E£5 for everyone and it is a wonderfully eerie time to be here. The reliefs really stand out in the spotlights, there are no tour groups, and your only company is likely to be a family of bats that flutter invisibly above you.

The story of the temple's construction is complex. It was the brain-child of the 18th dynasty Pharaoh Amenhotep III (1386-1349BC), and was built to house the statues of the Theban Triad of Mut, Amun and Khonsu, local gods who achieved national fame as Thebes became Egypt's capital during the New Kingdom. After Amenhotep III, his son Amenhotep IV (1350-1334BC) halted the work, created a new sun-worshipping religion – possibly the world's first monotheistic faith –

❑ The gods of Ancient Egypt

A frightening array of alien deities confront those who dare to delve into the text-books on Ancient Egypt. It is a confusing pantheon, and the reasons for this are twofold. Firstly, the faith of the ancient Egyptians evolved from the myriad of different cults practised by the early settlements along the Nile. As Egypt was united under Menes (3100BC) so a standardised religion had to be formulated and, not wishing to upset anyone, the Old Kingdom legislators tried to incorporate as many of the village gods as possible into this new pantheon. Such a fractured beginning could only lead to a complex religion riddled with inconsistencies, which is how it appears to us today.

Secondly, the beliefs and practices of the Ancient Egyptians developed greatly over time. Indeed such was the Egyptian fondness for deifying their pharaohs that it can become difficult to keep up with who was and who wasn't a god. For instance, the Old Kingdom architect, Imhotep, was being worshipped in the Ptolemaic era as the god of medicine and healing.

Isis, Osiris, Horus and Seth

The Egyptian pantheon was the loom upon which legends were woven. The most important concerns the battle between Osiris and Seth. These two were brothers, the grandsons of the Creator, Atum-Re. After Atum-Re had retired, his mantle passed on to his children, and in turn to Seth and Osiris. Seth, unhappy with having to share the earth with Osiris, murdered him, hacked up the body and scattered it all over Egypt. Isis, the wife of Osiris and sister of both of them, tracked down the remains of her husband-brother and reassembled them to bring him back from the dead. Osiris revived long enough for them to produce a son, Horus, who avenged the murder of his father by contending Seth's claim to rule the earth. Backed by his parents the challenge was successful: Horus ruled the earth, Seth was banished into the desert, and Osiris went to rule the Underworld.

The temples and rituals

The Egyptian gods were represented on earth by statues which, so worshippers believed, came to life when no mortal was watching. The temples were built as residences for these statues, which would be housed in a small sanctuary at the very back of the temple, the Holy of Holies. High priests were appointed to perform the daily rituals - including washing the statue and entertaining it – that would keep the god in good humour and ensure the good fortune of the local people. The general public were not allowed inside the temples but annual festivals were organised – such as the Opet Festival (see p282), or the Festival of the Beautiful Meeting – where the statues from one temple were taken to visit statues housed in another temple. This allowed the people the privilege of seeing their gods and was usually followed by weeks of festivities.

and moved the capital away from Thebes to al-Amarna. Whilst superficially this may have been a religious conversion, there is little doubt that it was politically motivated too: the priests at Thebes had been exercising far too much control over the throne and by creating a new religion Amenhotep hoped to wipe out their power in an instant.

Unfortunately for him the religion never really took off, and his nephew Tutankhamun (yes, that Tutankhamun) returned the capital to

Thebes and completed the main temple. Ramses II added an extension, Alexander the Great – a huge fan of Egyptian religion – built the Barque Sanctuary, and the Romans dedicated a portion of the inner temple to their own gods. Finally in 1077 the eastern section of Ramses II's courtyard metamorphosed into the Abu al-Haggag Mosque.

The temple Before the temple entrance are four statues of Ramses II and a giant obelisk, originally one of a pair. The other now stands in La Place de la Concorde in Paris, sent as a gift by Mohammed Ali in return for the clock that adorns his mosque in Cairo. The pylon behind is also Ramses' handiwork, and is decorated with his favourite design: Scenes from the Battle of Kadesh (see p22).

Passing through the pylons you come to the **Second Courtyard**, with the back of the Abu al-Haggag Mosque encroaching onto the yard on the left. The reliefs in this courtyard depict the Festival of Opet. Both Luxor and Karnak temples were dedicated to the same gods – the Theban Triad – and every year the statues from Karnak would be carried by priests onto a barque, which was then drawn downstream to their other home at Luxor. This procession presaged three weeks of rampant festivities. The reliefs show some of these celebrations, including musicians, acrobats and dancers.

This celebratory theme is continued into the **Colonnade** next door – the design is Amenhotep's, but most of the reliefs here are Tutankhamun's. Beyond is the **Hypostyle Hall**, after which come three small chambers, the middle one later converted by the Romans for their own worship. A small **Offering Hall**, with some excellent reliefs of the Opet procession on the wall, separates this chamber from the **Sanctuary of the Barque**, where the sacred boat was placed after bearing the gods down the Nile. The Sanctuary was built by Alexander the Great and he is depicted on the walls making offerings to the gods. Straight ahead lies the **Holy of Holies**, while on your left is a small entrance to the **Divine Birth Room**, with Khnum (he's the one who looks like a sheep) fashioning the spirit of Amenhotep III on his potter's wheel.

On leaving, you can visit the **mosque**, the final resting place of Sheikh Abu al-Haggag, a descendant of the Caliph Ali. The entrance lies to the east of the temple.

Karnak Temple الكرنك
(0600-1830 summer, -1730 winter; E£10, E£5 students; sound and light E£33, check at tourist office for times.). An even more colossal and impressive collection of structures lies just 3km from Luxor Temple. The most agreeable way to get here is to take a stroll along the Nile, although you may prefer to catch a minibus from opposite the bus station in Luxor (25pstr) as you'll have plenty of walking to do at the site. Note that this place gets packed. Try to turn up first thing in the morning if possible.

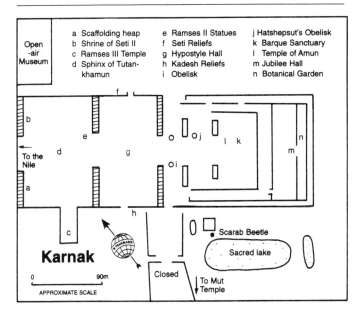

Open-air Museum	a Scaffolding heap	e Ramses II Statues	j Hatshepsut's Obelisk
	b Shrine of Seti II	f Seti Reliefs	k Barque Sanctuary
	c Ramses III Temple	g Hypostyle Hall	l Temple of Amun
	d Sphinx of Tutan-khamun	h Kadesh Reliefs	m Jubilee Hall
		i Obelisk	n Botanical Garden

Karnak

To the Nile

Scarab Beetle

Sacred lake

Closed

To Mut Temple

0   90m
APPROXIMATE SCALE

The temple The temple is once more a New Kingdom design, but, like Luxor Temple, was altered and extended considerably over the years. Although most of the buildings were constructed around 1500-1000BC, nearly every New Kingdom pharaoh, and a few later ones, seem to have changed the original design in some way.

The whole complex is surrounded by walls built by King Nectanebo, 380-342BC, and it is reasonable to surmise that he had a hand in the enormous pylon that stands between you and the complex too. Whoever it belongs to, it was never completed – it is undecorated, and the pile of detritus (**a**) lying against one tower inside the complex is probably ancient scaffolding that was never removed.

(**b**) Immediately on your left are three small shrines used to house the barques of the three main Gods of Thebes.

(**c**) Built in a much more ostentatious style, Ramses III's shrine lies behind the southern wall.

(**d**) The Great Court. Lined with pillars and adorned with statues, this is the largest section of the complex.

(**e**) Back in the main courtyard there are some columns interspersed with a few statues: the face of the Sphinx resembles Tutankhamun, whilst the other statues guarding the way to the temple are of Ramses II; his wife stands in miniature by his knees.

(**f**) Through the second pylon we arrive at the hypostyle hall. The 12 central pillars here are each 22.5m high, and used to hold aloft the roof, while the other pillars are about 7.5m shorter and were probably merely decorative. The hall was completed during the reign of Ramses II, although it was his father, Sety I, who actually initiated the project. The reliefs in this section are good, and some still retain their original colour. On the columns are pictures of the pharaohs making offerings to the gods.

(g) The reliefs on the exterior of the north wall commemorate Sety's recapture of Palestine. Look for the Lebanese cutting down their cedar trees, and the Canaanites cowering inside their city walls.

(h) On the exterior of the south wall are, once again, scenes of Ramses II's battle at Kadesh,

(i) Heading east once more, we soon come to the second biggest obelisk in the world (29.58m tall), made from Aswan granite and erected on the orders of Hatshepsut to commemorate 16 years on the throne. Its twin (j) lies scattered in pieces throughout the site (you can see its top near the sacred pool). Near to the erect obelisk is a statue of Thutmose II kneeling in front of an altar.

We are now in the Temple of Amun proper (k). A pair of granite columns either side of the central aisle mark the entrance into the Sanctuary of the Holy Barque (l), built by a brother of Alexander the Great. The exterior of this sanctuary depicts Amun crowning the king; the colour on the south wall is still vivid in places.

(m) A gap in the wall to the east brings us to the Jubilee Hall of Thutmose III. The main hall here was used by the Byzantines as a church. You can still see the faces of saints on the pillars.

(n) Beyond the main hall to the east is an entry into the botanical garden, so-called because of the pictures of wildfowl and animals on the walls.

South of the main complex is the **Sacred Lake** which was used for ritual purification; a granite scarab beetle stands by the north-west corner. From here look to the west and you can see the beginning of a **Processional Way** which used to join up with the Avenue of Sphinxes at Luxor Temple. Before heading off to Luxor yourself, have a quick peek at the small **open-air Museum** (E£5, E£2.5 students at the museum's entrance) in the north-west corner of the compound. On display here is a Middle Kingdom temple which originally stood near the third pylon.

Luxor Museum

(0900-1230; also 1600-2100 winter, 1700-2200 summer; E£15, E£8 students). In contrast to the Cairo Museum, this place has been thoughtfully laid out. Don't miss the statue of Thutmose III (No 61 in the catalogue). Other exhibits to look out for include some caricature sculptures of Amenhotep III (No 156), a calcite sculpture of both Amenhotep III and Sobek, the crocodile deity, (No 107) and a display of blocks from Amenhotep's dismantled mortuary temple which have been found all over Luxor. Downstairs is a new room dedicated to more statues of Amenhotep III, from a cache discovered in 1989 at Luxor Temple.

The West Bank

For those with only a passing interest in ancient Egypt, the New Kingdom attractions on the West Bank can be seen in one very full day although it's possible to spend weeks exploring the area. However you decide to travel around – whether by bike (E£4 per day), donkey (as little as E£12 if hiring from the West Bank, E£40 if taking an all-inclusive package from your hotel), or taxi (E£25pp if it's a full cab) – be sure to bring sun-cream, shades, a hat and plenty of water. A torch is very useful, for the 'in-tomb' lighting, if it's working at all, is often inadequate. A small bundle of

❏ Life and death in Ancient Egypt

In common with most religions today, the Egyptians believed in life after death for the pure and righteous. Upon dying the heart of the deceased was weighed by Horus to determine whether his spirit deserved to live on after his body had expired: worthy, and the spirit was led to the blissful underworld of Osiris; unworthy, and it became dinner for Ammut, a crocodile monster.

Except that it was not that simple. After dying, the spirit was supposed to perform a number of spells before he/she could enter into the hereafter. These spells were written down in manuals drawn up by priests – the *Book of the Dead* and the *Book of Gates* were two – excerpts of which decorate the walls in most of the New Kingdom tombs.

A complex set of burial rites and traditions had to be observed by the deceased relatives too. Firstly, the body had to be transported by funeral barque (a barge or ferry) to the west side of the Nile. Once there, the mummification could begin, a process that took up to 70 days. Firstly the internal organs had to be removed and placed in special Canopic jars; then the bandages were wrapped round the body in a style imitating the first mummification, performed by Isis on Osiris (see p269). Finally the body was placed in a tomb, the walls of which were decorated with pictures of food, games, weapons and treasures for the spirit of the deceased to enjoy. Small models – shabtis – were interred for the same purpose. Visitors to these tombs today will also find a false door painted on the tomb walls, through which the spirit could come and go as it pleased.

Royal burial

The rules of death for royalty were a little different from those that applied to your average man in the Sharia. Being gods already and indeed reincarnations of Horus, pharaohs were exempt from having their hearts weighed by Horus; their entry into Osiris' underworld was a formality. To smooth the way, however, their personal effects and treasures (including, some believe, their slaves) were buried with them.

Their tombs were, of course, very grand affairs, the construction of which began many years before the pharaoh died. Many pharaohs built mortuary temples near their tombs, where loyal subjects could come and worship them. Often a statue of the expired pharaoh was placed in a small room – the serdab – so that he could watch the faithful coming to worship him. In this way the spirit of the pharaoh could enjoy the adulation of his people, long after the flesh had been swathed in bandages and hidden away.

change for baksheesh could also prove useful. Set off early – the first ferry is at 6am (last one 9pm), and all the attractions open then too (shutting at 5pm). Tickets for each site can be bought in two places. If you're a student, you must go to the kiosk beyond the Colossi of Memnon; non-students can buy their tickets there, or from the tourist-ferry launch on the West Bank. Tickets are valid on the day of purchase only.

The Temple of Hatshepsut معبد هاتشيبسوت (E£6, E£3 students). The most stunning façade on the whole of the West Bank belongs to the mortuary temple of Queen Hatshepsut, where the wide horizontal lines of the

temple contrast spectacularly with the steep vertical cliffs which form its backdrop. Queen Hatshepsut was the enigmatic widow of Thutmose II. On Thutmose's death she assumed power for 15 years (1498-1483BC) until their son, Thutmose III, took over. The nature of her demise is not recorded, although it is reasonable to suppose that Thutmose III may have played a part: when he came to power he immediately attempted to obliterate his mother from history by defacing her image wherever it was found. (She's had the last laugh, however. While her temple is still admired and enjoyed by thousands each day, his temple was destroyed by landslides long ago, and today it lies in ruins to the south of hers.)

The temple is split into three horizontal sections, although the upper level is undergoing restoration and is currently closed to the public. Before climbing the ramp to the first section, look at the **porticoes** on the right, where the extremely faint reliefs depict the conveying of Hatshepsut's obelisks to Karnak Temple. The reliefs at the back of the porticoes on the next level are in a much better state. To the left of the ramp is an account of a trading expedition to a place called Punt on the coast of Somalia. The detail here is incredible; note the baboons swinging off the rigging, and the domed huts of the African natives. At the end of the expedition Hatshepsut offers the spoils to the god Amun.

To the left of this portico is a temple for the cow-like goddess of love and joy, Hathor. On your right as you walk in you see Hathor suckling Hatshepsut; on your left, she licks the queen's hand. Such scenes are clearly meant to display Hatshepsut's divine right to be sovereign to a sceptical public used to having a male king. Interestingly, nobody knows why only some of the queen's images have been defaced here.

To the south of Hatshepsut's temple is the temple of the Middle Kingdom pharaoh, **Mentuhotep** (2060-2010BC), built five centuries earlier and clearly an influence on Hatshepsut's design. The secret tomb of her architect, **Senenmut,** lies to the east; from here a path heads up the cliff-face to arrive, after a 40-minute scramble, at the Valley of the Kings.

Valley of the Kings وادي الملوك

(E£10 for 3 tombs, E£5 students. Tickets for Tutankhamun's tomb sold separately: E£20, E£10 students). Just buy one ticket to the valley, for you can buy more at the valley entrance.

The cemetery complex was the final resting place for over four centuries of New Kingdom pharaohs and nobles, 62 corpses in total, beginning with Pharaoh Thutmose I (1524-1518BC – see p21). The valley was chosen in the hope of hiding the inordinate treasures, buried along with the pharaohs, from the legions of grave robbers. This ploy failed in every case except one: Tutankhamun, whose fabulous hoard survived intact to be displayed in the Cairo Museum. Many tombs are closed now but those which are open furnish visitors with a good idea of the basic royal tomb layout. Listed here are four of the best.

● **Thutmose III** (1504-1450BC – Queen Hatshepsut's reign c1498-1483BC). Hidden away in a small cut between the cliffs, the obvious question is how did the pallbearers get the sarcophagus up here in the first place? Now the entrance is reached by a metal staircase, after which a narrow corridor descends deep into the mountainside. Halfway along the corridor an unfathomable well awaits the unwary. This was a typical feature of most tombs, possibly dug as a trap for robbers. Beyond lies an ante-chamber, its four walls decorated with over 700 'matchstick' deities. The empty sarcophagus still resides in the final chamber, with an image of the Sky God Nut, her arms outstretched to envelop the king, etched into the quartzite. On the pillar by the door is an image of the king in the solar barque along with his mother – a strange companion considering the hatred he showed for her after her death (see p286).

The walls, as usual, are decorated with text from the *Book of the Dead* (see p285). The small rooms surrounding this chamber are storage rooms.

● **Ramses III (1182-1151BC)** Ramses III, along with his son Merneptah, successfully defended Egypt from the invasions of the Peoples of the Sea and the Libyans. He was also the pharaoh who built Medinat Habu (see p288). The entrance to his tomb is guarded by two figures of Ma'at, the goddess of truth. The long first corridor has many small storage rooms running off to the sides. Halfway along, the corridor ends abruptly, shifts

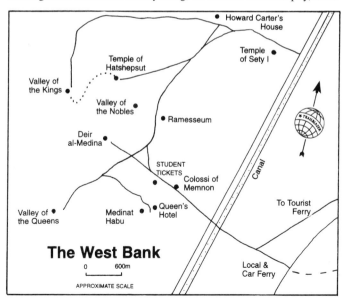

Howard Carter's House

Temple of Sety I

Temple of Hatshepsut

Valley of the Kings

Valley of the Nobles

Ramesseum

Deir al-Medina

STUDENT TICKETS

Colossi of Memnon

Canal

Valley of the Queens

Medinat Habu

Queen's Hotel

To Tourist Ferry

The West Bank

0   600m

APPROXIMATE SCALE

Local & Car Ferry

to the right, and then continues. This kink marks the end of Sethnakt's attempt to excavate the tomb (his own is featured below), and the rest of the corridor is Ramses III's work.

Scenes from *The Book of the Dead* fill the next walls, before the corridor widens into a chamber where the frescoes depict the four races of man: Asians, Libyans, Negroes and Egyptians. Unfortunately, beyond here the tomb has been closed off.

● **Ramses IX (1126-1108BC)** This short and exquisite tomb lies near the entrance to the complex. Ramses IX was the one of the last New Kingdom pharaohs, before the Libyans took control of the country. On the right-hand wall of the first corridor is a picture of the king semi-reclining, his arms (and formerly his phallus before he was cruelly emasculated by a prudish tourist) extended towards the life-giving sun, here pushed across the sky by a scarab beetle. For further proof of the skill of the artists, look at the details on the first supporting arch. Whilst the quality of the artwork further on deteriorates and the tomb was never fully completed, the designs here show a level of inventiveness and individuality that is not exceeded in any other tomb.

● **Tausert/Sethnakt (1187-1185BC/1185-1182BC)** Originally designed as a tomb for the wife of Sety II, Queen Tausert's tomb was later usurped by the 19th-dynasty pharaoh Sethnakt, who had given up excavating a tomb of his own (see Ramses III above). He replaced all images of her with those of himself, and installed his own huge granite sarcophagus in the final chamber. The designs on the wall are remarkable not just for their detail but also for their excellent state of preservation.

● **Tutankhamun (1334-1325BC)** While Howard Carter's discovery of this tomb is a fascinating tale (see p302), the tomb itself is the dullest of them all. The interior is very plain, with only King Tut's sarcophagus *in situ*, as a consolation for all those who have just parted with E£20.

Medinat Habu مدينة حابو (E£6, E£3 students). The last mortuary temple to be built on the West Bank, Medinat Habu is dedicated to the worship of Ramses III (1182-1151BC), although it began life as a temple to Amun built by Queen Hatshepsut. The entrance is flanked by giant towers. In these towers are rooms that were once the preserve of Ramses III himself. If the reliefs on the walls are to be believed the pharaoh was often entertained by a bevy of females here, and some written records also detail an assassination attempt made on the king in this room.

Moving on to the first courtyard, the small temple to your right is a remnant from Hatshepsut's day; once again her son Tuthmose III has obliterated his mother from the reliefs. After this is the temple proper. All

(Opposite) A typically chaotic Egyptian street scene, this time in Luxor.

along the inside of the north wall are scenes of Ramses' successes against invaders; the shields decorating the first Pylon are a list of all his conquered foes. Moving through two courtyards (the first contains statues of the king) and the hypostyle hall you reach the sanctuary proper, where the statues of the Theban Triad resided once a year during the 'Feast of the Valley' – a similar celebration to the Opet Festival. Before leaving the site, visit the small warren of rooms to the south of the first courtyard. This was originally the pharoah's quarters during state visits.

Valley of the Queens وادي الملكات (E£6, E£3 students). This series of approximately 75 tombs lies to the west of Medinat Habu. These were the burial chambers for the pharaohs' queens and their sons, and though smaller and less spectacular than those in the Valley of the Kings the tombs nevertheless contain some vivid and beautiful wall-paintings.

Amongst those currently open is the **Tomb of Prince Khaemwese**. Here the murals show the young prince, his hair cut in the youthful, partly-shaven style, being led by his father Ramses III before the gods. The second corridor is devoted to the *Book of the Gates*; the knife-wielding chaps on the walls are the gate-keepers. Finally on the back wall the pair meet Osiris, the king of the Underworld, whilst the tiny figure of Horus stands watching on the lotus-blossom.

Also in the valley is the **Tomb of Amonhikhopeshef**. The tiny granite sarcophagus indicates that this poor fellow, the brother of Khaemwese, must have died very young. Nevertheless he has been buried with all the pomp accorded his elder brother. Nearby, the **Tomb of Queen Titi** is also open but in a very bad state of repair.

● **Tomb of Queen Nefertari** (0830-1600 winter, 0730-1700 in summer;E£100, E£50 students). Since its reopening last year, crowds have flooded back to see the burial place of Ramses II's wife. The authorities have had to limit the number of visitors to 150 per day so buy your tickets early if you want to see it. The tomb was closed because of the threat from Thebes' rising water table but it has now been fully restored to its former splendour.

The Ramesseum الرامسيوم (E£6, E£3 students). Whilst this building has the standard layout of most New Kingdom mortuary temples, the size and style are unmistakably Ramses II's: gigantic, self-glorying and full of those familiar scenes from the Battle of Kadesh. Such self-glorification has attracted the envy of lesser men, and unfortunately the Ramesseum is now in a very bad state of repair. Many of the statues have been beheaded, nearly half of the columns in the hypostyle hall have fallen and most

---

(Opposite) Top: Taking a midday siesta on the Corniche by Luxor Temple. **Bottom:** Although no longer a god to the Egyptians, Ramses III still watches over his people at Medinat Habu (see p288).

of the reliefs have been worn down. Nevertheless, it's worthwhile wandering amongst the ruins and dreaming of how this place used to be. A small building to the north of the Ramesseum proves that, while Ramses II was undoubtedly a fearless warrior and a ruthless leader of men, he never forgot his mum; it is a small temple built in her honour.

Other sights on the West Bank
During the New Kingdom era it became accepted practice for the nobles of the day to be buried in a style only slightly less flamboyant than that of their pharaoh. Over 400 of these **Tombs of the Nobles** exist among the houses of Qurna village. Each have been numbered, and those of particular interest have been grouped together and require a special ticket costing E£6 (E£3 students) each. If you wish to buy just one ticket, see the tombs of Ramose, Userhet and Khaemhet.

To the south-west is the temple of **Der el-Medina** (E£6,E£3 students). It's pretty crummy compared to the other attractions on the West Bank, although the ruined village nearby, formerly the home of the artists and labourers who built the temples, is interesting. Back near the student ticket booth are the **Colossi of Memnon** (free). These two giant statues of Amenhotep III originally guarded the entrance to his mortuary temple but apart from this duo and a few stone sculptures in the fields behind (look out for the crocodile!) little else remains.

To the north of the West Bank stands the **Temple of Sety I** (E£6, E£3 students). Sety was responsible for the revival in Egypt's fortunes following the chaos of the Middle Kingdom. His temple is in a reasonable condition, although currently undergoing restoration. The artwork in the hypostyle hall is particularly fine.

Moving on
● **Train** Tourist trains to Cairo (9.5hrs) currently follow this timetable:

Depart	1st cl (student)	2nd cl (student)
1130	E£48 (E£31)	E£28 (E£21)
2330	E£51 (E£34)	E£31 (E£24)

● **Bus** By the time the buses reach Luxor they are already full. This usually means that, unless you are very lucky, you could be standing in the central aisle for your entire journey which is not very pleasant if you happen to be travelling all the way to Cairo, an 11-hour journey. Buses depart at 1630 (E£22) and at 1900 (E£39).

● **Servis** The servis taxis leave from the north of the city. Qena ﻗﻨﺎ is the most northerly destination of Luxor's servis taxis (E£2).

Cairo
القاهرة

This little world, the great Cairo....the most admirable and the greatest city seen upon the earth....the Microcosmus of the greater world.... **William Lithgow, 1614**

Egypt's capital can both captivate and infuriate. One minute you could be dumb-struck with awe at the foot of the pyramids, and the next you could be battling with an over-insistent papyrus seller or wilting under the heat and the tedium in a queue at Mogamma.

The reason why the Cairo experience can be such a roller-coaster ride is simple: the streets of the capital are crammed with over fifteen million souls – an incredible 75,000 people per square mile. The extraordinary cacophony generated on the streets – diesel engines revving, hawkers shouting, horns blaring – is the sound of people trying to eke out a living amid the bedlam. Consequently, your happiness is not their first priority, although your money could well be.

Nevertheless, there's also plenty of glamour amongst the clamour. While the city's present battle is to provide for its people, much of Cairo's rich history has been preserved and there are some great places to explore. The Cairenes too (when you finally meet them) are as warm and friendly as their Middle Eastern neighbours. The capital does seem over-powering at first but once you've become accustomed to the suffocating noise, immune to the persistent hassle and addicted to the blue, lead-laden air, you may even find you're enjoying yourself.

HISTORY

It may look decrepit in parts, but Cairo is, by the standards of the Near East, a fairly modern city. Nearby is an ancient ford used in pharaonic times, whilst the first Old Kingdom capital, Memphis, lies just a few km to the south of the city. The metropolis itself, however, is a mere baby, founded by the all-conquering Muslims a mere 1350 years ago. Amr Ibn al-As was the Muslim leader who ousted the Byzantines and established al-Fustat – 'the Camp' – within the borders of modern Cairo, in 640AD.

The Tulunids

Since then, Cairo has been the seat of more than its fair share of empires and dynasties. The first, founded by Ahmad Ibn Tulun in 868AD, was a relatively minor affair. Tulun was a bit of a loose cannon, an Abbassid general charged with overseeing Egypt who preferred to run the country without interference from Baghdad. Consequently, two years after arriving Tulun stopped paying tributes to his Abbassid paymasters and declared himself the sole ruler of newly-independent Egypt. The dynasty lasted just 38 years before the Abbassids returned to take back Egypt and crush the city, al-Qata, that he had founded to the north of al-Fustat.

The Fatimids

Sixty-four years later and the Fatimids under General Gawhar arrived. Their homeland was North Africa, their conquests stretched as far as Arabia; what they needed, therefore, was a new capital somewhere in between. The site of Amr Ibn al-As' al-Fustat was ideal. The Fatimids called their new capital al-Qahira (the Conqueror) – after the planet al-Qahir (Mars) which was in the ascendancy at the time. The Fatimid era was a chequered one. While the city became the capital of an empire and an important religious and academic centre – the world's oldest university, al-Azhar Mosque, was established at this time – it also suffered from plagues, drought and the infamous Caliph al-Hakim (see p308). Eventually the population dwindled and the city declined. The end of the Fatimid era was nigh. Upon hearing the news that the Frankish Crusaders had designs on the city and were approaching fast, al-Qahira was torched.

The Ayyubids

Three years later, Saladin al-Ayyubi, the Crusader's greatest foe and the founder of the Ayyubid dynasty, took over what was left of al-Qahira. His greatest legacy to the city is the huge citadel, the largest in the Arab world, that sits atop a hill to the east of Ibn Tulun's mosque. Once more the academics, merchants, philosophers and politicians were drawn to al-Qahira, and the city grew more wealthy and beautiful as a result.

This prosperity continued under the Mamlukes. After Baghdad had been destroyed by Genghis Khan's Mongols (and the last Baghdad Caliph had been rolled up in a carpet and trampled to death by horses), Baybars established a new Caliphate in Egypt by installing on the throne an Abbassid nobody who had fled to Cairo from Baghdad. It gave the Mamluke Empire a shade more credibility and temporarily moved the centre of the Islamic world away from Baghdad to Egypt. Although the Ottomans (who followed the Mamlukes) neglected the city, their rebellious pasha Mohammed Ali built a tremendous mosque inside Saladin's citadel, while the French and British developed picturesque suburbs on the new islands that emerged as the Nile continued its shift westwards.

Cairo today

Cairo's population is still growing, creating an enormous strain on the city's infrastructure. While parts of the city are continually being modernised in an attempt to maintain Cairo's international prestige, other, poorer sections such as the notorious 'City of the Dead', have been neglected for years. It is a problem exacerbated by natural disasters, such as the 1992 earthquake that did great damage to the city. Immigrant work-ers from both rural Egypt and abroad continue to arrive in great numbers, and yet somehow this 'Mother of all Cities' still finds the resources to support them all. Whether she can continue to do so in the long-term only time will tell.

LOCAL TRANSPORT

● **The airport** Cairo airport has two terminals, 'Old' and 'New', which lie about two km apart. The bus stop is at the Old Terminal. You will probably arrive at the New Terminal, however, so head out to the car park where almost any bus that drives by will take you to the old terminal for 50pstr. Bus No 400 (one of the large red, orange and white buses) will take you to Midan Tahrir in Central Cairo for just 50pstr. A taxi can cost as little as E£10 if you bargain hard but the average price is double this.

● **Metro** On the only underground network in Africa the carriages are clean and comfy, and some of the bigger stations even have televisions on the platform. If your journey is less than eight stops the fare is just 30pstr. The first few carriages are women only, and men are subjected to a small fine if they are caught in one. The three main stops are: **Sadat** (Midan Tahrir), **Nasser** (for Tawfikia St), and **Mubarak** (Ramses Station).

● **Bus** The buses run to an extensive network. The main terminus lies in front of the Nile Hilton at Midan Tahrir, and there is a smaller one at Midan Ataba ميدان العتبة. The standard fare is usually 25-50pstr. The only disadvantage with this form of transport is that bus numbers are written in Arabic only, although somebody will usually shepherd you onto the right bus if you ask. Bus numbers are given in the relevant sections below.

● **Taxi** These are also inexpensive, although it is impossible to pay as lit-tle as the locals. The meters invariably do not work, so it is a case of hag-gling once again. A trip from the tourist office to Midan Tahrir is about E£2; cross the bridge to Dokki and it rises to E£5.

● **Ferry** The ferry plies a scenic route up and down the Nile from the TV station to the Old City. Virtually useless as a means of getting from A to B, it's a pleasant way to get an alternative view of the capital (50pstr).

● **Tram** The tram (25pstr) is really only useful if you wish to go from the Ramses Hilton to the train station and have a lot of time to kill.

ORIENTATION

Part transport terminus, part government office, and part hotel complex, the centre of Cairo is Midan Tahrir ميدان التحرير. South of it is Garden City جاربين سيتي, home to many of the foreign embassies. Still further south is Old Cairo, now the centre of the Egyptian Coptic religion. Continuing clockwise there's Roda Island, and on the Nile's west bank, Gizaالجيزة. To the west of Midan Tahrir is a second island, Geziraجزيرة الجزيرة, with the

European-designed suburb of Zamalek on its northern end. On the west bank beyond Gezira is Dokki الدقي. The twin industrial neighbourhoods of Bulaq and Shubra lie to the north of Midan Tahrir. It is doubtful that you will visit either of these.

To the east is the downtown area, and beyond that, Islamic Cairo. Still further east is the City of the Dead مدينة الأموات, a vast Mamluke cemetery that today is home to many of Cairo's destitute citizens; it's the strangest, eeriest place to wander around.

SERVICES

(Cairo ☎ area code 02)

● **Bookshops** Bibliophiles are spoilt for choice in Cairo. The **American University** has a sizeable collection of new books in its store, particularly on the Middle East. The entrance to the AU is opposite McDonald's on Sharia Mohammed Mahmud. Bring your passport. The **Anglo-Egyptian Bookshop** on Sh M Farid شارع محمد فريد is also full of interesting tomes, although the majority are textbooks. There is also a small second-hand market on the walls behind Ezbekiya Gardens but the selection is usually very disappointing.

● **Changing money** You will have no trouble finding a bank in Cairo. The branches of AMEX and Thomas Cook are centrally located, and are marked on the map. (AMEX address: 15 Sh Qasr el-Nil, PO Box 2160). Many of the big hotels have now installed electronic cash dispensers for credit cards in their lobbies. Rates vary from hotel to hotel.

❏ **Embassies and consulates**

For buses to Dokki, go to the south of Midan Tahrir and take almost any bus (see the Central Cairo map on p299).

• **Australia** (☎ 777900) Cairo Plaza Tower, South Bld
• **Canada** (☎ 3543110) Africa-Arab Bank Bldg, Shari Khalil Agra, Garden City
• **Jordan** (☎ 3485566) 6 Sh Gohaini, Dokki. Visa: 0900-1100 Sat-Thu. One photo, pick up same day 1230-1300. Aus free, Can E£91, UK E£63, US E£70.
• **Lebanon** (☎ 3610474) 5 Sh Ahmed Nassim, Giza. Visa: Mon-Fri 1000-1200. One photo and photocopy of passport picture required. One-day process; E£68 all nationalities.
• **Libya** (☎ 3610474) 7 El-Salah Ayub, Zamalek
• **Sudan** (☎ 3549661) 3 Sh El-Ibrahim, Garden City. Visa: Sat-Thu 0900-1100. Four photos required, a letter of recommendation, and five photocopies of the application form, five to six day process, US$57 all nationalities.
• **Syria** (☎ 3358232) 13 Abdel Rahman Sabri, Dokki. Visa: NB! This is your **last opportunity** to buy a Syrian visa; 0900-1100 Sat-Thu; two photos and letter of recommendation, three-day process. Aus, Can free (letter still required), UK E£182, US E£123.
• **UK** (☎ 3540850) 2 Ahmed Ragheb, Garden City
• **USA** (☎ 3557371) 5 Latin America, Garden City

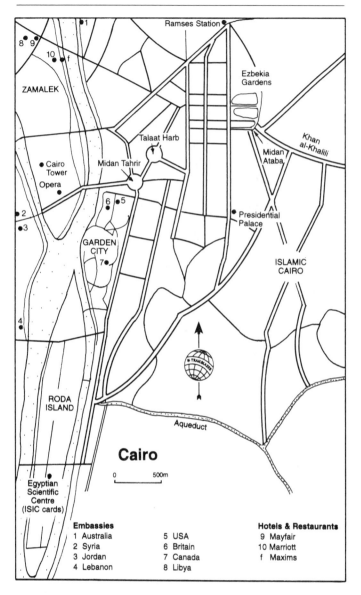

ZAMALEK

Ramses Station

Ezbekia
Gardens

Talaat Harb

Khan
al-Khalili

Midan
Ataba

Cairo
Tower

Midan Tahrir

Opera

Presidential
Palace

GARDEN
CITY

ISLAMIC
CAIRO

RODA
ISLAND

Aqueduct

Cairo

0   500m

Egyptian
Scientific
Centre
(ISIC cards)

Embassies
1 Australia
2 Syria
3 Jordan
4 Lebanon

5 USA
6 Britain
7 Canada
8 Libya

Hotels & Restaurants
9 Mayfair
10 Marriott
f Maxims

● **Post** The main GPO lies hidden away in the shadow of a flyover to the east of Opera Square ميدان الاوبيرا. Opening hours are 0800-1800 everyday except Friday. The Poste Restante is round the corner through a door marked 'Private Boxes'; collect from counter No 11.

● **ISIC Cards** Most hotels will also be able to arrange ISIC cards for about E£30, or you can save yourself E£8 by visiting the supplier at the **Egyptian Scientific Center** (0930-1400 and 1600-2000, Friday 1000-1400), 23 al-Manial Street, above the National Bank of Egypt on Roda Island. They also sell GO25 cards, invaluable if you are going to Turkey. Catch the metro to el-Malek el-Saleh and cross the bridge from there.

● **Photography** The Kodak store on Sh Adli is the best place to buy film. Many of the camera shops in the big hotels also stock reliable film, although these places are very expensive.

● **Telephone** There is a 24-hour telephone office next to the tourist office. This place charges for a minimum of three minutes but it's cheaper than using a phonecard.

● **Tourist information** From 0830-2000 every day the gallant boys and girls of the tourist office on Sh Adli dispense little nuggets of wisdom to bewildered tourists. They're a smashing bunch. Ayman Youssef is particularly knowledgeable and a bit of a local star: his other job is as a film critic for the local press.

● **Tours** A few hotels offer tours to Giza, Memphis and Saqqara for about E£15 but this is for the transport only; entrance fees and food are extra. Alternatively, for US$40 Misr Travel (just of Midan Tahrir on Talaat Harb) will escort you in luxury around the West Bank necropolis with everything included. Other travel agents run similar tours.

● **Travel agents** Egypt's strict airline controls ensure that flights out of Egypt are rarely cheap. If you have the time and inclination head to Eilat in Israel and fly from there. If you do have to fly from Cairo, avoid a company called Wondertours. The number of complaints I have received about this company is phenomenal and the tourist office has a file full of similar cases. Your best bet is to visit the airline offices directly; see the map (p299) for the three cheapest: Egyptair, Tarom and Malev.

● **Visas** A trip to the Mogamma building on Midan Tahrir should be on everybody's itinerary even if you've already registered your visa. This is *the* high-temple to the demi-god bureaucracy, where the priests of paperwork, the clerks, ensure that the sacred rituals of red tape continue to be observed punctiliously every day.For tourists, the first floor is where it's at: registering takes place at window No 45, while the other 90 or so windows can help with all manner of other requests, from visa extensions to re-entry visas. While you're waiting in the queue treat yourself to a cup of tea and a shoe shine, or even change some money. The whole show kicks off at 0830 and continues through to 2000 (closed Fridays).

WHERE TO STAY

Cairo's hostels used to be legendary. Many of the nastier hovels were mythologised in travellers' tales as appalling paragons of filth. Alas, most of these pits have been replaced by a new breed of budget hostel where clean linen, matching crockery and MTV are the norm. The *Sun Hotel* [1] (☎ 5781786) is among the latter. Ideally located on the corner of Midan Tahrir and Talaat Harbطلعت حرب, this blemish-free establishment boasts all of the above, plus a hearty breakfast, and all for only E£15 (dorm). They will also store luggage free of charge. It's way up on the ninth floor; unfortunately, the lift works only when it feels like it. Nearby, the *Ismalia Hotel* [2] (☎ 3563122) on Midan Tahrir is of a very similar standard to the Sun, but a little more scruffy.

For those who'd rather save every piastre possible, and at the same time undergo the 'Cairo hovel experience', there are still a few dirt cheap places around. The *Sultan*فندق السلطان(E£7 dorm) and *Sultan II* (E£6 dorm) hostels [3] (☎ 771925) share the same building on Sharia Tawfikia شارع التوفيقية, a small market street off Talaat Harb. The Sultan II, up on the fifth floor, is definitely the ugly sister: the lift doesn't work, the water supply is temperamental, and the whole place is in a bad state of repair. Nevertheless, there is a really friendly spirit at the Sultan II, and it's E£1 cheaper. Both hostels have kitchens for you to use, and the staff are very helpful.

If you're looking to escape from fellow travellers then you have three choices: the peaceful *Amin Hotel* فندق الأمين [4] at 38 Falaky Square (☎ 3933813; E£16.55/24 sgl/dbl); the *Gresham* [5] (☎ 5759043) at 20 Talaat Harb, where the latticed reception and comfortable lounge are let down by some slightly tatty rooms (E£35/45 sgl/dbl); or the spotless *Petit Palais* فندق بيتيت [6] (☎ 3911863), near Midan Opera, which has some of the smartest rooms in the budget range (E£15/20/35 dorm/sgl/dbl).

No guide to budget Cairo would be complete without mentioning the *Oxford Pension* [7] (☎ 5758173; E£11pp, bargaining possible), the venerablegranddaddy of Cairo's flea-pits. The nicotine-stained hallways still echo to the ghostly footsteps of previous residents but these days it seems deserted; a large family of cats were the only guests when I visited.

Medium and top-range hotels

Don't be misled by the scruffy neighbourhood in which it stands, or the tatty exterior of the hotel itself, for the *Windsor Hotel* فندق الويندزور [8] (☎ 5915277), now over 100 years old, is still a cut above most accommodation. Reputedly the bar, a former watering-hole for British officers, is the oldest in Cairo, but nowadays the biggest draw seems to be that Michael Palin (ex-Monty Python) stayed here during his 80-day jaunt around the world (Room 16). Some of the bedrooms are lovely, and the hotel still preserves some nice touches such as uniformed bellboys and a delightful crank-handled lift. Rooms start at US$22/30 sgl/dbl rising to US$31/42 for en suite 'luxury rooms'. Another recommended place is the ***Mayfair Hotel*** [9] (☎ 3407315), occupying some very valuable real estate near the Dutch and French embassies. The grey-beige combination of the décor may depress after a while but it is surgically clean and, being in Zamalek, imbued with funereal silence; often the only noise to be heard is the swish of the maid's duster. Rooms cost US$22/37 for a single/double, rising to US$34/49 with shower and air-conditioning.

Finally, if you've got the money, a stay in a 19th century palace could be in order. The ***Marriott*** [10] (☎ 3408888), near the 26th July Bridge in Zamalek, was built by Khedive Ismail, a descendant of Mohammed Ali, as part of the celebrations for the opening of the Suez Canal. Today it appears to have more restaurants than residents; but at only US$90 for a room with Nile view (US$72 garden view) it's good value.

WHERE TO EAT

Whatever you do and wherever you go in this great city, don't miss the opportunity to visit that hallowed Cairene institution, the ***café***. There are thousands all over the city, each with its own distinctive character. Don't miss the hand-painted establishment in the alley off Tawfikia St [a], and also the one near the pedestrian overpass on Midan el-Falaki [a] which catches the raking afternoon sun perfectly (and also stocks beer).

Cairo has some of the best street stalls in the Near East where one can usually 'refuul' for less than E£1. If you're staying at the Sultan Hotel you will probably have already been tempted by some of the goods in the market on Tawfikia Street, but you may not be aware of the foody heaven that takes place every evening in an alley off ***Midan Orabi*** [b]. There are lots of different restaurants and street stalls to choose from here and a corresponding number of dishes to try, from the humble 30pstr felafel to the full five-course feast.

Connoisseurs of Goshari should go to the ***Tahrir Goshari*** [c] on Sh Tahrir. By common consent this is the best in Cairo. To quote one exasperated Cairene: 'Ramadan would be easier to endure if this place had never existed'. Not far away, on Talaat Harb, is the ***Felfela*** [d], a trendy Egyptian fast-food joint. Everything, including fuul sandwiches, is a little more expensive here but only by 10pstr or so. Their restaurant round the corner *is* beyond most budgets, however, although I hear it does the best pigeon in the whole of Egypt.

One place where you wouldn't think of looking for budget food is the Marriott Hotel but every Friday at ***Harry's Pub*** [10] they hold a barbecue for just E£10, while on Saturday it's Chinese food (E£10) and on Sunday roast beef (E£15). Opposite the American University there are branches of ***McDonald's*** [e] and ***Pizza Hut*** [e].

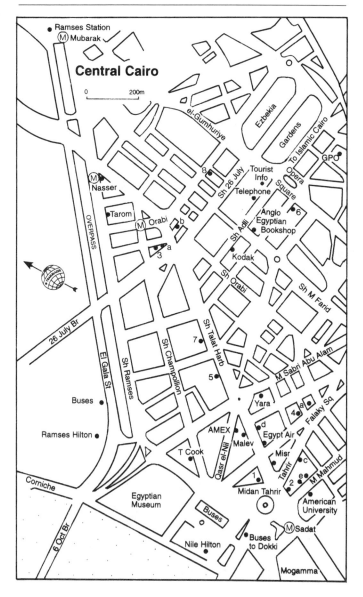

Central Cairo

If you're planning to celebrate your last night in the Near East you may like to try *Maxim's* [f, on main Cairo map, p299], a floating restaurant moored near the Marriott. It departs at 1930 and again at 2300. The two-hour cruise up and down the Nile costs E£70-80, for which you get a main course, salad and dessert, not to mention a band and belly-dancing. If you can tear yourself away from the dancer's navel for a second you'll notice the scenery outside is interesting too.

NIGHTLIFE

There are plenty of places to go for an evening out, although a knowledge of Arabic is required to make the most of them. The best is the **Sufi Dancing** at the al-Ghouri Mausoleum (2100 Wed and Sat, free). There is also the **opera** (☎ 341926), and the **Balloon theatre**, which holds folk shows every evening at 2100 for which they charge as little as E£5.

WHAT TO SEE

The Pyramids الاهرام
(0700-1700; E£10, E£5 students). Not even the plagues of persistent camel drivers and souvenir hawkers that swarm at their feet can fully diminish the unadulterated splendour of the three Great Pyramids of Giza, the only surviving Wonders of the Ancient World.

The two largest, which originally housed the bodies of the fourth-dynasty king Cheops (2589-2566BC) and his son Chefren are breathtaking enough today, but all we are really seeing is the substructure. Both were originally dressed in a cloak of limestone (a little still remains at the summit of Chefren's Pyramid), which would have made a dazzling spectacle for the Ancient Egyptians as it glistened in the sunlight.

Bus No 82 from platform 8 at Midan Tahrir drops you on the Pyramid's Road just a couple of hundred metres from the site. Alternatively, take bus No 84 from Ataba Sq. Entering from the Pyramids Road, on your right is the ticket booth for entry into the complex whilst on the left is a separate booth selling tickets into Cheops' Pyramid, the largest (and most claustrophobic) of the three tombs.

● **Pyramid of Cheops** (0900-1630, separate ticket required; E£10, E£5 students). As the splendid aspect over this 'corrugated, unsightly mountain of stone' (as Twain described it) hoves into view from the Pyramids Road, reflect for a moment on some of the statistics that surround this tomb. At 137m tall it is the largest pyramid in the world, covering a total land area of 13 acres and using nearly 2,400,000 cubic metres of stone. It has been estimated that this tomb took 30 years to complete and approximately 100,000 slaves helped in the construction. Despite such colossal figures, Cheops' pyramid was built with incredible accuracy, necessary in order to prevent the whole structure from collapsing on top of itself. Even 4500 years later it is still difficult to fully comprehend the techniques used. And if all this doesn't blow you away, just remember: when these pyramids were built not even the wheel had been properly developed!

Walking through the entrance in the northern face, two passages confront the visitor. The tunnel heading down (usually closed) leads to an unfinished burial chamber, while another passage ascends steeply for about 50m before splitting in two. The cramped horizontal tunnel leads to the **Queen's Chamber**, while the passage up (known as the **Great Gallery**) arrives eventually at the undecorated granite **King's Chamber**, which still contains the lidless sarcophagus of the king. The small, flat section between the gallery and the chamber originally housed four giant granite slabs used to seal the tomb; now only their niches remain.

Around the pyramid are other buildings of note. The three unimpressive mounds to the east are actually more tombs, this time for the bodies of Cheops' queens. To the south there's a **Boat Museum** (0900-1700 summer, 0900-1600 winter; E£10, E£5 students) housing a restored barque under special, temperature-controlled conditions. The boat was one of five such barges discovered buried around the pyramid; whether they ever had a practical purpose or were merely symbolic, to be used by the king for his journey to the underworld, has never been ascertained.

● **Pyramid of Chefren** Once 10m shorter than Cheops', thanks to the retention of the limestone sheathing on its summit it now measures just 50cm less than his father's. (It looks bigger, simply because it stands on higher ground.) Although this pyramid is currently closed, the mortuary complex that lies outside is open for all to see.

The mortuary complex begins with the **Valley Temple** at the foot of the hill, in front and to the right of the Sphinx's paws. Produce your ticket to the pyramid complex to be admitted here. This was where Chefren's body was mummified by priests before his internment. Chefren's **Mortuary Temple** (see p285) used to stand next to the east face of the pyramid, and these two temples were linked by a **Ceremonial Walkway**, of which only the foundations now remain. It is believed that the funeral procession would have started in the valley temple, from where they would have borne the body along the causeway, through the mortuary temple for the last rites, and then into the pyramid to deposit the body.

You can also visit the **Tombs of the Nobles** to the west of the pyramid, which date from Chefren's time, and those of his family to the east.

● **The Sphinx** For as long as anyone can remember this lion-bodied, Chefren-faced sculpture has always been surrounded in both myth and scaffolding. According to a large stele found between its paws, Tuthmose IV (1419-1386BC) saved the Sphinx from asphyxiation in the sand (trying saying that after three Stellas) and was rewarded with the kingship for his pains. After having its beard shot off by the Turks, and now suffering from the more insidious torture of pollution which is causing its body and face to crumble, the Sphinx probably wishes it had remained buried up to its sandstone scalp.

● **Pyramid of Mycerinus** The smallest of the three giants – at 62m it's not even half as tall as the other two – belongs to Mycerinus, another son of Cheops who rose to become pharaoh. Uncompleted at the time of his death (the pyramid never received its limestone sheathing), inside it's the most complex of the three pyramids and the only one that has interior decorations on the walls.

Museum of Egyptian Antiquities

(0900-1700 daily; E£10, E£5 students). Housed in the neo-classical mansion to the north of Midan Tahrir, this is a fascinating warehouse of pharaonic relics. Every era of ancient Egypt up to and including the Roman occupation is included, the undoubted highlight being the priceless treasures of Tutankhamun.

The rest of the museum is laid out in chronological order, beginning on the left and continuing clockwise. Although there is far too much to describe here, most of the exhibits are clearly labelled and the guides for hire at the ticket booth (E£10) are usually very knowledgeable. Make sure you don't miss the **Narmer Palette** by the entrance. This stone tablet depicts Menes wearing the crowns of Upper and Lower Egypt and beat-

---

❏ **Tutankhamun's treasures**

Tutankhamun was a relatively minor New Kingdom pharaoh who ruled for just nine years. It is believed that during his reign the high priests were the real rulers, and King Tut was a mere puppet in their hands.

The treasures were recovered from his tomb on Luxor's West Bank in 1922 by Howard Carter, an English archaeologist who had spent many fruitless years digging in the Valley of the Kings. While his sponsor, Lord Carnarvon, pestered him to admit defeat, Carter carried out one last excavation underneath some workmen's huts. Sure enough the sealed tomb was discovered, and his relief soon turned to incredulity when he realised that the tomb was untouched by robbers, its treasures still intact.

And what treasures! Tutankhamun's gilt complex fills the whole of the rear corridor of the Museum of Egyptian Antiquities in Cairo, half of the eastern one, and all the adjoining rooms too. Over **1700 items** are on display, including the most famous relic of all: the gold and lapis lazuli **funerary mask** of the young king. Other Tut treasures include: his gilded **wooden shrines** along the rear corridor; the 143 pieces of **jewellery** that were found on the body inside his **golden sarcophagus**; the **funerary bed**, again covered with sheet gold; and the fabulous **wooden throne**, gilded and encrusted in jewels, with a picture of the king in conversation with his wife on the back. Also on display throughout the exhibition are a series of photos, taken in 1922 at the West Bank site, that show the original position of the treasures in the tomb.

ing up the people of the Delta. It may look unremarkable, but this is probably the world's oldest surviving example of a historical record, being
approximately 5000 years old. Look out for the **animal rooms** (Nos 48
and 53), which contain the mummified remains of apes, ibises, croco-
diles, cats and fish; wildlife preservation, pharaonic-style!

And then there's the **mummy room**. After decades spent stored away,
some New Kingdom pharaohs have deigned to receive tourists once more
(E£30, E£15 students). It gives you the weirdest feeling, after hearing so
much about them, to finally meet the rulers of Ancient Egypt face to face.
Thutmose II, Sety I and Ramses II are the star attractions.

Islamic Cairo ميدان الاسلام

No trip to Egypt's capital would be complete without a visit to the Islamic
Quarter. Much of the area is a claustrophobic mélange of winding alleyways and covered souks, a romantic, aromatic labyrinth that evokes better than any other place on our route the mysterious medieval city of *A
Thousand and One Arabian Nights*.

The quarter offers the visitor a crash-course in 1350 years of Islamic
architecture, beginning with Ibn Tulun's simple ninth-century mosque –
the oldest in Cairo and the only surviving building from Ibn Tulun's reign
– and finishing with Mohammed Ali's vain nineteenth-century attempt to
emulate the glory of the Aya Sofya. Once your architectural interest
begins to wane there's always the Khan al-Khalili, Cairo's main bazaar,
where you can peruse the less august delights of stuffed camels and fake
mother-of-pearl jewellery boxes.

As it would still take days to see all of the sights in Islamic Cairo we
have listed only the major buildings. For those whose interest in minarets
is minimal, I recommend a tour from the citadel to al-Azhar Mosque via
the Street of Saddlemakers. For a more in-depth study, buy a copy of
Parker and Sabin's *Islamic Monuments in Cairo – a practical guide*
(American University in Cairo Press), which suggests walking tours and
gives detailed descriptions of the buildings en route.

Bus No 57 leaves from Ataba Sq to Midan Saladin ميدان سلاح الدين.
Alternatively, walk east from Midan Ataba. Don't come on a Friday,
when many buildings are closed to sightseers. Keep your arms and legs
covered, and your eyes and ears open. Remember to bring plenty of
change too: this quarter runs on baksheesh.

Mosque of Ibn Tulun [a] (see map on p307) جامع ابن طولون   (0830-1700;
E£3, E£1.5 students). The mud-brick walls of Tulun's mosque are a ten-
minute walk from Midan Saladin. Built in 876, this mosque lay at the
heart of Tulun's capital, al-Qata, surrounded by the city's most important
administrative offices. Following the destruction of Tulun's city by the
Abbassids in 905 the mosque fell into disrepair. For the next three centuries it was used as a khan (inn) by visiting traders, until in 1296 Amir

Husam al-Din Lagin, an accomplice in the murder of the then sultan, al-Ashraf Khalil, sought refuge within its walls. Al-Ashraf had been a brave and successful general, famous for his defeat of the Crusaders at Acre in 1291 that finally drove out the knights from the Near East. But he was also a cruel and exacting ruler. His murder, whilst hardly unexpected, plunged Egypt into near anarchy. Whilst hiding within, Lagin vowed to restore the mosque if ever he survived to become sultan. And so it came to pass that later the same year he ascended the throne and, true to his word, the restoration of Tulun's mosque began.

On entering one is struck by the scale and space of the mosque. Covering 2.5 sq km of prime Cairene real estate, in its heyday it could house most of Tulun's army, including their horses, within its walls. There is little filling the void today except for a beautiful thirteenth-century minbar that stands adjacent to the qibla wall (on your left as you enter), and a fountain in the centre. Both are Lagin's work. But it is the tranquillity flowing throughout the building that is so attractive; if one finds the pace of Cairo too stressful this is the perfect place to seek refuge, much as Lagin did 700 years ago. Before you leave, climb the minaret for the excellent panorama.

After the simplicity of the mosque, the **Gayer-Anderson Museum** (0800-1600; E£8, E£4 students) next door provides the contrast. John Gayer-Anderson, a keen historian and antiques dealer, lived in these two houses during the 1930s and spent much of his time restoring them to their original Ottoman splendour. Each room has a different theme. The exquisite Damascene ceilings and intricate mashrabiyyah screens that veil the windows are two of the highlights.

● **The Citadel** (0800-1800 summer, 0800-1700 winter; E£10, E£5 students). On the eastern side of Midan Saladin stands the mighty citadel, the heart of the capital for over 700 years.

Facing the roundabout is the infamous **al-Azab Gate**, the site of the murder of 470 Mamluke leaders by the Ottoman Pasha Mohammed Ali in 1811. After laying on a sumptuous feast for all of them within the citadel, Pasha Ali trapped the Mamlukes by the gate as they made their way home, and slaughtered every one. This massacre finally ended Mamluke influence in Egypt after 639 years. (Although the last Mamluke sultan was killed in 1517, the Mamlukes had continued to wield influence in the courts of Egypt until Pasha Ali's intervention 300 years later). Today the al-Azab gate is closed; the entrance is up the hill to the north of the gate.

Little remains of Saladin's original twelfth-century citadel; a large map inside the entrance shows how the fortress has been altered down the years. The most eye-catching structure inside is **Mohammed Ali's Mosque** (closed on Friday) straight ahead after the entrance. Completed in 1848 the mosque, with its clustered semi-domes and pencil-shaped

---

❏ **Mohammed Ali**

In 1798 Napoleon's troops landed in Egypt. It was the beginning of a century-long war of attrition between the European empires, waiting to take over the Ottoman territories as soon as the empire crumbled. After Britain had chased Napoleon's troops out a new Ottoman Pasha of Albanian descent, Mohammed Ali, ruled Egypt for the Ottomans. His first task was to rid the country of the Mamlukes, who still wielded considerable influence in the country. Having achieved that in one gory episode (see p304), Pasha Ali began modernising Egypt's infrastructure. Having achieved that in double-quick time too, he decided to conquer the Near East. It wasn't long before Jordan and Syria were his, and he probably would have continued too if it hadn't have been for the European powers who forced him to sign a power-sharing pact with the sultan. In return, Ali was made governor of Egypt for life, a hereditary title.

---

minarets, is clearly an attempt to emulate the architectural achievement of the Aya Sofya. Although it may fare badly when compared to Istanbul's gem, there is no doubt that this mosque remains an imposing structure. Mohammed Ali rests in a little mausoleum to the right of the entrance. To the east of his mosque is **Gawhara Palace**, named after Ali's wife.

The other mosques in the citadel are not as impressive, having been stripped of much of their better features by Mohammed Ali. Some of the citadel's museums are worth a visit, however. The assassination room of the **Police Museum** is particularly good. It begins with an account of an attempt made on the life of Ramses III, and concludes with a report of the farcical attempt to kill Gamel Nasser made by the Muslim Brothers: six bullets were fired at the former president, and all of them missed.

● **Madrassa of Sultan Hassan [b]** مدرسة السلطان حسن (0800-1800, -1700 in winter; E£6, E£3 students). Sultan Hassan (1354-61), a grandson of Qalawun (see below), was assassinated a year before his madrassa was completed. As befits a building constructed during the troubled Mamluke period, this school for religious education is built like a fortress, with the minarets resembling lookout towers. These fortifications were often necessary, too, not least when the last Mamluke sultan, Tumanbay, used the madrassa as a refuge from the Ottoman soldiers. He was eventually forced to evacuate when the Ottomans began to pepper the walls with cannon-fire.

There are actually four schools inside the madrassa – one in each of the liwans – although sightseeing is restricted to the central courtyard and the mausoleum of Hassan's family. One clever architectural quirk is that while the whole building appears to be uniformly rectangular from the outside, the interior actually bends almost 30 degrees along its north-south axis. This ensures that while the building aligns with the street and faces the citadel, its qibla (direction towards the Ka'aba) points to Mecca. The western minaret is the second tallest in Cairo, measuring some 80m;

for a little baksheesh you may well have the opportunity to climb it.

Opposite is the **Mosque of al-Rifai [c]** (same times and prices as Hassan), which complements the grand style of its neighbour. This madrassa may look Mamluke in style but in fact it was built some five hundred years later in 1869. Today it houses an important mausoleum containing, amongst others, the bodies of King Fuad, Khedive Ismail and the Shah of Iran. **Tickets** for both buildings are obtainable from the office to the north of the Hassan Madrassa.

● **Sharia al-Surugiyyah, Street of Saddlemakers** شارع سعد الماكرس Return to the walkway that runs between these two buildings and head west away from the citadel. Cross the road and continue straight on, until you come to the al-King Restaurant. The road running alongside is Sharia al-Surugiyyah, a narrow stall-lined street that runs north towards the Khan al-Khalili. On the right-hand side you pass the **Madrassa of Ganim al-Bahlawan [d] 1510** (E£3, E£1.50 concessions) and the **Madrassa of Inal al-Yusufi [e] 1392** (E£3, E£1.50). Continuing you reach the Fatimid **Mosque of Salah Talei [f] 1160** (E£3, E£1.50) and eventually pass through **Bab Zweila [g]**. This Fatimid city gate, built in 1092 and one of three extant in Cairo today, used to be the site of public executions.

After this is the defunct **Mosque of Sultan Mu'ayyad Sheikh [h]** (E£3, E£1.50). Now overgrown and shabby, the main attraction of this mosque (1420) is the minaret atop Bab Zweila, which for an extra E£1 baksheesh you can climb. Eventually you arrive at the main east-west thoroughfare, Sharia al-Azhar. Just before it is the **Mausoleum of al-Ghouri [i]** on the right, a beautiful 16th-century building which honours the penultimate Mamluke sultan of Egypt. Both the mausoleum and the **madrassa** which stands opposite were badly damaged by the earthquake that struck Cairo in 1992, yet there is still much to admire about both.

● **Al-Azhar Mosque [j]** جامع الأزهر (E£6, E£3 concessions). This is the oldest university in the world and the centre of Islamic theology. Established by the Fatimid conqueror Gawhar in AD970, the university is now much more than just this one building. Indeed, there are over 90,000 students affiliated to al-Azhar, distributed amongst eight campuses in Egypt. The university still teaches the intricacies of Koranic Law, as it has always done, although other subjects have been added to the curriculum. The head of the mosque (the Sheikh al-Azhar) has throughout history always wielded immense power in Egypt, both in theological circles where he is the ultimate authority on Islamic matters and in political circles, too.

The building is a pot-pourri of different architectural styles – there are even a couple of Mamluke madrassas incorporated within – but the basic style of teaching remains the same. Sometimes you can still see the pupils sitting around the feet of the sheikh (teacher), or sitting by themselves memorising Koranic texts.

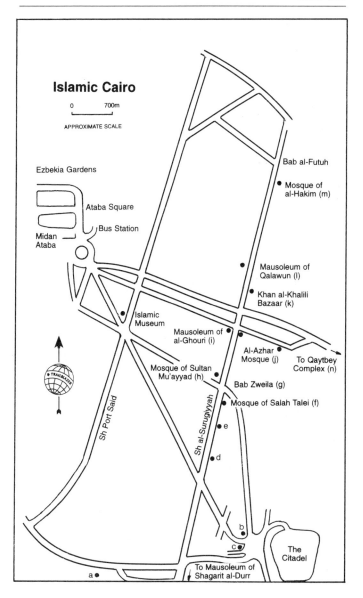

Islamic Cairo

0   700m

APPROXIMATE SCALE

Ezbekia Gardens

Ataba Square

Bus Station

Midan
Ataba

Islamic
Museum

Mausoleum of
al-Ghouri (i)

Mosque of Sultan
Mu'ayyad (h)

Sh Port Said

Sh al-Suruqiyyah

Bab al-Futuh

Mosque of
al-Hakim (m)

Mausoleum of
Qalawun (l)

Khan al-Khalili
Bazaar (k)

Al-Azhar
Mosque (j)

To Qaytbey
Complex (n)

Bab Zweila (g)

Mosque of Salah Talei (f)

e

d

b

c

a

To Mausoleum of
Shagarit al-Durr

The
Citadel

● **Khan al-Khalili Bazaar [k]** خان الخليلي Cross Sharia al-Azhar from Sh Suru-giyyah and you throw yourselves at the mercy of the merchants in the main Khan al-Khalili bazaar. It's a fascinating place to do your shopping but for the moment save your piastres and head straight on to ...

● **Mausoleum of Qalawun [l]** ضريح قلاوون (1285) More than just a mausoleum, this huddle of buildings, made on the orders of Sultan Qalawun (the father of al-Ashraf Khalil – see above), includes a hospital and madrassa too. The hospital was the most technically advanced of its day; minstrels and narrators were provided to distract the patients. A hospital for eye diseases still practises here. The minstrels, however, have gone.

● **Mosque of Caliph al-Hakim [m]** جامع الحكيم At the northern end of Khan al-Khalili is al-Hakim's Mosque (1093). Despite all his faults, the crazy caliph proved to be a skilful general. His conquests included Jerusalem and Palestine, and with the wealth accumulated he was able to finance this beautiful mosque. Being a Fatimid building the architectural style, including monumental entrance and elaborate facade, borrows heavily from the mosques of North Africa. Later rulers have been less appreciative of this style: the Ayyubids used it as a gaol for Crusader prisoners, Napoleon made it his stables, and Nasser converted it into a school.

● **Mausoleum of Qaytbey [n]** ضريح قايتبي This one's a bit tricky to find. One km east of the al-Azhar mosque, in what is known as the Northern Cemetery, stands this tomb of one of the last Mamluke sultans, al-Ashraf Qaytbey. As well as his mausoleum there's also a madrassa and ruined

---

❏ **Al-Hakim**

Caliph al-Hakim bi-Amr Allah – 'Ruler by God's command' – was Egypt's pottiest Fatimid caliph. His childhood, if you ignore the time he killed his tutor in a fit of temper, seemed relatively normal. But following his accession to the throne in 996AD, al-Hakim began to truly bark. His reign was characterised by laws that bore out his prejudices: Christians were forced to wear heavy wooden crosses; women, whom he despised, were kept off the streets by his edict proscribing the production of their shoes; and anybody who offered even the slightest resistance to his madcap policies felt the full force of his wrath.

Sunlight was a bugbear for the caliph, so he passed a law forbidding his subjects from working during the day. One of al-Hakim's own nocturnal activities was to ride his favourite donkey, Moon, out into the desert. One night, in 1013, he mysteriously failed to return. The identities of his abductors were never discovered – after all, half of the city were possible suspects – and although Hakim's donkey was found, the beast remained silent. From these inauspicious beginnings emerged one of the major faiths in the region. Just before his disappearance, Hakim decided he wished to be treated as a god and so declared his divinity to his loyal subjects. One of them, al-Darazi, believed him, and following his master's demise fled to Syria to preach his late master's word. The converts to this new religion became known as the 'Darazi' after this first preacher; today we know them as the Druze.

commercial centre here. Qaytbay was an energetic and ambitious ruler, and his reign (1468-1492) was the second-longest in Mamluke history. This complex is just the best of many structures built during his rule.

Saqqara سكارا

(0730-1700 summer, 0730-1600 winter; E£10, E£5 students). To get to Saqqara, 25km to the south of Giza , head back on to the Pyramids Road and walk down to the first canal (about 20 minutes away). The road that runs along the west bank of the canal leads to Saqqara; a minibus leaves from the junction to Saqqara village, about four km from the Step Pyramid, for 50 pstr. As an alternative, consider hiring a camel from Giza to pass by the three pyramids at Abu Sir on your way to Saqqara. About E£45 will get you a ride on one of these flatulent fur-balls.

About 60 pyramids were built along the west bank of the Nile, of which the Great Pyramids are merely the most spectacular. Such ambitious projects could never have been attempted without first perfecting the techniques on more modest structures. One of the earliest prototypes, the first to be made of stone, is in the necropolis at Saqqara. The Third Dynasty **Step Pyramid** (2680BC) was built by the master Old Kingdom architect Imhotep for his pharaoh, Djoser. The method used in its construction – building a ramp that wound round the pyramid which grew as the pyramid grew – was probably emulated at Giza.

In front of the Step Pyramid is a large forecourt, the venue for the bizarre 'Heb Sed' festival. The king, upon reaching 30 years in office, would undergo a ritual 're-coronation' during this ceremony, which involved undertaking a series of tasks to prove he was still a worthy ruler. These included running around a course in the courtyard in order to prove his fitness. The buildings that surround the courtyard were shrines to the gods, whose statues would sit inside and watch the king. To the north of the pyramid by the entrance (now closed) is the serdab, wherein sits a statue of the king watching his adoring public. This statue is a copy; the original is inside the entrance of the Cairo Museum.

Around Djoser's complex are many other tombs worth visiting. The ruins to the south include the pyramid and mortuary temple of the Fifth Dynasty (2500-2345BC) **Pharaoh Unis** (currently closed), the **Funerary Complex of Sekhemkhet** (ditto), and the **Tombs of Three Persian**

❏ **Camel fair**
(E£2) The camel fair at Imbaba, near the airstrip to the north-west of the city, has become a popular Friday event for both tourists and camel-lovers. Catch the No 71 bus from Ataba Sq to join in the fun. The action begins first thing in the morning and has usually petered out by midday. Prices begin at E£1000 for the moth-eaten, three-legged variety, rising to about US$1500 for the thoroughbred. Go on, treat yourself – think how much you'll save in train fares.

Noblemen (find the man with the keys). If Unis' tomb has re-opened have a look inside. Although the exterior appears to be just a pile of dirt left behind by tomb excavators, the interior was one of the first to be decorated, setting a trend that would really catch on during the New Kingdom. Unis' daughter **Idut** also has a tomb here and it's beautiful. The princess appears larger than life on the murals to emphasise her importance. The corridor is decorated with an ongoing saga between the crocodile and two hippopotami, in mortal combat in the second room. On the walls of the final chamber is a list of food used in preparation for a great feast, as well as the false door, here painted to resemble granite.

To the north of the Step Pyramid is another example of classic Old Kingdom art. Beyond the crumbling **Pyramid of Userkaf** is the complex **Tomb of Mereruka**, a sixth-dynasty nobleman. At the entrance is the man himself, relaxing after a stressful life by painting at his easel. Other scenes show Mereruka with his sons participating in their favourite pastimes: catching fish, hunting and beating the fellahin (farmers) for non-payment of taxes. The quality of artwork here is only matched in Saqqara by the **Tomb of Akhethotep and Ptahhotep**, the father-and-son mausoleum lying 500m away, to the west along the road that splits the Pyramid of Userkaf from the Tomb of Mereruka. Nearby is the **Serapeum**, a spooky catacomb full of huge sarcophagi, in which lay the mummified bodies of sacred bulls

Cairo Tower برج القاهرة

(0900-2400; E£12). Gezira Island's main attraction is modern Cairo's pride and joy. The Cairo Tower, standing 187m high, houses a viewing platform and two restaurants. The best time to come is just before dusk, although this is also the busiest. If you want a panoramic view of the city but don't want to pay E£12, you have three options: go to Saladin's citadel, from where, on a clear day, you can still see the pyramids; plan a pre-dawn expedition up Cheops' Pyramid – illegal, dangerous and damaging to the pyramid but offering incomparable views; or learn Arabic and wear a jalabiyyeh – Egyptians pay E£3.50 at the Cairo Tower.

> ❏ **Other Attractions in Egypt**
> If Egypt is a buffet then we have merely nibbled on the vol-au-vents and sampled the savoury dips. There is so much more to this country, including the heavenly oases that stretch into the Libyan Desert. The best-known of these is the traveller's hangout at Siwa, where Alexander the Great consulted the Oracle. The result of this meeting was Alexandria, Egypt's second great metropolis which stands at the Northern end of the Nile Delta. All along the Nile are colossal temples: Dendera Temple at Qena, twinned with Edfu; Kom Ombo, just a short trip away from Aswan; and the temples at Abydos, Assyut et al. And all this is ignoring the coasts, both Red and Med, where one can enjoy the underwater delights of Hurghada, Sharm el-Sheikh and Marsa Matruh.

Other sights in and around Cairo

Cairo has plenty of other attractions to amaze and amuse. The **Coptic** and **Islamic Art Museums** are both fascinating, even if, before you go in, you have little interest in the two subjects. The latter can be combined with a tour around Islamic Cairo. The Coptic Museum is in the heart of **Old Cairo**, six km south of Central Cairo; it is said that this is where Jesus, Mary and Joseph lived after fleeing from Herod. The Roman **Fortress Babylon** was also once located here; there are still a few remains. To reach Old Cairo, take the metro to Mar Girgis station.

At the southern tip of Roda Island is a **Nilometer**, Cairo city's oldest monument (AD861). It is similar in function to Aswan's gauge.

Egypt's first capital was established at **Memphis** منفيس (24km from Cairo) at the point where Upper and Lower Egypt meet. There's little of interest now except some statues of Ramses II, Amenhotep's sarcophagus, and an alabaster table used in the mummification of bulls.

MOVING ON

● **Train** Although Ramses Station is a nightmare to negotiate, there are station officials around whose job it is to help the confused-looking traveller. The timetable for the high speed tourist trains is as follows:

Cairo to:	Depart	1st cl (student)		2nd cl (student)	
Luxor	0730	E£48	(E£31)	E£28	(E£21)
	2200	E£51	(E£34)	E£31	(E£24)
Aswan	0730	E£60	(E£38)	E£34	(E£25)
	2200	E£63	(E£41)	E£37	(E£28)

It is impossible to book 3rd or 2nd class non air-conditioned trains in Cairo. Just to turn up and jump on the next one. Currently the times for these trains to Luxor and Aswan are: 0740; 1215 and 1515 (both 2nd class only); 2115; 2210; and 2315 (2nd class only). Prices to Aswan are E£16.60/E£7.30 (2nd/3rd cl). To Luxor the fares are E£13.80/E£6.10. These fares, unbelievably, are also subject to a 50% student discount!

● **Bus** Buses to southern destinations leave from in front of the Ramses Hilton or alternatively from behind the Ramses train station. For Luxor (E£40), the bus leaves at 2115; for Aswan (E£50), at 1700 and 1900.

● **Servis** Regular departures from Ahmed Helmi Bus Station to Luxor (E£50). You can also catch a servis to Suez (for the Sinai) for E£4.50.

❑ **To Sudan**
Currently the Egyptian-Sudanese border south of Aswan is closed. It is still possible to cross into Sudan by ship, however. The boat, *el-Mahrosa*, sails from Port Suez (Tawfikia) to Suakin every Sunday. Tickets cost E£500/600 for 2nd/1st cl for the three-day journey. The only place to buy tickets in Cairo is Yara Travels, 38 Sabry Abu Alaam. Check the current political situation before travelling.

APPENDIX A: EMBASSIES

IN AUSTRALIA

Egyptian Consulate
335 New South Head Rd
Double Bay, Sydney
NSW 2028
(☎ 02-9362 3482/8)
(consulate in Melbourne)

Israeli Consulate
Westfield Towers
300 William St
Sydney, NSW 2011
(☎ 02-9358 5077)

Jordanian Embassy
20 Roebuck St
Redhill, Canberra
ACT 2603
(☎ 06-295 9951)

Syrian Embassy
41 Alexandra Ave
South Yarra
Victoria 3141
(☎ 03-9867 5131)

IN CANADA

Egyptian Embassy
454 Laurier Ave East
Ottawa, Ontario K1N 6R3
(☎ 613-234 4931)
(Consulate in Montreal)

Israeli Embassy
Suite 1005
50 O'Connor St
Ottawa, Ontario K1P 6L2
(☎ 613-567 6450)
(consulates in Montreal
and Toronto)

Jordanian Embassy
Suite 701
100 Bronson Ave
Ottawa, Ontario K1R 6G8
(☎ 613-238 8090)

IN CANADA (cont)

Lebanese Embassy
640 Lyon St,
Ottawa, Ontario K1S 3Z5
(☎ 613-236 5825)
(consulates in Montreal)

Turkish Embassy
197 Wurtemburg St
Ottawa, Ontario K19 8L9
(☎ 613-789 3442)

(For **Syrian visas**, contact
consulate in USA)

IN UNITED KINGDOM

Egyptian Consulate
2 Lowndes St
London SW1X 9ET
(☎ 0171-235 9719)

Israeli Embassy
2 Palace Green
London W8 4QB
(☎ 0171-957 9500)

Jordanian Embassy
6 Upper Phillimore Gdns
London W8 7HB
(☎ 0171-937 3685)

Lebanese Consulate
15 Palace Garden Mews
London W8 4RE
(☎ 0171-229 7265)

Syrian Embassy
8 Belgrave Square
London SW1X 8PH
(☎ 0171-245 9012)

Turkish Consulate
Rutland Lodge
Rutland Gardens
London SW7 1BW
(☎ 0171-584 6235)

IN USA

Egyptian Embassy
3521 International Court
NW, Washington
DC 20008
(☎ 202-244 4319)

Israeli Embassy
3514 International Drive
NW, Washington
DC 20008
(☎ 202-364 5500)
(consulates in Atlanta,
Boston, Chicago,
Houston, Los Angeles,
Miami, New York,
Philadelphia and San
Francisco)

Jordanian Embassy
3504 International Drive
NW, Washington
DC 20008
(☎ 202-966 2664)

Lebanese Consulate
9 East 76th St
New York
NY 10021
(☎ 212-744 7905)

Syrian Embassy
2215 Wyoming Ave NW
Washington DC 20008
(☎ 202-232 6313)
(consulate in Houston)

Turkish Embassy
1714 Massachusetts Ave
NW, Washington
DC 20036
(☎ 202-659 0744)
(consulates in New York,
Chicago, Houston and Los
Angeles)

APPENDIX B: TURKISH & ARABIC LANGUAGE

Turkish

Turkish is such a logical and phonetic language that it was used as the basis for Esperanto. At first the multitude of accents may appear alien but in fact they are an aid to pronunciation. For example, the curved accent above a 'g' tells us that the g should be soft (as in giant) as opposed to hard (as in get) if it is absent. The other important point is that every letter in Turkish is pronounced. If you see the combination 'th' as in marathon, in Turkish this would be pronounced marat-hon.

Arabic

Sometimes I caught fragments of their language – an impenetrable labyrinth of consonants which sounded more musical to my ear than the noise which came out of their tape-recorders – **Jonathan Raban** *Arabia through the Looking Glass*

Arabic is a frustrating language to learn and there are plenty of different versions to try. The Arabic spoken in Jordan and the Levantine countries differs from that spoken in Egypt and both differ from the Modern Standard Arabic that is written in newspapers or Arabic spoken in the mosque.

Then there's the transliteration problem: as yet, no system has been formulated that adequately describes the subtle nuances of Arabic pronunciation using only the blunt 26 letters of the Roman alphabet. Consequently, you will see one Arabic word spelt in many different ways in Roman script depending on the transliteration technique used (eg the Arabic for 'castle', *qasr*, is also be written *kasr*). Similarly, the Arabic word for 'the', *al*, is often written *el* or even modified depending on the word that follows (eg Khan al-Saboun is usually written Khan as-Saboun). In this book we use 'al' except for restaurant/hotel names where 'el' is in the name.

But all these transliteration problems are as nothing compared to the traumas encountered when trying to pronounce the language. There are certain sounds in Arabic that the Western tongue just wasn't designed to make. Here are a few: an apostrophe in the text is a glottal stop produced by tightening the back of the throat – as in a hiccup. The '**kh**' sound is another produced at the back of the throat; imagine saying the word 'kettle' whilst gargling; the sound produced at the beginning should be an approximation of kh. And then there is the '**dh**' sound, similar to a gargling, back-of-the-throat version of the Latin 'th'.

You will hear certain Arabic words and phrases time and again. *Inshallah* (God willing) is probably the most common, and you will hear it being uttered every time you ask about a future event – eg 'Is this bus leaving soon?', or 'Are you open tomorrow?'. Another common phrase, particularly in Egypt, is 'shwoyer, shwoyer', which literally translates as 'slowly slowly' or 'calm down'.

Note that all the letters pronounced 'j' outside Egypt are pronounced as a hard 'g' everywhere in Egypt apart from Alexandria.

BASIC VOCABULARY

English	Turkish	Arabic	
airport	hava alani	المطار	mataar
aeroplane	ucak	الطائرة	tayara
bank	bank	البنك	bank
baths	hamam	حمام	hamaam
beach	kumbasi	شاطيء	shatt
bicycle	bisiklet	دراجة	bisklatt

English	Turkish	Arabic	
bus	otobus	باص	baas
café	kahvehane	مقهى	mak-hah
church	kilise	الكنيسة	kaniisa
clock tower	saat kulesi	برج الساعة	burj as-sa'a
embassy	sefarethane	السفارة	sifaara
ferry	feribot	زورق	jenniyeh
good	iyi	جيد	kuwayis, tayeb
hill	tepe	التل	jabal, tel
hospital	hastane	المستشفى	mustashfa
hotel	otel	فندق	funduk
laundry	camasir	مصبغة	masbagha
market	pazar, carsi	السوق	souk
mausoleum	turbe	ضريح	dariha
monastery	manastir	دير	deir
mosque	cami	الجامع	masjid
museum	muze	المتحف	madhaf
passport	pasaport	جواز سفر	jawaaz safar
police	polis	الشرطة	buliis
port	liman	مرفأ	mina'a
post office	postane	دائرة البريد	maktab al-bariid
restaurant	restoran	مطعم	mata'am
room	oda	غرفة	ghurfa
servis taxi	dolmus	خدمة (تاكسي)	servees, dolmush
shower	dus	دوش (حمام)	duush
station	istasyon	محطة	mahataat
street	sokak, caddesi	شارع	sharia
taxi	taksi	تاكسي (سيارات الأجرة)	taksi
telephone	telefon	هاتف	talifawn
temple	mabet	معبد	kanis
ticket	bilet	تذكرة	tadhkara
toilet	tuvalet	تواليت - حمام	bayt mayy
tourist office	turist bureau	مكتب السياحة	saayih maktab
tower	kule	البرج	majdal
train	tren	القطار	qitaar

FOOD AND DRINK

English	Turkish	Arabic	
beer	bira	البيرة	biira
bread	ekmek	الخبز	khubz
breakfast	kahvalti	الفطور	futu'ur
cheese	peynir	جبنة	jibneh
chicken	pilic	دجاج	djaj
coffee	kahve	قهوة	qahwa
doner kebab	kebap	الشاورما / الدونر كباب التركي	shwaarma
fish	balik	السمك	samaka
fruit	meyve	فواكه	fa'akiha
ice cream	dondurma	بوظة	buuza, dondurma
juice	ozsu	عصير	a'asiir

English	Turkish	Arabic	
lamb	kuzu	لحم الغنم	saru'uf
pizza	pizza	البيتزا	pizza
pork	domuz eti	لحم خنزير	lahm khanziir
salad	salata	السلطة	salata
soup	corba	الحساء	shorba
spicy	baharli	بهارات	behar
tea	cay	الشاي	chai
vegetarian	et dusmani	نباتي	nabati
water	su	الماء	mayy

NUMERALS

English	Turkish		Arabic	
1	bir	١	واحد	wahid
2	iki	٢	اثنين	ithnayn, tnaan
3	uc	٣	ثلاثة	tala'ata, tlaat
4	dort	٤	أربعة	arba'a
5	bes	٥	خمسة	khamsa
6	alti	٦	ستة	sita'a
7	yedi	٧	سبعة	saba'a
8	sekiz	٨	ثمانية	tamanya
9	dokuz	٩	تسعة	tissa'a
10	on	١٠	عشرة	a'ashra
11	on bir	١١	احدى عشر	ihdashr
12	on iki	١٢	اثنى عشر	itnaysh
13	on uc	١٣	ثلاثة عشر	tala'atash
14	on dort	١٤	أربعة عشر	arba'ata'ash
20	yirmi	٢٠	عشرون	ishri'in
21	yirmi bir	٢١	واحد وعشرون	wahid wa ishri'in
30	otuz	٣٠	ثلاثون	talathi'in
40	kirk	٤٠	أربعون	arba'ati'in
50	elli	٥٠	خمسون	khamsi'in
60	altmis	٦٠	ستون	sitti'in
70	yetmis	٧٠	سبعون	saba'i'in
80	seksen	٨٠	ثمانون	tamaani'in
90	doksan	٩٠	تسعون	tis'i'in
100	yuz	١٠٠	مائة	miyya
200	iki yuz	٢٠٠	مئتين	mittayn
1000	bin	١٠٠٠	ألف	elf
2000	iki bin	٢٠٠٠	ألفين	alfayn
3000	uc bin	٣٠٠٠	ثلاثة آلاف	tala'athat aalaaf
1,000,000	bir milyon			malaayin

USEFUL PHRASES

English	Turkish	Arabic	
hello	merhaba	مرحباً (السلام عليكم)	maharba, sala'am wa aleikhoom
goodbye	gule gule	وداعاً (مع السلامة)	ma asala'am (to a man)
			ma asala'meh (to a woman)
yes	evet	نعم	na'am, aywa
no	hic	لا	la

English	Turkish	Arabic	
please	lutfen	رجاءً (من فضلك)	min fadlak
sorry	uzgun	آسف	samahini
thank you	tesekkur ederim	شكراً	shukram
What is your name?	Adiniz ne?	ما إسمك ؟	Ma asmak?
You are welcome	Bir sey degil	على الرحب والسعة	Ahlan wasahlan
I would like....	Istiyorum	أنا أرغب (أريد)	Min fadlak, laazimnii
How much?	Ne kadar?, Kac?	ما القيمة (كم)	Kam?
cheap	ucuz	رخيص / غالي	rashi'is
expensive	pahal	مفتوح / مغلوق	ghaali
How long (time)?	Kac saat?	كم من الوقت ؟	Gaddaysh
Monday	Pazartesi	الاثنين	Yawm al-Ithnayn
Tuesday	Sali	الثلاثاء	Yawm al-Tala'ata
Wednesday	Carsamba	الأربعاء	Yawm al-Arbaa
Thursday	Persembe	الخميس	Yawm al-Kamis
Friday	Cuma	الجمعة	Yawm al-Jumba'a
Saturday	Cumartesi	السبت	Yawm al-Ahad
Sunday	Pazar	الأحد	Yawm al-Sabt

APPENDIX C: GLOSSARY

Agora – Roman meeting hall. Usually little more than open space.

Apse – Recess in a church, usually semi-circular and arched.

Barque – Pharaonic boat used to carry the dead or statues of the gods.

Basilica – Style of church made popular in Byzantine times, with a long hall surrounded by pillars.

Burqa – Black, full-length robe worn by Islamic women.

Calèche – Horse-drawn carriage.

Canopic Jars – Jars used to store the internal organs of mummy. Placed in burial chamber.

Capitals – The decorated tops of pillars.

Caravanserai – see Khan.

Colonnade – Covered walkway lined with pillars.

Cruciform – In the shape of a cross.

Decapolis – Roman trading union consisting of ten major Asian cities.

Diaspora – The exiled Jewish community across the world.

Haj – The pilgrimage to Mecca, one of Islam's five tenets that must be carried out at least once by all Muslims.

Hammam – Public bath.

Heb Sed – Ancient Egyptian festival where the Pharaoh would celebrate 30 years on the throne by proving, by a series of tests, that he was still fit to govern.

Holy of Holies – The sanctuary at the back of the temple which housed the statues of the gods.

Hypostyle Hall – Columned hall in a Pharaonic temple.

Intifada – Series of strikes and terror activities organised by the PLO.

Kibbutz – Communal settlement in Israel, once just agricultural but now with industry, too.

Khan – Inn built to accommodate visiting traders.

Koran – Holy book of Islam, dictated to scribes by Mohammed.

Jalabiyyeh – Ankle-length tunic of the Arab.

Janissary – Ottoman guards, the personal soldiers of the sultan.

Liwan – Vaulted hall that opens into central courtyard in a mosque.

Loge – Private section in a mosque for the sultan's personal use.

Madrassa – Islamic college for the study of the Koran. Usually a mosque and courtyard stands in the centre, surrounded by the classrooms and libraries of the college.

Mamissi – Divine birth-room of a Pharaonic temple, where the rituals of the king's divine birth were performed.

Maristan – Hospital.

Mashrabiyyah – Wooden screen of intricate latticework.

Mausoleum – Stately tomb.

Minaret – Tower in mosque from which the faithful are called to prayer.

Minbar – Pulpit in a mosque.

Mihrab – Niche in the interior wall of the mosque that points towards Mecca.

Monotheistic – Belief in one god only.

Mortuary Temple – Temple dedicated to the worship of a late Pharaoh.

Moshav – Privately-run settlement in Israel, combining industry and agriculture.

Muezzin – Member of mosque who calls faithful to prayer five times per day.

Nargileh – Also called the hubbly-bubbly, this is the water-pipe used to smoke tobacco.

Narthex – Porch or enclosed entrance of the church.

Nilometer – Central column in a pit marked with graduations, used to measure the level of water in the Nile.

Nome – Administrative district in ancient Egypt.

Nymphaneum – Roman fountain, often consecrated as holy ground.

Opet Festival – Ancient Egyptian festival, also called 'Festival of Beautiful Meeting', where god from one temple would visit god of neighbouring temple.

PLO – The Palestinian Liberation Organisation, an Arab organisation dedicated to win back Palestine from the Jews

Pylon – Monumental entrance, made of two adjoining giant towers, to a Pharaonic temple.

Qibla – Mihrab wall.

Ramadan – Holy month in the Muslim calendar.

Sarcophagus – Coffin

Serdab – Small chamber near mortuary temple where statue of late Pharaoh was placed, so that they could communicate with mortal world.

Souk – Market.

Stele – Commemorative stone tablet (plural: stelae).

Tetrapylon – Roman crossroads, often marked with a statue at each corner.

Talmud – Jewish holy book.

Torah – Jewish holy book, first five books of Old Testament.

Valide sultan – Sultan's mother

Vizier – Government minister in both ancient Egypt and the Ottoman Empire.

Yarmulka – Head covering to be worn when visiting holy Jewish sights.

INDEX